Transport Law in China

Transport Law in China

Second Edition

James Zhengliang Hu

This book was originally published as a monograph in the International Encyclopaedia of Laws/Transport Law.

Founding Editor: Roger Blanpain
General Editor: Frank Hendrickx
Volume Editor: Eric Van Hooydonk

Wolters Kluwer

Published by:
Kluwer Law International B.V.
PO Box 316
2400 AH Alphen aan den Rijn
The Netherlands
E-mail: lrs-sales@wolterskluwer.com
Website: www.wolterskluwer.com/en/solutions/kluwerlawinternational

Sold and distributed by:
Wolters Kluwer Legal & Regulatory U.S.
920 Links Avenue
Landisville, PA 17538
United States of America
E-mail: customer.service@wolterskluwer.com

ISBN 978-94-035-0309-7

e-Book: ISBN 978-94-035-0319-6
web-PDF: ISBN 978-94-035-1254-9

This title is available on www.kluwerlawonline.com

The Author

Prof. Dr James Zhengliang Hu, LLM, PhD (Dalian), is a Professor of maritime and transport law, Director of Institute of Maritime Law and PhD supervisor in maritime and shipping law at Shanghai Maritime University. He was a visiting scholar at the University of Antwerp and a visiting professor at the Catholic University of Leuven, Belgium. He was a draftsman of Chinese Maritime Code, Chinese Port Law, Chinese Shipping Law (not adopted yet) and various Chinese maritime and shipping regulations. He acts as a legal advisor to the Ministry of Transport (MOT) and the Maritime Safety Administration (MSA) of the People's Republic of China. He is a member of the Board of Standing Directors of China Maritime Law Association, an arbitrator of China Maritime Arbitration Commission (CMAC) and of Shanghai Arbitration Court of International Shipping. He is also a practising maritime lawyer at Wintell & Co Law Firm. His research interests include maritime law, shipping policies and law, port law, transport law and maritime procedural law. He published nearly twenty books and many articles, mainly in the area of maritime and shipping law.

The Author

Table of Contents

List of Abbreviations

AL	The Arbitration Law of China
Art.	Article
AUL	The Auction Law of China
BIMCO	Baltic and International Maritime Council
CAAC	Civil Aviation Administration of China
CAL	The Civil Aviation Law of China
CC	The Civil Code of China
CCP	Collision Compensation Provisions
CCPIT	China Council for the Promotion of International Trade
CCS	China Classification Society
Ch.	Chapter
CIETAC	China International Economic and Trade Arbitration Commission
CIF	Cost, Insurance and Freight
Cl.	clause
CLC	International Convention on Civil Liability for Oil Pollution Damages
CMAC	China Maritime Arbitration Commission
CMG	China Merchants Group
CMI	Comité Maritime International
CMIC	Agreement of International Railway Through Transport
CNY	Chinese Yuan
COLREGs	International Regulations for the Prevention of Collisions at Sea
COSCO SHIPPING	China COSCO Shipping Corporation Limited
CPC	The Civil Procedure Code of China
CPI	China Shipowners' Mutual Assurance Association
DACR	Regulations on the Domestic Cargo Transport of China Civil Aviation (Domestic Air Cargo Regulations)
DWT	Deadweight Tonnage

List of Abbreviations

EDI	Electronic Data Interchange
EPL	The Environmental Protection Law of China
F.P.A.	Free from Particular Average
FCL	Full Container Load
HL	Highway Law of China
IACR	Regulations on the International Cargo Transport by Civil Aviation in China (International Air Cargo Regulations)
IATA	International Air Transport Associations
ICE LIBOR	London Inter-Bank Offered Rate
IL	The Insurance Law of China
ILO	International Labour Organization
IMF	International Monetary Fund
IMO	International Maritime Organization
ISM	International Safety Management
ISM Code	International Safety Management Code
LCL	Less Than Container Load
LDC	Convention on the Prevention of Marine Pollution by Dumping of Wastes and Other Matters
LLMC	Convention on the Limitation of Liability for Maritime Claims
MARPOL	International Convention for the Prevention of Pollution from Ships
MC	The Maritime Code of China
MEE	The Ministry of Ecology and Environment of China
MEPL	The Marine Environmental Protection Law of China
MOC	The Ministry of Commerce of China
MOR	Ministry of Railways
MOT	The Ministry of Transport of China
MSA	The Maritime Safety Administration of China
mt	metric tons
MTO	Multimodal Transport Operator
MTSL	The Maritime Traffic Safety Law of China
NPC	The National People's Congress of China
P&I	Protection & Indemnity
PAL	Athens Convention Relating to the Carriage of Passengers and Their Luggage by Sea
para.	paragraph
PICC	The People's Insurance Company (Group) of China Limited

PICC P&C	PICC Property & Casualty Company Limited
PRPT	Provisions on Railway Passenger Transport
RDC	Running Down Clause
RL	The Railway Law of China
s.	section
SAR	International Convention on Maritime Search and Rescue
SDR	Special Drawing Right
SMPL	The Special Maritime Procedure Law of China
SOLAS	International Convention on Safety of Life at Sea
SPC	The Supreme People's Court of China
SSE	Shanghai Shipping Exchange
STCW	International Convention on the Standards of Training, Certification and Watch-keeping for Seafarers
SWB	Sea Waybill
TCT	Time Charter on Trip Basis
UNCLOS	United Nations Convention on the Law of the Sea
W.A.	With Average
WRC	Nairobi International Convention on the Removal of Wrecks
YAR	York-Antwerp Rules

Preface

As encouraged by Prof. Marc A. Huybrechts, who is the chief editor of the International Encyclopaedia of Transport Law and was my academic supervisor when I was studying maritime and shipping law in Belgium, I finalized the first edition of the monograph on China Transport Law in 2002, the first comprehensive introduction to Chinese transport law presented in English, covering each of the main legal aspects of maritime, road, rail, air and multimodal transport, inland navigation as well as the related legal issues. The first edition was revised in 2014, and the present edition was submitted in 2023.

The domain of Chinese transport law is so vast that the present monograph can only be an introduction to this subject. Hopefully, however, it will serve as reliable access to the various sources of transport law in China.

The author cited the various international treaties which China has ratified, acceded to or approved as the Chinese laws and regulations enacted regarding maritime and other modes of transport up to September 2023, the abbreviations of which are contained in Chapter 2 of Part II. Readers are requested to pay attention to the development of the Chinese legislation in this area since laws and regulations will be enacted or amended in developing China, especially the Maritime Code (MC) will expectedly be revised in the very near future. Meanwhile, China may ratify or accede to more international treaties in the area of transport. While the author has tried to make this monograph as practicable as possible, the monograph is also prepared by reference to the most reliable academic sources available. Noticeably, not many case judgments regarding transport law are quoted since China is not a case law country. However, case judgments, especially those published by the Supreme People's Court (SPC) as the guiding cases or model cases, have more and more important reference values.

I would like to thank the Faculty of Law of the Catholic University of Leuven for its provision of a study facility in 2001 when I was a visiting professor, which enabled me to finish preliminary preparation of the first edition of the monograph. Special thanks to my wife, Liu Min, for her continuous and greatest encouragement and support.

General Introduction

§1. General Background of the Country

I. Geography

1. The People's Republic of China (hereinafter referred to as 'China' in this Monograph), lying in East Asia, is the third largest country in the world in terms of territorial area. It covers a land area of about 9.6 million square kilometres and an area of the inner and territorial sea of about 3 million square kilometres in the Yellow Sea, East China Sea and South China Sea from north to south. It has approximately 18,000 kilometres of coastline and 22,000 kilometres of land frontiers. It borders fourteen countries, i.e., North Korea in the east, Vietnam and Laos in the south, Myanmar, India, Bhutan and Nepal in the southwest, Pakistan, Afghanistan, Tajikistan, Kyrgyzstan and Kazakhstan in the west, and Mongolia and Russia in the north. The neighbouring countries are South Korea and Japan across the Yellow Sea and the Philippines, Malaysia, Indonesia and Brunei across the South China Sea.

2. Beijing, previously called 'Peking', has been the capital of China since the establishment of the People's Republic on 1 October 1949 and is situated in the Hebei Plan in the north of China. Besides Beijing, Shanghai, Tianjin, Chongqing, Shenyang, Dalian, Qingdao, Nanjing, Hangzhou, Ningbo, Suzhou, Wuhan, Xi'an, Zhengzhou, Chengdu, Kunming, Changsha, Guangzhou, Shenzhen, Xiamen, Guangzhou, Haikou are among the most important major cities in Mainland China.

China has twenty-two provinces, five autonomous regions, four municipalities directly under the State Council and two special administrative regions (SARs).

The twenty-two provinces are Heilongjiang, Jilin and Liaoning in the northeast; Hebei and Shanxi in the north; Shandong, Jiangsu, Anhui, Zhejiang, Jiangxi, Fujian and Taiwan in the east; Guangdong and Hainan in the south, Hunan, Hubei, Henan in the centre; Yunnan, Sichuan, Guizhou in the southwest; Shaanxi and Gansu in the west. The five autonomous regions where people of minority nationalities live in compact communities and regional national autonomy is carried out are Tibet in the west, Inner Mongolia, Xinjiang Uygur and Ningxia Hui in the northwest and Guangxi Zhuang in the southwest. The four municipalities directly under the State Council are Beijing and Tianjin in the north, Shanghai in the east, and Chongqing in the southwest. The SARs are Hong Kong and Macau.

All parts of China except Hong Kong, Macau and Taiwan are called Mainland China.

...currently a special province of China. It is separated geographically ...land by the Taiwan Straits and has not been under the central gov-...nce 1949, at the end of the Chinese Civil War. All affairs, including poli-...economy, military affairs, etc., are dominated by the Taiwan local government ...ead of the central government of China. In the past decades, however, trade, ...ncluding maritime trade between the two sides, increased significantly.

II. Demography

4. China is a populous country with a population of proximately one-fourth of the total population in the world and is the second largest country in the world in terms of population, about 145 inhabitants per square kilometre. In accordance with the result of the seventh national census conducted on 1 November 2020, the total population in Mainland China was 1,443.50 million. The population in Hong Kong, Macau and Taiwan on 1 November 2020 was respectively 7.47 million, 0.68 million and 23.56 million.

5. There are altogether fifty-six nationalities in China.

The Han nationality is the largest one, accounting for 91.11% of the population of China in accordance with the result of the seventh national census and is distributed all over the country. Its people speak and write Mandarin Chinese, but there are many dialects.

Other nationalities which are called minority nationalities are, alphabetically, Achang, Baizu, Benglong, Blang, Bonan, Bouyei, Chaoxian, Daizu, Daur, Derung, Dongxiang, Dongzu, Ewenki, Gaoshan, Gelao, Ginzu, Hani, Hezhen, Huizu, Jingpo, Jino, Kazak, Kirgiz, Lahu, Lhoba, Lisu, Lizu, Manzu, Maonan, Miaozu, Monba, Mongol, Mulam, Naxi, Nuzu, Oroqen, Primi, Qiangzu, Russ, Salar, Shezu, Suizu, Tajik, Tatar, Tujia, Tuzu, Uygur, Uzbek, Vazu, Xibe, Yaozu, Yizu, Yugur, Zangzu, Zhuangzu. Most of the minority nationalities have their own languages. Among them, the majority live in compact communities in the autonomous regions. These minority nationalities account for 8.89% of the total population of China.

In accordance with the result of the seventh national census, the total population living in cities or towns was 901.99 million, accounting for 63.89% of the population of China, while 509.79 million people, accounting for 36.11%, were living in rural areas.

III. Information on Political and Legal System of the Country: Form of Government

6. The prevailing *Constitution of the People's Republic of China* (hereinafter referred to as '*Constitution*'), promulgated in 1982 and latest amended on 11 March 2018, sets up a socialist State under the people's democratic dictatorship led by the working class and based on the alliance of workers and peasants. The socialist system is the basic system of China. All powers in China belong to the whole people. The National People's Congress (hereinafter referred to as 'NPC') and the local people's congresses at various levels are the organs through which the people exercise the State powers.

7. NPC is the highest organ of State powers. Its permanent body is the Standing Committee of NPC. The State Council, i.e., the central government of China, is the executive body of the highest organ of the State powers and of the State administration.

Laws and resolutions are to be adopted by a majority vote of all the deputies to NPC or members of its Standing Committee. NPC is composed of deputies elected from the provinces, autonomous regions and municipalities directly under the State Council and the armed forces. All minority nationalities are entitled to appropriate representation.

8. The *Constitution* also sets out the principle of democratic centralism applied by all the State organs of China. NPC and the local people's congresses at various levels are constituted through democratic elections and are responsible to the people and subject to the people's supervision. All the administrative, judicial and procuratorial organs of the State are created by the people's congresses to which they are responsible and by which they are supervised. The division of functions and powers between the central and local State organs is guided by the principle of giving full scope to the initiatives and enthusiasm of the local authorities under the unified leadership of the central authorities.

9. The age of eligibility for election is 18 for NPC and local people's congresses.

NPC is elected for a term of five years and meets in session once a year and is convened by its Standing Committee.

10. The President and Vice President of China are elected by NPC. Chinese citizens who have the right to vote and to stand for election and have reached the age of 45 are eligible for election as the President or the Vice President.

The term of office of the President and Vice President is the same as that of NPC.

In pursuance of the decisions of NPC or its Standing Committee, the President promulgates laws and other national statutes, appoints or removes the premier, vice premiers, State councillors, ministers in charge of ministries or commissions, auditor-general and secretary-general of the State Council, confers State medals or titles of honour, issues orders of special pardons, proclaims martial law or a State of war, and issues mobilization orders.

11. Regional autonomy is practised in the areas where people of minority nationalities live in compact communities where organs of self-government are established to exercise the powers of autonomy. All the national autonomous areas are integral parts of China. All the minority nationalities have the freedom to use and develop their own spoken and written languages and to preserve or reform their own folkways and customs.

12. NPC exercises the functions and powers of amending the *Constitution*, supervising the enforcement thereof, enacting and amending basic laws governing criminal offences, civil affairs, State organs and other nationwide important matters. Its Standing Committee is competent for interpreting the *Constitution*, supervising its enforcement, enacting, amending and interpreting laws. The division of powers in enacting and amending laws is specified in the *Law on Legislation* adopted by NPC on 15 March 2000 and amended in March 2015 and in March 2023.

The State Council is competent for the adoption of administrative measures, enactment of administrative rules and regulations in accordance with the *Law on Legislation*, issuance of decisions and orders in accordance with the *Constitution* and laws for education, including academic education, cultural affairs, social welfare, health, economy, local and provincial governments, public function and scientific research as well as other functions and powers as NPC or its Standing Committee may assign to it.

13. The provinces, autonomous regions or municipalities directly under the State Council are headed by the people's congresses at the same level, i.e., the provincial level. The lower localities, including municipalities next to the provincial level or districts within the municipalities directly under the State Council, counties or districts at county level within the capitals of provinces, autonomous regions, and townships, are headed by the people's congresses at the same level. The local people's congresses at various levels are the local organs of the State powers at the corresponding levels. The local governments at various levels are the local executive bodies of the State powers as well as the local organs of the State administration at the corresponding levels.

The governors, mayors or heads of localities at various levels assume the overall responsibilities for the local people's governments at the corresponding levels. The local people's congresses at their respective levels elect and have the power to recall the governors and deputy governors, the mayors and deputy mayors, or the heads and deputy heads.

14. The people's courts of law are the judicial organs of the State. The Supreme People's Court (hereinafter referred to as 'SPC'), located in Beijing, is the highest judicial organ of the State. Currently, SPC has six circuit courts, i.e., in Shenzhen, Shenyang, Nanjing, Zhengzhou, Chongqing and Xi'an, which exercise judicial power over administrative and civil cases on behalf of SPC.

A people's high court is established in a province, autonomous region or municipality directly under the State Council. The people's intermediate courts are established at the level next to the provincial one, and the people's basic courts are established at county level. Special courts of law, including the maritime courts are established as introduced in Chapter 3 of Part I *infra*.

The people's courts exercise judicial power independently and in accordance with the provisions of laws and are not subject to interference by any administrative organs, public organizations or individuals.

SPC, as the highest judicial organ in China, supervises the administration of justice by the people's courts at various local levels and by the special people's courts. The people's courts at higher levels supervise the administration of justice by those at lower levels.

IV. Economy and Transport

15. As the largest developing country in the world, China's economy has been developing over the past forty years. According to the China National Bureau of Statistics (NBS), the gross domestic product (GDP) of Mainland China reached CNY 121.02 trillion or approximately USD 18 trillion in 2022 and ranked the second largest in the world only after the United States. In 2022, the volume of commodity export in Mainland China reached USD 3.359 trillion, the volume of commodity import reached USD 2.72 trillion, and the total volume of commodity export and import reached USD 6.31 trillion and ranked first in the world.

16. The rapid development of the economy has stimulated the development of transport. The government has been making tremendous investments in the development of infrastructures of transport in the past decades.

§2. General Introduction to Transport

I. Basic Statistics Relating to Transport

17. China has the complete five means of transport, i.e., shipping, railway transport, highway transport, aviation transport and pipeline transport.

According to the *Statistical Bulletin on the Development of the Transportation Industry in 2022* issued by the Ministry of Transport (hereinafter referred to as 'MOT'), in Mainland China in 2022, the total operational cargo transport volume and turnover of operational cargo transport reached 50.67 billion mt and 22,616.1 billion mt×km respectively. The turnover of containers reached 296 million TEUs in the scaled ports. The total passenger transport volume was 55.87 billion person-times tons, and the total turnover of passenger transport was 1,292.12 billion person×km. These two figures were a more than 30% decrease as compared with 2021 due to the serious influence of the COVID-19 pandemic.

The following are statistics concerning the passenger and freight traffic and their respective turnover in Mainland China in 2022.

Table 1 Passenger Traffic/Turnover of Passenger Traffic

Mode	*Passenger Traffic (Million Person-Times)*	*Turnover of Passenger Traffic (Million Person-Times×Km)*
Railway	1,673	657,530
Highway	3,546	240,754
Waterway	116	2,260
Aviation	252	391,387
In total	5,587	1,292,154

Table 2 Freight Traffic/Turnover of Freight Traffic

Mode	*Freight Traffic (Million Tons)*	*Turnover of Freight Traffic (Million Tons×Km)*
Railway	4,984	3,594,569
Highway	37,119	6,895,804
Waterway	8,554	12,100,314
Aviation	6	25,410
Pipeline	660	350,009
In total	50,663	22,616,096

The following are statistics concerning the length of transport routes and main operating transport vehicles in Mainland China by the end of 2022.

Table 3 Length of Transport Routes

Railways	155,000 km
Highways	5,354,800 km
Inland waterways	128,000 km

Table 4 Main Operating Transport Vehicles

Railway locomotives	22,100
Railways passenger wagons	77,000
Railway freight wagons	997,000
Automobiles	12,220,800
Motor vessels	121,900
Aeroplanes	4,165

II. Shipping

18. In Mainland China, as compared with the other four transport means, ping still plays the most important role in foreign trade transport. Nearly 90% of th Chinese import and export cargoes are carried by sea. The volume of waterway freight traffic and turnover of waterway freight traffic were 16.9% and 53.5%, respectively, of the total volume and turnover in 2022.

According to the *Review of Maritime Transport 2022* published by the United Nations Conference on Trade and Development (UNCTAD), the Chinese merchant fleet in the mainland ranked second with a percentage of 12.74% of the world merchant fleet in terms of deadweight tonnage (DWT), while Hong Kong ranked fifth with a percentage of 5.12% of the world merchant fleet by 1 January 2022. Meanwhile, the Chinese merchant fleet in the mainland ranked first and Hong Kong ranked eighth in terms of the commercial value in the world by 1 January 2022.

19. The following are statistics concerning the general water-borne transport by the end of 2022 in Mainland China.

Table 5 General of Water-Borne Transport

Vessels	121,900
Coastal vessels	10,997
Ocean vessels	1,387
Inland vessels	109,500
Net deadweight of vessels	297,758,100 tons
Net deadweight of coastal vessels	93,703,100 tons
Net deadweight of ocean vessels	51,557,700 tons
Net deadweight of inland vessels	152,497,300 tons
Passenger carrying capacity	861,800
Container carrying capacity	2,987,200 TEUs
Operating berths	21,323
Berths at seaports	5,441
Berths at inland ports	15,822
Turnover of sea and inland ports	15,685,000,000 mt
Turnover of seaports	10,131,000,000 mt
Turnover of inland ports	5,554,000,000 mt
Freight traffic	8,554,000,000 mt
Inland freight traffic	4,402,000,000 mt
Sea freight traffic	4,151,000,000 mt
Turnover of freight traffic	12,100,314,000,000 mt×km

… inland freight traffic	1,902,573,000,000 mt×km
…ver of sea freight traffic	10,197,741,000,000 mt×km
…ssenger traffic	116,000,000 person-times
Turnover of passenger traffic	2,260,000,000 person-times×km

20. The largest shipping companies such as China COSCO SHIPPING Corporation Limited, known as 'COSCO SHIPPING', China Merchants Energy Shipping Co., Ltd. and SINOTRANS & CSC Holdings Co., Ltd. under China Merchants Group, known as CMG, are mainly invested by the State and thus called State-owned enterprises, although some companies thereunder are listing companies involving numerous big or small shareholders. However, these enterprises are independent legal persons in law, like private companies and enjoy a high degree of autonomy in their business operations.

COSCO SHIPPING is headquartered in Shanghai. It is the merged entity of China Ocean Shipping (Group) Company (COSCO) and China Shipping (Group) Company (China Shipping). By the end of 2022, the total fleet of COSCO SHIPPING comprises 1,394 vessels with a total DWT of 113.82 million tons, ranking the first in the world. Its container fleet capacity is 3.02 million TEUs, ranking third in the world. Its dry bulk fleet of 437 ships with total DWT of 45.14 million tons, tanker fleet of 228 tankers with total DWT of 29.18 million tons, and general and specialized cargo fleet of 175 ships with total DWT of 5.78 million tons, are all at the top of the world's list. COSCO SHIPPING has also invested in port terminals, logistics, shipping finance, shipbuilding and ship repairs.

CMG is headquartered in Hong Kong and was founded in 1872 as the first commercial corporation in China. China Merchants Energy Shipping Co., Ltd, under CMG, operates and manages a fleet with a total capacity ranking second among the non-financial shipowners in the world. Its oil tanker fleet and bulk carrier fleet are leading in the world. CMG has also invested in port terminals, logistics, shipping finance, shipbuilding and ship repair.

21. China has concluded bilateral shipping agreements with nearly seventy countries or regions. In Mainland China, shipping companies engaging in international shipping business and branch companies of foreign shipping enterprises may be solely invested by foreign companies subject to approval by the MOT and the Ministry of Commerce (hereinafter referred to as 'MOC'). Foreign enterprises have invested in many projects in port construction in Mainland China. All the major seaports and inland ports are open to ships flying foreign flags.

III. Coastal Ports

22. The principal coastal ports are linked with each other and with other Chinese and even Asian destinations by highways, railways or even pipelines. They offer a wide choice of liner and tramp services for the carriage of goods to and from

the maritime forelands. Goods are transported to and from hinterlands by traditional means like inland waterways, railways, highways or even pipelines. The goods arriving at those ports are either immediately transferred to ships or are unloaded on the quay and stored temporarily in the open air or in warehouses. In order to guarantee an efficient performance, ports have all the essential infrastructure like good access by waterways, docks, locks, sites and superstructure, e.g., warehouses, storage spaces, loading and unloading installations and also the specialist work-force.

Ningbo-Zhoushan, Tangshan, Shanghai, Qingdao, Guangzhou, Suzhou, Rizhao and Tianjin were among the leading ten global ports in the world in terms of throughput of freight traffic in 2022, and Ningbo-Zhoushan ranked first with its throughput of freight traffic of 1.22 billion mt. Shanghai, Ningbo-Zhoushan, Shenzhen, Guangzhou, Qingdao, Tianjin and Hong Kong were among the leading ten global container ports in the world in terms of throughput of container freight traffic in 2023, and Shanghai ranked first with its throughput of container freight traffic of 47.30 million TEUs.

23. The following are statistics regarding the principal coastal ports in Mainland China.

Table 6 General of Principal Coastal Ports in 2022

Operating sea berths	5,441
Throughput of principal coastal ports	10,131,000,000 mt
Throughput of passengers	38,474,300 person-times

Table 7 Throughput of Leading Ten Coastal Ports in 2022

Port	*Freight Traffic (Million Tons)*	*Port*	*Container Freight Traffic (Million TEUs)*
Ningbo-Zhoushan	1,261.34	Shanghai	47.30
Tangshan	768.87	Ningbo-Zhoushan	33.35
Shanghai	727.77	Shenzhen	30.04
Qingdao	657.54	Qingdao	25.67
Guangzhou	655.92	Guangzhou	24.86
Suzhou	572.76	Tianjin	21.02
Rizhao	570.57	Xiamen	12.43
Tianjin	549.02	Suzhou	9.08
Yantai	462.57	Beibuwan	7.02
Beibuwan	371.34	Rizhao	5.80

IV. Inland Waterways and Ports

24. The inland water systems in Mainland China are flourishing and facilitate inland navigation. There are mainly three inland water systems, i.e., the Changjiang River in the middle, the Pearl River in the south and the Heilongjiang River bordering Russia in the north, all of which are in the direction from west to east. Each system consists of rivers and lakes.

Among the three rivers, the Changjiang River, the lower reaches of which are called the Yangtze River, plays the most important role in the inland navigation in China. The Changjiang River, with a navigable length of over 64,818 km, is the longest river in China and the third longest in the world. Its main navigable waterways across six provinces, *viz.* Sichuan, Hunan, Hubei, Jiangxi, Anhui, Jiangsu and two municipalities directly under the State Council, *viz.* Shanghai and Chongqing and links twenty-three lakes. Its estuary lies in Shanghai and connects the East China Sea. Suzhou (Taicang and Changshu and Zhangjiagang), Nanjing, Nantong, Huzhou, Zhenjiang, Jiangyin, Taizhou, Chongqing, Foshan, Jiaxing, Yueyang, Wuhan, Wuhu, Anqing, Jiujiang and Chizhou, etc., are the major inland ports.

25. The following are statistics regarding inland waterways and ports in 2022 in Mainland China.

Table 8 General of Inland Waterways & Ports in 2022

Length of inland waterways	128,000 km
Operating berths	15,882
Throughput of principal inland ports	5,554,000,000 mt
Turnover of inland freight traffic	1,902,573,000,000 mt×km

Table 9 Throughput of the Leading Ten Inland Ports in 2022

Port	*Freight Traffic (Million Tons)*	*Port*	*Container Freight Traffic (Million TEUs)*
Suzhou	572.76	Suzhou	9.08
Taizhou	364.44	Foshan	3.22
Jiangyin	350.62	Nanjing	3.20
Nantong	285.08	Jiaxing	2.85
Nanjing	271.55	Wuhan	2.70
Zhenjiang	225.42	Nantong	2.24
Jiujiang	180.61	Wuhu	1.25
Wuhu	135.04	Chongqing	1.13
Wuhan	130.74	Yueyang	1.01
Chizhou	130.63	Jiangmen	0.98

Besides the three rivers mentioned *supra*, the Great Canal, which was originally put into operation in 1293 and linked four provinces, *viz.* Hebei, Shandong, Jiangsu and Zhejiang and one municipality directly under the State Council, *viz.* Beijing, in the direction from north to south with a length of 1,423 km, also plays an important role in inland water transport.

V. General Introduction to Other Means of Transport

A. *Railway*

26. There is a gigantic railway network in Mainland China consisting of State-owned railways, joint venture railways, local railways and industrial railways. By the end of 2022, the total length of railways reached 155,000 km, ranking second in the world. In particular, the length of high-speed railways with speeds of 200 to 350 km per hour reached more than 42,000 km, which is about 50% of the total length of high-speed railways in the world.

Within the railway network, the principal trunk national railways are Jingguang (Beijing-Guangzhou) and Jingjiu (Beijing-Kowloon), connecting north and south in the middle, Jinghu (Beijing-Shanghai) connecting north and east, Jiaoliu (Datong-Liuzhou) connecting north and south in the west, Baocheng (Baoji-Chengdu) and Chengkun (Chengdu-Kunming) in the southwestern area, Longhai (Lianyungang-Lanzhou) and Lanxin (Lanzhou-Urumqi) connecting east and northwest, Jingbao (Beijing-Baotou) and Baolan (Baotou-Lanzhou) connecting east and west in the north, Hukun (Shanghai-Kunming) connecting east and west in the middle, Hada (Harbin-Dalian) and Binzhou-Binsui in the northeast, Jingshen (Beijing-Shenyang) connecting north and northeast.

More than ten international railways connect seven neighbouring countries. Among these railways, three connect Russia, three connect North Korea, two connect Vietnam, two connect Kazakhstan, two connect Myanmar, one connects Mongolia, and one connects Laos. There are more than ten international railway passenger transport routes, including, *inter alia*, Beijing–Pyongyang (North Korea), Beijing–Hanoi (Vietnam), Kunming–Hanoi (Vietnam), Beijing–Ulaan Bator (Mongolia), Huhhot–Ulaan Bator (Mongolia), Urumqi–Druzhba-Alamto (Kazakhstan), Beijing–Moscow (Russia), Shenyang–Moscow (Russia), Harbin–Vladivostok–Chabarovsk (Russia), Kunming–Vientiane (Laos).

The Asia-Europe land bridge between Lianyungang in China at the east end and Rotterdam in the Netherlands at the west end links the Pacific and Atlantic regions via railways with a length of 10,800 km. The China Railway Express (CR Express), operated by China Railway Corporation provides regular container freight services between China and several European countries, including Russia, Poland, Germany, France and Spain, from 2011.

27. The following are statistics regarding railway transport in 2022 in Mainland China.

Table 10 General of Railway Transport in 2022

Length of railways	155,000 km
State-owned railways	134,000 km
High-speed railways	42,000 km
Railway locomotives	22,100
Railway passenger wagons	77,000
Railway freight wagons	997,000
Passenger traffic	1,672,960,000 person-times
Turnover of passenger traffic	657,753,000,000 person-times×km
Freight traffic	4,984,240,000 mt
Turnover of freight traffic	3,594,569,000,000 mt×km

B. Highway

28. A huge highway transport network exists in Mainland China and ranks second in the world in terms of length. Highway transport remains the most important mode of domestic passenger and freight transport in terms of covering areas. The network links with all the neighbouring countries.

Highways can be divided into State-owned, local and joint venture ones from the point of investment.

29. The following are statistics regarding highway transport in 2022 in Mainland China.

Table 11 General of Highway Transport

Length of highways	5,354,800 km
Expressways	177,300 km
Transport automobiles	12,220,800
Passenger automobiles	554,200
Cargo automobiles	11,666,600
Passenger traffic	3,546,000,000 person-times
Turnover of passenger traffic	240,754,000,000 person-times×km
Freight traffic	37,119,000,000 mt
Turnover of freight traffic	6,895,804,000,000 mt×km

C. Civil Aviation

30. By the end of 2022, there were sixty-six airlines in Mainland China. Three principal airlines are China International Airlines (Air China), China Southern Airlines (China Southern) and China Eastern Airlines (China Eastern). These principal airlines, together with Hainan Airlines, Shanghai Airlines, Shenzhen Airlines, Xiamen Airlines, Shandong Airlines, Juneyao Airlines, Tianjin Airlines and China Cargo Airlines in Mainland China, are members of the International Air Transport Associations, known as 'IATA', founded in Havana in 1945. Besides, Cathay Pacific, Dragonair, Hong Kong Airlines and Hong Kong Express Airways based in Hong Kong and Air Macau based in Macau are members of IATA.

There were 254 civil transport airports in Mainland China by the end of 2022, among which the passenger traffic of eighteen airports was over 10 million person×time, and the freight and post traffic of fifty-one airports was over 10,000 mt. Beijing, Shanghai and Guangzhou are the busiest airports. Other principal airports include Chengdu, Shenzhen, Kunming, Xi'an, Chongqing, Hangzhou, Xiamen, Changsha, Nanjing, Urumqi, Dalian, Qingdao, Zhengzhou, Sanya, Shenyang and Haikou, etc.

By the end of 2022, there were 661 general air companies with a total number of 3,186 aeroplanes.

China has concluded bilateral civil air transport agreements with 129 countries and regions.

31. In 2022, the total air traffic turnover in Mainland China was 59.928 billion tons×km, the total air passenger traffic was 0.252 billion person-times, and its turnover was 391.387 billion person-times×km, the total air freight and post traffic was 6,076,100 mt, and its turnover was 2.541 billion person-times×km. As compared with the figure for 2021, the figures experienced a drop of about 30% due to the spread of the COVID-19 pandemic.

32. The following are statistics regarding civil aviation transport in 2022 in Mainland China.

Table 12 General of Civil Aviation Transport

Airports	254
Airlines	66
Air routes	4,670
Domestic	4,334
Hong Kong and Macau	27
International	336
Length of repeated air routes	10,327,900 km
Domestic	8,651,100 km
International	1,676,800 km

Length of non-repeated air routes	6,998,900 km
Domestic	5,461,500 km
International	1,537,400 km
Aeroplanes	4,165
Flights	598,932
Flight hours	6,275,600
Passenger traffic	251,713,200 person-times
Domestic	249,852,500 person-times
Hong Kong and Macau	469,200 person-times
International	1,860,800 person-times
Freight and post traffic	6,076,100 mt
Domestic	3,437,900 mt
Hong Kong and Macau	147,400 mt
International	2,638,200 mt
Total traffic turnover	59,928,000,000 mt×km
Domestic	38,786,000,000 mt×km
Hong Kong and Macau	230,000,000 mt×km
International	21,142,000,000 mt×km
Passenger traffic turnover	391,387,000,000 person-times×km
Domestic	380,501,000,000 person-times×km
Hong Kong and Macau	651,000,000 person-times×km
International	10,887,000,000 person-times×km
freight and post traffic turnover	25,410,000,000 mt×km
Domestic	5,230,000,000 mt×km
Hong Kong and Macau	173,000,000 mt×km
International	20,179,000,000 mt×km

D. Pipelines

33. Pipelines have become more and more important and are irrefutably a necessary complement to the traditional traffic infrastructure. Transport through pipes is, in certain cases, even vital for the establishment of industrial plants. This explains why there is still a boom of pipelines in the ports of coastal cities importing or exporting oil, gas or liquefied chemical products.

Traditionally, pipelines as a means of transport are mainly used to transport crude oil from oil fields to the near major seaports in China. Now pipelines are also used to transport natural and other gases and oil products, especially natural gases, from the western part to the eastern part of China. Remarkably, there are four pipelines which transport the imported natural gas or crude oil from neighbouring countries. The China-Myanmar oil and gas pipeline is used to transport from Myanmar part of the crude oil imported by China from the Middle East and Africa to China as a result of which, the transport of the crude oil and natural gas is not through the Malacca Strait, the Indian Ocean and the South China Sea. The China-Kazakhstan crude oil pipeline transports crude oil from Kazakhstan to China. The China- Middle Asia natural gas pipeline transports natural gas from Turkmenistan to China via Uzbekistan and Kazakhstan. The China-Russia crude oil pipeline transports crude oil from Russia to China.

A network of pipelines has been formed with a total length of 118,000 km. In 2022, the pipeline transport volume reached 860 million tons, and its turnover reached 562.18 billion ton×km.

VI. Ministry or Department Responsible for Transport Policy

34. In Mainland China, the four means of transport, i.e., shipping, railway transport, highway transport and aviation transport, are subject to the administration of a single department under the State Council, i.e., MOT, after the reform of central governmental organs.

MOT is directly responsible for the maritime transport, inland navigation and road transport. The National Railway Administration under MOT is responsible for railway transport. The Civil Aviation Administration of China (hereinafter referred to as 'CAAC') under MOT is responsible for civil aviation transport. The transport through pipelines is the responsibility of the enterprises of which the main enterprise engaged in transport through pipelines is the China Petroleum Pipeline Bureau (CPP) under China National Petroleum Corporation (CNPC).

The aforementioned governmental authorities issue orders and directives, promulgate provisions within their respective powers in pursuance of the laws, especially the *Law on Legislation*, adopted by NPC or its Standing Committee, and the administrative rules and regulations, decisions and orders issued by the State Council. To this extent, they are competent for making transport policies in macrocosm and also responsible for the implementation of the laws adopted by NPC or its Standing Committee, the rules, regulations and policies made by the State Council.

35. The transport authorities under the local governments are responsible for the implementation of the laws adopted by NPC or its Standing Committee, the rules, regulations and policies made by the State Council, MOT and the local people's congresses or governments at the same or higher levels, and for handling specific administrative matters within their respective powers and responsibilities.

Part I. Introduction

Chapter 1. Definitions and Notions

§1. Maritime Law and Transport Law

36. Maritime law, or admiralty law, is a body of legal norms that regulate the relations arising from maritime transport and those pertaining to ships.[1]

37. In China, maritime law is deemed basically as a special part of civil law. The main body of maritime law is the civil and commercial legal rules that deal with contracts of carriage of passengers or goods by sea, charter parties, contracts of towage, contracts of marine insurance, maritime torts such as ship's collision and marine pollution from ships, limitation of liability for maritime claims, ownership of, mortgage and maritime lien on ships, all of which relate to ships as the tools of maritime transport or other maritime operations.

38. Apart from civil and commercial legal rules, maritime law is also shaped by rules in the nature of administrative law, international law, labour law, procedural law and even criminal law.

The legal rules dealing with ship's registration and nationality, right of navigation, maritime safety, prevention of marine pollution and other similar matters are in the nature of administrative or international law. The legal rules dealing with the rights and obligations of the master and crewmembers during their employment on board ships and other labour relations between the masters or crewmembers and their employers are in the nature of labour law. Special legal rules dealing with maritime litigation and arbitration are part of procedural law. The legal rules dealing with crimes committed on board ships or at sea are part of criminal law.

39. Transport law is much broader than maritime law in terms of the scope of regulation.

Besides maritime transport, transport law regulates all other types of transport, *viz.*, railway transport, highway transport, aviation transport and even pipeline transport.

So far, a few legal rules and provisions that are common to all types of transport are contained in Chapter XIX, 'Contract of Carriage' of Book Three 'Contracts' of the Civil Code of China (hereinafter referred to as 'CC'). Separate legal rules are

1. Si, Y. & Hu, Z. *e.a.*, *Maritime Law*, Beijing, 1999, 3.

shaped in special laws for maritime transport, railway transport, and aviation transport. Currently, however, no separate legal rules in the nature of civil and commercial law are shaped for highway transport or pipeline transport.

§2. THE LAW OF THE SEA

40. The law of the sea is deemed as a body of legal norms that regulate the relations between States or between a State and other legal identity regarding the use and control of the sea and its resources. Use and control of the sea and its resources relates to, *inter alia*, the navigation of ships at sea in respect of freedom on the high seas, the right of innocent passage in the territorial waters of other States, control of the coastal State over foreign ships navigating in the inner waters of the State as well as prevention of marine pollution from ships, which is also deemed as part of maritime law in China. Consequently, the law of the sea and maritime law overlap in some aspects so far as ships are concerned.

41. Basically, the law of the sea is part of public international law. Thus, its main sources are international treaties and international customs and usages. In China, there are also domestic laws and regulations in this regard.

The law of the sea has been codified in the *United Nations Convention on the Law of the Sea*, known as 'UNCLOS' or 'Montego Bay Convention', signed at Montego Bay on 10 December 1982 and came into force as of 16 November 1994.

In pursuance of the decision made by the Standing Committee of NPC on 15 May 1996, China ratified the UNCLOS. At the same time, the following was declared by the Chinese Government:

- China has the sovereignty and jurisdiction over its exclusive economic zone and continental shelf within an area of 200 nautical miles by virtue of the provisions of the UNCLOS.
- China shall negotiate with the neighbouring countries for the division of borderlines of respective jurisdiction overseas in accordance with international law and the principle of equity.
- China re-declares its sovereignty over the islands listed in Article 2 of the *Law on the Territorial Sea and Contiguous Zone* adopted on 25 February 1992.
- China re-declares that the provisions contained in the UNCLOS regarding innocent passage in the territorial waters do not prejudice its right to require foreign warships to obtain permission from and to inform the Chinese Government in advance in accordance with its laws and regulations.

42. Besides the *Law on the Territorial Sea and Contiguous Zone*, other laws and regulations of China relating to or in connection with the control of the seas include, *inter alia*:

- The *Law on the Exclusive Economic Zone and Continental Shelf*, adopted by the Standing Committee of NPC on 26 June 1998.

- The *Maritime Traffic Safety Law* (MTSL), adopted by the Standing Committee of NPC on 2 September 1983 and revised on 29 April 2021.
- The *Regulations on the Administration of Foreign Ships*, adopted by the State Council in 1979.
- The *Regulations on the Registration of Vessels*, adopted by the State Council on 2 June 1994.
- The *Regulations on the Prevention and Control of Pollution of Marine Environment from Vessels*, adopted by the State Council on 2 September 2009.

43. The law of the sea is not the object of the present study, except those contents thereof overlapped by maritime law.

Chapter 2. The Main Sources of Transport Law

§1. Maritime Law

I. Treaties

44. International maritime treaties in various forms have been playing an essential role in modern international maritime law. This is because maritime transport or other operations of ships often have cross-border or international features.

Before 1980 when China began to carry out the policies of reform and opening to the outside world, China was not active in shaping, acceding to or ratifying international treaties in the area of maritime law.

Up to now, China has ratified or acceded to most of the treaties adopted by the former Inter-governmental Maritime Consultative Organization (IMCO) or the current International Maritime Organization (IMO), a United Nations agency established in London of which China is a Member State of council of Grade A, mainly regarding safety of ships and prevention of marine pollution. However, China has not ratified or acceded to some international maritime commercial treaties up to now, especially those shaped by Comité Maritime International (CMI) at an earlier time. However, many contents of such treaties are absorbed into the *Maritime Code* (hereinafter referred to as 'MC') adopted by NPC on 7 November 1992 and coming into force as of 1 July 1993.

45. So far, China has ratified or acceded to the following international treaties in the area of commercial maritime law:

- The *International Convention for the Unification of Certain Rules of Law relating to Collisions between Vessels*, known as '1910 Collision Convention', signed in Brussels on 23 September 1910.
- The *Athens Convention relating to the Carriage of Passengers and Their Luggage by Sea*, known as '1974 PAL', signed at Athens on 13 December 1974, and its Special Drawing Right (SDR) Protocol of 1976.
- The *Convention on the Limitation of Liability for Maritime Claims*, known as 'LLMC', signed in London on 19 November 1976, but only applicable in Hong Kong.[2]
- The *International Convention on Salvages*, signed in London on 28 April 1989.
- The *International Convention on Civil Liability for Oil Pollution Damages*, known as '1969 CLC', signed at Brussels on 29 November 1969, its SDR Protocol of 1976 and Protocol of 1992 (the 1969 CLC as amended by its Protocol of 1992 is called '1992 CLC').

---

2. By virtue of the agreement concluded between the government of China and that of the UK, the international treaties ratified or acceded to by the UK should be ceased to apply in Hong Kong on 1 Jul. 1997 when the sovereignty over Hong Kong was returned to China and China should ratify or accede to these treaties to be applicable in Hong Kong on the same date in order to maintain the prosperity and stability in Hong Kong.

- The *International Convention on the Establishment of an International Fund for Compensation for Oil Pollution Damage*, known as '1971 Fund Convention', signed in Brussels on 18 December 1971, as amended by its Protocol of 1992, also known as '*1992 Fund Convention*', but only applicable in Hong Kong.[3]
- The *International Convention on Civil Liability for Bunker Oil Pollution Damage*, known as '2001 Bunker Convention', signed in London on 23 March 2001.
- The *Nairobi International Convention on the Removal of Wrecks*, known as 'WRC', signed in Nairobi on 18 May 2007.

46. The international treaties that China has ratified or acceded to regarding maritime safety and prevention of marine pollution from ships include, *inter alia*:

- The *International Convention on Ship Load Lines*, known as 'LL', signed in London on 5 April 1966.
- The *International Convention on the Measurement of Ship Tonnages*, signed in London on 23 June 1969.
- The *International Convention relating to Intervention on the High Seas in Cases Oil Pollution Casualties*, known as 'Intervention Convention', signed in Brussels on 29 November 1969, its Protocol of 1973 and Amendment of 1991.
- The *Protocol relating to Intervention on the High Seas in Cases of Pollution by Substances Other than Oil*, 1973, known as 'Intervention Prot. 1973', signed in London on 2 November 1973 and its Amendment.
- The *Convention on the Prevention of Marine Pollution by Dumping of Wastes and Other Matters*, known as 'LDC', signed in London on 13 November 1972, and its Amendments.
- The *International Convention on Safety of Containers*, signed in Geneva on 2 December 1972, known as 'CSC', and its Amendments of 1981, 1983, 1991 and 1993.
- The *Convention on the International Regulations for the Prevention of Collisions at Sea*, known as 'COLREGs', signed in London on 20 October 1972 and its Amendments.
- The *International Convention for the Prevention of Pollution from Ships*, signed in London on 2 November 1973 as amended by its Protocol of 1978, known as 'MARPOL 73/78' and its Amendments.
- The *International Convention on Safety of Life at Sea*, known as 'SOLAS', signed in London on 1 November 1974 and most of its Protocols and Amendments.
- The *Convention on International Maritime Satellite Organization*, known as 'INMASAT', signed in London on 3 September 1976 and its Amendment of 1985.
- The *International Convention on the Standards of Training, Certification and Watch-keeping for Seafarers*, known as 'STCW', signed on 7 July 1978 and its Amendments.
- The *International Convention on Maritime Search and Rescue*, known as 'SAR', signed in Hamburg on 27 April 1979.

3. *Ibid.*

- The *United Nations Convention on the Law of the Sea*, known as 'UNCLOS', signed in Montego on May 10 December 1982.
- The *Convention on Suppression of Unlawful Acts against the Safety of Maritime Navigation*, known as 'SUA', signed in Rome on 10 March 1988.
- The *Protocol for the Suppression of Unlawful Acts against the Safety of Fixed Platforms Located on the Continental Shelf*, signed in Rome on 10 March 1988.
- The *International Convention on Oil Pollution Preparedness, Response and Co-operation,* known as 'OPRC', signed in London on 30 November 1990.
- The *Protocol on Preparedness, Response and Co-operation to Pollution Incidents by Hazardous and Noxious Substances,* signed in London on 15 March 2000, but only applicable in Macau.

47. China has ratified the Maritime Labour Convention, known as 'MLC', adopted by the International Labour Organization (ILO) and signed in Geneva on 23 February 2006 and its Amendments.

48. Another international treaty relating to maritime transport that China has ratified is the *United Nations Convention on a Code of Conduct for Liner Conferences*, known as '*LINER CODE*', signed in Geneva on 6 April 1974.

49. China adheres to the principle that international treaties ratified or acceded to or approved by China have priority over Chinese law in foreign-related relations to the extent of repugnance.

As provided for in Article 268 of MC and Article 96 of the *Marine Environmental Protection Law* (MEPL), if any international treaty concluded or acceded to by China contains provisions differing from those contained in Chinese law, the provisions of the relevant international treaty shall apply unless the provisions are those on which China has announced reservations. As a principle, international treaties are not applicable if no foreign-related relation exists.

Except for the provisions of the treaties on which China has announced reservations, the treaties shall have a direct effect on foreign-related relations in China and are not subject to domestic legislation for the purpose of giving effect thereto. So far as domestic relations are concerned, the treaties are not applicable unless the effect is given by the Chinese government or in domestic law.

The *Law on the Procedure in the Conclusion of Treaties* adopted by NPC on 28 December 1990 governs the procedures in the ratification of, accession to or approval of the multilateral or bilateral agreements by the Chinese Government.

50. China is not a party to the following international treaties in the area of maritime commercial law:

- The *International Convention for the Unification of Certain Rules of Law relating to Bills of lading*, known as 'Hague Rules', signed in Brussels on 25 August

1924, its Protocol known as 'Visby Rules', signed at Brussels on 23 February 1968, and its SDR Protocol, signed in Brussels on 21 December 1979.[4]
- The *International Convention for the Unification of Certain Rules relating to Maritime Liens and Mortgages*, signed in Brussels on 10 April 1926.
- The *International Convention for the Unification of Certain Rules concerning the Immunity of State-owned Ships*, signed in Brussels on 10 April 1926.
- The *International Convention for the Unification of Certain Rules relating to Arrest of Seagoing Ships*, signed in Brussels on 10 May 1952.
- The *International Convention for the Unification of Certain Rules relating to Civil Jurisdiction in Matters of Collision*, signed in Brussels on 10 May 1952.
- The *Convention relating to Civil Liability in the Field of Maritime Carriage of Nuclear Materials*, known as '*Nuclear 1971*', signed in Brussels on 17 December 1971.
- The *United Nations Convention on the Carriage of Goods by Sea*, known as '*Hamburg Rules*', signed in Hamburg on 31 March 1978.
- The *United Nations Convention on International Multimodal Transport of Goods*, signed in Geneva on 24 May 1980.
- The *United Nations Convention on Conditions for the Registration of Ships*, signed in Geneva on 7 February 1986.
- The *International Convention on Maritime Liens and Ship Mortgages*, signed in Geneva on 6 May 1993.
- The *International Convention on Liability and Compensation for Damage in Connection with the Carriage of Hazardous and Noxious Substances by Sea*, known as 'HNS', signed in London on 3 May 1996 and its Protocol of 2010.
- The *International Convention on the Arrest of Ships*, signed in Geneva on 12 March 1999.
- The *United Nations Convention on Contracts for the International Carriage of Goods Wholly or Partly by Sea*, known as '*Rotterdam Rules*', signed in Rotterdam on 23 September 2009.

51. Expectedly, China will take different approaches towards the aforementioned treaties. In detail, it will not ratify or accede to those treaties adopted at an earlier time and have been replaced or will be replaced by new treaties or have become obsolete *ex facto*, but will ratify or accede to those shaped in modern time, when, as in the normal course, many or most of the other trade and shipping powers have become parties to them, unless the ratification or accession will or may be in conflict with the fundamental interests of China.

Noticeably, although many international treaties are not ratified or acceded to by China, as mentioned *supra*, references have been made to some treaties or some contents thereof have been adopted in shaping the relevant Chinese laws or regulations. As typical examples, Chapter XI 'Limitation of Liability for Maritime Claims' of MC is a reproduction of the LLMC 1976, and the basic rules contained in the Hague-Visby Rules are incorporated in Chapter IV 'Contract of Carriage of Goods by Sea' of MC.

4. The Hague Rules as amended by the Visby Rules and the SDR Protocol is known as the Hague-Visby Rules.

II. Domestic Laws and Regulations

52. As the main source of maritime law, the statutes include MC and other laws, regulations and provisions dealing with matters of maritime transport and/or other matters relating to ships.

53. MC deals with the following subject matters:

- 'General Provisions' including the scope of application, principled provisions regarding cabotage, ship's registration and nationality and governmental administration on maritime transport (Chapter I).
- 'Ships' covering the ownership of ships, mortgages and maritime liens on ships (Chapter II).
- 'Masters and Crew', including the basic provisions and the functions and powers of shipmaster (Chapter III).
- 'Contract of Carriage of Goods by Sea' governing, *inter alia*, bills of lading, voyage charter parties and multimodal transport contracts (Chapter IV).
- 'Contract of Carriage of Passengers by Sea' (Chapter V).
- 'Charter Parties' covering time charter parties and bareboat charter parties (Chapter VI).
- 'Contract of Sea Towage' (Chapter VII).
- 'Collisions of Ships' (Chapter VIII).
- 'Salvages at Sea' (Chapter IX).
- 'General Average' (Chapter X).
- 'Limitation of Liability for Maritime Claims' (Chapter XI).
- 'Contract of Marine Insurance' (Chapter XII).
- 'Limitation of Time' (Chapter XIII).
- 'Application of Law in Relating to Foreign-related Matters' (Chapter XIV).
- 'Supplementary Provisions' (Chapter XV).

Two points need to be mentioned concerning the scope of application of MC. First, as defined in Article 2 in Chapter I of MC, the maritime transport, as referred to in MC, means the carriage of goods and passengers by sea, including the river-sea direct transport, but the provisions concerning contract of carriage of goods by sea contained in Chapter IV do not apply to the maritime transport of goods in coastal trade, *viz.*, maritime transport of goods between the ports or other places in China. Second, Article 3 in Chapter I of MC defines a 'ship' as a 'seagoing ship or other mobile unit, but does not include a ship or craft to be used in military or public service purposes nor a small vessel of less than 20 tons gross tonnage'. Therefore, MC does not apply to inland vessels unless an inland vessel is involved in collision or salvage with a ship defined in Article 3 of MC.[5]

54. Besides MC, the following laws govern special matters of maritime transport and other matters relating to vessels:

---

5. For details, *see* Ch. 9 and Ch. 12 of Part II.

- The *Maritime Traffic Safety Law* (hereinafter referred to as 'MTSL') governing maritime safety, adopted on 2 September 1983 and latest revised on 29 April 2021.
- The *Marine Environmental Protection Law* (hereinafter referred to as 'MEPL') governing marine environmental protection, including prevention of marine pollution from ships and principled civil liability for marine pollution damage, adopted on 23 August 1982 and latest amended on 4 November 2017.
- The *Special Maritime Procedure Law* (hereinafter referred to as 'SMPL') governing maritime litigation procedures, adopted on 25 December 1999.
- The *Port Law* governing the issues of port operations, etc., adopted on 28 June 2003.

55. The following are the regulations and provisions promulgated by the State Council or the MOT (previously the Ministry of Communications: MOC) governing or in connection with the matters of maritime transport and other matters relating to ships:

- The *Regulations Governing Administration on Foreign Ships*, promulgated by the State Council on 18 September 1979.
- The *Regulations Governing Registration of Ships*, promulgated by the State Council on 2 June 1994 as amended.
- The *Measures regarding Registration of Ships*, promulgated by MOT on 13 December 2016.
- The *Provisions Regarding the Limitation of Liability for Ships with a Gross Tonnage not Exceeding 300 Tons and Those Engaging in Transport Services between the Ports of the People's Republic of China as well as Those for Other Coastal Operation*, promulgated by the former MOC on 15 November 1993 after approval by the State Council.[6]
- The *Provisions regarding the Limitation of Liability in the Carriage of Passengers between the Ports of the People's Republic of China*, promulgated by the former MOC on 15 November 1993 after approval by the State Council.[7]
- The *Regulations Governing Transport of Passengers by Waterways*, promulgated by the former MOC on 12 December 1995 as amended.[8]
- The *Provisions Regarding Administration on Ship's Pilotage*, promulgated by the former MOC on 30 November 2001 as amended.
- The *Regulations Governing Administration on Traffic Safety in Rivers*, promulgated by the State Council l on 28 June 2002 as amended.
- The *Regulations on Vessel's Crew*, promulgated by the State Council l on 10 April 2007 as amended.
- The *Regulations on the Prevention and Control of Pollution of Marine Environment from Ships* (hereinafter referred to as 'Ships Pollution Regulations'), promulgated by the State Council l on 9 September 2009 as amended.

6. *See* Ch. 4 of Part II.
7. *See* Ch. 15 of Part II.
8. This statute also applies to the carriage of passengers in inland navigation. *See* Ch. 3 of Part III.

– The *Regulations Governing Administration on Domestic Waterway Transportation*, promulgated by the State Council on 13 October 2012 as amended.

56. Noticeably, the domestic carriage of goods by sea and the domestic carriage of goods by inland waterway (collectively called 'domestic carriage of goods by waterway') were regulated by the *Regulations Governing Domestic Carriage of Goods by Waterway* (hereinafter referred to as '2000 Cargo Regulations') promulgated by the former MOC on 17 July 2000. However, the 2000 Cargo Regulations were abolished in 2016. Nevertheless, the contracts of domestic carriage of goods by waterway or the waybills often provide that the contracts are subject to the 2000 Cargo Regulations. Consequently, the 2000 Cargo Regulations are in fact still playing their important role in regulating domestic carriage of goods by waterway.

57. By virtue of Article 99 of the *Law on Legislation* adopted on 1 July 2000 as latest amended on 13 March 2023, the regulations and provisions promulgated by the State Council or the ministries under it or by the local people's congresses or local governments shall not be in conflict with laws adopted by NPC or its Standing Committee; the regulations and provisions promulgated by the ministries under the State Council or the local governments shall not be in conflict with those promulgated by the State Council. Otherwise, they shall be null and void to the extent of conflict.

In addition, the powers of the State Council, the ministries under it, the local people's congresses or local governments in promulgating regulations and provisions are limited to the scope and issues as stipulated in the *Law on Legislation*. Otherwise, any statutory provisions made beyond their respective statutory powers shall be null and void.

58. As provided for in the *Law on Legislation*, the power of construing laws rests with the Standing Committee of NPC, and that of construing regulations or provisions rests with the State Council or the ministries under it, the local people's congress or local government that promulgated them. In addition, SPC has the power of construing law in the application thereof in the trials of cases by courts of law at various levels.

III. Shipping Customs and Usages

59. Shipping customs and usages are deemed as one of the sources of maritime law in China.

Paragraph 2 of Article 268 of MC provides that international customs and usages may be applied to matters for which neither the relevant laws of China nor any international treaty concluded or acceded to by China contains relevant provisions. By virtue of Article 276, the application of international shipping customs and usages shall not be contrary to the social public interests. These articles are contained in Chapter XIV 'Application of Law in Relating to Foreign-related Matters' and thus are applicable only in foreign-related matters.

In the case of domestic matters, Article 10 of CC contains similar provisions, i.e., where there is no provision of law, customs, and usages that may be applied provided that they shall not be contrary to the public order and good morality.

Noticeably, shipping customs and usages may be applicable. The word 'may' means that the application of any proven shipping customs and usages is within the discretion of a court of law. Unlike the applicable statutory provisions, therefore, a court of law is not mandatorily obliged to apply shipping customs and usages.

60. Shipping customs and usages are understood to be practices in shipping activities which are followed by the people in their shipping business and the contents of which are reasonable, certain and notorious to these people. A typical example may be the York-Antwerp Rules (YAR) that are universally followed in the adjustment of general average.

A shipping custom and usage shall not be applied where a provision to the contrary is contained in any applicable statutory law or international treaty or contained in the contract concluded by the parties concerned, or its application will be contrary to the public order.

§2. Road Transport

I. International Treaties

61. China has concluded bilateral agreements with respect to road transport with Russia, Mongolia, Vietnam, Pakistan and some other neighbouring countries. However, these bilateral agreements are not in the nature of civil law.

China has not acceded to any international convention concerning road transport, including the. *Convention on the Contract for the International Carriage of Goods by Road*, known as 'CMR'.

II. Domestic Laws and Regulations

62. The *Highway Law* (hereinafter referred to as 'HL') and the *Road Traffic Safety Law* are the two special laws in connection with road transport in China, but both regulate administrative matters only and have no concern with the matters in the nature of civil law in road transport.

HL was adopted by the Standing Committee of NPC on 3 July 1997 and latest, amended on 4 November 2017. The subject matters covered by HL are 'General Principles' (Chapter I), 'Highway Planning' (Chapter II), 'Highway Construction' (Chapter III), 'Highway Maintenance' (Chapter IV), 'Highway Administration' (Chapter V), 'Chargeable Highways' (Chapter VI), 'Supervision & Inspection' (Chapter VII) and 'Legal Liability' (Chapter VIII).

The *Road Traffic Safety Law* was adopted by the Standing Committee of NPC on 28 October 2003 and latest amended in 2021. The subject matters covered by this

Law are 'General Principles' (Chapter I), 'Vehicles and Drivers' (Chapter II), 'Road Passage Conditions' (Chapter III), 'Rules of Road Passage' (Chapter IV), 'Traffic Accident Handling' (Chapter V), 'Enforcement and Supervision' (Chapter VI) and 'Legal Liability' (Chapter VII).

63. So far, the issues of civil law in road transport are concerned; the laws applicable are the basic laws, mainly CC, as listed in §7 *infra*.

64. The following are the main regulations and provisions concerning or in connection with road transport, some of which regulate matters of administrative law:

- *The Regulations on Road Transport,* promulgated by the State Council on 30 April 2004 and latest amended on 29 March 2022.
- The *Provisions on the Administration on International Road Transport*, promulgated by the MOT on 26 September 2022.
- The *Provisions on the Administration on Road Cargo Transport and Terminals*, promulgated by MOT on 16 June 2005 and latest amended on 26 September 2022.
- The *Provisions on the Administration on Road Passenger Transport and Terminals*, promulgated by MOT on 6 July 2020 and amended on 26 September 2022.
- The *Provisions on the Administration on Road Dangerous Cargo Transport*, promulgated by MOT on 23 January 2013 and latest amended on 18 November 2019.

§3. Rail Transport

I. International Treaties

65. China is a party to the Agreement of International Railway through Transport, known as 'CMIC', and the Agreement concerning International Carriage of Passengers by Rail, signed at Warsaw in November 1951 and was amended later. Other parties thereto include, *inter alia*, Albania, Bulgaria, Hungary, Vietnam, North Korea, Mongolia, Poland, Romania, Russia and other countries of the Commonwealth of the Independent States, Czech and Slovakia.

China is not a party to any other multilateral treaties concerning international carriage by rail.[9]

9. China is not a party to the *Convention concerning International Carriage by Rail*, known as 'COTIF', signed at Berne on 9 May 1980 and amended by the Protocol of 3 Jun. 1999. The Convention as so amended is known as 'COTIF 1999' the appendixes of which include, *inter alia*, the *Uniform Rules concerning the Contract for International Carriage of Passengers and Luggage by Rail*, known as 'CIV', and the *Uniform Rules concerning the Contract for International Carriage of Goods by Rail*, known as 'CIM'.

II. Domestic Laws and Regulations

66. The *Railway Law* (hereinafter referred to as 'RL'), adopted by the Standing Committee of NPC on 7 September 1990 and amended on 27 August 2009 and on 24 April 2015, is the main law regulating railway transport in China.

RL is a mixture of civil and administrative rules. The provisions in the nature of civil law are mainly contained in Chapter II 'Operations of Railway Transport'. The provisions mainly in the nature of administrative law are contained in Chapter I 'General Principles', Chapter III 'Railway Construction', Chapter IV 'Railway Security & Protection' and Chapter V 'Legal Liability'.

67. The following are the main regulations and provisions concerning railway transport:

- The *Administrative Regulations on Safety of Railways*, promulgated by the State Council on 17 August 2013.
- The *Provisions on Railway Passenger Transport* (hereinafter referred to as 'PRPT'), promulgated by the MOT on 3 November 2022.

68. SPC promulgated the Explanations concerning Certain Issues in the Trial of Cases of Compensation for Damages in the Railway Transport (hereinafter referred to as 'RCE') on 27 October 1994 as amended on 23 December 2020, and the Explanations concerning Certain Issues in the Trial of Cases of Compensation for Loss of Life or Personal Injury in the Railway Transport (hereinafter referred to as 'RPCE') on 3 March 2010 as amended on 23 December 2020 and on 24 November 2021. The two judicial interpretations contain some explanations of the provisions of RL.

§4. Inland Navigation

I. International Treaties

69. China is not a party to the *Budapest Convention on the Contract for the Carriage of Goods by Inland Waterways*, known as 'CMNI', adopted in Budapest on 3 October 2000.

II. Domestic Laws and Regulations

70. So far, there is no specific law regulating inland navigation in China. Some general rules applicable to inland navigation are contained in basic laws as listed in §7 *infra*.

71. The main administrative statutes governing or applicable to inland navigation are as follows:

- The *Regulations Governing Registration of Ships*, promulgated by the State Council on 2 June 1994 and amended.
- The *Regulations Governing Transport of Passengers by Waterways*, promulgated by the former MOC on 12 December 1995 and amended on 26 August 1997 and on 2 January 2014.
- The *Regulations Governing Administration on River Traffic Safety*, promulgated by the State Council on 28 June 2002.
- The *Administrative Regulations Governing Domestic Waterway Transportation*, known as 'Waterway Regulations', promulgated by the State Council on 13 October 2012 and amended on 6 February 2016 and on 1 March 2017.
- The *Administrative Provisions Governing Domestic Waterway Transportation*, promulgated by MOT on 3 January 2014 and latest amended on 24 February 2020.

72. The above administrative statutes govern the registration of inland vessels and administration of passenger and cargo transport in inland navigation. There is no specific law or administrative statute regulating such matters of civil law relating to inland navigation and inland vessels as collision, salvage, general average, limitation of liability, hull and cargo insurance, vessel's real rights, including ownership, mortgage and maritime lien, although limited general rules contained in basic laws as cited in §7 *infra* are applicable to such matters of civil law. However, these basic laws do not fit in well with the needs of inland navigation. Consequently, China needs provisions of specific laws regulating relations in the nature of civil law arising from inland waterway transport and those relating to inland vessels.

§5. Air Transport

I. International Treaties

73. There are many international treaties in the area of civil aviation. China has accepted, ratified or acceded to the following ones:

- The *Convention on International Civil Aviation*, signed in Chicago on 7 December 1944 and based upon which the International Civil Aviation Organization (ICAO) was established to which China has been a member of the Council since 15 February 1974.
- The *International Air Service Transit Agreement*, signed in Chicago on 7 December 1944, but only applicable in Hong Kong and Macau.
- The *Protocol relating to an Amendment to the Convention on International Civil Aviation (Article 93bis)*, signed at Montreal on 27 May 1947.
- The *Protocol relating to the Amendment to Article 45 of the Convention on International Civil Aviation*, signed at Montreal on 14 June 1954.
- The *Protocol relating to the Amendment to Articles 48(a), 49(e) & 61 of the Convention on International Civil Aviation*, signed at Montreal on 14 June 1954.
- The *Protocol relating to the Amendment to Article 50(a) of the Convention on International Civil Aviation*, signed at Montreal on 21 June 1961.

- The *Protocol relating to the Amendment to Article 48(a) of the Convention on International Civil Aviation*, signed at Rome on 15 September 1962.
- The *Protocol on the Authentic Trilingual Text of the Convention on International Civil Aviation*, signed in Buenos Aires on 24 September 1968.
- The *Protocol relating to the Amendment to Article 50(a) of the Convention on International Civil Aviation*, signed in New York on 12 March 1971.
- The *Protocol relating to the Amendment to Article 56 of the Convention on International Civil Aviation*, signed at Vienna on 7 July 1971.
- The *Protocol relating to the Amendment to Article 50(a) of the Convention on International Civil Aviation*, signed at Montreal on 16 October 1974.
- The *Protocol on the Authentic Quadrilingual Text of the Convention on International Civil Aviation*, signed at Montreal on 30 September 1977.
- The *Protocol of Amendment to the Convention on International Civil Aviation (Final Clause)*, signed at Montreal on 30 September 1977.
- The *Protocol relating to the Amendment to Article 83bis of the Convention on International Civil Aviation*, signed at Montreal on 10 May 1980.
- The *Protocol relating to the Amendment to Article 3bis of the Convention on International Civil Aviation*, signed at Montreal on 10 May 1984.
- The *Protocol relating to the Amendment to Article 56 of the Convention on International Civil Aviation*, signed at Montreal on 6 October 1989.
- The *Protocol relating to the Amendment to Article 50(a) of the Convention on International Civil Aviation*, signed at Montreal on 10 October 1990.
- The *Protocol of Amendment to the Convention on International Civil Aviation (Final Paragraph, Arabic Text)*, signed at Montreal on 29 September 1995.
- The *Protocol of Amendment to the Convention on International Civil Aviation (Final Paragraph, Chinese Text)*, signed at Montreal on 1 October 1998.
- The *Convention for the Unification of Certain Rules relating to International Carriage by Air*, known as 'Warsaw Convention', signed at Warsaw on 12 October 1929.
- The *Protocol to Amend the Convention for the Unification of Certain Rules relating to International Carriage by Air signed at Warsaw on 12 October 1929*, known as '1955 Hague Protocol', signed at the Hague on 28 September 1955, the Warsaw Convention as amended this Protocol being known as 'Warsaw Convention as amended at the Hague, 1955'.
- The *Convention on the Recognition of Rights in Aircraft*, signed at Geneva on 19 June 1948, but only applicable in Macau.
- The *Convention Supplementary to the Warsaw Convention for the Unification of Certain Rules relating to International Carriage by Air Performed by a Person Other than the Contracting Carrier*, known as '1961 Guadalajara Convention', signed at Guadalajara on 18 June 1961, but only applicable in Hong Kong.
- The *Convention on Offences and Certain Other Acts Committed on Board Aircraft*, signed at Tokyo on 14 September 1963.
- The *Convention for the Suppression of Unlawful Seizure of Aircraft*, signed at The Hague on 16 December 1970.
- The *Convention for the Suppression of Unlawful Acts against the Safety of Civil Aviation*, signed at Montreal on 23 September 1971.

- The *Protocol for the Suppression of Unlawful Acts of Violence at Airport Serving International Civil Aviation Supplementary to Convention for the Suppression of Unlawful Acts against the Safety of Civil Aviation done in Montreal on 23 September 1971*, signed at Montreal on 24 February 1988.
- The *Convention on the Marking of Plastic Explosives for the Purpose of Detection*, signed in Montreal on 1 March 1991, but only applicable in Hong Kong.
- The *Convention for the Unification of Certain Rules for International Carriage by Air*, known as '1999 Montreal Convention', signed at Montreal on 28 May 1999, which prevails over the Warsaw Convention, the 1955 Hague Protocol, the 1961 Guadalajara Convention, the 1972 Guatemala City Protocol and the 1975 Montreal Protocols in international carriage by air between States parties to this Convention.
- The *Convention on International Interests in Mobile Equipment*, signed at Cape Town on 16 November 2001.
- The *Protocol to the Convention on International Interests in Mobile Equipment*, signed at Cape Town on 16 November 2001.

74. China has not accepted, ratified, acceded to, or denounced the following international treaties in the area of civil aviation:

- The *International Air Transport Agreement*, signed in Chicago on 7 December 1944.
- The *Convention on Damage Caused by Foreign Aircraft to Third Parties on the Surface*, known as '1952 Rome Convention', signed at Rome on 7 October 1952.
- The *Protocol to Amend the Convention on Damage Caused by Foreign Aircraft to Third Parties on the Surface*, signed at Montreal on 23 September 1978.
- The *Protocol to Amend the Warsaw Convention of 1929 as Amended by the Hague Protocol of 1955*, known as '1971 Guatemala City Protocol', signed at Guatemala City on 8 March 1971.
- The *Additional Protocol No. 1 to Amend the Warsaw Convention of 1929 as Amended by The Hague Protocol of 1955*, signed at Guatemala City on 25 September 1975.
- The *Additional Protocol No. 2 to Amend the Warsaw Convention of 1929 as Amended by The Hague Protocol of 1955*, signed at Guatemala City on 25 September 1975.
- The *Additional Protocol No. 3 to Amend the Warsaw Convention of 1929 as Amended by The Hague Protocol of 1955*, signed at Guatemala City on 25 September 1975.
- The *Additional Protocol No. 4 to Amend the Warsaw Convention of 1929 as Amended by The Hague Protocol of 1955*, signed at Guatemala City on 25 September 1975.
- The *Convention on Compensation for Damage Caused by Aircraft to Third Parties*, signed at Montreal on 2 May 2009.
- The *Convention on Compensation for Damage Resulting from Acts of Unlawful Interference Involving Aircraft*, signed in Montreal on 2 May 2009.

II. Domestic Laws and Regulations

75. As compared with other modes of transport, China has a more complete domestic law system in air transport.

76. The *Civil Aviation Law* (hereinafter referred to as 'CAL'), adopted by NPC on 30 October 1995 and latest amended on 29 April 2021, is the main law regulating air transport in China.

CAL is a combination of civil and administrative law. The subject matters in the nature of civil law are mainly contained in Chapter IX 'Public Air Transport' and Chapter XII 'Liability for Damage to Third Parties on the Surface'.

The provisions of Chapter IX of CAL are mainly a reproduction of the Warsaw Convention as amended at The Hague in 1955 as introduced *infra*, especially so far as international carriage of passengers and baggage is concerned. Other issues, mainly in the nature of administrative law, are contained in Chapter I 'General Principles', Chapter II 'Nationality of Civil Aircraft', Chapter III 'Rights of Civil Aircraft' including ownership and mortgage and lien and lease, Chapter IV 'Airworthiness Management of Civil Aircraft', Chapter V 'Airmen', Chapter VI 'Civil Aircraft', Chapter VII 'Air Navigation', Chapter VIII 'Public Air Transport Enterprise', Chapter X 'General Aviation', Chapter XI 'Search and Rescue and Accident Investigation', Chapter XIII 'Special Provisions Governing Foreign Civil Aircraft', Chapter XIV 'Application of Law to Foreign-related Matters', Chapter XV 'Disciplinary and Special Criminal Liability' and Chapter XVI 'Supplementary Provisions'.

Besides CAL, the basic laws as listed in §7 *infra* are applicable to the matters of air transport, provided that they are not repugnant to CAL.

77. The following are the main regulations and provisions regarding air transport:

- The *Regulations on the Registration of Rights in Civil Aircrafts*, promulgated by the State Council on 21 October 1997.
- The *Implementation Provisions of the Registration of Rights in Civil Aircrafts*, promulgated by CAAC on 1 September 1999.
- The *Regulations on the Registration of Nationality of Civil Aircrafts*, promulgated by the State Council on 21 October 1997.
- The *Administrative Provisions on Services for Passengers in Public Air Transport*, hereinafter referred to as 'PSP', promulgated by MOT on 3 March 2021.
- The *Regulations on the Domestic Cargo Transport of China Civil Aviation*, known as 'Domestic Air Cargo Regulations' and hereinafter referred to as 'DACR', promulgated by CAAC on 1 March 1996.
- The *Regulations on the International Cargo Transport by Civil Aviation in China*, known as 'International Air Cargo Regulations' and hereinafter referred to as 'IACR', promulgated by CAAC on 21 April 2000.
- The *Provisions on Limit of Liability of Carrier in Domestic Air Transport*, promulgated by CAAC on 28 February 2006.

§6. Multimodal Transport

I. International Treaties

78. China has not ratified the *United Nations Convention on International Multimodal Transport of Goods*, signed in Geneva on 24 May 1980 and not in force yet.

II. Domestic Laws and Regulations

79. Up to now, there is no specific law in China governing multimodal transport of goods or passengers. Multimodal transport is currently regulated by various chapters of several laws and administrative regulations, mainly as follows:

- section 8 'Special Provisions regarding Multimodal Transport Contract' of Chapter IV 'Contract of Carriage of Goods by Sea' of MC applicable to international multimodal transport of goods with one mode of transport being international carriage by sea;
- section 4 'Multimodal Transport Contract' of Chapter XIX 'Contract of Carriage' of Book Three of CC.

§7. Basic Laws

I. Principle of Application

80. In contrast with a special law, a basic law regulates a much broader category of relations. For example, *CC* regulates all kinds of civil law relations, while MC regulates only those relations arising from maritime transport or pertaining to ships. Therefore, in contrast with MC, CC is a basic law, and MC is a special law. Another example is, in contrast with the provisions governing marine insurance contained in Chapter XII of MC, the *Insurance Law* (IL) is a basic law.

China adheres to the principle that where both special law and basic law contain provisions concerning a certain matter, the special law has priority over the basic law to the extent of repugnancy. However, where no provision is contained in any special law, the basic law shall apply. Subject to this principle, basic laws are very important sources of transport law in China.

II. Main Basic Laws Applicable to Transport

81. So far, several laws of general application apply to the transport of various modes subject to the principle mentioned *supra*.

The basic laws mainly include the following:

- The *Civil Code* (CC), applicable to all kinds of civil relations, adopted by NPC on 28 May 2020 which is a codification of the *General Principles of Civil Law* of 1986, the *Security Law* of 1995, the *Contract Law* of 1999, the *Real Rights Law* of 2007 and the *Tort Liability Law* of 2009 and consequently abolished these laws.

- The *Civil Procedure Code* (hereinafter referred to as 'CPC'), applicable to all kinds of civil litigations, adopted by NPC on 9 April 1991 and latest amended on 1 September 2023.
- The *Insurance Law* (hereinafter referred to as 'IL'), regulating various kinds of insurance including property insurance, life insurance and liability insurance, adopted by the Standing Committee of NPC on 30 June 1995 and latest amended on 24 April 2015.
- The *Arbitration Law* (hereinafter referred to as 'AL'), applicable to all kinds of arbitration, adopted by the Standing Committee of NPC on 31 August 1994 and amended on 1 September 2017.
- The *Auction Law* (hereinafter referred to as 'AUL'), applicable to all kinds of sale by auction, adopted by the Standing Committee of NPC on 5 July 1996 and latest amended on 24 April 2015.
- The *Law on the Application of Law in Foreign-related Civil Relations*, adopted by the Standing Committee of NPC on 28 October 2010.

82. Besides these basic laws, the judicial interpretations promulgated by SPC within its powers defined in the *Law on the People's Courts* as authentic interpretations of laws also have the force of law, provided that they are not repugnant to the laws. SPC has the power to interpret various laws concerning specific issues of application of law in trial of cases. SPC may make the judicial interpretations for the application in a single case. SPC may also make judicial interpretations for general application, and the following are examples:

- The *Opinions on Certain Issues regarding Application of Civil Procedure Code of the People's Republic of China*, (hereinafter referred to as 'CPC Interpretations'), promulgated on 18 December 2014 and latest amended on 10 April 2022.
- The *Interpretations on Certain Issues regarding Application of Special Maritime Procedure Law of the People's Republic of China*, (hereinafter referred to as 'SMPL Interpretations'), promulgated on 3 December 2002.
- The *Interpretations on Certain Issues regarding Application of Arbitration Law of the People's Republic of China*, (hereinafter referred to as 'AL Interpretations'), promulgated on 26 December 2005.
- The *Interpretations on Certain Issues regarding Application of Insurance Law of the People's Republic of China,* (hereinafter referred to as 'IL Interpretations'), promulgated on 14 September 2009 and amended 6 May 2013.
- The *Interpretations on Certain Issues regarding Application of Law on the Application of Law in Foreign-related Civil Relations of the People's Republic of China (Part One)*, (hereinafter referred to as 'ALFCR Interpretations'), promulgated on 10 December 2012.
- The *Interpretations on Certain Issues Regarding Application of the Book of General Provisions of Civil Code of the People's Republic of China*, (hereinafter referred to as 'CC General Provisions Interpretations'), promulgated on 24 February 2022.

- The *Interpretations on Certain Issues regarding Application of the Security Regime of Civil Code of the People's Republic of China*, (hereinafter referred to as 'CC Security Regime Interpretations'), promulgated on 31 December 2022.

Chapter 3. Jurisdiction and Courts

§1. Governing Laws and Statutory Provisions

83. Civil litigation in China is governed by CPC and the CPC Interpretations. Civil arbitration in China is governed by AL and the AL Interpretations, as well as the provisions concerning arbitration contained in CPC and the CPC Interpretations. It needs to be mentioned that civil litigation or civil arbitration covers commercial litigation or commercial arbitration. Besides, the recognition and enforcement of foreign arbitration awards are also governed by the *New York Convention on the Recognition and Enforcement of Foreign Arbitration Awards of 1958*, known as '1958 New York Convention', to which China is a party and which has priority over Chinese law and the judicial interpretations adopted by SPC.

84. Maritime litigation and arbitration is also governed by SMPL and various provisions adopted by SPC, including, *inter alia*, the *Scope of Cases to Be Seized by Maritime Courts* adopted on 13 May 1989, and the *Provisions Concerning Jurisdiction over Foreign-related Maritime Litigations* adopted on 31 January 1986.

85. As introduced in Chapter 2 of this part *supra*, SMPL as a special law has priority over CPC as a basic law in the matters of maritime litigation and arbitration to the extent of repugnancy between them. However, where SMPL contains no provision, CPC shall apply. The SMPL Interpretations also have priority over CPC and the CPC Interpretations. Subject to this principle, the CPC Interpretations have a binding effect on maritime litigations; the AL Interpretations and the provisions concerning arbitration of the CPC Interpretations have a binding effect on maritime arbitrations.

86. SMPL and the SMPL Interpretations are applicable to maritime litigations both in the first and second instances as well as in the retrial procedures.

87. The aforementioned laws and the judicial interpretations adopted by SPC applicable to maritime litigation are also applicable to the litigation of disputes arising from or in connection with the inland navigation in the water areas adjacent to the sea, so far as these disputes are within the jurisdiction of maritime courts as introduced in §2 *infra* in the cases of litigation. The statutory provisions applicable to maritime arbitration are also applicable to the arbitration of disputes arising from or in connection with inland navigation in the water areas adjacent to the sea.

§2. Maritime Litigation and Arbitration

I. Maritime Jurisdiction and Court

88. Six maritime courts as professional courts of law were first established in China in 1984 in accordance with the *Decision on the Establishment of Maritime*

Courts in Coastal Cities adopted by the Standing Committee of NPC on 14 November 1984. Among them, five are located in the biggest coastal cities, *viz.* Dalian, Tianjin, Qingdao, Shanghai, Guangzhou, and the other one is located in Wuhan, the biggest city located in central China along the Yangtze River. Four other maritime courts were established one after another in four major coastal cities, i.e., Ningbo, Xiamen, Haikou and Beihai afterwards. In 2019, Nanjing Maritime Court was established in Nanjing, a big city located in east China along the Yangtze River. Thus, up to now, there are eleven maritime courts in China. Some of them have branches in the neighbouring cities. So far, China is the unique country in the world which has professional courts of law in the trial of maritime cases and SMPL as the special maritime procedure law for maritime litigations.

Each maritime court has its statutory basic jurisdiction area. That is, a maritime court shall have jurisdiction as the Court of First Instance over maritime cases occurring in a certain geographical area.

The geographical jurisdiction areas of the eleven maritime courts are divided as follows:

- Dalian Maritime Court: Liaoning Province and its stretched water areas.
- Tianjin Maritime Court: Tianjin Municipality directly under the State Council, Hebei Province and their stretched water areas.
- Qingdao Maritime Court: Shandong Province and its stretched water areas.
- Shanghai Maritime Court: Shanghai Municipality directly under the State Council and its stretched water areas.
- Nanjing Maritime Court: Jiangsu Province and its stretched water areas, and the water areas of the Yangtze River and its tributaries within Jiangsu Province.
- Ningbo Maritime Court: Zhejiang Province and its stretched water areas.
- Xiamen Maritime Court: Fujian Province and its stretched water areas.
- Guangzhou Maritime Court: Guangdong Province and its stretched water areas.
- Haikou Maritime Court: Hainan Province and its stretched water areas.
- Beihai Maritime Court: Guangxi Zhuang Autonomous Region and its stretched water areas.
- Wuhan Maritime Court: water areas of the Yangtze River and its tributaries except those within Jiangsu Province.

89. Like in other civil cases, the jurisdiction is exercised over maritime cases by virtue of the statutory jurisdiction by levels, geographical jurisdiction, exclusive jurisdiction, jurisdiction by agreement, designated jurisdiction and other statutory jurisdiction.

It needs to be mentioned that maritime cases include cases arising from or in connection with transport or vessels in the inland navigation in the water areas adjacent to the sea. Maritime cases also include cases from or in connection with multimodal transport, provided that one mode of transport is either maritime transport or inland navigation in the water areas adjacent to the sea.

90. With respect to jurisdiction by levels, the jurisdiction over a maritime case of first instance rests with the maritime court and that over maritime cases of second instance, i.e., the final instance, rests with the high people's court located in the province, municipality directly under the State Council or autonomous region where the maritime court is located. However, as exceptions, a high people's court may exercise jurisdiction over a case of first instance if the case has significant influence in its jurisdictional area, in which case the jurisdiction over the case of second instance rests with SPC; SPC may exercise jurisdiction over a case of first instance if the case has significant influence in the whole State, in which case the first instance is also the final instance (Articles 20 and 21, CPC). A superior court of law may try a case of first instance within the jurisdiction of its inferior court of law or submit a case of first instance within its jurisdiction to its inferior court of law after approval by its superior court of law (Article 39, CPC).

As another exception to the principle that the second instance of a case is the final instance by virtue of the provisions of Articles 209 and 210 of Chapter XVI 'Trial Supervision Procedures' of CPC, a case may be retried where the judgment, award or reconciliation statement[10] of the case has already become effective and is found wrongful indeed. There are three circumstances for retrial of case. First, where the president of a court of law at various levels considers necessary for the retrial, he or she shall submit it to the adjudicatory committee of the court for discussion and decision. Second, SPC may retry a case, or a superior local court of law may retry a case made by an inferior local court of law at various levels. Third, a party or parties may apply to the court of law which made the judgment or award or the court of law at the next higher level for retrial, in which case the enforcement of the judgment or award shall not be stopped if it has not been enforced.

91. With respect to the geographical jurisdiction, by virtue of Article 6 of SMPL, the jurisdiction of maritime courts over maritime cases of first instance is further as follows:

- litigation arising from a maritime tort, e.g., ship's collision or allision, is subject to the jurisdiction of the maritime court in the place where the tortuous act was committed, the accident occurred, the defendant has domicile or residence, the offensive ship arrived earliest or is arrested, or her homeport is located;
- litigation arising from a contract of carriage of goods or passenger is subject to the jurisdiction of the maritime court of the place where the port of loading or discharge or transhipment of the goods, or embarkation or disembarkation of the passenger, is located, or the defendant has domicile or residence;
- litigation arising from a time charter party or bareboat charter party of a seagoing ship is subject to the jurisdiction of the maritime court of the place where the port of delivery or redelivery of the ship or her homeport is located or the defendant has domicile or residence;

10. A reconciliation statement is a judicial document issued by a court containing the result of the agreement concerning resolution of the disputes of the case reached by the parties thereto through the court's reconciliation. As provided for in CPC, a court is obliged to conduct reconciliation upon the voluntariness of the parties to a case during the trial. A reconciliation statement is enforceable upon application of a party to the court where the other party fails to voluntarily perform its obligation thereunder.

- litigation arising from a contract of marine insurance is subject to the jurisdiction of the maritime court of the place where the subject matter of insurance is located, the accident causing loss or damage occurred, or the defendant has domicile or residence;
- litigation arising from a contract of seafarer's employment is subject to the jurisdiction of the maritime court of the place where the contract was concluded, the port of embarkation or disembarkation of the seafarer is located, or the plaintiff or the defendant has domicile or residence;
- litigation arising from a maritime security is subject to the jurisdiction of the maritime court of the place where the security object is located or the defendant has domicile or residence, or, in the case of ship mortgage, her homeport is located;
- litigation arising from ownership, right of possession or use of a ship, or maritime lien on a ship is subject to the jurisdiction of the maritime court of the place where the ship or her home port is located or the defendant has domicile or residence.

In a maritime case, as a principle of geographical jurisdiction, if there is no maritime court in the province, municipality directly under the State Council or autonomous region where the defendant has his domicile or residence, or principal place of business in the case the defendant is an enterprise or institution, then the nearest maritime court has jurisdiction over the case, unless otherwise expressly provided for in law.

92. With respect to the exclusive jurisdiction, by virtue of Article 7 of SMPL, the jurisdiction of maritime courts over maritime cases of the first instance is as follows:

- Litigation arising from coastal port operation is subject to the jurisdiction of the maritime court of the place where the port is located.
- Litigation arising from marine pollution damage due to ship's discharge, leakage or dumping of oil or other harmful substance, production or operation at sea, or ship's dismantling or repair is subject to the jurisdiction of the maritime court of the place where pollution or the result thereof occurred, or preventive measures were taken.
- Litigation arising from contract of exploration or exploitation within Chinese territorial seas or other waters within Chinese jurisdiction is subject to the jurisdiction of the maritime court of the place where the contract was performed.

93. With respect to the jurisdiction by agreement, by virtue of Article 8 of SMPL, where all the parties involved in dispute are foreigners, stateless persons or foreign enterprises or organizations and have chosen by agreement in writing the jurisdiction of a Chinese maritime court, the maritime court so chosen shall have jurisdiction over the dispute, even if the place or places having genuine link with the dispute are not located in China.

Where one or all the parties involved in dispute are Chinese citizens or enterprises or organizations, the parties can only choose by agreement in writing the jurisdiction of a maritime court of the place where the defendant or the plaintiff has domicile or residence or the contract concerned was concluded or performed, or the subject matter is located, or where it has genuine link otherwise with the dispute, provided that the statutory provisions of exclusive jurisdiction contained in Article 7 of SMPL are not derogated (Article 35, CPC).

94. With respect to other statutory jurisdictions, the following is provided for in SMPL or CPC:

- application for recognizing ownerless property at sea shall be submitted to the maritime court of the place where the property is located (Article 9, SMPL);
- application for declaring death due to a marine accident shall be submitted to the maritime court of the place where the competent authority handling the accident is located or to the maritime court having entertained the related maritime case (Article 9, SMPL);
- where dispute exists between a maritime court and a local court of law regarding jurisdiction, the dispute shall be settled by agreement or, if no settlement is agreed upon, subject to the common superior court of law for designating jurisdiction (Article 10, SMPL);
- application for enforcement of a maritime arbitration award made by a Chinese arbitration organ, or for recognition and enforcement of a judgment or award made by a foreign court of law or of a foreign arbitration award shall be submitted to the maritime court of the place where the property subject to enforcement is located, or the person against whom the enforcement is applied for has domicile or residence or, where there is no maritime court located in such a place, to the intermediate court of law located in such a place (Article 11, SMPL);
- application for arrest of a ship, attachment on cargo or bunkers or stores on board a ship, or other maritime claim preservation made before filing of a lawsuit shall be submitted to the maritime court of the place where the property to be preserved in located (Article 13, SMPL); such an application made after the filing of a lawsuit shall be submitted to the maritime court which has entertained the case;
- where arrest of a ship, attachment on cargo or bunkers or stores on board a ship, or other maritime claim preservation has been enforced by a maritime court, and no litigation or arbitration procedure has started with respect to the related maritime dispute, any party concerned may file a lawsuit in respect of the maritime dispute with the maritime court which has taken the maritime claim preservation or other maritime court with jurisdiction over the dispute, unless a valid agreement of jurisdiction or arbitration between the parties exists (Article 19, SMPL);
- litigation arising from payment for salvage at sea is subject to the jurisdiction of the maritime court of the place where the salvage service was rendered or the salved ship arrived earliest (Article 32, CPC);
- litigation arising from general average is subject to the jurisdiction of the maritime court of the place where the ship concerned arrived earliest, the general average was adjusted, or the voyage concerned was terminated (Article 33, CPC);
- litigation arising from one of the other maritime contracts is subject to the jurisdiction of the maritime court of the place where the defendant has domicile or residence or the contract has been performed (Article 24, CPC);

- in other cases, a maritime claim against a citizen, legal person or other organization is subject to the jurisdiction of the maritime court of the place where the defendant has domicile or residence (Article 22, CPC).

95. It is clear that from the above statutory provisions regarding jurisdiction of maritime courts,[11] two or even more maritime courts may have jurisdiction over a single case of dispute. Almost inevitably, the plaintiff has a choice, even a big choice, for filing a lawsuit with a maritime court with jurisdiction. The plaintiff always wants to choose a maritime court in which the litigation will be most convenient for it and will be most beneficial in other aspects. In China, the laws and other statutory provisions are the same for the whole State, no matter where the litigation is brought by the plaintiff. However, China is not a case law State, and the admiralty practice may differ slightly in different maritime courts; thus, together with other elements, such as the convenience of the availability of evidence, the final result may be different if litigation is brought in a different maritime court. Such a choice of court may be called 'forum shopping'.

As provided for in Article 36 of CPC, where two or more courts of law have jurisdiction over a case, the plaintiff may file a lawsuit with any of the courts and, where the plaintiff files a lawsuit with two or more courts with jurisdiction, the case shall subject to the jurisdiction of the court having entertained the case earlier or earliest.

More or less similar provisions are contained in the laws of other shipping countries in the world, and consequently, courts of two or more countries may have jurisdiction over a case of dispute, resulting in a conflict of jurisdictions. Consequently, 'forum shopping' widely exists. Due to the lack of sufficient uniformity of maritime law in the international community, quite often, it is difficult for the defendant to anticipate the result of litigation depending upon where the litigation is brought against him.

II. Maritime Litigation Procedures

96. Whether a case is tried by a maritime court, high court of law or even SPC, as the case may be, maritime litigation is subject to the common civil procedures provided for in CPC unless otherwise provided for in SMPL.

CPC contains the following four parts:

- Part I 'General Provisions' covering the tasks, scope of application and general principles (Chapter I), jurisdictions (Chapter II), trial organization (Chapter III), challenge against the judicial bench (Chapter IV), litigation participants (Chapter V), evidence (Chapter VI), periods and service (Chapter VII), reconciliation (Chapter VIII), property preservation and advance enforcement (Chapter IX),

11. More details are contained in the *Provisions Concerning Jurisdiction over Foreign-related Maritime Litigations*, adopted by SPC on 31 Jan. 1986, and the *Scope of Cases to Be Seized by Maritime Courts*, adopted by SPC on 13 May 1989.

compulsory measures against acts obstructing civil litigation (Chapter X), and litigation costs (Chapter XI).
- Part II 'Trial Procedures' covering the ordinary trial procedure for first instance (Chapter XII), simplified trial procedure (Chapter XIII), trial procedure for second instance (Chapter XIV), special trial procedure (Chapter XV), trial supervision procedure (Chapter XVI), procedure for hastening debt recovery (Chapter XVII), and procedure for publicizing public notice for assertion of claims (Chapter XVIII).
- Part III 'Enforcement Procedures' covering the general provisions (Chapter XIX), application for and transfer of enforcement (Chapter XX), enforcement measures (Chapter XXI), and suspension and termination of enforcement (Chapter XII).
- Part IV 'Special Provisions governing Foreign-related Civil Litigations' covering the general principles (Chapter XXIII), jurisdiction (Chapter XXIV), service and periods (Chapter XXV), arbitration (Chapter XXVI), and judicial assistance (Chapter XXVII).

97. SMPL governs the following matters:

- General principles (Chapter I).
- Jurisdiction (Chapter II).
- Maritime claim preservation covering general provisions, arrest and auction sale of ship,[12] and attachment on an auction sale of the cargo carried by ship (Chapter III).
- Maritime compulsory order (Chapter IV).
- Maritime evidence preservation (Chapter V).
- Maritime security (Chapter VI).
- Service (Chapter VII).
- Trial procedures for the trial of cases of ship's collision,[13] general average,[14] marine insurer's subrogation claim,[15] and simplified trial, hastening debt recovery and publicizing public notice for assertion of claims (Chapter VIII).
- Procedure for the establishment of fund of limitation of liability for maritime claims (Chapter IX).[16]
- Procedure for the registration of claims and compensation (Chapter X).[17]
- Procedure for hastening maritime lien (Chapter XI).[18]
- Supplementary provisions (Chapter XII).

12. *See* Ch. 14 of Part II.
13. *See* Ch. 12 of Part II.
14. *See* Ch. 10 of Part II.
15. *See* Ch. 13 of Part II.
16. *See* Ch. 4 of Part II.
17. *See* Ch. 2 of Part II.
18. *See* Ch. 2 of Part II.

III. Maritime Arbitration

A. Arbitration Organizations

98. Before the enactment of AL on 31 August 1994, there were only two arbitration organizations in China, *viz.* China Maritime Arbitration Commission, known as 'CMAC', and China International Economic and Trade Arbitration Commission, known as 'CIETAC', established in 1958 under China Council for the Promotion of International Trade, known as 'CCPIT', based in Beijing.[19] After the enactment of AL, arbitration committees have been established in each capital of provinces, autonomous regions or municipalities directly under the State Council and even in many big cities by virtue of AL, besides CMAC and CIETAC. Both CMAC and many local arbitration commissions are qualified for maritime arbitrations.

Chinese law does not widely recognize ad hoc arbitrations.

An arbitration commission consists of a director, deputy directors and members and is an institute legal person in law and a self-discipline organization independent of any administrative organs (Articles 12, 14 and 15, AL). Arbitration shall be done independently in accordance with law and shall not be subject to any interference from any administrative organs, social organizations or individuals (Article 8, AL).

99. Arbitrators are appointed by an arbitration commission. An arbitrator shall have the qualification either as engaged in arbitration for eight years, or as a lawyer for eight years, or as a judge for eight years, or as engaged in research or teaching of law with senior professional post, or as engaged in international economy and trade and so on with knowledge of law and with senior professional post or equal professional level (Article 13, AL).

B. Arbitration Agreement

100. An arbitration agreement reached before or after the dispute arose, either in the form of an arbitration clause contained in a contract or in other written forms, should contain the expression of the idea of resorting to arbitration, the items of arbitration and the chosen arbitration commission (Article 16, AL).

Where no provision or specific provision of the items of arbitration or arbitration commission is contained in an arbitration agreement, the agreement shall be invalid unless a supplementary agreement to this effect is concluded (Article 18, AL). By virtue of this statutory provision, therefore, an arbitration clause contained in a charter party stating 'any dispute arising from this charter party shall be referred to arbitration in China' is invalid because it does not contain the chosen arbitration commission. Even if the clause states 'arbitration in Beijing', it is also invalid because two arbitration commissions in Beijing are qualified for maritime arbitration, *viz.* CMAC and Beijing Arbitration Commission.

19. CCPIT is also called China Chamber of International Commerce (CCIC).

Where one party raises objection to the validity of an arbitration agreement, the party or parties may demand the arbitration commission concerned for decision or demand a court of law with jurisdiction for awarding (Article 20, AL). Any such objection shall be raised before the first hearing in arbitration.

An arbitration agreement exists independently of the related contract. Any change or termination of the contract shall have no effect on the arbitration agreement and vice versa (Article 19, AL).

Where a valid arbitration agreement exists, any party cannot file a lawsuit with a court of law, or if a lawsuit has been filed, the court of law shall not entertain the case (Article 5, AL), or if the court has entertained a case and the other party has raised objection to the jurisdiction, the court of law shall dismiss the case.

C. Arbitration Procedures

101. The arbitration procedures as provided for in Chapter IV of AL include the application for arbitration and entertainment, organization of arbitration penal, hearing and delivery of arbitration award. Every arbitration commission has its own arbitration rules containing more specific provisions of the arbitration procedures.

102. The applicant shall submit a written application together with the arbitration agreement and supporting evidence. The respondent may submit pleadings. Where one party applies for property preservation, application therefor shall be submitted to the arbitration commissions, and the latter shall submit it to a court of law with jurisdiction for decision.

An arbitration penal shall consist of three arbitrators unless the parties agree to the arbitration by a sole arbitrator or the amount in dispute is less than a certain amount,[20] in which case a sole arbitrator shall be agreed upon by the parties or designated by the director of the arbitration commission if the parties failed to reach such an agreement. Each party shall appoint one arbitrator. The third one as umpire shall be agreed upon by the parties or designated by the director of the arbitration commission if the parties fail to reach such an agreement. Where one party fails to appoint an arbitrator within the fixed time, the second arbitrator shall be designated by the director of the arbitration commission. One party may also ask the director to designate an arbitrator or the parties may ask the director to designate a sole arbitrator.

103. Hearing shall be held in arbitration unless the parties agree to a documentary trial only. The hearing procedure is similar to that in litigation in a court of law, but the hearing is not in public. The parties may reach a settlement during arbitration. The penal may reconcile the dispute during arbitration.

104. Arbitration award shall be based upon the majority opinion of the penal of the three arbitrators if the penal cannot reach the award unanimously or upon the

20. CNY1,000,000 under the Arbitration Rules of CMAC.

opinion of the umpire if the penal cannot reach a majority opinion. Arbitration award is final and binding upon both parties and is not subject to appeal.

D. Recognition and Enforcement of Arbitration Award

105. Application for the enforcement of a maritime arbitration award shall be submitted to the maritime court of the place where the property to be enforced is located, where the person against whom the enforcement is applied has domicile or residence, or where there is no maritime court located in such a place, to the intermediate court of law located in such a place (Article 11, SMPL).

The statutory conditions for the enforcement of various arbitration awards are not the same, depending upon whether the award involves a foreign element or not or whether the award is delivered by a Chinese arbitration commission or a foreign one.

By virtue of paragraphs 2 and 3 of Article 248 of CPC, where it proves an arbitration award without foreign element is delivered under any of the following circumstances, the enforcement of the arbitration award shall be refused by a court of law:

- no arbitration clause was contained in contract concluded between the parties, nor arbitration agreement was reached after the dispute arose;
- the matters decided in the arbitration award were not within the scope of the arbitration agreement or should not be subject to the jurisdiction of the arbitration commission;
- the organization of the arbitration penal or the arbitration procedure violated the statutory procedures;
- the evidence based upon which the arbitration award was delivered was forged;
- the other party concealed evidence which is sufficient to affect a justifiable award;
- the arbitrator or arbitrators committed corruption or malpractices, accepted bribes or perverted the law in delivering the arbitration award;
- enforcement of the award will violate social public interests.

If an arbitration award delivered by a Chinese arbitration commission is foreign-related, as provided for in Article 291 of CPC, where it proves the award is delivered under any of the following circumstances, the enforcement of the award shall be refused by a people's court:

- no arbitration clause is contained in contract concluded between the parties, nor arbitration agreement was reached after the dispute arose;
- the respondent was not served with the notice to appoint an arbitrator or to proceed with arbitration procedures or was unable to state its opinions due to causes for which it should not be responsible;
- the organization of the arbitration penal or the arbitration procedure was not in conformity with the arbitration rules;

- the matters decided in arbitration award were not within the scope of the arbitration agreement or should not be subject to the jurisdiction of the arbitration commission;
- enforcement of the arbitration award will violate social public interests.

106. Therefore, in the procedure of enforcement of an arbitration award with or without foreign element delivered by an arbitration organization in China, the supervision by court of law does not apply to matters of both substantial law and facts which have been decided in the arbitration award, but only to the matters of the arbitration agreement and arbitration procedure. Where an arbitration award is without foreign element, however, the court of law may refuse to enforce an arbitration award in the case of forged evidence based upon which the arbitration award was delivered or in the case of concealed evidence sufficient to affect a justifiable award.

Where the enforcement of arbitration award is refused by a court of law, the parties can refer the dispute to arbitration again or file a lawsuit with a court of law with jurisdiction (Articles 244, 282, CPC).

107. With respect to the recognition and enforcement of an arbitration award delivered by a foreign arbitration organization, both international treaty and domestic law shall be complied with. In case of conflict, the international treaty has priority over the domestic law.

China is a party to the *1958 New York Convention*. When acceding to this Convention on 2 December 1986, China made its reciprocal and commercial reservation to the effect that the Convention applies to commercial arbitration recognized by Chinese law on the basis of reciprocity only.

Where the country in which an arbitration award is delivered is not a party to the *1958 New York Convention*, nor has any bilateral agreement with China concerning recognition and enforcement of arbitration award, such an arbitration award shall be recognized and enforced only on the basis of the principle of reciprocity (Article 304, CPC).

Noticeably, in order to secure compliance with the *1958 New York Convention*, any refusal of recognition and enforcement of foreign arbitration award is subject to the approval of SPC.

§3. Litigation and Arbitration of Disputes in Other Modes of Transport

I. Litigation of Disputes

108. In China, cases of disputes arising from railway transport and other matters in connection with railways are subject to the jurisdiction of railway transport courts in the places at provincial level where there are railway transport courts. The railway transport courts in some places at provincial level were revoked in 2019, and therefore, such disputes are subject to the jurisdiction of the intermediate court of law for first instance and of the high court of law for second instance in these places.

The cases of disputes arising from transport other than maritime transport or inland navigation in the water areas adjacent to the sea and other matters with respect thereto are subject to the jurisdiction of ordinary courts of law, except where there are railway transport courts which entertain disputes arising from or with respect to railway transport.

109. There is no special law or provisions adopted by SPC governing the litigation procedures of disputes arising from transport other than maritime transport or inland navigation in the water areas adjacent to the sea and other matters with respect thereto. Thus, the provisions contained in CPC and the CPC Interpretations as introduced in §2 *supra* shall apply.

II. Arbitration of Disputes

110. Unlike CMAC in the cases of maritime disputes, there is no special arbitration organization in China with respect to arbitration of cases of disputes in other modes of transport than maritime transport or main inland navigation in the water areas adjacent to the sea. The parties may refer the disputes with foreign elements to arbitration in the CIETAC by virtue of an arbitration agreement. They may also refer the disputes with or without foreign elements to arbitration in other arbitration commissions established in accordance with AL.

111. AL, the AL Interpretations and the provisions contained in CPC and the CPC Interpretations governing arbitration as introduced in §2 *supra* shall apply to arbitration of cases of disputes in the other modes of transport. In addition, where recognition and enforcement of a foreign arbitration award of disputes in such other modes of transport is concerned, the *1958 New York Convention* shall apply.

Chapter 4. State Immunity and Transport Law

112. In China, a State-owned property means a property that is owned by the whole people of China.

As a socialist country, the scope and quantity of State-owned properties are larger than in a capitalist country. As provided for in the *Constitution*, the lands, minerals and other natural resources are owned by the State. Traditionally, many enterprises are invested by the State or governmental organs at various levels, although the number of such enterprises decreased along with the policies of reform and the setting up of a modern system of enterprises in the past three decades. However, so far as State-owned enterprises or properties operated by them are concerned, the State, via its governmental organs at various levels, acts as nominal owners only. These enterprises, as legal persons under the *Company Law*, are deemed as the owners in the sense of civil law of the properties invested by the State or governmental organs and operated by these enterprises. That is, the enterprises are taken as the owners of the properties invested by the State or governmental organs, although the enterprises themselves are owned by the whole people in the broadest sense. The State-owned lands, minerals and other natural resources are operated, used or exploited by individuals or enterprises in accordance with various laws.

113. China has never enacted any specific law concerning State immunity of State-owned properties. China is also not a party to the international treaties governing immunities of State-owned properties, including, *inter alia*, the *International Convention for the Unification of Certain Rules relating to the Immunity of State-owned Vessels*, signed in Brussels on 10 April 1926 and its Protocol signed in Brussels on 24 May 1934, and the *International Convention for the Unification of Certain Rules relating to the Precautionary Attachment of Aircrafts*, signed in Rome on 29 May 1933.

114. Some of the State-owned ships, aircraft or other means of transport are used for military or public services, while the others are used for commercial service. The treatment in law shall differ in the light of their different uses.

The State-owned ships, aircraft or other means of transport used for military or public services, i.e., non-commercial service, shall enjoy State immunity as a rule of international law and thus shall not be subject to arrest or attachment. SMPL expressly provides in paragraph 3 of Article 23 that ships engaged in military or public services shall not be arrested.

Where the State-owned ships, aircraft or other means of transport are used for commercial services, they are deemed as properties owned by legal persons in law[21] and shall, like the properties owned by individuals or private companies, be subject to arrest or attachment in accordance with law.

China never claimed State immunity of any State-owned ships or aircrafts used for commercial services, even in the time of thirty or forty years ago when China

21. Article 8 of MC provides: 'With respect to a State-owned ship operated by an enterprise owned by the whole people having a legal person status granted by the state, the provisions of this Code regarding the shipowners shall apply to this legal person.'

was very conservative. There is also no reported case judgment concerning State immunity of any State-owned ships. Instead, there are reported cases in which ships operated by State-owned companies were arrested by maritime courts in China.

Chapter 5. Transport Intermediaries and Auxiliaries

§1. Introduction

115. A contract of intermediary is subject to Chapter XXVI 'Contract of Intermediary' of Book Three 'Contracts' of CC. By virtue of Article 961 of CC defining a contract of intermediary, an intermediary means a natural or legal person who, upon entrustment by his principal, reports to the principal the chances of conclusion of contract or renders intermediary service for the conclusion of contract upon payment of reward by the principal as agreed.

A contract of intermediary is a kind of contract of entrustment in a broad sense. However, a contract of intermediary should be differentiated from another kind of contract of entrustment, i.e., contract of agency under Chapter XXIII 'Contract of Entrustment' of Book Three 'Contracts' of CC. An agent is a person who, either natural or legal, upon entrustment by his principal, handles business for and on behalf of the principal as entrusted upon payment of reward by the principal as agreed.

Consequently, it may be difficult to differentiate an intermediary from an agent. Theoretically, the main difference between an intermediary and an agent lies in the extent of service rendered. However, an agent may conclude contract with a third party either in the name of his principal as agent or in his own name,[22] while an intermediary never does so.

Due to the similarities in the legal nature and services between an intermediary and an agent, and for the convenience of presentation, agents are embodied in intermediaries in this chapter.

116. Transport auxiliaries are understood to be those natural or legal persons who render services related to transport of goods or passengers.

117. Within the category of transport intermediaries and auxiliaries in China, the important ones are freight forwarders, transport agents, transport brokers as well as shipping exchanges, although they may have different legal statuses depending upon the nature of services rendered by them upon entrustment by their principals.

118. So far, there is no specific law in China governing the activities of transport intermediaries and auxiliaries. Administrative regulations or provisions in this

22. Where an agent enters into a contract with a third party within the scope of agency in his own name, by virtue of Arts 925 and 926 of CC, if the third party knew the relation of agency at the time of conclusion of contract, the contract shall bind directly upon the principal and the third party; if the third party did not know and failed to fulfil the contractual obligations, the agent shall disclose the third party to his principal and thereupon the principal shall exercise the rights which the agent has under the contract as against the third party, except where the third party would not have entered into the contract, had he known the principal at the time of entering into the contract; if the third party did not know the relation of agency and the agent failed to fulfil the contractual obligations due to causes on the part of the principal, the agent shall disclose his principal to the third party and the latter may choose the agent or his principal as the other party to the contract.

respect do not provide their rights and obligations in the nature of civil law but govern their access to the markets, operation and other issues subject to governmental administration. Their rights and obligations in the nature of civil law shall be determined in accordance with CC and other basic laws.

§2. Freight Forwarders, Transport Agents and Brokers, Shipping Exchange

I. Freight Forwarders

119. Freight forwarders play very active roles in the transport market. Normally, a freight forwarder concludes a contract with a trader and thereupon makes arrangements for the transport of goods.

SINOTRANS Limited, under CMG, with its head office in Beijing and hundreds of branch companies over China and many offices or branches in other countries, is the largest freight forwarding company in China. A big coastal city has tens or even hundreds of freight forwarders of State-owned or private ownership or of Chinese-foreign joint ventures.

Freight forwarders are subject to the administration of MOT, but also subject to the administration of MOT where it acts as non-vessel operating carriers as mentioned in paragraph 120 *infra*.

120. In the transport practice, a freight forwarder sometimes concludes a contract of carriage or charter party with the owner or operator of means of transport for and on behalf of his principal, who is a cargo trader. In such a case, the freight forwarder acts as agent of his principal, and the contract thus concluded binds upon his principal. The legal consequences arising from his act done within the scope of agency shall be borne by his principal. The principal pays the agreed agency fees to the freight forwarder. Besides conclusion of contracts of carriage or charter parties, a freight forwarder often clears customs and port formalities for goods for and on behalf of his principal.

Sometimes, however, a freight forwarder concludes a contract of carriage or charter party with a cargo trader and another contract of carriage or charter party with the owner or operator of means of transport. Therefore, as against the cargo trader, the freight forwarder acts as a carrier or disponent owner and is entitled to the agreed freight or hire. As against the owner of means of transport, the freight forwarder is the shipper or charterer and is obliged to pay the agreed freight or hire to the carrier or the owner or operator of means of transport. The benefit of the freight forwarder lies in the difference of freights or hires in such a case. In liner shipping practice, a freight forwarder in such a case is often called a 'non-vessel operating carrier' under the *Regulations on International Seagoing Transport* promulgated by the State Council on 11 December 2001 and latest amended on 2 March 2019, which is quite similar to 'non-vessel operating common carrier' (NVOCC) under the American *Ocean Shipping Reform Act of 2022*.

In modern times, one of the main businesses of a big freight forwarding company is the multimodal transport of goods, in which case the freight forwarder becomes a multimodal transport operator (MTO). In addition, some large traditional freight forwarders have changed into logistic service providers in the supply chain, and consequently, their scope of service becomes wider to meet the various demands of their principals.

II. Transport Agents

121. In contrast with a freight forwarder, a transport agent accepts the entrustment of the owner or operator of transport means and renders transport services, including, *inter alia*, canvassing goods, making transport documents, collecting freights from a shipper or consignee for and on behalf of his principal.

Besides professional transport agencies, ship agencies often act as transport agents. For example, the branch companies based in port cities of China Ocean Shipping Agency, known as 'PENAVICO', or China Marine Shipping Agency, known as 'SINOAGENT', render their services as aforementioned for and on behalf of their principals, *viz.* shipowners, operators, bareboat or time charterers of ships in most cases, and at the same time they render services for the ship's calling at Chinese ports. Occasionally, a company, the main business of which is freight forwarding, acts as transport agent. So far, many companies set up in China and solely invested by foreign shipping companies act as transport agents for their respective mother companies.

Ship agencies are subject to the administration of MOT.

III. Transport Brokers

122. Transport brokers render their intermediary services mainly in the conclusion of charter parties of transport means and are entitled to brokerage commissions where the contracts are concluded between owners and charterers of transport means due to their services.

IV. Shipping Exchange

123. Shanghai Shipping Exchange, known as 'SSE', was established in 1996 as approved by the State Council. Its activities are regulated by the *Provisions on the Administration of Shanghai Shipping Exchange* promulgated by the former MOC (now MOT) in 1996, by which MOT and the Shanghai Municipal Government jointly exercise administration and supervision of it.

124. As a non-profit enterprise, SSE provides information on maritime transport supplies and demands by publishing container transport indexes and other shipping information, facilitates its members, either shipowners, ship's operators or cargo traders, for the negotiation of maritime transactions, including carriage by sea, ship's sale and purchase, and provides the traders with services of customs declaration, cargo inspection and quarantine for the import and export of cargoes via the freight forwarding company invested by it. In addition, as designated by MOT, SSE accepts the filing of tariffs by liner shipping companies.

Part II. Maritime Transport

Chapter 1. Ship

§1. Definition and Legal Status

125. In the Chinese language, the character pronounced as 'chuanbo' can embody the English words 'vessel', 'ship' and 'boat', although in English, normally a ship means a large vessel and a boat means a small one. The word 'ship' is used in the official English translation of some Chinese statutes, such as MC, while 'vessel' is used in others without obvious differences in meaning. For the convenience of elaboration, the word 'ship' is used *infra*, unless otherwise indicated.

There is no uniform definition of ship in the statutes since different statutes regulate different scopes of ships. Even different parts of a statute may not govern the same scope of ships. For example, Article 3 of MC contains a general definition of a ship as cited below, whereas paragraph 2 of Article 165 in Chapter VII 'Ship's Collisions' and Article 172 in Chapter IX 'Salvage at Sea' of MC contains a wider definition of ship.

126. Article 3 of MC provides: '"ship" as referred to in this Code means a seagoing ship and other mobile seagoing unit, but does not include a ship or craft used for military or public service purposes, nor a small vessel of less than 20 tons gross tonnage'.

To come within this definition, a ship must be a seagoing one. Therefore, an inland vessel is excluded from the scope of ship.

In principle, MC does not apply to inland vessels and small vessels of less than 20 tons gross tonnage. However, as an exception, MC applies to a collision between a ship, as defined in Article 3 thereof and an inland vessel or a small vessel or to salvage between a ship, as defined in Article 3 thereof and an inland vessel or a small vessel, provided that the inland vessel or small vessel is not used for military or public service purposes (Articles 165 and 172, MC).

Three opinions exist as to the meaning of the word 'mobile' adopted in Article 3 of MC *viz.* (a) self-movable only; (b) either self-movable or movable by way of motive power from outside; (c) either self-movable or movable by way of motive power from outside which can be supplied immediately at any time when required. Therefore, three corresponding opinions exist as to whether a floating barge or other craft without motive power is a ship, *viz.* (a) it is not a ship in any case; (b) it is a ship in any case; (c) it is a ship when it is under towage or is connected with a tug or other ship with motive power that enables it to move when required, while it is not a ship when not under towage or so connected. Currently, the majority view is that a floating barge or other craft without motive power is a ship as defined in Article 3 of MC.

127. MTSL has a much wider definition of vessel. Article 117 provides: '"vessels" mean all types of vessels, crafts, hydroplanes, submersibles, movable platforms and other movable installations which displace or do not displace waters'.

128. Ships are objects. As in the civil law countries, there is no action in rem in China. So, ships cannot be parties to legal relations but only be subject matters thereof.

Ships are movables. However, they are sometimes deemed immovable and can be mortgaged (section 2, Chapter II, MC; Chapter XVII, Book 2, CC).

§2. Registration and Nationality of Ships

I. Introduction

129. It is an international rule and practice that every ship, especially a seagoing ship, shall be duly registered in a State and sail under the flag of the State of registry. Without registration, a ship is not entitled to sail at sea.

As required by UNCLOS, to which China is a party, a genuine link shall exist between the State of registry and its ships, and each State shall effectively exercise its jurisdiction and control in administrative, technical and social matters over ships flying its flag (Articles 91 and 94).

Ship's nationality is obtained through registration. After being duly registered in a State, a ship has the nationality of the State of Registry and is qualified to fly its flag. A ship is subject to the exclusive jurisdiction of the State of Registry while sailing on the high seas, except the right of visit and the right of hot pursuit as provided for in Articles 110 and 111 of UNCLOS. The jurisdiction of the State of registry is called flag State control (FSC). While sailing, berthing or operating in the territorial or inner waters of another State, the ship is also subject to the jurisdiction of that coastal State.

130. The provisions concerning the jurisdiction of Chinese maritime traffic safety authorities, i.e., the central Maritime Safety Administration of China (MSA) or the departments directly under it, i.e., the local MSAs over foreign ship's sailing, berthing or operating in the Chinese coastal waters are contained in MTSL and the *Regulations Governing Administration on Ships of Foreign Nationalities of 1979*. The jurisdiction of a coastal state over foreign ships calling at its ports includes the port state control (PSC) in pursuance of the various IMO conventions and regulations as well as the domestic regulations.

131. MC expressly provides in Article 5 that ships are allowed to sail under the national flag of China after being registered as required by law and granted Chinese nationality, and ships illegally flying the Chinese flag shall be prohibited and fined by the authorities concerned.

II. Conditions for Registration and Chinese Nationality

132. China is not a country of the so-called State of Flag of Convenience. A State of flag of convenience carries out an open registry, and there is no requirement, or there are flexible requirements regarding shipowners or shareholders, place of their principal business, ship's manning, etc. Thus, the flag of convenience cannot meet the requirement of Articles 91 and 94 of UNCLOS because of the lack of a genuine link between the State of registry and its ships and of the effective exercise of jurisdiction and control by the State of registry in administrative, technical and social matters over ships flying its flag. Currently, the main States of flag of convenience are Panama, Liberia, Marshall Islands, Singapore, Malta, Bahamas, etc. Strictly speaking, Hong Kong's flag is also a flag of convenience.[23]

Strict conditions for ship's registration in Mainland China and Chinese nationality are currently contained in the *Regulations Governing Ship Registration of 1994*. For a ship to be registered in Mainland China and granted Chinese nationality, the following conditions shall be satisfied:

- the ship is owned by a Chinese individual or company duly registered in Mainland China as a Chinese legal person, or, where the company is a Chinese-foreign joint venture, the share of investment in the ship by the Chinese investors shall not be less than 50%;
- the master and crewmembers shall be Chinese citizens unless employment of foreign citizens is necessary, in which case the employment is subject to the approval of MOT.

A ship owned by a Chinese company solely invested by foreign citizens and/or companies is not allowed to be registered in Mainland China and granted Chinese nationality.

Where a ship is registered in Mainland China and sails under the Chinese flag, the certificates of competencies that the master, officers and engineers shall hold by virtue of the STCW Convention, which China has ratified, shall be issued by the Chinese competent authorities, *viz.* MSA or, in the case of a fishing vessel, the administration of fishing vessels and fishing ports.[24]

23. After the sovereignty over Hong Kong was returned to China on 1 Jul. 1997, Hong Kong maintains its independent ship registry and the ships duly registered in Hong Kong fly the flag of Hong Kong, as provided for in the *Basic Law of Hong Kong Special Administrative Region of China*.
24. Article 32 of MC provides the master, deck officers, chief engineer, engineers, electrical engineer and radio operator must hold appropriate certificates of competency. Similar provisions are contained in Art. 13 of MTSL.

The conditions for ship's registration and nationality are a reflection of a State's shipping policies. As a whole, such policies are developing in Mainland China in the direction of gradually opening to the outside world.

133. China does not recognize ship's double registrations or double nationalities but adheres to the principle that a ship shall only have one nationality. Therefore, if a ship of foreign nationality is to be changed into the Chinese nationality, the foreign nationality shall be cancelled or suspended before the Chinese nationality is granted and *vice versa.*

Where a ship of foreign nationality is chartered by a Chinese company on a bareboat charter or financial leasing basis, the charterer is able to apply for a ship's temporary Chinese nationality for the period of not exceeding two years after being duly registered, provided that a proof has been issued by the original ship's registry indicating that the ship's original nationality has been cancelled or suspended or shall be cancelled or suspended.

III. Formalities of Registration

134. By virtue of the *Regulations Governing Ship Registration of 1994*, in the application for the Chinese ship registration and nationality, the following documents shall be submitted to the ship registration authority together with an application in writing:

- A document evidencing the ownership of ship, e.g., a shipbuilding contract or a contract of sale of ship or a bill of sale, and the document of delivery and acceptance, or the certificate of ownership if the shipowners already have.
- A document evidencing cancellation of her original registration, if applicable.
- The valid technical certificates issued by China Classification Society, known as 'CCS', or a foreign classification society approved by Chinese maritime traffic safety authorities, including, *inter alia*, ship tonnage certificate, ship load line certificate, ship safety construction certificate, ship safety equipment certificate and prevention of oil pollution certificate.

135. After registration, a certificate of ship nationality will be issued. This certificate shall be carried onboard for inspection by coastal State authorities in the ports she calls at.

§3. Acquisition and Ownership

I. Acquisition According to Civil Law

136. The ownership of a ship is defined in Article 7 of MC as the shipowners' rights to lawfully possess, utilize, profit from and dispose of the ship in their ownership.

137. The modes of acquisition of property under civil law apply to ships. Therefore, a ship can be acquired by way of purchase from its original owners, from the sale by auction by court of law, or by way of shipbuilding, incorporation, inheritance, donation, etc.

II. Particular Modes of Acquisition

138. There are three particular ways of acquisition of ships, *viz.* abandonment under hull insurance, capture and confiscation.

Under hull insurance, where a ship becomes a constructive total loss, and the insured demands compensation from the insurer on the basis of total loss, the insured ship shall be abandoned by the insurer (Article 249, MC). If the insurer accepts the abandonment, all the rights and obligations relating to the ship shall be transferred to the insurer (Article 250, MC). Consequently, the insurer acquires the ownership of the ship that the insured has abandoned.

Acquisition by way of capture or confiscation is a matter of public law.

By virtue of the law of the seas, the States at war may capture ships of a hostile State, whether the ship is owned by the hostile State, a company in the State or its civilian, and consequently acquire the ownership of the ship captured. There is no specific statutory provision on this matter under Chinese law. In fact, capture of ships rarely occurs in modern times.

Confiscation of ship may occur where a ship is engaged in illegal trades, e.g., smuggling, or carrying contrabands, slaves or stowaways and thus seriously violates the international or national laws, as a result of which the ship may be arrested by a coastal State and confiscated. Consequently, the coastal State acquires the ownership of the ship confiscated. For example, by virtue of Article 82 of the *Customs Law* adopted by the Standing Committee of NPC on 22 January 1987 and latest amended on 4 November 2017, the customs may confiscate a ship that is specially used in smuggling or used in smuggling on many occasions.

III. Co-ownership

139. On some occasions, a ship is owned by co-owners by shares, i.e., part owners or joint owners.

By virtue of Articles 298 and 299 of CC, part owners are owners of a property with distributed shares, and joint owners are owners without distributed shares.

If a ship is invested by two or more persons, whether individuals or companies, the investors shall be part owners of the ship, holding shares in proportion to the amounts of their respective investments unless otherwise agreed upon. Where the ownership of a ship is acquired by way of heritage, then the successors are joint owners of the ship unless otherwise agreed upon.

Co-ownership is governed by civil law. In the case of part ownership, the part owners shall enjoy rights and bear obligations relating to their ship in accordance with their respective shares. In the case of joint ownership, the joint owners shall enjoy the rights and bear obligations relating to their ship in common.

140. MC in Article 16 contains special provisions concerning the establishment of mortgage on a ship owned by co-owners to the effect that the establishment shall unless otherwise agreed upon, be subject to the agreement of those co-owners who have two-thirds or more of the shares thereof. However, a part owner may establish a mortgage on the shares of a ship he owns. In the case of joint ownership, establishment of mortgage on a ship shall be subject to the agreement of all the joint owners.

IV. State-Ownership

141. Traditionally, many merchant ships were deemed State-owned under the socialist system in China. As introduced in Chapter 4 of Part I *supra*, however, along with the policies of reform and the setting up of modern system of enterprises, most previously Stated-owned ships are no longer owned by the State, *viz.* the whole people of China.

At the present stage, shipping companies in China may be State-owned, such as COSCO SHIPPING. Some are State organ holding companies. However, these companies are independent legal persons in terms of the *Company Law*. Thus, they shall enjoy rights and bear obligations relating to the properties registered as the properties of their respective companies independent of any other companies.

It is expressly provided for in Article 8 of MC that with respect to a State-owned ship operated by an enterprise owned by the whole people having the status of a legal person granted by the State, the provisions of MC regarding the shipowners shall apply to that legal person. Therefore, such a legal person is deemed as the shipowner and registered as such, although it is entrusted by the State to operate and manage such ships.

V. Registration of Ownership

142. The acquisition, transfer or extinction of ship ownership shall be registered with the ship registration authority, and no acquisition, transfer or extinction of ship ownership shall act against a third party unless registered (Article 9, MC).

Where a ship is co-owned by two or more legal persons or individuals, the co-ownership shall be registered with the ship registration authority, and no co-ownership of the ship shall act against a third party unless registered (Article 10, MC).

As expressly provided for in Article 225 of CC, the abovementioned third party shall be understood to be a third party acting in good faith, i.e., a person who did not know or should not have known that his transaction with the counterparty would cause harm to the legitimate rights and interests of persons other than his counterparty. For example, A, as the shipowner, sold a ship to B and then to C, and C acquired the ship and is duly registered as the new shipowner without knowledge that the ship had been sold to B. In such a case, B is unable to assert his ownership of the ship as against C, even if B has paid the purchase price to A because B is not duly registered as the shipowner, and C is a third party acting in good faith and is the registered shipowner.

143. By virtue of the *Regulations Governing Ship Registration of 1994*, in the application for the registration of ship ownership, the following documents shall be submitted to the ship registration authority together with an application in writing:

- a document evidencing the identity of shipowners, e.g., the certificate of company registration or the identity cards in case of a ship owned by individuals;
- a document evidencing the acquisition of ownership, e.g., a shipbuilding contract, a contract of sale of ship, a bill of sale or an effective court judgment, and document of delivery and acceptance;
- the ship's technical documents, e.g., the ship's survey certificates for a newly built ship or existing ship or the technical evaluation report for a ship purchased from abroad;
- a document evidencing cancellation of her original ownership registration, if applicable.

144. After registration, a certificate of ship ownership will be issued. This certificate shall be carried onboard for inspection by coastal state authorities in the ports she calls at.

Chapter 2. Maritime Liens and Mortgages

§1. Applicable Laws

145. Maritime liens are regulated by section 3 'Maritime Liens' and ship mortgages are regulated by section 2 'Ship Mortgages' of Chapter II 'Ships' of MC.

So far as mortgage is concerned, Sub-Book One 'General Rules' and Sub-Book Four 'Real Rights for Security' of Book Two 'Real Rights' of CC govern various kinds of real rights for securities, including mortgage, pledge and possessory lien. Therefore, in addition to those contained in section 2 of Chapter II in MC, the provisions of Chapter XVII 'Mortgages' of the said Sub-Book Four, together with those related provisions of the said Sub-Book One, shall be applicable to ship mortgages to the extent that they are not repugnant to provisions of section 2 of Chapter II in MC.

146. China is not a party to the International Convention for the Unification of Certain Rules Relating to Maritime Liens and Mortgages signed in Brussels on 10 April 1926, the International Convention for the Unification of Certain Rules Relating to Maritime Liens and Mortgages signed in Brussels on 27 May 1967, or the International Convention on Maritime Liens and Mortgages signed in Geneva on 6 May 1993 which China has signed, but subject to ratification. However, reference to the Convention of 1993 was made in shaping sections 2 and 3 of Chapter II of MC during the drafting thereof.

§2. Maritime Liens

I. Definition and Legal Nature

147. Maritime lien is defined in Article 21 of MC as the right of maritime claimant to take priority in compensation against shipowners, bareboat charterers or operators of a ship with respect to the ship that gave rise to the said claim.

Maritime liens secure specified maritime claims for which the shipowners, bareboat charterers or operators of a ship are responsible. Therefore, for a maritime claim to be secured by maritime lien, three conditions should be met: first, the claim should be specified in law as secured by maritime lien; second, the shipowners, bareboat charterers or operators of the ship are responsible for the claim; third, the claim was given rise to by the ship.

Maritime liens are in nature statutory proprietary rights on ship that the claimants of the specified maritime claims have by virtue of MC to secure the compensation for these claims, as a consequence of which the claimants have priority over other claimants whose claims are not secured by maritime lien in compensation in the distribution of proceeds of sale of the ship giving rise to the maritime claims. Thus, maritime liens shall be enforced by court of law by arresting and selling by auction the ship that gave rise to the said maritime claims (Article 28, MC). Arrest and sale by auction of the ship shall be executed by a maritime court upon application by a claimant in accordance with SMPL. A maritime court may appoint an auctioneer set up in accordance with AUL to perform a sale by auction of a ship. Traditionally, a ship was sold in a live auction hosted by the auction commission consisting of judges and auctioneers. Now, a ship is usually sold on a specified internet website as entrusted by the maritime court entertained the case.

Maritime liens are a special kind of security. However, they do not come into the scope of regulation of Sub-Book Four 'Real Rights for Security' of Book Two 'Real Rights' of CC.

148. In Anglo-American law, maritime liens are deemed indispensable from action in rem. However, Chinese law does not recognize action in rem but recognizes maritime liens in action in personam, *viz.* actions against the shipowners, charterers or operators of a ship who are responsible for the claims secured by maritime liens.

II. Categories of Maritime Liens

149. As maritime liens are statutory rights, the categories of maritime claims secured by maritime liens are stipulated in MC. During the drafting of MC, the idea followed regarding maritime lien is that the Chinese shipping industry needed funds to be financed by the banks, which usually secure their rights by means of ship mortgage, and as the maritime claims secured by maritime lien have priority over those secured by ship mortgages in compensation from the proceeds of sale by auction of a ship, the maritime claims secured by maritime lien should be limited in order to benefit the ship mortgagees. Thus, by reference to the *International Convention on Maritime Liens and Ship Mortgages* signed in Geneva on 6 May 1993, paragraph 1 of Article 22 of MC only stipulates the following five categories of maritime claims secured by maritime lien.

A. Claims for Seafarers' Wages, Etc.

150. Claims for wages, other remuneration, crew repatriation and social insurance costs made by the master and crewmembers of the complement in accordance with the relevant labour laws, administrative rules and regulations or articles of employment are secured by maritime lien.

Many seafarers serve onboard via seafarer recruiting companies in practice. On most occasions, a recruiting company enters into a contract with seafarers in its own name on the one hand and enters into a contract in its own name with the shipowners, bareboat charterers or operators of a ship on the other hand. Consequently, there is no direct contractual relation between a seafarer and the shipowners, bareboat charterers or operators of a ship. Instead, the employer of a seafarer is the recruiting company that shall bear the contractual responsibility for the payment of the seafarer's wages and other remuneration, etc. The prevailing labour laws, administrative rules and regulations contain no provision to the effect that, in such a case, the shipowners, bareboat charterers or operators of a ship shall also be responsible for the payment of seafarer's wages and other remuneration, etc. Thus, strictly speaking, the seafarer's claim for wages and other remunerations, etc., shall not be secured by maritime lien by virtue of Article 21 of MC.

Nevertheless, in admiralty practice, there are judgments made by maritime courts which confirm that a seafarer's claim for wages and other remunerations is still secured by maritime lien, even if there is no direct contractual relation between the seafarer and the shipowners, bareboat charterers or operators of a ship on which the seafarer is serving or served.[25] Such judgments are based upon the finding that there exists a relation *ex facto* between a seafarer and the shipowners, bareboat charterers or operators of a ship in order to protect the interests of seafarers.

Claims for seafarers' wages, etc., are listed as secured by maritime lien because the wages, etc., are normally their source of income and even of their families and therefore are necessary to be secured by maritime lien for protecting the seafarers' interests.

B. *Claims in Respect of Loss of Life or Personal Injury Occurred in the Operation of a Ship*

151. The claims cover loss of life or personal injury to the master, crewmembers, stevedores, passengers or any other persons, whether onboard or not, who have suffered loss of life or personal injury arising from the operation of a ship.

Claims in respect of loss of life or personal injury are listed as secured by maritime lien because loss of life or personal injury should have priority over property damage in compensation.

C. *Claims for Port Charges*

152. Claims for ship's tonnage dues, pilotage dues, harbour dues and other port charges are secured by maritime lien.

In China, ship's tonnage dues are State dues and are levied by the customs on ships engaged in international transport in terms of their gross registered tonnage. Pilotage dues are remunerations paid to the piloting stations in ports or other special water areas for their piloting services. Harbour dues on ships were levied by MSAs for the maintenance of port facilities in terms of their gross registered tonnage. However, harbour dues on ships have not been levied anymore since 1 October 2015. Other port charges to be secured by maritime lien should be in the nature of expenses payable to the port authority, local or state government, or port operators by virtue of specified regulations or rules and do not include the expenses of commercial services rendered by stevedores in loading or discharge of cargo and tugs, etc.

Claims for port charges, etc., are listed as secured by maritime lien because port charges, etc., involve the protection of the State's economic interests.

25. For example, judgments made by Ningbo Maritime Court in 1999 and the People's High Court of Zhejiang Province in 2000 in the case of M.V. 'Hua Mao 3' and M.V. 'Hua Mao 6'.

D. Claims for Salvage Payment

153. Salvage payment, as defined in Article 172 of Chapter IX 'Salvage at Sea' in MC means any reward, remuneration or special compensation for salvage operations to be paid to the salvor by the salved party, *viz.* the owners of the salved ship, cargo or other properties on board the ship. Salvage payment may be based on the principle of 'no cure, no pay' or the employed salvage services. However, the salvage payment to be paid by the owners of the salved cargo or properties other than a ship is not secured by maritime lien.

Claims for salvage payment are listed as secured by maritime lien because salvage is beneficial to the maritime safety and to preserve the ship from peril, enabling the compensation of other claims.

E. Claims for Loss of or Damage to Property under Tortuous Liability

154. Compensation claims for loss of or damage to property resulting from tortuous acts in the course of operation of a ship are secured by maritime lien.

However, claims for loss of or damage to properties under contractual liability are not secured by maritime lien, even if they can be founded in tort by virtue of the principle of competition between contractual liability and tortuous liability by virtue of Article 186 of CC, which provides that, where the breach of contract by one party causes damage to the personal or property interests of the other party, the other party may choose the party committed breach of contract to bear contractual liability or liability in tort. The underlying philosophy is that a party to a contract could choose the counterparty beforehand, whereas a person who suffered loss of or damage to property caused by another person without contractual relation could not choose and anticipate the committer of tortuous act causing the loss or damage and, therefore, the loss of or damage to property resulting from tortuous act should be compensated for before the compensation for the loss or damage resulting from breach of contract.

The property in this category includes ships, cargo, port installations and other physical property, whether movable or fixed, whether in water or ashore.

However, by virtue of paragraph 2 of Article 22 of MC, claims for oil pollution damage caused by a ship carrying more than 2,000 tons of oil in bulk as cargo that has or should have a valid certificate attesting that her owners have oil pollution liability insurance coverage or other appropriate financial security are not within this category.[26] This is because compensation for this kind of loss or damage to property is already secured by liability insurance or other financial security as provided for in the *International Convention on Civil Liability for Oil Pollution Damage of 1992* or domestic law, and there is no need for further security by means of maritime lien. Now, the liability for oil pollution damage not within this scope is, on most occasions, also insured, or other appropriate financial security is provided

26. For oil pollution liability insurance or financial security, *see* §4 in Ch. 13 of this part *infra*.

under the *International Convention on Civil Liability for Bunker Oil Pollution Damage of 2001* or domestic law. Thus, where the liability for oil pollution damage caused by a ship is insured, or other appropriate financial security is provided, claims for such oil pollution damage are not secured by maritime lien.

III. Enforcement of Maritime Liens

A. *Persons Entitled to Enforce Maritime Lien*

155. Any maritime claimant whose claim is secured by maritime lien by virtue of Articles 21 and 22 of MC is entitled to enforce maritime lien.

Maritime lien is transferable. Therefore, where a maritime claim secured by maritime lien is transferred from the claimant to a third person, the maritime lien shall be transferred to that third person accordingly (Article 27, MC). Thus, the transferee who is subrogated in the right of maritime claim of the original claimant is entitled to enforce maritime lien to the extent of such subrogation.

B. *Properties Subject to Enforcement*

156. Maritime liens are on a ship only under MC and can only be enforced on the ship, giving rise to the maritime claims secured by maritime lien. Freight accrued since the commencement of the voyage during which the claims giving rise to the maritime lien arose or the accessory rights of a ship are not subject to maritime lien, although they are subject to enforcement by virtue of Article 2 of the *International Convention for the Unification of Certain Rules Relating to Maritime Liens and Mortgages of 1926* to which China is not a party.

A ship giving rise to maritime lien has the same definition as in Article 3 of MC. Therefore, the hull, machinery and appurtenances are all subject to enforcement, even if any part of them may be ashore during ship repair.

Ships excluded from the scope of ship defined in Article 3 of MC are not subject to maritime lien. As discussed in Chapter 1 of this part *supra*, these excluded ships include inland vessels, seagoing vessels of less than 20 tons gross tonnage and ships or crafts used for military or public service purposes.

C. *Amount to Be Enforced*

157. A claimant whose claim is secured by maritime lien is entitled to put forward his claim in full. The amount of claim shall include the interests accrued and costs paid to the maritime court or arbitration organization for the judgment or arbitration award confirming the claim.

Where it happens a claim secured by maritime lien by virtue of Articles 21 and 22 of MC are also subject to limitation of liability provided for in Chapter XI of MC, MC does not contain specific provisions concerning the amount of compensation for such a claim. The academic views diverge in this respect. It is certain, however, that maritime lien does not exclude the application of limitation of liability. The maritime claims specified in Article 207 of Chapter XI 'Limitation of Liability for Maritime Claims' are subject to limitation of liability if applied for by the shipowners, bareboat charterers or operators of a ship and approved by a maritime court by virtue of SMPL. Where a claim subject to limitation of liability is compensated for either from the limitation fund or directly by the shipowners, bareboat charterers or operators of a ship, any sum of the claim not compensated for due to the limitation of liability cannot be compensated for in the enforcement of maritime lien.

In addition, the application of limitation of liability is not conditional upon the establishment of a limitation fund by virtue of Article 213 of MC, except in the case of claims for oil pollution damage from a ship. Thus, where no limitation fund is established, but the shipowners, bareboat charterers or operators of a ship apply for limitation of liability, a claim which is subject to limitation of liability and secured by maritime lien shall be allowed in the distribution of the proceeds of sale of ship since the claim is secured by maritime lien. In such a case, the amount of the claim to be distributed in the proceeds of sale shall not exceed the sum due in accordance with the rules of limitation of liability because it is fully doubtful the claimant can get extra benefit from the absence of limitation fund and failure of the shipowners, bareboat charterers or operators of a ship to compensate for the claim in the procedure of limitation of liability. This rule is reflected in Article 30 of MC, stipulating that maritime liens shall not affect the implementation of the limitation of liability for maritime claims provided for in Chapter XI of MC.

D. Enforcement Procedure

158. Maritime liens shall be enforced by a maritime court by arresting and selling by auctioning the ship, giving rise to the maritime claims (Article 28, MC). The enforcement procedures are stipulated in SMPL, covering arrest and sale by auction of the ship, registration of claims secured by maritime lien and distribution of proceeds of sale. Thus, the provisions of section 1 'General Provisions' and section 2 'Arrest and Sale by Auction of Ship' contained in Chapter III 'Maritime Claim Preservation' as well as Chapter X 'Registration of Claims and Compensation' of SMPL shall apply to the enforcement of maritime liens. The procedures of arrest and sale by auction of ship are discussed in Chapter 14 of this part *infra*.

159. By virtue of Chapter X of SMPL, the claimants shall, after the maritime court that executed arrest of the ship has publicized the notice of forced sale by auction of the ship, register their claims with the maritime court within the period of time specified in the notice; where a claim is not so registered, the right of the claimant for compensation from the proceeds of sale by auction of the ship shall be deemed as waived (Article 111). However, such a waiver does not mean extinction of the claim, and the claimant can otherwise make it against the party liable by virtue of applicable law.

In his application for the registration of claim, the claimant shall submit to the maritime court a written application together with the documents evidencing his claim, e.g., a judgment, award, reconciliation statement, arbitration award with legal effect, or a notarized document or other documents evidencing maritime claim (Article 113).

The maritime court shall examine the application and make an award, either granting registration if the judgment, award, reconciliation statement, arbitration award or notarized document is true and legal or the claim is supported by other evidence, or refusing registration if the claim is not supported by evidence (Articles 114 and 115). However, where the applicant submits documents other than a judgment, award, reconciliation statement, arbitration award or notarized document, he is required to file a lawsuit with the maritime court to confirm his claim in the form of a judgment or award to be made by the maritime court and such judgment or award is final and not subject to appeal in order to expedite the distribution of proceeds of sale by auction of the ship (Article 116).

The maritime court shall, after the trial and confirmation of the registered claims, convene a meeting of all the creditors for the negotiation of distribution of the proceeds of sale by auction of the ship (Article 117). Where an agreement is reached among all the creditors and approved by the maritime court, the agreement shall have legal effect; where no such agreement is reached, the maritime court shall make an award by virtue of MC and other applicable laws for the distribution of the proceeds of the sale (Article 118).

The interest on the proceeds of sale shall also be distributed. The surplus, if any, after the compensation for all the registered and confirmed claims and the expenses listed in Article 24 of MC as introduced *infra* shall be refunded to the original shipowners (Article 119).

IV. Ranking

160. In pursuance of Article 23 of MC, the claims secured by maritime lien set out in paragraph 1 of Article 22, as mentioned and discussed *supra*, shall be satisfied in the order listed, *viz.* from A to E. However, claims for salvage payment set out in sub-paragraph D, which arose later than those under sub-paragraphs A through C, shall have priority over them. In case there are two or more maritime claims under sub-paragraphs A, B, C or E of paragraph 1 of Article 22, they shall be satisfied at the same time regardless of their respective occurrence; where they cannot be paid in full, they shall be paid in proportion. Should there be two or more maritime claims for salvage payment, the one or those arising later shall be satisfied first.

The reason why the claims for salvage payment arising later than those claims listed before it shall have priority and why, so far as two claims salvage payment are concerned, the later one shall have priority over the former one is that, without the salvage or the later salvage, the ship would become a total loss and consequently those claims listed before it or the claim for payment for the former salvage would have no chance to be satisfied. For this reason, the satisfaction for claims for salvage payments always follows the reverse priority rule, *viz.* 'first in time, last in right'.

161. As provided for in Article 24 of MC, the legal costs for enforcing the maritime liens, the expenses for preserving and selling the ship giving rise to the claims, the distribution of the proceeds of sale of the ship and other expenses incurred for the common interests of the claimants shall be deducted and paid first from the proceeds of sale, although not secured by maritime lien in nature. This is because the occurrence of these costs and expenses is necessary for, and is the precondition of, the proceeds and distribution thereof to become realistic.

The legal costs for enforcing maritime liens cover the costs paid to the maritime court as application fees for the arrest of the ship giving rise to the claims and the costs paid to the maritime court for the trial of the case of claims secured by maritime lien. The expenses for preserving the ship cover the expenses of watching the ship under arrest by court marshals, policemen from the border control or other persons as appointed by the maritime court, as well as the expenses of bunkers supplied to and port charges for the ship under arrest, provisions supplied to the master and crewmembers remaining on board, if these expenses are not paid by the shipowners, bareboat charterers or operators. The expenses for preserving the ship occur from the time the ship is arrested by a maritime court. Watching expenses may normally occur only in respect of the arrest of a foreign ship unless the master and crewmembers of a domestic ship went ashore after arrest and watchmen were appointed by the maritime court.

162. In the distribution of proceeds of sale of a ship defined in Article 3 of MC, where claims secured by maritime lien, possessory lien and ship mortgage exist simultaneously, the maritime lien shall have priority over the possessory lien, and the possessory lien shall have priority over the ship mortgage by virtue of paragraph 1 of Article 25 of MC.

As provided for in paragraph 2 of Article 25 of MC, the possessory lien only means the right of a shipbuilder or repairer to secure the shipbuilding or repairing costs by means of detaining her in his possession when the other party to the contract fails to pay. Possessory lien shall be extinguished when the ship builder or repairer no longer possesses the ship he has built or repaired.

Therefore, the ranking in the compensation from the proceeds of sale of a ship is defined in Article 3 of MC as the legal costs and expenses referred to in Article 24 of MC, the claims secured maritime lien, the claims secured by possessory lien, the claims secured by ship mortgage and other maritime claims.

Noticeably, such other maritime claims may include claims secured by possessory lien other than that of a shipbuilder or repairer. Such claims shall be satisfied after claims are secured by ship mortgage but shall have priority over other claims without security.

163. In the case of a ship excluded from the scope of ship defined in Article 3 of MC, particularly an inland vessel, no maritime lien occurs, as discussed *supra*. Therefore, a claim that would be secured by maritime lien if the ship giving rise to it was one defined in Article 3 of MC shall be deemed as a claim without security unless it is secured by possessory lien, as discussed below. The absence of maritime liens with respect to inland vessels has given rise to the question of how to protect the claims of the master and crewmembers' claim for unpaid wages, etc., and the claims for loss of life or personal injuries. One academic view is to make the provisions of maritime liens contained in MC applicable to inland vessels after the revision of MC, expectedly in a couple of years to come.

Possessory lien may occur by virtue of Chapter XIX 'Possessory Lien' of Sub-Book Four 'Real Rights for Security' of Book Two 'Real Rights' of CC. Article 447 of CC provides where a debtor fails to pay off his due debt, the creditor may exercise lien on the movable property of the debtor and lawfully in possession of the creditor and has priority in compensation with respect to the movable property unless the parties have agreed that the movable property is not subject to possessory lien. The said movable property of the debtor includes the movable property owned by the debtor and the movable property owned by a third party but in the lawful possession of the debtor. By virtue of Article 448 of CC, the movable property subject to possession lien shall be in the same relation with the claim secured by it, i.e., the claim arises with respect to the movable property concerned, with the exception that where the creditor and the debtor are both enterprises, the creditor may exercise lien on the movable property in his lawful possession during the course of usual business transactions with the debtor, the same relation is not required.

A creditor's possessory lien may occur under a contract of custody, carriage, or procession and work if the debtor fails to fulfil his debt. A shipbuilding contract and a contract of ship repair are within the category of contract of procession and work. A contract of salvage may be dealt with by reference to a contract of procession and work. Therefore, a shipbuilder, ship repairer or salvor of a ship may have possessory liens on the inland vessels.

By virtue of Articles 394 and 448 of CC, both claims secured by mortgage and those by possessory lien, have priority in compensation. Other claims without security of mortgage or possessory lien shall rank after the mortgage and possessory lien and shall rank equally in compensation. Article 456 of CC further provides that, where there exist mortgage and possessory lien on the same movable property, the claim secured by possessory lien shall have priority in compensation over that secured by mortgage.

V. Extinction of Maritime Liens

A. *Extinction of Maritime Claim*

164. Maritime liens on ship are in nature right in rem on ship to secure the payment or compensation of specified claims and are thus subordinate to the claims. As subordinate rights, their existence is conditional upon the existence of the claims they secure. Thus, where a claim secured by maritime lien is extinguished, the maritime lien securing this claim shall be extinguished at the same time (Article 393, CC). A claim shall be extinguished by the debtor's fulfilment of the debt, enforcement of an effective judgment or arbitration award, the creditor's waiver of the claim, or setting off claims the creditor and the debtor have against each other, etc.

B. Loss of Ship

165. Where a ship is lost, any maritime lien on her shall be extinguished (Article 29, MC). To bring out the extinction of maritime lien, the ship should become an actual total loss. If a ship only suffers partial loss or constructive total loss, maritime lien still exists on the damaged ship or her wreck.

C. Expiration of Time-Bar

166. By virtue of Article 29 of MC, where a maritime claim secured by maritime lien has not been enforced by the claimant within one year from the time of occurrence of maritime lien, the maritime lien shall be extinguished. This specified one-year period shall not be suspended or discontinued. Such a short period of time, which is normally shorter than the time bars for maritime claims, may urge the claimants whose claims are secured by maritime lien to enforce maritime lien in time in order to avoid accumulations of maritime liens on a ship which may be harmful to the interests of the later claimants and to the interests of purchaser of the ship.

The extinction of maritime lien due to expiration of the one-year time limitation, however, does not bring out the extinction of claim itself that was secured by maritime lien.

D. Forced Sale of Ship

167. Where a ship is sold by auction by a maritime court, any maritime lien on her shall be extinguished (Article 29, MC).

Once the ship is sold by auction by a maritime court, the claimants' maritime liens shall be transferred to the priorities in the compensation from the proceeds of sale in accordance with law.

E. Failure to Enforce in the Case of Voluntary Transfer of Ownership

168. As a rule, where the ownership of a ship transfers on voluntary basis, e.g., through voluntary sale of a ship, maritime liens on the ship shall not be extinguished but shall still attach to the ship. However, where the transferee applies to a maritime court for making public notice of the transfer when the transfer is effected, and the claimants whose claims are secured by maritime liens fail to enforce maritime liens in accordance with law within sixty days of the public notice, those maritime liens shall be extinguished (Article 26, MC).

169. Chapter XI 'Maritime Lien Hastening Procedure' of SMPL specially applies to the application of transferee as provided for in Article 26 of MC *supra*.

By virtue of Articles 120 and 121 of SMPL, the transferee of a ship may apply to the maritime court located in the place where the ship is delivered, or the transferee has his domicile for hastening the claimants to enforce maritime liens in order to bring out extinction of maritime liens attached to the ship.

The applicant shall submit to the maritime court an application indicating the facts and reasons for hastening maritime liens, the contract of ship transfer, the ship's technical certificates and other documents (Article 122).

The maritime court shall, after receipt of these documents, examine the application and make an award, either granting or refusing the application. Where the application is refused, the transferee may apply to the court for reconsideration (Article 123).

After the award granting the application has become effective, the maritime court shall publicize via newspapers or other news media to hasten the claimants whose claims are secured by maritime lien to enforce the maritime liens within sixty days by way of registering their maritime liens with the maritime court (Article 124). If a claimant fails to register, he shall be deemed as having waived his maritime lien (Article 125). Where no person has registered maritime lien within the period of sixty days, the maritime court shall, based upon the application of the transferee, make a judgment declaring that no maritime lien is attached to the ship transferred and publicize the contents of the judgment correspondingly (Article 126).

170. Noticeably, so far as extinction of maritime liens is concerned, where the nationality of a ship changes, the maritime liens on her shall not be affected. Maritime liens are regulated by *lex fori* in accordance with Article 272 of MC and thus are irrelevant to the change of ship's nationality.

There exist arguments in China as to whether maritime liens on a ship shall be extinguished when a ship is sold by governmental organs like customs or border control after confiscation. It seems the majority view supports extinction of maritime liens in such a case because such enforced sale is very similar to the enforced sale by auction of a maritime court.

VI. Choice of Law

171. As provided for in Article 272 of Chapter XIV 'Application of Law in Relation to Foreign-related Matters' of MC, the law of the place where the court hearing the case is located shall apply to the matters pertaining to maritime liens.

Therefore, MC follows the principle of *lex fori* that coincides with *lex fori arresti*. Where a maritime lien case is heard by a Chinese maritime court, MC and SMPL shall be applied in deciding, *inter alia*, whether the maritime claims are secured by maritime liens, the priority of compensation and the amount of each claim to be compensated for in the proceeds of sale as well as the procedures of enforcing maritime liens, regardless of the nationality of a ship, the place or places of the occurrences giving rise to the claims.

§3. SHIP MORTGAGES

I. General Concepts

172. A ship mortgage is defined in Article 11 of MC as 'the right of preferred compensation enjoyed by the mortgagee of a ship from the proceeds of the sale by auction enforced in accordance with law where and when the mortgagor fails to pay his debt to the mortgagee secured by the mortgage on that ship'.[27]

173. Ship mortgage, or mortgage on ship, is a special kind of mortgage covered by Chapter XVII 'Mortgages' of Sub-Book Four 'Real Rights for Security' of Book Two 'Real Rights' of CC. Therefore, the provisions concerning mortgages contained in CC as the basic law shall apply to ship mortgages to the extent that MC does not contain any special provision to the contrary.

Article 394 of CC provides that, in order to ensure the payment of a debt, a debtor or a third party mortgages his property to the creditor without transferring the possession of the property, and where the debtor fails to pay due debt or any circumstance as agreed upon by the parties concerned for realizing the mortgage happens, the creditor has the right to seek preferred payments from the property.

Article 410 of CC further provides that where the debtor fails to pay due debt or any circumstance as agreed upon by the parties concerned for realizing the mortgage happens, the mortgagee may reach an agreement with the mortgagor to convert the property into money according to the market value of the mortgaged property for repayment or have his credit satisfied with priority in the proceeds of the sale by auction or voluntary sale of the property; if such an agreement causes harm to the interests of another creditor, however, the other creditor may apply to a court of law for dismissing the agreement within one year from the date on which the other creditor knew or should have known the cause of dismissal; where the mortgagee and the mortgagor have not reached an agreement as to the means of realizing the mortgage, the mortgagee may apply to a court of law for selling the mortgaged property, either by auction or not.

174. As compared with the above provisions of CC, mortgage on a ship defined in Article 3 of MC can only be enforced by way of preferred compensation enjoyed by the mortgagee of that ship from the proceeds of the sale by auction as provided for in Article 11 of MC. That is, the mortgagee is not entitled to convert the ship into money for repayment, nor have his credit satisfied with priority in the proceeds of voluntary sale of the ship. The reason is that although conversion of a ship into money or voluntary sale by agreement between the mortgagee and the mortgagor is convenient, time-saving and economical, a mortgaged ship normally has a big value and may at the same time involve other claims, especially the claims secured by maritime line and, therefore, conversion or voluntary sale may affect the interests of other claimants and even the mortgagor.

27. In practice, the mortgagor may be the debtor itself or a third person. The person obliged to pay the debt is always the debtor. Therefore, the expression 'the mortgagor fails to pay his debt' is inaccurate and an accurate expression should be 'the debtor fails to pay his debt'.

175. Traditionally, mortgages could be established on real assets only and not on movables, which were the subjects of pledges in law. Modern civil law has developed to grant mortgages on certain movables. By virtue of Article 395 of CC, aeroplanes, ships and other transport vehicles, etc., can be used for mortgage. In this regard, it is said in the maritime law circle in China that a ship is movable but is deemed a real asset so far as mortgage is concerned.

A ship mortgage is a proprietary right on the mortgaged ship. This right confines the owners of the mortgaged ship at their disposal of her, although, unlike pledge, a ship mortgage does not transfer the possession of the mortgaged ship from the mortgagor to the mortgagee.

Once a mortgage is established on a ship, the ownership of the mortgaged ship shall not be transferred without the consent of the mortgagee (Article 17, MC). However, Article 406 of CC provides that unless otherwise agreed upon by the parties, the mortgagor can transfer the mortgaged property during the period of mortgage and notify the mortgagee thereof; where the mortgaged property is transferred, the mortgage shall not be affected; upon proving that the transfer may cause harm to the mortgage, the mortgagee may require the mortgagor to use the amount of transfer for advance payment for the debt for deposit. Nevertheless, a ship as a means of transport is not often transferred, and, more importantly, her value may be adversely affected at the hands of different owners. Consequently, the majority view in the circle of maritime law in China supports maintaining the provisions of Article 17 of MC. Now, Article 17 of MC is applicable to mortgage on a ship defined in Article 3 of MC, whereas Article 406 of CC is applicable to inland vessels and other vessels not defined in Article 3 of MC.

II. Creation of Ship Mortgage

A. *Persons Entitled to Grant Ship Mortgage*

176. The owners of a ship or those so authorized by the owners may establish mortgage on a ship (paragraph 1, Article 12, MC). Thus, only the shipowners or persons authorized by the shipowners may establish mortgage on a ship.

The right to establish mortgage on a ship is, in nature, a reflection of the ownership of a ship. In shipping practice, the persons authorized by the shipowners to establish mortgage on a ship on their own behalf may include, *inter alia*, charterers under a charter party by demise with hire purchase or operators of a ship upon agreement. In practice, such authorization rarely occurs in China.

Where a ship is State-owned and operated by an enterprise which is a legal person as granted by the State, this enterprise is deemed as the owner of the ship concerned under Article 8 of MC and is entitled to establish mortgage on the ship.

177. In the case a ship is owned by co-owners,[28] special provisions governing establishment of ship mortgage are provided for in law.

28. *See* Ch. 1 of Part II *supra*.

In the case of part ownership of a ship, the establishment of mortgage shall be subject to the agreement of those co-owners who have two-thirds or more of the shares thereof unless otherwise agreed upon (paragraph 1, Article 16, MC). Otherwise, a mortgage established on a ship by a co-owner or co-owners holding less than two-thirds of the shares thereof shall stand null and void. The mortgage established by part owners of a ship in accordance with the requirement set out in paragraph 1 of Article 16 of MC shall not be affected by virtue of the division of ownership thereof (paragraph 2, Article 16, MC).

MC does not contain any provision governing the situation of joint ownership of a ship. Nevertheless, Article 301 of CC provides that any disposal of property owned by joint owners is subject to the agreement by all of them unless otherwise agreed upon. Therefore, in the case of joint ownership of a ship, the establishment of mortgage shall be subject to the agreement of all the joint owners unless otherwise agreed upon.

B. Ships Subject to Mortgage

178. Like the case of maritime lien, mortgage can be established on a ship defined in Article 3 of MC. Any freight or accessory rights of a ship are not subject to ship mortgage.

Mortgages on inland vessels or seagoing vessels of less than 20 tons gross tonnage are subject to Chapter XVII 'Mortgages' of Book Two of CC.

Where a mortgage is established on a ship, it shall cover her hull, machinery and appurtenances, even if any part of them may be ashore during ship repair. Equipment added to the mortgaged ship or other improvement made to her after the establishment of mortgage shall be subject to mortgage automatically unless the mortgage deed provides otherwise.

179. A ship under construction is not a ship before it becomes technically movable. However, so far as ship mortgage is concerned, it is deemed as a ship. Thus, mortgage may be established on a ship under construction (paragraph 1, Article 14, MC).

Article 74 of the *Measures Regarding Registration of Ships of 2016* defines a ship under construction as the keel laying or similar construction stage or later stage. However, it is not clear whether the scope of a ship under construction includes the materials, machines and equipment which has not been used for construction, but are planned to be used.

Under a shipbuilding contract, the parties are free to negotiate the transfer of ownership of the ship under construction from the shipbuilder to the ordering party. Sometimes, it is agreed upon in the contract that the ownership of the ship under construction transfers pro rata to the ordering party as the construction progresses against the payment by instalments of construction price and is thus further agreed upon that the ordering party is entitled to establish mortgage on the ship under construction for that part of her ownership he has acquired during the construction. It rarely occurs the shipbuilder allows the ordering party to establish mortgage on a ship under construction for all or any part of the ownership the ordering party has not acquired.

Therefore, the shipbuilding contract determines whether and to what extent the ordering party is entitled to establish mortgage on the ship under construction. Thus, to ensure the validity of mortgage on the ship under construction, the shipbuilding contract shall be submitted to the ship registration authority in the registration of the mortgage thereon (Article 14, MC).

180. Where a ship is under arrest or seizure by a maritime court or is under control and custody by a governmental organ in accordance with law, no mortgage can be established thereon (Article 399, CC). The reason is the right of shipowners to dispose of their property is confined by law under these circumstances.

C. *Amount of Secured Claim*

181. MC contains no provision concerning the extent and amount of claim to be secured by a ship mortgage.

By virtue of Article 389 of CC, the extent of security by mortgage includes the principal credit sum and its interests, penalties for breach of contract, compensation for loss or damage and the costs for the custody of the mortgaged property and enforcing the mortgage, unless the mortgage deed provides a smaller extent of security.

The amount of credit secured by mortgage is subject to the agreement between the mortgagor and the mortgagee. This means the amount of credit secured by ship mortgage may exceed or be less than the value of a ship. Where a further second mortgage is established on a ship, amount of credit secured by the mortgage shall not exceed the surplus in value of the ship.

182. Section 2 of Chapter XVII 'Mortgages' of Book Two of CC contains provisions governing mortgage for a maximum amount, which means the mortgaged property secures the credits that will happen successively during a certain period of time within a maximum amount as agreed upon between the mortgagor and the mortgagee (Article 424, CC). A mortgage deed for a maximum amount can be attached to a loan agreement or a contract concluded for the successive transactions of a certain kind of commodity. Therefore, the mortgage for a maximum amount is applicable to the ship mortgage to secure the repayment of all the present and future debts within a certain maximum amount under a loan agreement.

D. *Remedies of Mortgagee*

183. Ship mortgage is a kind of right in rem on the mortgaged property. Consequently, if the mortgaged ship is lost or seriously damaged, the mortgagee losses its primary protection of the ship mortgage. Therefore, insurance of the mortgaged ship is crucial for the protection of interests of the mortgagee.

The mortgagor is obliged to have the mortgaged ship insured unless the mortgage deed provides otherwise. In the case the ship is not insured, the mortgagee has the right to place the ship under insurance coverage, and the mortgagor shall pay for the premium thereof (Article 15, MC). In case the mortgaged ship is lost, with respect to the compensation paid from the insurance coverage on account of the loss of the ship, the mortgagee shall be entitled to enjoy priority in compensation over other creditors (Article 20, MC). Article 390 of CC offers wider protection of interests of the secured creditor, i.e., where the secured property is lost, damaged or requisitioned, etc., during the period of security, the secured creditor may enjoy priority in compensation from the insurance indemnity, payment of compensation for loss or damage or reward of requisition. This provision is applicable to a ship mortgage.

III. Formalities Relating to Creation of Ship Mortgage

A. *Mortgage Deed*

184. A mortgage deed is a contract concluded between the mortgagor and the mortgagee for the establishment of mortgage on a property.

A mortgage deed shall be concluded in writing (paragraph 2, Article 12, MC; Article 400, CC). By virtue of Article 469 of CC, the form in writing includes, *inter alia*, telegram, telex, telefax, electronic data interchange (EDI), e-mail and other forms of electronic data message that can visibly indicate the loaded contents. As regards ship mortgage, the validity of a mortgage deed is not subject to notarization, registration or other formality.

185. MC does not contain any provision concerning the contents of ship mortgage deed. However, besides the names and addresses of the parties, a ship mortgage deed shall include the following contents by virtue of Article 400 of CC:

- kind and amount of the principal credit secured;
- period of the repayment of debt by the debtor;
- name, tonnage, nationality, owners and other details of the mortgaged ship;
- extent of security by mortgage;
- other items as deemed necessary by the parties.

B. *Registration of Ship Mortgage*

186. A ship mortgage shall be registered with the ship registration authority jointly by the mortgagor and the mortgagee (paragraph 1, Article 13, MC).

At present, a mortgage on a ship other than a fishing vessel flying the Chinese flag shall be registered with MSA located at her homeport. A mortgage on a fishing vessel shall be registered in the administration of fishing vessels and fishing ports located at her homeport.

187. The registration authority shall register a mortgage on a Chinese ship in accordance with the *Regulations Governing Registration of Ships of 1994* and the *Measures regarding Registration of Ships of 2016*. The documents to be submitted to the registration authority as required include:

- application in writing signed by the mortgagor and the mortgagee;
- certificate of ship ownership or, in the case of a ship under construction, the shipbuilding contract or a document sufficient to prove the acquirement of ownership;
- mortgage deed;
- in the case of co-ownership of a ship, a document indicating consent of part owners holding two-thirds or more of the shares thereof or of all the joint owners;
- in the case mortgage has already been established on the ship, a document indicating the existing ship mortgage.

188. In accordance with paragraph 2 of Article 13 of MC, the main items for the registration of a ship mortgage shall be:

- the name and address of the mortgagee and the mortgagor;
- the name and nationality of the mortgaged ship and the authority that issued the certificate of ownership and the certificate number thereof;
- the amount of credit secured, the interest rate and the period for repayment.

The above information about the registration of a ship mortgage shall be recorded in the Book of Ship Registration and is accessible to the public for inquiry (paragraph 3, Article 13, MC).

189. Concerning the legal effect of mortgage registration, no ship mortgage may act against a third party unless registered (Article 13, MC). As explained in paragraph 142 *supra*, the third party mentioned in paragraph 1 of Article 13 of MC shall mean a third party acting in good faith. Therefore, the registration of ship mortgage is a must for the mortgagee to exert its right of mortgage on a ship against any third party acting in good faith other than the mortgagor, although the mortgage without registration is still valid between the mortgagor and the mortgagee.

IV. Ranking

190. Where two or more mortgages are established on a ship defined in Article 3 of MC, the ranking between or among the mortgages shall be determined according to the dates of their respective registration, and the mortgagees shall be paid out of the proceeds of the sale by auction of the ship in the order of registration of their respective mortgages; the mortgages registered on the same date shall rank equally for payment (Article 19, MC).

However, Article 410 of CC contains slightly different and more specific provisions. That is, where there are two or more mortgages on the same property, the registered mortgages shall be compensated for in the order of registration or rank equally in compensation if the order is the same; the registered mortgage shall have priority over the unregistered one; the unregistered mortgages shall rank equally in compensation. Therefore, the mortgages registered on the same date shall not rank equally for payment. Instead, the strict order in terms of the exact time of registration shall be followed. These provisions are applicable to mortgages on ships not defined in Article 3 of MC. However, the provisions of Article 410 of CC that the registered mortgage shall have priority over the unregistered one and that the unregistered mortgages shall rank equally in compensation are also applicable to mortgages a ship defined in Article 3 of MC as they are not repugnant to Article 19 of MC.

191. So far as a ship defined in Article 3 of MC is concerned, where the claims respectively secured by maritime lien, possessory lien and ship mortgage exist simultaneously together with other claims without security, as discussed *supra*, the claim secured by ship mortgage shall rank after the claims secured maritime lien or by possessory lien but shall rank before other claims (paragraph 1, Article 25, MC). If a ship mortgage is not registered and thus cannot act against a third party acting in good faith, the claim concerned shall be deemed as a claim without security and rank with other claims not secured by maritime lien or possessory lien and equally for payment pro rata, if the fund available is insufficient.

In the case of a ship excluded from the scope of ship defined in Article 3 of MC, claims secured by possessory lien on a ship shall have priority in compensation over claims secured by ship mortgage by virtue of Article 456 of CC. Other claims without security of mortgage or possessory lien, including the claims that would be secured by maritime lien by virtue of MC if she were a ship defined in Article 3 of MC shall rank after the claims secured by the mortgage or possessory lien and shall rank equally in compensation.

V. Validity Period of Ship Mortgage

192. Neither MC nor CC contains provision regarding the validity period of ship mortgage or the registration thereof. It shall be understood that a duly established ship mortgage is valid before it is extinguished, and its registration is valid so long as the ship mortgage stands valid.

VI. Transfer of Ship Mortgage

193. A ship mortgage can be transferred by the mortgagee. The transfer of ship mortgage follows the transfer of the credit it secures. Thus, Article 18 of MC provides that in the case the mortgagee has transferred all or part of his credit secured by the mortgage to another person, the mortgage shall be transferred accordingly. In order words, the transfer of ship mortgage is conditional upon the transfer of the credit it secures. In addition, by virtue of Article 407 of CC, a mortgage cannot be transferred independently of the credit it secures or be used as security for other credit; where the credit is transferred, the mortgage securing the credit shall be transferred simultaneously unless the law provides or the parties have agreed otherwise.

The credit secured by a ship mortgage is a contractual right. A contractual right is transferable partly or wholly by agreement between the transferor and the transferee subject to notice of the transfer to the debtor unless the right is not transferable in nature or the contract or the applicable law prohibits it from transfer (Articles 545 and 546, CC). Thus, the mortgagee is obliged to notify the mortgagor of the transfer. Otherwise, the transfer shall have no effect on the mortgagor. Where the mortgagor is a third person other than the debtor, the mortgagee shall also notify the mortgagor of the transfer of credit. Such notification cannot be withdrawn unless the transferee agrees (paragraph 2, Article 546, CC). A ship mortgage is, in nature, a right subordinate to the credit it secures. Thus, where the credit secured by the ship mortgage is transferred, the transferee obtains the credit together with its subordinate mortgage (Article 547, CC).

194. Transfer of a ship mortgage shall be registered with its original registration authority. An application in writing shall be submitted together with an agreement of such transfer signed by the transferor and the transferee. If not registered, the transfer may not act against a third party acting in good faith.

VII. Extinction of Ship Mortgage

195. Same as maritime lien on a ship, a ship mortgage is also in nature right in rem on ship to secure the payment of specified claims and is subordinate to the credit it secures. Therefore, the causes of extinction of a ship mortgage are contained in Article 20 of MC and Articles 393 and 419 of CC are very similar to those of maritime lien as discussed in §2 *supra*, although there exist minor differences.

A. *Extinction of Claim Secured by Ship Mortgage*

196. Where a claim secured by a ship mortgage is extinguished, the ship mortgage securing this claim shall be extinguished at the same time (Article 393, CC).

B. *Realization of Ship Mortgage*

197. Where a ship mortgage is realized, i.e., the debtor or other person, including the mortgagor on behalf of the debtor, repays the debt to the mortgagee, the ship mortgage shall be extinguished at the same time (Article 393, CC).

C. *Loss of Ship*

198. Where the mortgaged ship is lost, the mortgage on her shall be extinguished (Article 20, MC). Like the case of maritime lien, to bring out the extinction of a ship mortgage, the ship should become an actual total loss. If the ship only suffers partial loss or constructive total loss, the ship mortgage still exists on the damaged ship or her wreck.

Where a ship mortgage is extinguished due to loss of the mortgaged ship, the mortgagee shall have priority in compensation over other creditors from the insurance indemnity on account of the loss of ship (Article 20, MC). The insurance indemnity in such a case shall be deemed as the mortgaged property.

MC does not provide whether the mortgagee shall have priority over other creditors in compensation from the insurance indemnity or the compensation payment by a liable third party on account of damage to the mortgaged ship or from compensation payment on account of governmental requisition of the ship. By virtue of Article 390 of CC, the mortgagee shall have such priority; where the period of repayment for the secured credit has not expired, the said insurance indemnity or compensation payment shall be deposited. This article is applicable in the case of mortgage on a ship defined in Article 3 of MC.

D. *Waiver of Ship Mortgage by Mortgagee*

199. By virtue of Article 409 of CC, the mortgagee may waive the mortgage or its priority in compensation. By virtue of Article 393 of CC, a ship mortgage shall be extinguished due to the waiver thereof by the mortgagee.

E. *Expiration of Time-Bar*

200. Article 419 of CC provides that the mortgagee shall enforce the mortgage within the time limitation for the principal credit. After the expiration of this time period, the mortgagee loses its right to resort to legal protection of mortgage on the ship through a maritime court or arbitration. However, this time period does not confine the mortgagor to fulfil the debt voluntarily.

This time period is subject to suspension or discontinuance.

Suspension of time limitation occurs where, during the last six months within the period of time limitation, the creditor is prevented from enforcing its right due to force majeure or other obstacle. When the cause of suspension no longer exists, counting of the period of time limitation shall be resumed (Article 266, MC; Article 194, CC).

Time limitation shall be discontinued as a result of starting court proceedings, submitting the case for arbitration or submitting an application for the arrest of ship by the mortgagee or the admission to fulfil the debt by the debtor/mortgagor, unless the mortgagee withdraws his legal action or submission for arbitration (Article 267, MC). The period of time limitation shall be counted anew from the time of discontinuance. Noticeably, by virtue of Article 196 of CC, time limitation shall also be discontinued when the creditor demands the debtor to fulfil his debt, even if fulfilment is refused by the debtor. Article 196 of CC shall only apply to the mortgages a ship excluded by Article 3 of MC.

F. *Forced Sale of Ship*

201. Neither MC nor CC contains provisions to the effect that a ship mortgage shall be extinguished on account of forced sale of the mortgaged ship. However, it should be understood that such a sale shall bring out the extinction of all the rights in rem on the ship, including mortgage and therefore the purchaser shall have a clean title to the ship, no matter whether the claim of the applicant for forced sale is secured by ship mortgage or not.

Once a mortgaged ship is sold by auction by a maritime court, the creditor's right initially secured by the ship mortgage shall be transferred to the priority in compensation from the proceeds of sale in accordance with MC or CC.

VIII. Voluntary Transfer of Ownership of Ship

202. As introduced in paragraph 175 *supra*, the ownership of a mortgaged ship shall not be transferred without the consent of the mortgagee (Article 17, MC). In other words, a voluntary transfer of ownership of a mortgaged ship without the consent of mortgagee is invalid and therefore the mortgage is not extinguished.

Also, as introduced in paragraph 175 *supra*, Article 406 of CC provides that unless otherwise agreed upon between the mortgagor and the mortgagee, a mortgaged property can be transferred without the consent of the mortgagee. In such a case, the mortgage shall be extinguished and the mortgagee has the rights provided for in Article 406 of CC. This Article is not applicable to a ship defined in Article 3 of MC but applicable to a ship not defined in this article.

IX. Choice of Law

203. MC follows the principle of the law of flag or *lex rei sitae* with respect to ship mortgages. Article 271 of Chapter XIV 'Application of Law in Relation to Foreign-related Matters' of MC provides that the law of the flag State of the ship shall apply to ship mortgages. Where a ship mortgage is established during the period she is under a bareboat charter or a mortgaged ship is bareboat chartered after the establishment of a mortgage on her and the ship's flag changes during the period of charter, the law of the original country of her registry shall apply to the ship mortgage.

In the enforcement of a ship mortgage through arrest by a court of law and sale of auction, the procedural matters shall be subject to the law of the State where the court is located or *lex fori arresti* because the enforcement is a matter of procedural law in which the principle of *lex fori* is always followed in China.

Chapter 3. Shipmaster and Crew

§1. Shipmaster

I. Introduction

204. Under MC and other related Chinese laws, the word ‘crew’ includes the master and other crewmembers on board a ship. Traditionally, however, the functions of the master are different from those of other crewmembers in international treaties due to his unique position.

Crew means the entire complement of a ship (Article 31, MC). Practically, crewmembers shall be on the list of crew on board a particular ship. The number of crew to be manned on board a ship shall meet the minimum standard quota. The crewmembers shall hold the qualified and valid certificates (paragraph 2, Article 33, MTSL), details of which are provided for in the *Regulations Concerning Minimum Safety Manning on Ships* promulgated by the former MOC (now MOT) on 30 June 2004 and amended on 28 November 2018.

The master of a ship is the person who takes the position of master onboard and has the command of her both in law and *ex facto*.

II. Appointment of Master

205. A master is appointed by the owners or bareboat charterers or manager of a ship.

In order to qualify for his position on board a merchant ship flying the Chinese flag, the master shall meet the following two basic requirements:

(1) possessing Chinese citizenship, with the only exception that where it is indeed needed, a foreigner may take the position of master on board a Chinese ship after approval of MOT as provided for in Article 7 of the *Regulations Governing Ship Registration of 1994*;
(2) holding an appropriate certificate of competency issued by MSA, even if he is a foreigner (Article 33, MC).

206. Where death occurs to the master, or he becomes unable to perform his functions and duties as the master for whatever reasons, the deck officer with the highest rank, *viz.* the chief officer in most cases, shall act as the master before a new master is appointed to take command before the ship sails from her next port of call (Article 40, MC).

III. Public Functions and Duties of Master

207. As provided for in section 2 of Chapter III ‘Crew’ of MC and the *Regulations on Vessel’s Crew of 2007*, the master has the following functions in the nature of public law that cannot be deviated from by the articles of his employment concluded with his employer. The functions embody both the rights and duties of a master.

Noticeably, Article 38 of MTSL provides that the master is responsible for the management and command of a ship and has the power to independently make decisions with respect to ensuring the safety of lives at sea, ship's security and prevention of pollution from the ship. Article 24 of the *Regulations on Vessel's Crew* further provides that the master has the right of independent action and shall bear final responsibility with respect to ensuring the safety of lives and property in waters, ship's security and prevention of water pollution from the ship. In fulfilling this responsibility, the master may exercise the following rights: deciding ship's voyage plan, refusing to commence or continue a voyage if the ship does not meet the safety navigation conditions, refusing to carry out any direction given by his employer or the shipowners which is illegal or may cause danger to the persons, property and the ship's safety or pollution to the water environment; timely rectifying or stopping the manoeuvre orders given by a pilot if they may cause threat on ship's navigation safety or pollution to the water environment, and requiring change of pilot when necessary; ordering incompetent a crewmember to leave his post; other rights which may be exercised in case of emergency as introduced *infra*.

A. *Function in the Management and Navigation of Ship*

208. By virtue of Article 35 of MC, the master shall be responsible for the management and navigation of a ship. He has the power to give orders which shall be carried out by other crewmembers, the passengers and all other persons, including the representative of shipowner, if any, on board the ship.

As provided for in Article 20 of the *Regulations on Vessel's Crew*, in the exercise of this function, the master shall: ensure that the ship and other crewmembers carry the certificates, documents and the related navigation materials as required by law; prepare ship's emergency response plan and ensure its effective implementation; ensure the ship's seaworthiness and crew's fitness at the beginning of a voyage; ensure the minimum safety manning and crew being on duty; comply with the directions and orders given by maritime safety authority regarding traffic safety and prevention of pollution, and submit an accident report to maritime safety authority in case of occurrence of ship's traffic accident and pollution accident on water; carry out crew's routine training and examination; be on duty on the bridge when the ship is entering or leaving a port, getting or leaving berth, navigating in a congested or dangerous area, in bad weather conditions or on the occurrence of traffic accident, pollution accident or in other emergencies, and directly take command of the ship when necessary; ensure the safety of persons on board. Article 35 of MC further provides that the master shall take necessary measures to protect the ship and all persons on board, the documents, postal matters, goods as well as other property carried on board.

This duty shall not be absolved even with the presence of a pilot, whether the pilotage is compulsory or not (Article 39, MC).

B. Function as a Quasi-Police Officer

209. By virtue of Article 36 of MC, to ensure the safety of a ship and all persons on board, the master has the power to confine or take other necessary measures against any person who has committed a crime or violated laws or regulations onboard and to guard against his or her concealment, destruction or forging of evidence.

Having taken any of the above measures, the master shall make a written report of the case which shall bear the signature of himself and two or more other persons onboard and be handed over together with the offender to the authority concerned for disposition.

C. Function as a Public Notary

210. By virtue of Article 37 of MC, the master shall issue a certificate to evidence a birth or death occurred onboard in the presence of two witnesses and make entries in the logbook of such an occurrence. The death certificate shall be attached with a list of personal belongings of the deceased. Attestation shall be given by the master to the will, if any, of the deceased. Both the death certificate and the will shall be kept by the master and handed over to the family members of the deceased or organization concerned.

D. Function in Case of Emergency

211. As required by Article 38 of MC, where a sea casualty occurs on the ship, threatening the lives and properties onboard, the master shall, with other crewmembers and other persons under his command, make best efforts to run the rescue. Article 38 of MC and Article 24 of the *Regulations on Vessel's Crew* further provides that if the foundering or loss of the ship becomes inevitable, the master may decide to abandon the ship but shall report to the shipowners for approval except in case of urgency. It needs to be mentioned that the provision of master's decision to abandon the ship is subject to the shipowners' approval except in case of urgency was made in order to avoid master's reckless abandonment of a ship, but is now not in conformity with the master's power of making independent decision and final responsibility with respect to ensuring the safety of lives as provided in Article 38 of MTSL. Consequently, such a provision shall not be applicable anymore because Article 38 of MTSL is a provision of new law.

In addition, upon abandoning a ship, the master shall take all measures first to evacuate the passengers safely from the ship in an orderly way and then make arrangements for the other crewmembers to evacuate, while he shall be the last to evacuate. Before leaving the ship, the master shall direct the other crewmembers to do their utmost to rescue the logbooks, radio logbooks, sea charts, documents and papers used in the current voyage, as well as the valuables, mail and cash money.

If the master is not the last person to evacuate or seriously violates this statutory provision otherwise, he may be sanctioned with criminal liability under the *Criminal Code*.

IV. Private Functions of Master

212. In the early times, when remote communication was not available or very limited between the master and the shipowners or the cargo owners after a ship sailed from her home port, the master was deemed as the decision-maker of the ship and cargo under commercial law. However, due to the development of remote communications, especially satellite communication, and the widespread use of ship agency while a ship calls at a foreign port, the traditional function under commercial law of the master as a representative of the shipowners or the cargo owners has decreased in the modern time. As a result, the master represents the shipowners and/or the cargo owners only under limited statutory circumstances.

A. *Acting on Behalf of Shipowners*

213. The master of a ship in distress has statutory authority to conclude a contract for salvage operation on behalf of the shipowners (paragraph 2, Article 175, MC).

In addition, where the shipowners are the carrier under a contract of carriage of goods by sea, the master has statutory authority to act on behalf of the shipowners under the following circumstances:

- the master has the authority to sign bills of lading on behalf of the carrier (Article 72, MC);
- where the delivery of goods has not been taken at the port of discharge, or the consignee has delayed in taking delivery or refused to take delivery of the goods, the master may discharge the goods into warehouse or other appropriate place (Article 86, MC);
- where, due to force majeure or any other cause not attributable to the fault of the carrier or the shipper, the ship is unable to discharge the goods at the port of destination as agreed upon in the contract of carriage unless the contract is agreed otherwise, the master shall be entitled to discharge the goods at a safe port or place near the port of destination, provided that the master shall inform the shipper or the consignee timely and take the interests of the shipper or the consignee into consideration in deciding the discharge of goods (Article 91, MC).

214. Under other circumstances, the master can act on behalf of the shipowners only upon specific authorization of the shipowners. Thus, without such an authorization, the master cannot represent the shipowners in a lawsuit,[29] whether the shipowners are the plaintiff or the defendant, or select or hire crewmembers, charter out the ship, borrow money, give a respondentia, or order ship repair, bunkers, stores, provisions or port services.

B. Acting on Behalf of Cargo Interests

215. The master of a ship in distress has statutory authority to conclude a contract for salvage operation on behalf of the owners of the goods onboard (paragraph 2, Article 175, MC). Under other circumstances, the master cannot act on behalf of the cargo interests without authorization of them.

V. Liability of Master

216. Theoretically, the liability of a master during his service is threefold, i.e., civil, disciplinary and criminal. Sometimes, a single act of the master may involve two or even three forms of his liability.

A. Civil Liability of Master

217. Civil liability of a master during his service can be divided into contractual liability and tort liability.

Contractual liability of a master shall be determined by the articles of employment concluded with his employer and the *Labour Law* adopted by the Standing Committee of NPC on 5 July 1994 and latest amended on 29 December 2018, the *Labour Contract Law* adopted by the Standing Committee of NPC on 29 June 2007 and amended on 28 December 2012, or the labour regulations governing such employment as well as Book Three 'Contracts' of CC.

It is understood that, however, by the implication of principles of labour contract law, a seafarer shall not be held liable for economic losses caused by him to his employer during his service under a contract of employment unless caused by gross negligence or intentional act of the seafarer. That is to say, a seafarer shall not be held liable for losses due to his light negligence or fault within the scope of his employment, although he may be given sanctions by his employer with decrease in salary or position or even be discharged from employment. Where a seafarer proves that the losses occurred during his service were due to force majeure or other cause not attributable to him, he shall be exonerated from any liability for the losses. These principles are applicable to the case of a master.

Where a third person suffers damage or loss due to an act or omission of a master done within the scope of his employment, by implication of the rule contained in

29. As an exception, serving of a judicial document relating to arrest of ship by a maritime court on the master shall be deemed as having served on the owners of the offending ship (para. 2, Art. 80, SMPL).

Article 1191 of CC stipulating that the enterprise as employer shall bear civil liability in tort to the third party arising from the operational activities done by its staff members, it is fully doubtful that the third person can hold the master personally liable in tort. Instead, the third party may direct his claim against the shipowner or other employer of the master.

So far, there is not reported case in China in which a master was held liable in contract to his employer or in tort to a third party.

B. Disciplinary Liability of Master

218. Disciplinary liability of a master mainly occurs as a result of a maritime accident such as collision or marine pollution, etc. Where a maritime accident occurs, MSA or an administration on fishing vessels and fishing ports in the case of a fishing vessel shall, as a statutory investigation organ, investigate the accident with the power to ascertain the causes of the accident and to fix the responsibilities therefor (Article 83, MTSL).

The investigation organ has the power to impose disciplinary sanctions on the master or other crewmembers who are responsible for the accident in light of the circumstances of violation of the MTSL or the related maritime safety regulations or provisions. The disciplinary liabilities include warning, withholding or revocation of certificate of competency and fines.

If the master or other crewmember does not accept the disciplinary sanction imposed on him, he may apply to MSA's superior office or the superior administration on fishing vessels and fishing ports in the case of a fishing vessel that imposed the sanction for reconsideration in accordance with the *Administrative Reconsideration Law* adopted by the Standing Committee of NPC on 29 April 1999 and latest amended 1 September 2017. He may also file an administrative lawsuit directly with the court of law having jurisdiction against the administrative organ that imposed on him the disciplinary sanction in accordance with the *Administrative Litigation Law* adopted by the Standing Committee of NPC on 4 April 1989 and latest amended 27 June 2017. An administrative lawsuit may also be filed with a court of law if the master or other crewmember does not accept the decision of reconsideration.

C. Criminal Liability of Master

219. Criminal liability of a master or other crewmembers shall be imposed only by a court of law in accordance with the *Criminal Code* and the *Criminal Procedure Code*. Except for the *Criminal Code*, there is no special Chinese law stipulating criminal liability of a master or other crewmembers. The reported cases indicate that criminal liability may be imposed on a master as a result of a maritime accident such as collision or oil pollution causing serious loss of life or personal injury or heavy loss or damage to property or serious pollution damage to the marine or other water environment.

§2. CREW

I. Introduction

220. The international treaties with respect to the labour relations of seafarers are mainly adopted by ILO, established by virtue of the *Peace Treaty of 1919*. These treaties mainly aim at protecting the rights of seafarers while serving onboard regarding the conditions and hours of work, accommodations onboard, and welfare onboard or even after disembarkation. As introduced in §1 of Chapter 2 of Part I *supra*, China has ratified the *Maritime Labour Convention* adopted by ILO in 2006.

221. Article 34 of MC provides that, as regards the employment of crewmembers and other labour-related rights and obligations, the provisions contained in relative laws and administrative rules and regulations shall apply. Currently, the contracts of employment of seafarers and their rights and obligations are mainly determined by the *Maritime Labour Convention of 2006* and other ILO treaties that China has acceded to, the *Regulations on Vessel's Crew* and the *Administrative Rules concerning the Seafarers' Working and Living Conditions on Ships* promulgated by MOT of 26 July 2013 and amended on 7 December 2018 as well as the *Labour Contract Law*, the *Labour Law* and the relevant regulations and provisions that regulate ordinary labour relations.

The *Maritime Labour Convention of 2006* is a codification of sixty-eight existing seafarers-related treaties adopted by ILO for the main purpose of protecting seafarers' rights and interests. It contains the principled provisions of the fundamental rights and principles, seafarers' employment and social rights as well as the implementation and enforcement responsibilities. It also contains specific mandatory regulations and non-mandatory codes governing the minimum requirements for seafarers to work on a ship, the conditions of employment, accommodation, recreational facilities, food and catering, health protection, medical care and welfare of seafarers, the social security protection for the seafarers as well as compliance and enforcement. China strictly implements this *Convention*.

The *Regulations on Vessel's Crew* contains provisions on the registration, holding posts, training and occupational protection of crewmembers as well as provisions with respect to the services of crewmembers onboard. Basically, these Regulations do not regulate the seafarers' employment contracts. However, these Regulations provide that the employers and crewmembers shall participate in work-related injury insurance, medical insurance, pension insurance, unemployment insurance and other social insurance in accordance with the statutory stipulations.

The *Administrative Rules concerning the Seafarers' Working and Living Conditions on Ships* was adopted by virtue of the *Regulations on Vessel's Crew* and the *Maritime Labour Convention of 2006* for the main purpose of implementing this Convention. It contains the requirements for the seafarers' accommodation, recreational facilities, food and catering, medical care, health protection, repatriation, payment of wages, embarkation agreement, and special protection for the underage seafarers, as well as administrative supervision and inspection.

The *Labour Contract Law* is a basic law regulating labour contractual relations in China and contains general provisions and those of conclusion of employment contract, performance of and amendments to employment contract, termination of employment contract and special provisions. The *Labour Law* is another basic law regulating labour relations in China. This Law was shaped at the time of the planned economy. Some of them have become obsolete in the current market economy. In case of repugnancy between the *Labour Contract Law* and the *Labour Law*, the former shall have priority in application.

Now, China has become the biggest country in terms of the number of crewmembers on board ships and has a significant share in exporting seafarers' services in the world market. Consequently, special legislation dealing with maritime employment contracts has become a need in China.

II. Maritime Employment Contract

A. *Conditions of Employment of Seafarers*

222. To be employed on board a ship, a seafarer shall meet the following requirements, whether he is the master or other crewmember:

- being qualified for his position as an ordinary crewmember in the first place and for his special position on board a ship as required by the STCW Convention, the *Regulations Governing the Competency Examinations and Certificating of Seafarers on Board Seagoing Ships* promulgated by the MOT on 6 July 2020 and other relevant provisions concerning seafarers' training and certificating, and holding a certificate indicating that he has undergone training in lifesaving, firefighting and first aid;
- to be engaged in international voyages, holding a seamen's book issued by MSA or other competent authority (Article 33, MC);
- being in good health condition, and, if engaged in international voyages, holding a Health Certificate for International Traveler and an International Certificate of Vaccination issued by the customs after health examination and vaccination.

223. The master and other crewmembers on board a Chinese merchant ship shall hold appropriate certificates of competency issued by MSA or other competent authorities (paragraph 2, Article 13, MTSL).

B. *Recruiting of Seafarers*

224. Employment of seafarers can be divided into two forms in terms of the length of employment period, i.e., permanent employment and temporary employment.

Traditionally, under the system of planned economy, almost all the shipping companies were State-owned, and all the seafarers were employed on a permanent basis. As a statutory labour relation between a seafarer and a shipping company, the seafarer was entitled to serve and also was obliged to serve on board until his retirement, unless his health condition was not fit for the service onboard anymore or his position was changed by the shipping company from a ship to ashore. Now, under the system of market economy, such employment has become rare, even if in a State-owned shipping company. Instead, more and more seafarers are employed on a temporary basis under the articles of employment concluded with their employers. The length of employment is to be agreed upon in the contracts.

Regarding the means of recruiting seafarers, a seafarer concludes the articles of employment directly with the shipowners, bareboat charterers or manager of a ship in some cases. In other cases, a seafarer is employed via an intermediary of seafarer recruiting company. A seafarers recruiting company concludes in its own name two contracts, i.e., a seafarers recruiting contract with the shipowners, bareboat charterers or manager of a ship on the one hand and articles of employment with seafarers on the other. Occasionally, a seafarers recruiting company concludes articles of employment with seafarers as an agent of the shipowners, bareboat charterers or manager of a ship. Where a seafarer is to serve on board a foreign ship, it requires the intermediary service of a company with qualification for recruiting seafarers to serve on a foreign ship as approved by MOT.

C. *Obligations of Seafarer*

225. The main obligations of a seafarer include, *inter alia*:

- to board the ship on time at the beginning of and during service;
- to perform the service he is employed for;
- to obey the orders of the master within his powers;
- not to violate any laws or regulations concerning customs and immigration control, etc., during service.

D. *Obligations of Employer*

226. The main obligations of the shipowners, bareboat charterers or other employers include, *inter alia*:

- to pay to the seafarers the agreed wages, other service allowances and expenses onboard;
- to ensure the safety and appropriate conditions for the work and life of seafarers onboard and to provide appliances for labour protection;
- to repatriate seafarers to the port of embarkation or their hometowns when their services onboard terminate;
- to have the seafarers' personal injury or loss of life insured at a Protection & Indemnity (P&I) Club or an insurance company and to fulfil other requirements of regulations concerning social security and labour accidents.

E. Termination of Maritime Employment Contract

227. By virtue of Article 36 of Chapter IV of the *Labour Contract Law*, a maritime employment contract may be terminated by agreement between a seafarer and his employer.

228. By virtue of Articles 37 and 38 of Chapter IV of the *Labour Contract Law*, a maritime employment contract may be terminated by a seafarer under the following circumstances:

- the seafarer notifies the employer in writing thirty days in advance;
- the employer fails to provide the contractual labour protection or conditions;
- the employer fails to pay the labour remuneration in full;
- the employer fails to pay the social insurance premiums;
- the employer violates law or statutory provisions, causing harm to the seafarer in other aspects;
- the labour contract becomes invalid because the contract was concluded contrary to the real intention of the seafarer due to the employer's use of deception or coercion or taking advantage of the seafarer's difficulties;
- the employer uses violence, threats or unlawful restriction of personal freedom to compel the seafarer to work, or is instructed in violation of rules and regulations or is peremptorily ordered to perform dangerous operations which threaten his personal safety.

229. By virtue of Articles 39 and 40 of Chapter IV of the *Labour Contract Law*, a maritime employment contract may be terminated by the employer under the following circumstances:

- the seafarer is proved during the probation period unable to satisfy the conditions for employment;
- the seafarer materially breaches the employer's disciplines or regulations;
- the seafarer commits serious dereliction of duty or practices graft, which causes substantial damage to the employer;
- the seafarer has additionally established an employment relation with another employer which materially affects the performance of his tasks with the first employer, or the seafarer refuses to rectify the matter after the same is brought to his attention by the employer;
- the seafarer causes the employment contract to be invalid because the contract was concluded contrary to the real intention of the employer due to the seafarer's use of deception or coercion or taking advantage of the employer's difficulties;
- the seafarer is sanctioned with criminal liability in accordance with the law.

In addition, subject to a written notice of thirty days in advance or one month's wage in lieu of the notice, the employer may terminate the contract where a seafarer is no longer fit for his original employment or another work arranged for him by the employer after a set period of medical care for an illness or non-work-related injury, or where a seafarer is incompetent and remains incompetent after training or adjustment of his position or where a major change in the objective circumstances relied upon at the time of conclusion of the contract renders it not performable, and the employer and the seafarer are unable to reach an agreement on amending the contract after consultations.

230. By virtue of Article 42 of Chapter IV of the *Labour Contract Law*, a maritime employment contract cannot be terminated by the employer under the following circumstances:

- the seafarer is engaged in operations exposing him to occupational disease hazards and has not undergone a pre-departure occupational health check-up or is suspected of having contracted an occupational disease and is being diagnosed or under medical observation;
- the seafarer has been confirmed as having lost or partially lost his capacity to work due to an occupational disease contracted or a work-related injury sustained with the employer;
- the seafarer has fallen ill or sustained a non-work-related injury, and a set period of medical care has not expired;
- the seafarer is a female employee in her pregnancy, confinement or nursing period;
- the seafarer has been working for the employer continuously for not less than fifteen years and is less than five years away from his legal retirement age;
- other circumstances which are stipulated in laws or administrative statutes under which the employer cannot terminate the employment contract with the seafarer.

Chapter 4. Liability and Limitation of Liability in Maritime Law

231. The general statement and discussion on the liability and limitation of liability of the shipowners in this chapter does not cover the liability and limitation of liability of the carrier, actual carrier, their servants or agents for loss of life of or personal injury to passengers or loss of or damage to passenger's luggage under a contract of carriage of passenger by sea which will be discussed in §3 of Chapter 15 of this part *infra*, nor for loss of or damage to goods carried under a contract of carriage of goods by sea, i.e., the limitation of liability called 'package or unit limitation of liability' which will be discussed in §7 of Chapter 6 of this part *infra*, nor that of the shipowners for oil pollution damage from a ship which will be discussed in §4 of Chapter 13 of this part *infra*.

The limitation of liability discussed below is called limitation of liability for maritime claims or global limitation of liability.

§1. Liability of Shipowners, Their Servants and Agents

I. Application of Law

232. Unless otherwise provided for in MC, other special laws or regulations governing the liability of the shipowners, their servants or agents, the general provisions contained in CC shall apply in the determination of liability of the shipowners, their servants or agents.

The general provisions of civil liability are contained in Chapter VIII 'Civil Liability' of Book One 'General provisions' of CC. More detailed provisions of liability for breach of contract are contained in Chapter VIII 'Liability for Breach of Contract' of Book Three 'Contracts' of CC. And more detailed provisions of tort liability are contained in Book Seven 'Tort liability' of CC.

The following are the main provisions of civil liability of general application contained in CC:

- where impossibility of fulfilment of civil obligations is caused by force majeure, i.e., unpredictable, unavoidable and irresistible objective situations, liability shall be discharged unless otherwise provided for in law (Article 180, CC); in a case of contract, the liability for breach of contract shall be discharged partly or wholly in accordance with the degree of influence of force majeure on the fulfilment, but the impossibility of fulfilment shall be notified to the other party, and a proof of force majeure shall be provided within reasonable period of time (Article 590, CC);
- a party to a contract shall bear liability for breach of contract if it fails to fulfil its contractual obligation or the fulfilment of the contractual obligation does not conform to the agreement (Article 577, CC);
- where one party to a contract breaches the contract, the other party shall take appropriate measures to mitigate the loss; otherwise, the innocent party is not

entitled to claim for the loss exaggerated due to lack of such measures; the reasonable expenses incurred by the innocent party in mitigating the exaggeration of loss shall be borne of the party in breach of the contract (Article 591, CC);
- any person infringes on other people's civil rights and interests through his own fault or intent shall assume tort liability; if a person is presumed to be at fault according to the law and unable to prove that he is not at fault, then he shall assume tort liability (Article 1165, CC); if any person infringes on other people's civil rights and interests, and any legal provision specifies that he shall assume tort liability, such a provision shall govern, whether he is at fault or not (Article 1166, CC);
- if two or more persons jointly commit a tort and cause damages to other people, they shall bear joint and several liability (Article 1168, CC);
- where the person who suffers infringement has fault in the occurrence or exaggeration of the same damage, the liability of the tortfeasor may be reduced (Article 1173, CC);
- where working personnel of an employer cause damages to others due to performance of their tasks, the employer shall bear tort liability; if, during a period of labour dispatch, the seconded working personnel cause damages to others due to performance of their tasks, the party accepting such labour dispatch shall bear tort liability; if the seconding party commits fault, it shall bear liability correspondingly (Article 1191, CC);
- the civil legal acts implemented by an agent in its principal's name within its scope of agency shall be binding upon the principal (Article 162, CC), and therefore the principal shall bear civil liability for loss or damage suffered by a third party due to such acts.

II. Liability of Shipowners

233. In the case of contractual relations, unless otherwise provided for in Chapter IV 'Contract of Carriage of Goods by Sea', Chapter V 'Contract of Carriage of Passengers by Sea', Chapter VI 'Charter Parties' or Chapter VII 'Contract of Sea Towage' of MC, the shipowners shall bear liability for breach of contract for loss of or damage to property, whether onboard or not, or loss of life of or personal injury to stevedores or other persons, whether onboard or ashore.

In the case of non-contractual relations, unless otherwise provided for in Chapter VIII 'Collisions at Sea' of MC, MEPL and the related regulations, the shipowners shall bear tort liability for loss of or damage to property, whether onboard or not, or loss of life of or personal injury to stevedores or other persons, whether onboard or ashore, caused by their fault or intentional act.

III. Liability of Shipowners' Servants or Agents

234. Where loss of or damage to property, or loss of life of or personal injury to stevedores or other persons, is caused by the acts or omissions of the master, other crewmembers, pilot and other servants or employees or agents done in the course of their employment or agency, the shipowners as the employer or principal shall bear civil liability. The shipowners' servants or agents shall not bear civil liability therefor unless done not within the scope of employment or agency and not recognized by the shipowners retroactively, or their acts or omissions are illegal in nature and not instructed or otherwise required, recognized or acquiesced by the shipowners.

§2. Applicable Laws

I. International Treaties

235. China has not ratified or acceded to the International Convention for Unification of Certain Rules Relating to the Limitation of the Liability of Owners of Seagoing Vessels of 1924, nor the International Convention relating to the Limitation of the Liability of Owners of Seagoing Ships of 1957, known as 'CLC 1957'. China has ratified the LLMC of 1976 as amended, but this Convention is applicable only in Hong Kong.

II. Domestic Legislation

236. The limitation of liability is governed by Chapter XI 'Limitation of Liability for Maritime Claims' of MC and the following two by-laws promulgated by the former MOC as empowered by paragraph 2 of Article 210 and paragraph 2 of Article 211 of MC, respectively, and coming into force on 1 January 1994:

(1) The Provisions Regarding the Limitation of Liability for Ships with a Gross Tonnage not Exceeding 300 Tons and Those Engaging in Transport Services between the Ports of China as well as Those for Other Coastal Operations in China which set out limits of liability for ships engaging in international services and not exceeding 300 tons of gross tonnage or ships engaging in transport services between Chinese ports or other coastal operations in China.
(2) The *Provisions Regarding the Limitation of Liability in the Carriage of Passengers between the Ports of China,* which set out limits of liability for loss of life or personal injury in the carriage of passengers by sea between Chinese ports.

237. The provisions of Chapter XI of MC are more or less a reproduction of LLMC. However, the limits of liability provided for in this chapter that are the same as those contained in LLMC are not applicable to small ships of less than 300 gross tonnage and those engaging in the transport services between Chinese ports or other coastal operations in China as well as for the carriage of passengers and their luggage between two Chinese ports. The limits of liability for these excluded ships are governed by the aforesaid two by-laws. The limits of liability for ships engaging in domestic transport or coastal operations stipulating are much lower than those stipulated in LLMC. This is because when MC was adopted in 1992, the economic development level and the people's living standards in China were low, and the limits of liability contained in LLMC appeared too high so far as the domestic transport or coastal operations were concerned, but the limits of liability applicable to international transport should be in line with the international convention which was widely accepted. On the other hand, the economy was developing rapidly and therefore it was not appropriate to set fixed limits of liability for ships engaging in domestic transport or coastal operations. This is why paragraph 2 of Article 210 and paragraph 2 of Article 211 of MC empowered the former MOC to set limits of liability for such ships, and consequently, the aforesaid two by-laws were adopted.

238. SPC promulgated the Certain Provisions on the Trial of Cases of Disputes Relating to Limitation of Liability for Maritime Claims on 27 August 2010.

§3. Persons Entitled to Limit Liability

239. Under Chapter XI of MC, three categories of persons are entitled to limit liability for maritime claims, *viz.*:

(1) the shipowners, including charterers or operators of a ship or salvor (Article 204, MC);
(2) the servants or agents of the shipowners, including charterers or operators of a ship or salvor for whose acts they are responsible, *viz.* the persons done within the scope of their employment or agency, where claims are lodged against the said servants or agents (Article 205, MC);
(3) the liability insurer liable for the maritime claims to the same extent as the assured, provided that the assured may limit his liability (Article 206, MC).

240. Noticeably, unlike in Article 1 of LLMC, the shipowners in Article 204 of MC do not include the manager of a ship. This is because, at the time of shaping MC, there were no ship managers in China, and it was even difficult to understand the meaning of ship manager. However, there is a big market of ship management market now in China and therefore ship managers shall be added to the persons entitled to limit liability when MC is revised in the near future.

As regards the servants or agents of the shipowners, including charterers or operators of a ship or those of a salvor, where their acts or omissions are done within the scope of their employment or agency, claims cannot be lodged against them, but only against their employers or principals under Article 1191 or Article 162 of CC as introduced in §1 *supra*. It should be understood that their entitlement to the limitation of liability as provided for in Article 205 of MC does not change their legal status under CC.

Regarding the liability insurer, a claimant cannot make direct claim against the liability insurer of shipowners or other persons liable for maritime claims, with the exception of claims for oil pollution damage caused by ships under the current Chinese law as discussed in Chapter 13 of this part *infra*. Similarly, therefore, its entitlement to the limitation of liability as provided for in Article 206 of MC does not change its legal status under this rule.

§4. Claims Subject to Limitation

241. As expressly provided for in Article 207 MC, a person liable may limit his liability with respect to the following maritime claims, whatever the basis of liability may be and whatever the way the claims are lodged:

– the claims in respect of loss of life or personal injury or loss of or damage to property, including damage to harbour works, basins and waterways and aids to navigation occurring onboard or in direct connection with the operation of ship or with salvage operations, as well as the consequential damages resulting therefrom;
– the claims in respect of loss resulting from delay in delivery in the carriage of goods by sea or from delay in the arrival of passengers or their luggage;
– the claims in respect of other loss resulting from infringement of rights other than contractual rights occurring in direct connection with the operation of ship or salvage operations;
– the claims of a person other than the person liable in respect of measures taken to avert or minimize loss for which the person liable may limit his liability and further loss caused by such measures. However, with respect to the remuneration for which a person liable pays as agreed upon in the contract, the person liable may not invoke the provisions on limitation of liability in relation to his obligation for payment.

242. The claims listed as (d) and (e) as follows under the title of 'claims subject to limitation' in paragraph 1 of Article 2 of LLMC are not listed in Article 207 of MC and are thus not subject to limitation of liability in China:[30]

– the claims in respect of the raising, removal, destruction or the rendering harmless of a ship that is sunk, wrecked, stranded or abandoned, including anything that is or has been on board such a ship;
– the claims in respect of the removal, destruction or rendering harmless of the cargo of the ship.

§5. Claims Excepted from Limitation

243. As provided for in Article 208 of MC, the provisions of the limitation of liability contained in Chapter XI of MC shall not be applicable to the following claims:

30. Paragraph 1 of Art. 17 of the *Certain Provisions on the Trial of Cases of Disputes Relating to Limitation of Liability for Maritime Claims* promulgated by SPC confirms that the claims subject to limitation provided for in Art. 207 of MC do not include claims in respect of the raising, removal, destruction or the rendering harmless of a ship that is sunk, wrecked, stranded or abandoned, or claims in respect of the removal, destruction or the rendering harmless of the cargo of the ship.

- the claims for salvage payment or contribution in general average;
- the claims for oil pollution damage under international convention on civil liability for oil pollution damage to which China is a party, i.e., the *International Convention on Civil Liability for Oil Pollution Damage of 1992*, known as '1992 CLC';
- the claims for nuclear damage under international convention on limitation of liability for nuclear damage to which China is a party;
- the claims against the shipowners of a nuclear ship for nuclear damage;
- the claims by the servants of the shipowners, including the charterers or operator of a ship or salvor, if under the law governing the contract of employment, the shipowners or salver is not entitled to limit its liability or if it is by such law only permitted to limit its liability to an amount greater than that provided for in Chapter XI of MC.

244. China has ratified 1992 CLC and, therefore, the limitation of liability for oil pollution damage covered by 1992 CLC shall be subject to this Convention. Nevertheless, the limitation of liability for oil pollution damage not covered by this Convention, including limitation of liability for bunker oil pollution damage covered by the *International Convention on Civil Liability for Bunker Oil Pollution Damage of 2001*, known as 'Bunker Convention', which does not set out separate limitation of liability, shall be subject to Chapter XI of MC.

As regards claims for nuclear damage, China has not ratified or acceded to the *Convention Relating to Civil Liability in the Field of Maritime Carnage of Nuclear Materials of 1971* and, therefore, the limitation of liability for nuclear damage is subject to Chapter XI of MC.

As regards claims by the servants of the shipowners, including the charterers or operator of a ship or salvor, the current Chinese law governing the contract of employment of seafarers does not contain any provision allowing the shipowners or salvor to limit its liability, nor can the shipowners or salvor limit liability to its agents under a contract of agency.

§6. Counterclaims

245. As provided for in Article 215 of MC, where a person entitled to limitation of liability has a counterclaim against the claimant arising out of the same occurrence, their respective claims shall be set off against each other in the first place, and the limitation shall apply only to the balance. This is called the rule of single liability.

§7. Conduct Barring Limitation

246. Following the criteria commonly contained in the modern maritime conventions, Article 209 of MC provides that a person liable shall not be entitled to limit his liability if it is proved that the loss resulted from his act or omission done with intent to cause such loss or recklessly with the knowledge that such loss would probably result. Consequently, entitlement to limit liability is very rarely lost in judicial practice in China.

§8. General Limits of Liability

I. Basis of Calculation

247. The limits of liability are stated in 'Units of Account' *viz.* the SDRs as determined by the International Monetary Fund (IMF) to which China is a party.

The amount of the Chinese currency CNY in terms of SDR shall be calculated on the date of the judgment by a court of law or of the arbitration award by an arbitration organization or the date mutually agreed upon by the parties on the basis of the method of conversion established by the authorities in China in charge of foreign exchange control (Article 277, MC), i.e., the State Administration on Foreign Exchanges.

The limits are determined in accordance with the gross tonnage of ship as calculated by the tonnage measurement rules contained in *Annex I of the International Convention on Tonnage Measurement of Ships of 1969,* which China has ratified.

The limits of liability under Articles 210 and 211 of MC as mentioned *infra* shall apply to the aggregate of all claims that arise on any distinct occasion against the shipowners or the salvor and any person for whose act, neglect or fault the shipowners or the salvor is responsible (Article 212, MC).

II. Limits of Liability for Ships Engaging in International Trade Exceeding 300 Tons of Gross Tonnage

A. *In Respect of Claims for Loss of Life or Personal Injury to Persons Other than Passengers*

248. As provided for in paragraph 1(1) of Article 210 of MC, the limits of liability in respect of the claims for loss of life of or personal injury to persons other than passengers shall be:

(a) 333,000 SDR for a ship with a gross tonnage ranging from 300 to 500 tons;
(b) for a ship with a gross tonnage in excess of 500 tons, the limit under (a) above shall be applicable to the first 500 tons, and the following amounts in addition to that set out under (a) shall be applicable to the gross tonnage in excess of 500 tons:
   - for each ton from 501 to 3,000 tons: 500 SDR;
   - for each ton from 3,001 to 30,000 tons: 333 SDR;
   - for each ton from 30,001 to 70,000 tons: 250 SDR;
   - for each ton in excess of 70,000 tons: 167 SDR.

B. In Respect of Claims Other than for Loss of Life or Personal Injury

249. As provided for in paragraph 1(2) of Article 210 of MC, the limits of liability in respect of the claims other than for loss of life or personal injury shall be:

(a) 167,000 SDR for a ship with a gross tonnage ranging from 300 to 500 tons;
(b) for a ship with a gross tonnage in excess of 500 tons, the limit under (a) above shall be applicable to the first 500 tons, and the following amounts in addition to that set out under (a) shall be applicable to the gross tonnage in excess of 500 tons:
  - for each ton from 501 to 30,000 tons: 167 SDR;
  - for each ton from 30,001 to 70,000 tons: 125 SDR;
  - for each ton in excess of 70,000 tons: 83 SDR.

250. Where the amount calculated for claims for loss of life or personal injury under paragraph 1(1) of Article 210 is insufficient for payment of claims thereof in full, the amount calculated for the claims other than for loss of life or personal injury under paragraph 1(2) of Article 210 shall be available for payment ratably of the unpaid balance of the claims for loss of life or personal injury and the claims other than for loss of life or personal injury (paragraph 1(3), Article 210, MC). However, without prejudice to the right of claims for loss of life or personal injury, the claims in respect of damage to harbour works, basins and waterways and aids to navigation shall have priority over other claims other than for loss of life or personal injury (paragraph 1(4), Article 210, MC).

C. Limits of Liability of Salvor Not Operating from Ship or Operating Solely on Salved Ship

251. By virtue of paragraph 1(5) of Article 210 of MC, the limits of liability of any salvor engaged in international salvage not operating from any ship or for any salvor operating solely on the ship to or in respect of which it rendered salvage service shall be calculated according to a ship of gross tonnage of 1,500 tons. In such a case, therefore, the liability of salvor shall be limited to 333,000 + (1,500 – 500) × 500 = 833,000 SDR for the claims for loss of life or personal injury, and 167,000 + (1,500 – 500) × 167 = 334,000 SDR for the claims other than for loss of life or personal injury.

Where a salvor operates from a salvage ship engaging in international salvage exceeding 300 tons of gross tonnage, the limits of its liability for the claims for loss of life or personal injury and for the claims other than for loss of life or personal injury shall be calculated according to paragraph 1(2) and paragraph 1(2) of Article 210 respectively, as introduced *supra*, in terms of the gross tonnage of the salvage ship.

III. Limits of Liability for Ships with Gross Tonnage Not Exceeding 300 Tons and Those Engaging in Transport Services Between Chinese Ports or Other Coastal Operations

A. Limits of Liability for Ships with Gross Tonnage Not Exceeding 300 Tons Engaging in International Trade

252. As provided for in Article 3 of the Previsions Regarding the Limitation of Liability for Ships with a Gross Tonnage not Exceeding 300 Tons and Those Engaging in Transport Services between the Ports of China as well as Those for Other Coastal Operations in China, the limit of liability for a ship with a gross tonnage not exceeding 300 tons and engaging in international transport services or international operation shall be:

(a) In respect of the claims for loss of life or personal injury:
- 54,000 SDR for a ship with a gross tonnage exceeding 20 tons but not exceeding 21 tons;
- for a ship with a gross tonnage in excess of 21 tons, 1,000 SDR per ton in addition shall be applicable to the part in excess of 20 tons.

(b) In respect of the claims other than for loss of life or personal injury:
- 27,500 SDR for a ship with a gross tonnage exceeding 20 tons but not exceeding 21 tons;
- for a ship with a gross tonnage in excess of 21 tons, 500 SDR per ton in addition shall be applicable to the part in excess of 20 tons.

253. The provisions of paragraphs 1(3) and (4) of Article 210 of MC shall apply where the amount calculated for the claims for loss of life or personal injury is insufficient for payment or where there exist claims for damage to harbour works, basins and waterways and aids to navigation.

B. Limits of Liability for Ships Engaging in Transport Services Between Chinese Ports or for Other Coastal Operations

254. By virtue of Article 4 of the Previsions Regarding the Limitation of Liability for Ships with a Gross Tonnage not Exceeding 300 Tons and Those Engaging in Transport Services between the Ports of China as well as Those for Other Coastal Operations in China, the limits of liability for a ship engaging in transport service between the ports of China or coastal operation in China shall be calculated by 50% of the amount set out in Article 3 of this by-law if her gross tonnage does not exceed 300 tons or by 50% of the amount provided for in paragraph 1 of Article 210 of MC if her gross tonnage exceeds 300 tons.

IV. Limits of Liability for Loss of Life or Personal Injury to Passengers in the International Carriage by Sea

255. The limit of liability of the shipowner for loss of life or personal injury to passengers in the international carriage by sea shall be an amount of 46,666 SDR multiplied by the number of passengers whom the ship is authorized to carry according to the ship's relevant certificate, but the maximum amount of compensation shall not exceed 25,000,000 SDR (paragraph 1, Article 211, MC). The nationalities of passengers are irrelevant in the calculation of limit of liability.

V. Limits of Liability for Loss of Life or Personal Injury to Passengers in the Coastal Carriage Between Chinese Ports

256. By virtue of Article 4 of the *Provisions Regarding the Limitation of Liability in the Carriage of Passengers between the Ports of China*, the limit of liability for loss of life or personal injury to passengers in the coastal carriage between Chinese ports shall be an amount of Chinese currency CNY 40,000, i.e., proximately USD 4,300, multiplied by the number of passengers which the ship is authorized to carry according to the ship's relevant certificate, but the maximum amount of compensation shall not exceed CNY 21,000,000. The nationalities of passengers are irrelevant in the calculation of limit of liability.

It is well recognized that these limits are too low, and a significant increase thereof or the application of the same limits as in the international carriage is anticipated in the revision of MC in the near future.

§9. Procedure

I. Principles of Entitlement to Limitation of Liability

257. The shipowners, charterers, operator of a ship, or salvor or liability insurer against whom claims are made and who applies for limitation of liability after occurrence of a maritime accident may constitute a limitation fund with a maritime court having jurisdiction (Article 213, MC; paragraph 1, Article 101, SMPL). Therefore, the limitation of liability may be invoked by any one of them, notwithstanding that a limitation fund has not been constituted.

In the trial of a case concerned, if there is no sufficient evidence showing the situation of loss of right to limit liability. i.e., the loss or damage claimed for resulted from the act or omission of the person liable done with intent to cause such loss or damage or recklessly and with the knowledge that such loss or damage would probably result, the person liable is entitled to invoke the limitation of liability and this right shall not be lost due to the fact no limitation fund has been established nor corresponding security has been provided.[31]

258. However, where a ship has caused oil pollution damage, her owners, their liability insurer, or other person having provided financial security shall constitute a fund of limitation of liability with a maritime court having jurisdiction in order to invoke the right of limitation of liability (paragraph 2, Article 101, SMPL).

II. Procedures for Establishment of Limitation Fund

259. The procedures for the establishment of a limitation fund are provided for in SMPL and the *Certain Provisions on the Trial of Cases of Disputes relating to Limitation of Liability for Maritime Claims* promulgated by SPC on 27 August 2010.

The establishment of a limitation fund shall be applied for either before or during litigation but shall not be later than the time the judgment of first instance is rendered (paragraph 3, Article 101, SMPL).

Such an application in writing, if filed before litigation, shall be filed with the maritime court located in the place where the maritime accident occurred, the contract was performed, or the ship was arrested (Article 102, SMPL). If filed during litigation, the application shall be filed with the maritime court having entertained the case.

The establishment of a limitation fund shall not be subject to any jurisdiction or arbitration agreement between the parties (Article 103, SMPL).

The application for limitation of liability and establishment of a limitation fund does not mean the applicant's admission of any liability for the maritime claims.

The application shall indicate the sum of limitation fund, reasons for application, the names, addresses and means of communication of the parties with interests who are known to the applicant and shall be attached with supporting documents (Article 105, SMPL).

260. By Article 105 of SMPL, the maritime court, having received the application, shall notify these parties with interests of the establishment of limitation fund within seven days and make public notice via local newspaper or other news media at the same time, indicating the following contents:

– the name of the applicant;
– the facts and reasons of application;
– the items of establishment of limitation fund; and
– the other items that need to be notified.

31. The reply by SPC to the People's High Court of Zhejiang Province regarding the matter of application for the establishment of limitation fund of liability for maritime claim filed by Ningbo Overseas Shipping Company on 7 Dec. 1995.

261. After the maritime court makes a public notice, the claimants whose claims are subject to limitation of liability shall apply for registration of their respective claims with the court during the period indicated in the public notice; otherwise, their claims shall be deemed as waived (Article 112, MC). Where a claimant provides an effective judgment, award, reconciliation statement rendered by a court of law, arbitration award or notarized document as evidence of his claim, the maritime court shall confirm the claim if the court confirms such a document is a true copy after verification. Where a claimant provides other evidence of claim, he shall file a lawsuit with the maritime court for confirming his claim after registration thereof, unless there is an arbitration agreement in which case he shall refer the case to arbitration without delay. A judgment or award rendered by the maritime court in a lawsuit for confirming a maritime claim shall be binding upon the parties and not subject to appeal (Article 116, MC).

262. Any objection by a party with interest in the establishment of limitation fund shall be raised in writing and filed with the maritime court within seven days from the date of receipt of the notice or, where the notice has not been received, from the date of the public notice.

Having received the objection, the maritime court shall examine it and make an award within fifteen days. Where the objection is tenable, the application for the establishment of limitation fund shall be rejected. If untenable, the application for the establishment of limitation fund shall be granted. Any party who refuses to obey the award may file an appeal within seven days from the date of receipt of the award. The court of law of second instance shall make an award within fifteen days from the receipt of the appeal (Article 106, SMPL).

263. After the award granting the establishment of limitation fund has become effective, the applicant shall establish a limitation fund with the maritime court within the time limit set out in the award in the form of cash deposit or other forms approved by the court. The other forms to be approved by a maritime court are letters of security issued by a Chinese bank, a Chinese insurance company or another Chinese financial organ other than banks or the China P&I Club. Noticeably, a security issued by a foreign bank, a foreign insurance company or a foreign P&I club is not acceptable unless agreed to by the claimants.

The date of establishment of a limitation fund shall be the date the cash is deposited at the bank account designated by the maritime court or, where the establishment is in the form of security, the maritime court accepts the security. The sum of limitation fund shall be the principal amount of limit of liability set out respectively in Articles 210 and 211 MC or the said by-laws, together with the interests thereon from the date of the occurrence, giving rise to the liability until the date of the establishment of the fund (Article 108, SMPL; Article 213, MC). Where the establishment is the form of security, the amount of security shall be the sum of the fund plus the interests during the period of the validity of the fund (Article 108, SMPL).

264. After the establishment of limitation fund, any claimant shall not exercise any right against any assets of the applicant with respect to the claims subject to the limitation. Where any ship or other property belonging to the applicant has been arrested or attached, or another security has been provided by the applicant, the court shall order without delay the release of the ship from the arrest or the property from the attachment or the return of the security, as the case may be (Article 214, MC).

265. Where litigation has not started at the time of the establishment of limitation fund, any lawsuit regarding the related maritime disputes shall be filed with the maritime court with which the limitation fund has been established unless an agreement of jurisdiction or arbitration between the parties exists (Article 109, SMPL). The *Certain Provisions on the Trial of Cases of Disputes relating to Limitation of Liability for Maritime Claims* promulgated by SPC further provides in Article 4 that, after the establishment of limitation fund, the maritime court with which the limitation fund has been established shall have jurisdiction over the cases of disputes in which the maritime claimants make claims against the party liable relating to the maritime accident; where the maritime claimants have filed, or file lawsuits with other maritime courts, such maritime courts shall transfer the cases to the maritime court with which the limitation fund has been established unless an agreement of jurisdiction or arbitration between the parties exists. As a result, all the cases of claims subject to limitation of liability shall be adjudicated by the maritime court with which the limitation fund has been established so far as possible.

266. Where the application for the establishment of limitation fund proves wrongful, i.e., it finally proves the applicant is not entitled to limit liability, the applicant shall compensate for the losses suffered by the parties with interests resulting therefrom (Article 110, SMPL).

267. Where a limitation fund has been established, the amount of the fund, together with the interests, shall be distributed among all the registered claimants for all the claims subject to limitation of liability by agreement among the registered claimants in accordance with the provisions contained in MC or the said by-laws or, if no agreement can be reached, by an award rendered by the maritime court.

268. The payment to a claimant of his part of the limitation fund extinguishes the claim of the claimant against the applicant and other persons liable unless the applicant or any of the other persons loses the right to limit of liability by virtue of Article 209 of MC, even if the claim is not fully compensated for. Surplus of the limitation fund, if any, after the settlement of all the claims shall be returned to the applicant together with its interests.

269. Where no limitation fund has been established, but the person liable has applied for limitation of liability, and the application is granted by a maritime court having jurisdiction, each claimant may apply to the court to enforce the judgment or arbitration award in its favour within an amount due to it calculated in accordance with the statutory provisions of limitation of liability.

Chapter 5. Charter Parties

§1. Definitions and Varieties of Charter Parties

I. Definitions of Charter Party

270. A charter party or charterparty (C/P), in its general sense, is an agreement concluded between the shipowners who let out the ship as one party and the charterers who hire the ship as the other party for either a certain voyage or voyages or a fixed period of time against a fixed remuneration called freight or hire.

Besides the owners of a ship, the shipowners, as one party to a charter party, may be the charterers under an independent charter party (head charter party) or the operator of a ship. The charterers, as the other party, may be the owners of goods or other persons interested in the use of ship's service. On many occasions, the charterers, especially time charterers, charter a ship to carry as carrier the goods of a third person under a contract of carriage goods by sea. Where the shipowners under a charter party are the charterers under a head charter party, they are often called disponent owners in shipping practice.

A charter party is mainly for the purpose of carriage of goods by sea. Sometimes, it may be for other purposes, e.g., for the use of a ship as a floating warehouse under a bareboat charter party or in the case of ship other than a cargo ship. In this chapter, the charter parties discussed are for the purpose of carriage of goods by sea.

II. Varieties of Charter Parties

271. Charter parties can be basically divided into three kinds:

- voyage charter party or voyage charter defined in Article 92 of MC as a charter party under which the shipowners charter out and the charterers charter in the whole or part of the ship's space for the carriage by sea of the intended goods from one port or other place to another, and the charterers pay the agreed amount of freight;
- time charter party or time charter defined in Article 129 of MC as a contract under which the shipowners provide a designated manned ship to the charterers, and the charterers employ the ship during the contractual period for the agreed service against payment of hire;
- bareboat charter party or bareboat charter or charter party by demise defined in Article 144 of MC as a contract under which the shipowners provide an unmanned ship which the charterers shall possess, employ and operate during the contractual period for the agreed service against payment of hire.

272. Between a voyage charter party and a time charter party lies a time charter on trip basis (TCT) which is deemed as a special kind of time charter. The period of hire of a TCT is not a fixed time but is the actual time used for a designated voyage or voyages.

Occasionally, a bareboat charter contains a lease-purchase clause under which the ownership of the chartered ship shall be transferred from the shipowners to the charterers when the charterers have paid off the lease-purchase price to the shipowners as agreed upon in the contract (Article 154, MC). Such a charter party is called charter party by demise with hire purchase and is *ex facto* a mixture of a bareboat charter and a contract of sale and purchase of ship or, more precisely, is a bareboat charter in nature, but for the purpose of sale and purchase of the ship concerned.

§2. Applicable Laws

I. Domestic Laws

273. In China, charter parties are regulated mainly by MC and CC. So far, there is no international treaty governing charter parties.

274. In consideration of the lack of an international convention in the world governing the rights and obligations of the shipowners and the charterers under charter parties and that the national laws of most shipping countries either contain no provision governing charter parties or only set out non-compulsory provisions, leaving the shipowners and charterers to negotiate a charter party in a free market, the provisions in MC governing charter parties are mainly non-compulsory and are not in detail as compared with the complicated contents of charter parties. Consequently, the parties to a charter party have large freedom to negotiate a contract under MC.[32] The rights and obligations of the shipowners and the charterers are mainly determined by the terms and conditions of a charter party. For example, in the case of a voyage charter, the goods to be carried, port or other place of loading and discharge, laydays, laytime, freight, demurrage and dispatch money, etc., are subject to agreement between the shipowners and the charterers. In the case of a time charter, contents concerning trading limits, goods to be carried, period of hire, time and place of delivery and redelivery of ship, hire and its payment, etc., are also to be agreed upon between the shipowners and the charterers. Under a bareboat charter, besides ship's survey and insurance, cancellation of contract, etc., are also subject to agreement between the parties.

275. Charter parties are considered to have different legal natures under Chinese law. Consequently, MC deals with various charter parties in a slightly different way.

A voyage charter party is basically deemed as a contract of carriage of goods by sea. Therefore, Chapter IV 'Contract of Carriage of Goods by Sea' of MC sets out section 7 'Special Provisions Regarding Voyage Charter Party'. However, the legal nature of a voyage charter as a contract of carriage of goods by sea does not mean that it is not a charter party. By virtue of Article 94 of MC, the provisions of Article 47 regarding the carrier's obligation to exercise due diligence to make the ship seaworthy and those of Article 49 regarding the carrier's obligation not to deviate

32. Chinese law does not contain the term of 'freedom of contract'. What is expressly provided for in Art. 5 of CC is the parties' free will to conclude a contract or engage in other civil activities.

unreasonably shall apply compulsorily to the shipowners under a voyage charter party, while the other provisions contained in section 7 and other sections in Chapter IV of MC regarding the rights and obligations of the parties to a contract of carriage of goods by sea are not compulsorily applicable but shall apply to the shipowners and the charterers under a voyage charter only in the absence of relevant provisions or in the absence of provisions differing therefrom in the voyage charter.

A time charter party is not deemed as contract of carriage of goods by sea because the subject matter is not carriage of goods by sea, nor a contract of lease because the ship is not in the possession of charterers. Thus, a time charter party is not one of the typical contracts stipulated in Sub-Book Two 'Typical Contracts' of Book Three of CC.

A bareboat charter party is not deemed as a contract of lease, which is defined in Article 703 of CC, as a contract under which the leasers deliver the property of lease to the charterers for use and making profit, and the charterers shall pay hire. One of the features of a contract of lease is that the charterers possess the property of lease during the period of hire.

However, a time charter party and a bareboat charter party have a lot of similarities. In particular, the charterers use the ship and pay the hire as agreed. The main difference is that the shipowners are responsible for manning the master and other crewmembers and paying for them under a time charter party, while this is the responsibility of the charterers under a bareboat charter party.

The provisions governing time charters and bareboat charters are those contained in Chapter VI 'Charter Parties' of MC. In particular, section 2 'Time Charter Parties' of Chapter VI of MC governs time charters and section 3 'Bareboat Charter Parties' of Chapter VI of MC governs bareboat charters. However, Article 153 of section 3 provides that the provisions of Articles 134, 135, 142 and 143 of section 2 of Chapter VI of MC apply to bareboat charter parties.

By virtue of Article 127 of MC, the provisions regarding the rights and obligations of the shipowners and the charterers in Chapter VI are not compulsorily applicable but shall apply only where there are no provisions or no different provisions in this regard in a time charter party or bareboat charter party. However, Chapter IV including especially section 7 governing voyage charters and Chapter VI of MC governing time charter parties and bareboat charter parties also contain provisions not relating to the rights and obligations of the parties. These provisions shall apply compulsorily to charter parties. An example is the form of charter parties that, in accordance with Article 43 of MC in the case of a voyage charter, and Article 128 of MC in the case of a time charter or bareboat charter shall be in writing. In this respect, telegrams, telexes and telefaxes have the effect of being in writing (Article 43, MC). By virtue of Article 469 of CC, EDI, e-mail messages and other forms of electronic data messages which can indicate visibly the loaded contents also have the effect of being in writing.

276. Besides the provisions contained in section 7 of Chapter IV of MC governing voyage charter parties and Chapter VI of MC governing time charter parties and bareboat charter parties, charter parties are also subject to the relevant provisions of CC. However, the provisions contained in MC as special law shall have priority over those contained in CC as basic law in the case of repugnancy. Thus, the provisions contained in Book Three 'Contracts' of CC applicable to charter parties are mainly limited to those of Chapter II 'Conclusion of Contract', Chapter III 'Effect of Contract', Chapter VI 'Change & Transfer of Contract' and Chapter VII 'Termination of Contractual Rights & Obligations'. In addition, Chapter XIV 'Contract of Lease' shall be applicable to bareboat charter parties and Chapter XIX 'Contract of Carriage' shall be applicable to voyage charter parties to the extent that MC does not contain provisions to the contrary.

Noticeably, where the provisions contained in MC governing the rights and obligations of the parties are non-compulsorily applicable to a charter party, the parties are free to negotiate different terms of contract, and the terms so agreed upon shall have full effect, even if they are repugnant to those contained in CC except those regarding the effect of civil legal acts contained in section 3 of Chapter 6 'Civil Legal Acts' of Book One 'General Provisions' of MC.

II. Forms of Charter Parties

277. Various forms of charter parties of worldwide use, called standard forms, play very important roles in shipping practice. Charter parties are, on most occasions, formed and concluded on the basis of a chosen standard form. Typical examples of the forms are mainly those shaped by the Documentary Committee of Baltic and International Maritime Council, an international shipowners organization known as 'BIMCO', *viz.* Gencon 1994 and 2022 for voyage charters, Baltime 1976 and 2001 for time charters and Barecon 2001 for bareboat charters. NYPE 1993 and 2015, shaped by the Association of Ship Brokers and Agents of the United States known as 'ASBA', is also of worldwide use for time charters. The use of standard forms makes the conclusion of charter parties time-saving and economical.

The provisions contained in MC governing voyage charters, time charters and bareboat charters are laid down mainly by reference to the standard forms of Gencon 1976, Baltime 1976, NYPE 1946 and Barecon 1974, as revised in 1989, respectively.

278. Besides the standard forms of charter parties, many standard clauses and rules shaped by various non-governmental organizations are also of importance in shipping practice. Examples are the *Voyage Charter Party Interpretation Rules 2013* shaped by BIMCO, CMI, Federation of National Associations of Ship Brokers and Agents (FONASBA), International Association of Dry Cargo Shipowners (INTERCARGO) and the Baltic Exchange, and the International Safety Management (ISM) Clause shaped by BIMCO following the implementation of the *International Safety Management Code*, known as 'ISM CODE', adopted by IMO as part of the SOLAS Conventions.

279. Where a charter party is concluded on the basis of a form or clauses shaped by one party for the purpose of repeated use and without negotiation with the other party at the time of conclusion of the charter party, such a form or clauses are called 'form clauses' in China and are subject to the provisions of Articles 496, 497 and 498 of CC governing the use, effect and interpretation of form clauses.

§3. Voyage Charter Party

I. Obligations of Shipowners

A. *Compulsory Obligations of Shipowners*

280. As mentioned §1 *supra*, Chapter IV of MC puts the shipowners under a voyage charter party, basically in the same position as a carrier under a contract of carriage of goods by sea. Especially, Articles 47 and 49 of MC shall compulsorily apply to the shipowners, as a result of which the shipowners undertake compulsory obligations thereunder.

281. First, the shipowners shall be bound, before and at the beginning of the voyage, to exercise due diligence to make the ship seaworthy, properly man, equip and supply the ship and to make the holds, refrigerating and cool chambers and all other parts of the ship in which goods are carried, fit and safe for their reception, carriage and preservation.

This compulsory statutory obligation renders clause 1 'Owners' Responsibility Clause' in Gencon 1994 partly invalid.

282. Second, the shipowners shall carry the goods to the port of discharge on the agreed or customary or geographically direct route except for reasonable deviation.

This compulsory statutory obligation renders clause 2 'Deviation Clause' in Gencon 1994 or clause 22 'Liberty and Deviation' in Gencon 2022 partly invalid.

B. *Non-compulsory Obligations of Shipowners*

283. The shipowners undertake non-compulsory statutory obligations due to the application of the obligations of the carrier under Chapter IV of MC to the shipowners or the provisions contained in section 7 of Chapter IV by virtue of paragraph 2 of Article 94 of MC as mentioned in §1 *supra*.

284. First, the shipowners shall properly and carefully load, handle, stow, carry, keep, care for and discharge the goods carried unless the charter party provides otherwise.

Under an F.I.O.S.T. (free in, out, stowed and trimmed) clause, e.g., clause 4(a) of Gencon 2022, the charterers are obliged to properly and carefully load, handle, stow, and discharge the goods carried, and the shipowners are free of expenses, risks and liability from these cargo operations. However, where MC is applicable, if bad stowage constitutes unseaworthiness of the ship under an F.I.O.S.T. clause, the shipowners' obligation to exercise due diligence to make the ship seaworthy under

Article 47 MC is not discharged, and the shipowners shall be liable for loss of or damage or delay in delivery of goods resulting from ship's unseaworthiness if it proves that the shipowners, their servants or agents or independent contractors fail to make due diligence. Under Liner Terms, however, the shipowners shall be responsible for the expense risks from the cargo operations.

Other options between F.I.O.S.T. and Liner Terms include Liner In Free Out (L.I.F.O.), under which the shipowners are responsible for loading but not responsible for discharge of goods, and Free In Liner Out (F.I.L.O.) under which the shipowners are not responsible for loading, but r responsible for discharge of goods.

285. Second, the shipowners shall deliver the goods at the port or other place of discharge specified in the charter party within the time expressly agreed upon with the charterers.

Where a charter party contains a clause allowing the choice of the port or other place of discharge among the agreed picked ports or other places by the charterers and the charterers fail to choose within the time as agreed upon in the charter, the master may choose one among the agreed picked ports or other places to discharge the goods.

If the failure of the charterers to choose the port or other place of discharge has caused economic loss to the shipowners, the charterers shall be liable for compensation. On the other hand, if the master or shipowners arbitrarily choose the port or other place of discharge in disregard of the provisions in the charter party and, as a result, the charterers suffer loss, the shipowners shall be liable for compensation.

286. Third, the shipowners shall provide the agreed ship to the charterers within the laydays, i.e., the time or period of time fixed in the charter party when or during which the ship is expected ready to load unless the agreed ship is substituted by the shipowners as permitted in the chatter party or with the consent of the charterers (Articles 96 and 97, MC).

If the shipowners fail to provide the agreed ship or to provide within the laydays due to the fault on the part of shipowners and the failure has caused loss to the charterers, the shipowners shall be liable for compensation, unless the fault can be exempted by virtue of applicable law or the charter party.

If the ship provided by the shipowners or the ship substituted does not meet the requirements of the charter party, the charterers may reject the ship or cancel the charter party (Article 96, MC).

Where the shipowners fail to provide the ship and make her ready to load the agreed cargo at the port or other place of loading by the cancelling date, which is normally the last day of laydays, whether due to the fault of the shipowners or not, the charterers are entitled to cancel the charter party, provided that the delay is not attributable to the charterers. However, if the shipowners have notified the charterers of the delay of the ship and the expected date of her arrival at the agreed port or other place of loading, the charterers shall notify the shipowners whether to cancel the charter party within forty-eight hours of the receipt of the shipowners' notification. Should the charterers fail to notify, they shall be deemed as having waived the right to cancel the charter party (Article 97, MC). In such a case, the expected date of her arrival notified by the shipowners shall be the new cancelling date. A clause in a charter party to this effect is called an 'Anti-technicality clause'.

II. Obligations of Charterers

287. All the obligations of the charterers under a voyage charter provided for in Chapter IV of MC are non-compulsory by virtue of paragraph 2 of Article 94, as mentioned in §1 *supra.*

288. First, the charterers shall pay the shipowners the agreed freight (Article 69, MC).

The freight is normally calculated on the intaken or outtaken quantity of the goods as agreed. Sometimes, the freight is on a lump sum basis, irrespective of the actual quantity of goods supplied and loaded onboard.

The Charterers shall also pay dead freight to the shipowners except in the case of lump sum freight, demurrage, contribution in general average and other necessary charges paid by the shipowners for and on behalf of the charterers (Article 87, MC).

If the charterers fail to pay the freight and other expenses as agreed, the shipowners may exercise lien on the goods belonging to the charterers by virtue of Articles 87 and 88 of MC.

289. Second, the charterers shall provide the agreed goods, unless replaced by other goods, with the consent of the shipowners (paragraph 1, Article 100, MC).

If the charterers fail to provide the agreed goods and, as a result, the shipowners suffer loss, the charterers shall be liable for compensation. Where the charterers are entitled to replace the goods under the charter party, the shipowners shall be entitled to reject the goods replaced and cancel the charter party should the replacement of goods be detrimental to the interests of the shipowners (paragraph 2, Article 100, MC).

290. Third, the charterers shall load and/or discharge the goods within the laytime for loading and/or discharge.

On the one hand, where the charterers fail to load and/or discharge the goods within the laytime for loading and/or discharge, they shall pay demurrage to the shipowners. On the other hand, where the loading and/or discharge operation has been completed ahead of schedule, the charterers are entitled to despatch money. The rate of demurrage and despatch money shall be fixed in the charter party (Article 101, MC). The calculation of time on demurrage or time on dispatch is agreed upon by the charter party. Normally, the rate of despatch money is 50% of that of demurrage in practice.

Where no demurrage is agreed upon and the charterers fail to complete loading and/or discharge within the agreed laytime or within reasonable time in the case no laytime is agreed upon, e.g., under a customary quick despatch (C.Q.D.) clause, the Charterers shall be liable for damages for detention, if the delay in loading and/or discharge operation is caused by the fault on their part.

§4. TIME CHARTER PARTY

I. Obligations of Shipowners

291. All the obligations of the shipowners under a time charter provided for in section 2 'Time Charter Parties' of Chapter VI of MC are non-compulsory by virtue of Article 127, as mentioned in §1 *supra*.

292. First, the shipowners shall deliver the agreed ship within the period of time agreed upon in the charter party at the specified port or other place of delivery (paragraph 1, Article 131, MC).

By virtue of paragraph 2 of Article 131 of MC, if the shipowners fail to fulfil this obligation for whatever reasons, the charterers are entitled to reject the ship and cancel the charter party unless a later cancelling date is expressly agreed upon, provided that the delay in delivery is not attributable to the charterers. However, as in the case of a voyage charter as provided for in Article 97 MC, if the shipowners have notified the charterers of the anticipated delay in delivery and the expected time of her arrival at the port or other place of delivery, the charterers shall notify the shipowners of their decision whether to cancel the charter or not within forty-eight hours of the receipt of such notification, failing which the charterers shall be deemed as having waived the right to cancel the charter party and the expected date of her arrival notified by the shipowners shall be the new cancelling date.

The shipowners shall be liable for the charterers' economic loss resulting from the delay in delivery of the ship as agreed upon due to the shipowners' fault unless their fault can be exempted by virtue of the applicable law or the time charter party (paragraph 3, Article 131, MC).

293. Second, the shipowners shall, at the time of delivery, exercise due diligence to make the ship seaworthy and undertake that the ship delivered be fit for the agreed service (paragraph 1, Article 132, MC).

If the shipowners fail to fulfil this obligation, the charterers shall be entitled to cancel the charter party and claim for economic loss resulting therefrom (paragraph 2, Article 132, MC).

294. Third, if the ship is found during the period of hire at variance with the seaworthiness or other conditions agreed upon in the charter party, the shipowners shall take all reasonable measures to have them restored as soon as possible (paragraph 1, Article 133, MC).

This provision is called 'maintenance clause' by virtue of which the shipowners are obliged to exercise due diligence to maintain the ship in a seaworthy and efficient state during the period of hire.

Where the ship has not been operated normally for twenty-four consecutive hours due to her failure to maintain the seaworthiness or other conditions as agreed upon, the ship shall be on off-hire, and the charterers shall not pay the hire for the operating time so lost unless such failure is caused by the charterers (paragraph 2, Article 133, MC). Such a provision is called an 'off-hire clause'. Off-hire can be deducted from the payment of the next instalment of hire. In practice, many charter parties do not contain the restriction of twenty-four consecutive hours to the effect that any time lost is subject to off-hire.

Normally, this clause also covers loss of time resulting from the ship's lower speed than the agreed one. Where the ship's consumption of bunker in her engines is higher than the agreed quantity, the shipowners shall be liable for extra consumption of bunker and the expenses thereof can also be deducted from the hire in accordance with the charter party.

295. Fourth, the shipowners shall undertake that the master obey the charterers' instructions with respect to the operation of the ship during the period of hire, provided that such instructions shall not be inconsistent with the provisions of the charter party (Article 136, MC);

This provision, together with that of indemnity, is called 'employment and indemnity clause'. Indemnity means the charterers shall indemnify the shipowners against all consequences or liabilities for the losses suffered by the cargo owners or other third party arising from the master's obedience to the charterers' instructions with respect to the operation of the ship or from the use of the ship by the charterers in other respects causing responsibility or liability of the shipowners other than that agreed upon in the charter party, especially from any inconsistency between the time charter and the bills of lading or waybills signed by the charterers on behalf of the master or by the master at their request.

II. Obligations of Charterers

296. Like the obligations of the shipowners, all the obligations of the charterers under a time charter provided for in section 2 of Chapter VI of MC are non-compulsory by virtue of Article 127, as mentioned in §1 *supra.*

297. First, the charterers shall pay the hire as agreed upon in the charter party (Article 140, MC).

Where the charterers fail to pay the hire regularly and punctually, the shipowners shall be entitled to cancel the charter party by withdrawing the ship from the contractual service and to claim for any loss resulting therefrom. Some charter party provides a grace period to the effect that the shipowners shall notify the charterers of their failure in the payment of hire, and the charterers shall pay the hire within a fixed period of time, failing which the shipowners shall be entitled to cancel the charter party by withdrawing the ship. Furthermore, in the case the charterers fail to pay the hire or other sums of money as agreed upon in the charter party, the shipowners shall have a lien on the charterers' goods and other property onboard, including the bunker onboard supplied by the charterers and the earnings from the sub-charter or other sub-contract that the charterers concluded with a third party (Article 141, MC). In addition, some charter parties provide that the shipowners may withhold their performance of the charter party to compel the charterers to pay the hire while the ship is still on-hire.

298. Second, the charterers shall guarantee that the ship be employed in the agreed carriage between the safe ports or other places within the agreed trading area to carry the agreed lawful merchandise (Articles 134 and 135, MC).

Where the charterers fail to employ the ship in the carriage between the safe ports or other places within the trading area as agreed upon in the charter party, the shipowners shall be entitled to cancel the charter party and claim for any losses resulting therefrom. In particular, the charterers shall nominate a port or other place for loading or discharge of goods which is anticipated to be physically and legally safe for the ship's arrival, stay and departure without risks which cannot be avoided by a seaworthy ship and exercise of good seamanship of the master and other crew-members. Otherwise, the shipowners or master may require the charterers to re-nominate a safe one. If the charterers fail to re-nominate, the shipowners shall be entitled to cancel the charter party and claim for any losses resulting therefrom. Where the ship is lost or damaged, or the shipowners suffer loss otherwise due to the unsafety of the port or other place nominated by the charterers, the charterers shall be liable unless the unsafety or the loss or damage is due to force majeure or fault of the part of the shipowners.

Where the charterers fail to employ the ship to carry the agreed lawful merchandise, including carrying live animals or dangerous goods, without prior consent of the shipowners, they shall be liable for any loss suffered by the shipowners resulting therefrom.

299. Third, the charterers shall redeliver the ship to the shipowners at the agreed time of redelivery at the agreed port or other place of redelivery in the same good order and condition as it was at the time of delivery, fair wear and tear excepted (Article 142, MC).

As regards the time of redelivery, if, on the basis of reasonable calculation, the chartered ship may be able to complete her last voyage around the time of redelivery specified in the charter party and probably thereafter, the charterers are allowed to continue to use the ship in order to complete that voyage. During the extended period of time, the charterers shall pay the hire at the rate fixed in the charter party or, if the current market rate of hire is higher than that specified in the charter party, at the current market rate (Article 143, MC).

Where the ship, upon redelivery, is not in the same good order and condition as it was at the time of delivery, fair wear and tear excepted, the charterers shall be responsible for rehabilitation before redelivery or for compensation for the costs of repair to the ship's damage and operation loss resulting therefrom after redelivery, unless the ship's damage was caused by force majeure, attributable to the shipowners or the charterers' liability can be exempted by virtue of the provisions of the charter party (Article 142, MC).

In practice, the ship's technical condition and bunkers remaining onboard, which shall be paid for and taken over by the charterers on delivery and by the shipowners on redelivery, are determined via on-hire or off-hire survey conducted by two surveyors appointed by the shipowners and the charterers respectively or by a single surveyor jointly appointed.

III. Other Statutory Provisions

300. The charterers may sublet the chartered ship without prior consent by the shipowners unless otherwise provided for in the charter party but shall notify the shipowners of the sublet in time. The rights and obligations agreed upon in the head charter party shall not be affected by the sub-charter party, and the charterers of the head charter party remain responsible for the performance thereof (Article 137, MC).

301. The shipowners may transfer the ownership of the chartered ship to a third person without prior consent by the charterers unless otherwise provided for in the charter party but shall notify the charterers of the transfer in time. After transfer, the transferee and the charterers shall continue to perform the original charter party, and the rights and obligations agreed upon in the original charter party shall not be affected by the transfer. Therefore, where the transferee fails to perform the charter party, the shipowners remain responsible for the performance of the original charter party (Article 138, MC).

302. Where the chartered ship is engaged in salvage operations during the charter period, the charterers shall be entitled to half of the amount of the payment for the savage operations after deducting therefrom the salvage expenses, compensation for the damage, loss or other relevant costs arising from the salvage operations and the portion due to the master and other crewmembers (Article 139, MC).

§5. Bareboat Charter Party

I. Obligations of Shipowners

303. The shipowners under a bareboat charter party have the following non-compulsory obligations:

- The shipowners shall deliver the ship and her certificates to the charterers at the port or other place and time as provided for in the charter party and, at the time of delivery, exercise due diligence to make the ship seaworthy and the ship delivered shall be fit for the agreed service, failing which the charterers shall be entitled to cancel the charter party and claim for any loss resulting therefrom (Article 146, MC).
- During the charter period, if the ship is arrested due to any dispute over her ownership or debts owed by the shipowners, the shipowners shall guarantee that the interests of the charterers will not be affected and shall be liable for compensation for any loss suffered by the charterers thereby (paragraph 2, Article 149, MC).
- The shipowners shall not establish any mortgage on the ship during the charter period without consent in writing of the charterers, failing which the charterers shall be entitled to claim for any loss resulting therefrom (Article 151, MC).

II. Obligations of Charterers

304. Besides the obligations of the charterers under a time charter provided for in Articles 134,135, 142 and 143, as mentioned in §4 *supra*, the charterers under a bareboat charter party have the following non-compulsory obligations:

- The charterers shall be responsible for the maintenance and repair of the ship during the charter period (Article 147; MC).
- The charterers shall have the ship insured at their expense at the value agreed upon in the charter party and in the way consented to by the shipowners during the charter period (Article 148; MC).
- During the charter period, if the charterers' possession, employment or operation of the ship affects the interests of the shipowners or causes any loss to the shipowners, the charterers shall be liable for eliminating the consequences or compensating for the loss (paragraph 1, Article 149, MC).
- During the charter period, the charterers shall not assign the rights and obligations provided for in the charter party or sublet the ship under another bareboat charter party without the shipowners' consent in writing (Article 150, MC); otherwise, the shipowners can cancel the charter party and claim for loss resulting therefrom.

305. Noticeably, the charterers' primary obligation is to pay the hire agreed upon in the bareboat charter party. In the case of default of payment, a statutory grace period of seven consecutive days is provided for in paragraph 1 of Article 152 of MC. As a result, the shipowners may cancel the bareboat charter party by withdrawing the ship from the service only in the case of default of payment by the charterers for seven consecutive days or more after the time as agreed in the charter party for such payment, unless otherwise provided for in the charter party. Cancellation of the charter party is without prejudice to the shipowners' claim for the loss arising from the charterers' default.

In addition, should the ship be lost or missing, payment of hire shall cease from the day when she was lost or last heard of, and any hire paid in advance shall be refunded to the charterers in proportion (paragraph 2, Article 152, MC).

III. Other Statutory Provisions

306. The period of hire under a bareboat charter party shall not exceed twenty years; otherwise, the period of time exceeding twenty years shall be of no effect (paragraph 1, Article 705, CC).

307. By virtue of Article 725 of CC, where the ownership of the ship under a bareboat charter party is transferred by the shipowners, the bareboat charter party shall not be affected, and the shipowners and the charterers shall remain responsible for the performance of the charter party. Particularly, the right of the charterers in the use of the ship under the charter party shall not be affected by the transfer of ownership of the ship.

Chapter 6. Transport under Bill of Lading and Other Documents

§1. Definitions and Functions of Bill of Lading

I. Definition of Bill of Lading

308. Bills of lading (B/L) originated around the fourteenth century as a non-negotiable receipt issued by the shipowners for cargo received from a merchant who did not intend to travel with his goods.[33] Bills of lading have been playing a very important role in international trade, and their functions have been developed in modern times of maritime transport.

309. A bill of lading is defined in Article 71 of MC as 'a document which serves as evidence of the contract of carriage of goods by sea and the taking over or loading of the goods by the carrier, and based on which the carrier undertakes to deliver the goods against surrendering the same'.

This definition is the same as that contained in Article 1(7) of the Hamburg Rules.

II. Functions of Bill of Lading

310. From its definition cited *supra*, a bill of lading is deemed as having the following three functions.

A. *Evidence of Contract of Carriage of Goods by Sea*

311. A bill of lading is not a contract of carriage of goods by sea itself in nature but only an evidence thereof, no matter who is the holder thereof. This is because a contract of carriage had already been concluded between the carrier and the shipper before the issuance of bill of lading by the carrier, master of the carrying vessel or the agent of the carrier when the carrier or his agent accepted the demand (offer) of the shipper or its agent, commonly a freight forwarder, for the carriage of goods by sea. Therefore, the issuance of bill of lading is only a link in the performance of contract by the carrier.

However, a bill of lading serves not only as evidence of the existence of the contract of carriage of goods by sea but, more importantly, as evidence of the contents thereof. The forms of bills of lading of shipping companies are shaped in advance and known to the public. Before the conclusion of contract of carriage between the carrier and the shipper, the shipper normally has known or should have known the form and terms of the bill of lading to be issued. Where the form of bill of lading is provided by the shipper, the shipper knows or should have known every term of

33. Wilson, J., *Carriage of Goods by Sea*, London, 2008, 123.

the bill. The particulars of goods contained in the bill of lading are normally furnished by the shipper. Therefore, the contents of the bill of lading issued by the carrier or other person on its behalf shall be deemed as accepted by the shipper impliedly if no objection thereto was raised by the shipper before the conclusion of contract or issuance of bill. Unless the shipper can prove that an agreement to the contrary, known as a special agreement as referred to in the Hague Rules, has been reached with the carrier or, at the time of conclusion of the contract or before the issuance of bill of lading, the shipper did not know or should not have known the terms of the bill of lading because the bill issued is not in the agreed or the carrier's or usual terms, the contents of bill issued shall be deemed as those of the contract of carriage of goods by sea.

312. When a bill of lading is consigned or transferred to a third party, i.e., the consignee named in a straight bill or the endorsee of an order bill or the holder of a bearer bill, the rights and obligations between the carrier and the third party shall be determined in accordance with the bill of lading. In this respect, Article 78 of MC expressly provides that the relations between the carrier and the consignee or holder of the bill of lading with respect to their rights and obligations shall be determined by the clauses of the bill of lading, provided that the clauses of the bill shall not be repugnant to the mandatory provisions contained in Chapter IV thereof. Where a bill of lading is in the hands of a third party other than the shipper, the special agreement, if any, concluded between the carrier and the shipper besides the bill of lading shall have no effect on the third party unless the third party agreed to be bound by such agreement. However, the carrier and the shipper shall not be discharged from the obligations and liabilities under the bill of lading and/or special agreement to each other because of the consignment or transfer of the bill.

Unlike the Carriage of Goods by Sea Act, 1992 (1992 COGSA) in the UK or the Pomerence Act in the US, there is no bill of lading law in China now, except for the limited provisions of MC in this regard. As a result, some problems regarding the rights and obligations of a lawful holder of bill of lading as a consequence of consignment or transfer thereof are still not completely solved. As a principle in admiralty practice, however, it is decided that any person without holding an original bill of lading, including the consignee named in a straight bill cannot exert any right against the carrier on the basis of bill of lading.

B. Evidence of Taking over or Loading of Goods by Carrier

313. Where a bill of lading is in the hands of the shipper or regulates the relations between the carrier and the shipper, it serves as prima facie evidence of the taking over of goods in the case of a received-for-shipment bill or the loading of goods in the case of a shipped bill as described in it by the carrier. Therefore, the carrier is allowed to prove that the goods actually received or loaded were not consistent with those described in the bill and, thus shall not be responsible for the inconsistency.

However, where a bill of lading has been consigned or transferred to a third party acting in good faith in reliance on the description of the goods contained in the bill, it serves as conclusive evidence of the taking over or the loading of goods by the carrier. Thus, the carrier is estopped from proving any inconsistency between the goods actually received or loaded and those described in the bill unless the bill contains an express note of inconsistency or an effective 'unknown clause'.

The statutory provision in this respect is contained in Article 77 of MC, which provides that, except for the note, normally called as remark or reservation, made in accordance with the provisions of Article 75 of MC, the bill of lading issued by the carrier or the other person acting on his behalf is prima facie evidence of the taking over or the loading by the carrier of the goods as described therein; proof to the contrary by the carrier shall not be admissible, if the bill of lading has been transferred to a third party including a consignee who has acted in good faith. As a matter of construction, such a third party should also be in reliance on the description of goods contained therein. For example, a bill of lading contains a statement of 100 TV sets as description of goods, but only 95 TV sets are discharged and delivered to the consignee other than the shipper. The carrier proves the number of TV sets received and loaded at the port of loading was 95. In such a case, if the consignee paid for 100 TV sets as described in the bill of lading, he was in reliance on the statement of 100 TV sets and the statement constitutes a conclusive evidence as against the carrier; if the consignee paid for 95 TV sets as delivered to him, he was not in reliance on the statement and therefore the statement is still prima facie evidence.

314. By virtue of Article 75 of MC, if a bill of lading contains particulars concerning the description, mark, number of packages or pieces, weight or quantity of goods with respect to which the carrier or the other person issuing the bill of lading on his behalf has the knowledge or reasonable grounds to suspect that such particulars do not accurately represent the goods actually received or, where a shipped bill of lading is issued, loaded, or if he has had no reasonable means of checking, the carrier or such other person may make a note in the bill of lading specifying those inaccuracies, the grounds for suspicion or the lack of reasonable means of checking.

Therefore, a reservation in a bill of lading is effective only where the carrier or other person issuing the bill of lading on his behalf (a) has the knowledge that such particulars do not accurately represent the goods actually received or loaded, or (b) has reasonable grounds to suspect the accuracy of the particulars of goods described in the bill, or (c) has no reasonable means of checking the particulars. By this criterion, a reservation as to the quantity of bulk cargo is normally effective, because the carrier, the master or the carrier's agent issuing the bill of lading on his behalf normally does not know the accurate figure of the quantity of bulk cargo loaded. However, an effective reservation can protect the carrier only to a reasonable extent. That is, if the quantity of the alleged shortage of cargo exceeds a reasonable extent and thus the carrier or other person issuing the bill of lading on his behalf knew or should have known the inaccuracy, then the carrier cannot exempt his liability by virtue of such a reservation. A reservation as to the number of packages of packed cargo is normally invalid by the above criterion, unless contained in a container stowed and sealed by the shipper, but may be valid as to the weight thereof, unless the goods or the loaded container was duly weighed.

By virtue of the provisions of Article 75 of MC mentioned *supra*, a reservation shall specify the grounds for suspicion or the lack of reasonable means of checking. However, such specifications are seldom contained in the reservations. In shipping practice, a reservation is often in the form of an 'unknown clause' indicating 'shipper's weight', 'said to be', 'said to contain' or other similar statements. Nevertheless, such indications are normally confirmed by the maritime courts in China as satisfy the requirements of Article 75 of MC.

C. *Document Based upon Which Carrier Undertakes to Deliver Goods Against Surrendering the Same*

315. The carrier or his agent at the port of discharge or other destination shall deliver the goods to the consignee named in a straight bill of lading, or the endorsee contained in the endorsement of an order bill of lading, or the holder of a bearer bill, as the case may be, against surrendering the bill of lading (Article 71, MC).

316. The provisions of Article 71 of MC provide the statutory basis for solving the disputes of delivery of goods against a letter of undertaking without production of original bill of lading that occur very often in practice, especially in the carriage of oil or other liquefied goods in bulk, containerized goods or in international short sea trade, mainly because the ships sail faster than the transfer of bill of lading in the modern time. In other words, it is clear that delivery by the carrier or his agent of goods without production of original bill of lading is illegal, whether it is a named bill, order bill or bearer bill.

SPC promulgated the *Provisions on Certain Issues of Application of Law in the Trial of Cases of Delivery of Goods without Original Bills of Lading* on 26 February 2009. By virtue of this judicial interpretation, the carrier shall be held liable for the economic losses suffered by the lawful holder of bill of lading, except under the following circumstances: (a) the carrier delivered the goods to the customs or port authority at discharge port as required by the law of the place of the discharge port, (b) the goods were taken delivery of and sold by the customs at the discharge port due to the consignee's failure in customs declaration of the goods within the time stipulated in law, (c) the goods were sold by a court of law by virtue of an award as consequence of the carrier's lien on the goods, or (d) the carrier returned the goods to the shipper or delivered the goods to other consignee as required by the shipper of a named bill of lading as a result of his exercise of right of control on the goods as provided for in Article 829 of CC.[34] The loss suffered by the lawful holder of a bill of lading resulting from carrier's delivery of goods without production of bill of lading shall be calculated on the basis of the value of the goods at the time of loading plus freight and insurance premium, i.e., the Cost, Insurance and Freight (CIF) price of the goods. Where the carrier is liable for delivery of goods without

34. Article 829 of CC provides: 'Prior to the carrier's delivery of cargo to the consignee, the shipper may require the carrier to suspend the carriage, return the cargo, change the destination or deliver the cargo to another consignee, but shall compensate the carrier for any loss thus caused.'

production of bill of lading, the carrier cannot avail of the limitation of liability for loss of or damage to goods as provided for in Article 56 of MC.

D. Arguments Concerning Bill of Lading as Document of Title

317. In the English maritime law books, a bill of lading is described as having the function of a document of title to the goods. According to some authors, a bill of lading as a document of title represents the goods covered by it or is a symbol thereof and this function implies that the carrier is obliged to deliver the goods to the lawful holder of bill as against production thereof. However, there is no official concept of document of title under Chinese law. In addition, no prevailing Chinese law recognizes a bill of lading as representing the goods described in it or a symbol of the goods.

In Black's Law Dictionary, a document of title is described as 'including bill of lading, dock warrant, dock receipt, warehouse receipt or order for the delivery of goods, and also any other document which in the regular course of business or financing is treated as adequately evidencing that the person in possession of it is entitled to receive, hold and dispose of the document and the goods it covers'.[35]

318. In Article 440 of section 2 'Pledge on Rights' of Chapter VIII 'Pledge' of Book Two of CC, a bill of lading is listed as one of the rights which can be used for pledge like a draft, cheque, bond or deposit receipt. Thus, Chinese law enables the lawful holder of a bill of lading as pledger to use for pledge his right to take delivery of goods by virtue of MC and possess the goods covered by the bill or to dispose of the bill, by surrendering the bill to the pledgee.

319. It seems obvious, or at least there is a tendency, that the rights and obligations under a contract of carriage of goods by sea evidenced by a bill of lading divorce from the function of bill of lading as a document of title in the modern world. Following the Hamburg Rules, MC does not define bill of lading as a document of title.

However, this function of bill of lading can be understood to be existing conditionally in the area of documentary sale of goods and financing as commercial practice and usage in China, It enables a lawful holder of bill of lading to sell the goods by transferring or negotiating the bill to the buyer while the goods is in transit or to use it as security for repayment for a debt. The conditions on which a bill of lading serves as a document of title in documentary sale of goods may, as some English books often describe, include: (a) the bill must be transferable on its face; (b) the goods must be in transit at the time of the transfer; (c) the bill must be initiated by a person with good title; and (d) the transfer of the bill must be accompanied by an intention to transfer the ownership in the goods covered by the bill.

320. As regards the negotiability or transferability of a bill of lading, Article 79 of MC expressly provides that a straight bill is not negotiable, an order bill may be

35. Black, C., *Black's Law Dictionary*, St. Paul, 1979, 432.

negotiated with special endorsement or endorsement in blank, and a bearer bill is negotiable without endorsement. It is understood that a bearer bill is negotiable by delivery thereof.

§2. Contents and Issuance of Bill of Lading

I. Particulars to Be Contained

321. By virtue of paragraph 1 of Article 73 of MC, the particulars to be contained in a bill of lading shall include the following:

- the description of the goods, mark, number of packages or pieces, weight or quantity, and a statement, if applicable, as to the dangerous nature of the goods;
- the name and principal place of business of the carrier;
- the name of the ship;
- the name of the shipper;
- the name of the consignee;
- the port of loading and the date on which the goods were taken over by the carrier at the port of loading;
- the port of discharge;
- the place where the goods were taken over and the place where the goods are to be delivered in case of a multimodal transport bill of lading;
- the date and place of issue of the bill of lading and the number of original bills of lading issued;
- the payment of freight;
- the signature of the carrier or of a person acting on his behalf.

Noticeably, unlike a straight bill of lading, an order or bearer bill of lading does not indicate the name of consignee. Thus, the expression of 'the name of the consignee' contained in paragraph 1 of Article 73 of MC need be understood to mean the name or other description of the consignee.

Paragraph 2 of Article 73 further provides that the lack of one or more particulars in a bill of lading referred to in paragraph 1 of this Article does not affect the function of the bill of lading as such, provided that it nevertheless meets the requirements set forth in Article 71 of MC. However, it has never been decided, and is difficult to decide in fact, which particulars are musts and which can be lacked in a bill of lading.

322. In shipping practice, it often occurs, where a bill of lading is issued by the carrier's agent, the bill of lading does not indicate the name of carrier, but only indicates that the agent signed the bill 'for and on behalf of carrier as agent only'. Where a bill of lading is issued by the master or an agent 'for and on behalf of the master', it also does not indicate the name of carrier. Thus, it is often difficult for the consignee other than the shipper to identify the carrier.

In the admiralty practice in China, generally speaking, the carrier is identified as follows: (a) where a bill of lading indicate the name of carrier, the named carrier shall be identified as the carrier; (b) where a bill of lading is issued by a ship's agent without indicating the name of carrier, the carrier shall be identified by virtue of the provisions of agency contained in CC; (c) where a bill of lading is issued by the master or for and on behalf of the master, presumably the registered shipowners is identified as the carrier, but is allowed to prove that the ship is bareboat chartered out in which case the bareboat charterers shall be identified as the carrier, or otherwise prove another person is the carrier. However, the criteria for the identification of carrier have not been unified yet.

Where a bill of lading form of a shipping company is used, it does not necessarily mean this shipping company is the carrier. However, the *Regulations on International Maritime Transport of 2001* require registration of the forms of the bill of lading to be issued in China and each form shall indicate the name of the carrier. Thus, registration of the forms of the bill of lading is helpful for the consignee to identify the carrier

II. Obligation to Issue

323. As provided for in paragraph 1 of Article 72 of MC, on demand of the shipper, the carrier is obliged to issue to the shipper a received-for-shipment bill of lading where the goods have been taken over by the carrier for shipment, or a shipped bill of lading where the goods have been loaded onboard.

The bill of lading shall be issued in conformity with the mate's receipt (M/R) or dock receipt (D/R) in the case of containerized goods.

The carrier shall issue bill of lading within a reasonable time after the goods have been received or loaded onboard if so demanded by the shipper.

324. In some circumstances, the carrier is justified to refuse issuance of bill of lading as demanded by the shipper, e.g., where the shipper demands a freight prepaid bill of lading without payment of freight, or an anti-dated or advanced bill of lading, or a bill of lading not in conformity with the goods actually received or loaded by the carrier.

III. Issuers

325. Besides the carrier himself, a bill of lading may be issued by a person, normally the ship's agent at the port of loading, thus authorized by the carrier for and on behalf of him in accordance with paragraph 2 of Article 72 of MC.

The master of the carrying vessel has a statutory power to issue bill of lading in his own name. Such a bill of lading is deemed as have been signed on behalf of the carrier and is binding upon the carrier. The master can also authorize a person, normally the ship's agent at the port of loading, to issue bill of lading and the person so authorized shall issue for and behalf of the master.

§3. Types of Bills of Lading

I. Ordinary Bills of Lading

326. In accordance with the name of consignee contained in a bill of lading, bills of lading can be divided into:

– straight bill of lading indicating the name of consignee;
– order bill of lading stating the consignee is to order or to order by a certain person or company;
– bearer bill of lading simply stating the consignee is the 'bearer'.

327. In accordance with whether the goods have been loaded onboard or not, bills of lading can be divided into:

– shipped or onboard bill of lading issued after loading of the goods onboard indicating the name of the carrying ship and even the date of loading;
– received-for-shipment bill of lading issued after the taking over by the carrier of the goods for shipment, but before loading thereof.

As provided for in Article 74 of MC, if the carrier has issued on demand of the shipper a received-for-shipment bill of lading before the goods are loaded onboard, the shipper may surrender the same to the carrier as against a shipped bill of lading when the goods have been loaded onboard; the carrier may also note on the received-for-shipment bill of lading with the name of the carrying ship and the date of loading, and, when so noted, the received-for-shipment bill of lading shall be deemed as a shipped bill of lading.

328. In accordance with whether there is remark or reservation on the goods or not, bills of lading can be divided into:

– clean bill of lading without any remark or reservation as to the apparent order and condition of the goods;
– unclean or foul bill of lading with a remark or reservation indicating that the goods are not in apparent good order and condition.

329. In accordance with the mode of transport, bills of lading can be divided into:

– direct bill of lading in the sense that the goods shall be carried from the port or other place of loading to the port or other place of destination by the carrying ship without change of ship *en route*;
– ocean through bill of lading in the sense that the carriage of goods shall be performed by two or more ocean carriers successively;
– multimodal or combined or intermodal transport bill of lading issued in the case of multimodal transport of goods including international carriage by sea.

II. Other Bills of Lading

330. In international shipping practice, the following bills of lading are sometime issued, either as demanded by the shipper or due to commercial requirements:

- anti-dated bill of lading in which the date of issuance indicated is earlier than the actual date of issuance and the issuance of which by the carrier is deemed as illegal in admiralty practice;
- advanced bill of lading which is a shipped bill of lading issued before the loading of the goods and the issuance of which by the carrier is also deemed as illegal in admiralty practice;
- on deck bill of lading marked 'on deck' or 'stowed on deck' for the goods carried on deck;
- parcel bill of lading issued for the carriage of parcels;
- switch bill of lading issued to replace the bill of lading originally issued and indicate different port or other place of loading or discharge;
- minimum bill of lading issued for the goods where minimum freight is applicable;
- omnibus bill of lading issued for the goods of two or more consignments;
- separate bill of lading issued for part of the goods of a consignment;
- short form or simple bill of lading which does not contain detailed clauses at the back page as opposed to long form bill of lading.

§4. Bill of Lading Issued under Charter Party

I. Concept

331. A bill of lading issued under a charter party, or a bill of lading under a charter party, means a bill of lading issued for the goods carried under a charter party.

In the carriage of goods by sea under a charter party, when the goods have been loaded onboard, the charterers under CIF, cost and freight (CFR) or a similar term, or the shipper defined in Article 4(3)(b) of MC under free on board (FOB) or a similar term, usually demands the shipowners (carrier) to issue to him bills of lading for the purpose of settlement of exchange or documentary sale of goods. Thus, two contractual documents, i.e., the charter party and the bill of lading exist simultaneously for the same carriage of goods.

The two documents often do not coincide with each other, because a charter party is concluded between the shipowners and the charterers on the basis of the principle of freedom of contract, whereas the terms of bill of lading are subject to the compulsory statutory provisions of an international convention or national law.

II. Nature of Bill of Lading Issued under Charter Party

332. When a bill of lading issued under a charter party is in the hands of the charterers regulating the relations between the shipowners and the charterers, the contractual document binding upon them is the charter party. The bill of lading does not have the function of the evidence of contract, unless the charter party expressly provides to the contrary or otherwise the two parties have the intention that their legal relations shall be wholly or partly governed by the bill of lading.

When a bill of lading issued under a charter party is in the hands of a third party other than the charterers, the legal relations between the carrier *viz.* the shipowners under the charter party and the holder of bill of lading shall be governed by the bill of lading. In this regard, it is expressly provided for in Article 95 of MC that where the holder of bill of lading is not the charterers in the case of a bill of lading issued under a voyage charter, the rights and obligations of the carrier and the holder of bill of lading shall be governed by the clauses of the bill of lading.

III. Incorporation Clause

333. As the shipowners under a charter party is usually also the carrier under the bill of lading issued thereunder, the shipowners may hope that their rights and obligations under the charter party and those under the bill of lading with respect to the same carriage of goods are the same, although where they incur more liabilities to the holder of the bill of lading other than the charterers than those to the charterers under the charter party, they are entitled to make a recourse against the charterers for the extra liability by virtue of the employment and indemnity clause in the charter party. This is the main reason why an incorporation clause is usually contained in a bill of lading issued under a charter party to the effect that certain terms of the charter party shall be incorporated into the bill and that the holder of bill, though not a party to the charter party, shall be bound *ex facto* by the charter party incorporated to some extent.

By virtue of Article 95 of MC, where the clauses of a voyage charter party are incorporated into a bill of lading, the relevant clauses of the voyage charter party shall apply. This is a principled provision acknowledging the effect of an incorporation clause.

A typical incorporation clause is the one contained in the Congenbill Form of Bill of Lading 2022 that expressly provides: 'All terms and conditions, liberties and exceptions of the Charter Party, dated as overleaf are herewith incorporated. If the date of the Charter Party is not specified, the relevant charter party is deemed to be the voyage charter party that regulates the carriage of the cargo in respect of which this Bill of Lading has been issued.'

334. In admiralty practice in China, an incorporation clause is as a whole strictly construed in order to protect the interests of the holder of bill of lading other than the charterers. For example, if the date of the charter party to be incorporated is not clearly indicated at the front page of the bill of lading, an incorporation clause may not bring out the effect of incorporation. Strict attitude is also towards the incorporation into the bill of lading of the arbitration clause or even the paramount clause contained in the charter party. The incorporation of the arbitration clause is effective only if it meets the requirements of an effective arbitration agreement set forth in AL. In reality, it often does not meet the requirements, unless expressly accepted by the holder of bill of lading.

§5. International Conventions on Carriage of Goods by Sea

335. As introduced in §1 of Chapter 2 of Part I, China is not a party to the Hague Rules, the Hague-Visby Rules, the Hamburg Rules or the Rotterdam Rules. However, the Hague-Visby Rules and the Hamburg Rules had a significant value of reference in shaping the provisions of contract of carriage of goods by sea in Chapter IV of MC.

The provisions of Chapter IV of MC are a mixture of the Hague-Visby Rules and the Hamburg Rules and adopted a hybrid carrier's liability regime. In principle, they are mainly based upon the Hague-Visby Rules as amended by the SDR Protocol in essence, although they seemingly look more like a copy of the Hamburg Rules. The provisions concerning the carrier's obligations of exercising due diligence to make the ship seaworthy, care for cargo and no unreasonable deviation, and his exemptions and limitation of liability for loss of or damage to goods are basically incorporated from the Hague-Visby Rules. Those concerning the various definitions, carriage of live animals and deck cargo, legal status of the carrier's servants and agent and actual carrier, shipper's responsibilities, transport documents, etc., were laid down by reference to the corresponding provisions in the Hamburg Rules.[36] In addition, several provisions including, *inter alia*, the period of carrier's responsibility, the indemnity of loss of or damage to goods, the shipper's obligation of going through formalities for the carriage of goods, are of Chinese characters.

§6. Responsibilities of Carrier

I. Definitions

336. The carrier's responsibilities are governed by section 3 of Chapter IV of MC. The following definitions incorporated from the Hamburg Rules and contained in Article 42 of MC are concerned:

- 'Carrier' means the person by whom or in whose name a contract of carriage of goods by sea has been concluded with a shipper.
- 'Shipper' means (a) the person by whom or in whose name or on whose behalf a contract of carriage of goods by sea has been concluded with a carrier; (b) the person by whom or in whose name or on whose behalf the goods have been delivered to the carrier involved in the contract of carriage of goods by sea.

36. Hu, Z. & Huybrechts, M., 'The Underlying Principles & Highlights of the Maritime Code of P.R. China', XXX(3) *European Transport Law*, 1995.

- 'Actual carrier' means the person to whom the performance of carriage of goods or part thereof has been entrusted by the carrier including any other person to whom such performance has been entrusted under a sub-contract.
- 'Consignee' means the person who is entitled to take delivery of goods.
- 'Goods' includes live animals and containers, pallets or similar articles of transport supplied by the shipper for consolidation of the goods.

337. The adoption of the second kind of shipper as cited *supra*, i.e., the FOB seller in most cases, caused questions in admiralty practice in the past. In an FOB trade, the two shippers may exist in the same carriage of goods, i.e., the buyer who concluded a contract of carriage with the carrier is the shipper (a), and the seller who delivered to goods to the carrier or actual carrier is the shipper (b). In admiralty practice in China, if both shippers demand issuance of bills of lading, the carrier should issue the bills of lading to shipper (b). MC does not differentiate the two shippers concerning their rights and obligations. Thus, the question is whether the two shippers have the same rights and obligations. It seems necessary or at least advisable to differentiate the two shippers in respect of their rights and obligations to the effect that the rights and obligations of the shipper (b) shall be limited to those concerning delivery of goods to the carrier or actual carrier. However, if the shipper (b) fails to perform his obligations, the shipper (a) shall be liable for loss or damage suffered by the carrier or actual carrier resulting therefrom. Thus, the liability of the two shippers shall be joint and several to the extent that the shipper (b) is liable.

II. Period of Carrier's Responsibility

338. Different periods of carrier's responsibility for containerized goods and non-containerized goods are provided for in Article 46 of MC.

The responsibility of the carrier with regard to the containerized goods, whether of full container load (FCL) or of less than container load (LCL), covers the entire period during which the carrier is in charge of the goods, starting from the time the carrier has taken over the goods at the port of loading until the goods have been delivered at the port of discharge. This is because the containerized goods are normally taken over or delivered by the carrier in liner shipping at the container yards (CY) within the loading or discharge port or at container freight station (CFS) within or outside the loading or discharge port, as the case may be.

The responsibility of the carrier with respect to the non-containerized goods covers the period during which the carrier is in charge of the foods, starting from the time of loading of the goods onto the ship until the time the goods are discharged therefrom. However, the carrier may enter into any agreement with the shipper concerning the carrier's responsibility prior to loading onto and after discharging from the ship in the case of non-containerized goods. Therefore, a 'before and after clause' contained in a bill of lading is effective under MC.

The provision of period of carrier's responsibility concerning the containerized goods is incorporated from Article 4(1) of the Hamburg Rules and that concerning non-containerized is shaped by reference to Article 1(5) and Article 7 of the Hague Rules in essence.

339. It is expressly provided for in Article 46 of MC that the carrier shall be liable for the loss of or damage to the goods occurred during the period of responsibility, except as otherwise provided for. In the construction of this provision, however, the carrier's liability for loss of or damage to goods shall not be limited to those occurred during the period of responsibility. In other words, if loss of or damage to goods occurs after the expiration of the period of responsibility, but is caused by an occurrence that took place during the period of responsibility, the carrier shall also be held liable, unless his liability can be exempted by virtue of Articles 51, etc., of MC.

III. Main Obligations of Carrier

A. *Exercise of Due Diligence to Make Ship Seaworthy*

340. MC expressly provides in Article 47 that the carrier shall, before and at the beginning of the voyage, exercise due diligence to make the ship seaworthy, properly man, equip and supply the ship and to make the holds, refrigerating and cool chambers and all other parts of the ship in which goods are carried, fit and safe for their reception, carriage and preservation. This provision is a copy of Article 3(1) of the Hague Rules.

341. A seaworthy ship means she is in such a technical state as enables her to withstand all the risks she is reasonably expected to encounter during the contractual voyage.

In a narrow sense, the world 'ship' in Article 47 of MC refers to her hull and machinery. In a broad sense, ship's seaworthiness also cover her proper manning, equipment, supply of bunkers, stores and provisions and cargo-worthiness with respect to her holds, other cargo spaces and cargo handling gears. It is very important to note that, in the determination of ship's seaworthiness, the international conventions mainly adopted by IMO and ratified or acceded to by China shall be followed. These conventions include, *inter alia*, SOLAS, STCW, MARPOL 73/78, COLREGs and Load Line Convention, as mentioned in §1 of Chapter 2 of Part I *supra*. It needs to be mentioned that a lack of ISM as required by the ISM Code may constitute unseaworthiness of a ship.

342. In admiralty practice in China, the term 'voyage' is construed to mean the contractual or bill of lading voyage from the port or other place of loading to the port or other place of discharge, although a few scholars have the view that the term should mean the voyage between two ports, i.e., if there is a port of call during the contractual voyage, there are two voyages, i.e., one from the port of loading to the port of call and the other from the port of call to the port of discharge. Thus, the obligation to exercise due diligence only exists at the port or other place of loading and is not continuous during the voyage.

343. 'Due diligence' is not a legal term in Chinese traditional law. It means all reasonable measures that should be taken by the carrier under the circumstances of a particular case.

In addition, by virtue of the principle of vicarious liability or *respondent superior*,[37] the carrier shall be responsible for the fault or negligence of the master, other crewmembers, other servants or agents under his employment or agency, as well as the independent contractors such as ship repairer, ship surveyor or compass adjuster who were entrusted by the carrier to perform his obligation of the exercise of due diligence to make the ship seaworthy.

Where a ship proves unseaworthy, the carrier has the burden of proving exercise of due diligence based upon sufficient and reliable supporting evidence. In the admiralty practice in China, a valid certificate of seaworthiness or similar technical certificates issued by a classification society shall not constitute conclusive evidence of the ship's seaworthiness and the exercise of due diligence by the carrier and even cannot serve as prima facie evidence thereof. This is because almost all the ships carry onboard valid certificates showing her seaworthiness, whatever the titles of certificates are, but some ships are not in a completely seaworthy state de facto, especially where the certificates are issued by the so-called 'classification societies of convenience'. It is not abnormal in admiralty practice in China that the evidential effect of a technical certificate is overridden by a ship's survey report or other positive evidence showing the unseaworthiness of ship or the failure on the part of the carrier to exercise due diligence before and at the beginning of the voyage and thus the evidential effect of the certificate is denied by a maritime court.

B. Care for Goods

344. As provided for in Article 48 of MC, the carrier shall properly and carefully load, handle, stow, carry, keep, care for and discharge the goods carried. This provision is incorporated from Article 3(2) of the Hague Rules. Under a voyage charter party or otherwise, however, if the loading, stowage, handling or discharge of goods is performed by the shipper or consignee as agreed upon between the carrier and the shipper, the carrier shall not liable for loss of or damage to the goods arising from such operations by virtue of the carrier's immunity of liability of 'act of the shipper, owner of the goods or their agents' provided for in Article 51 of MC, provided that the carrier's obligation of exercise of due diligence to make the ship seaworthy shall not be relieved.

C. Without Unreasonable Deviation

345. As required by paragraph 1 of Article 49 of MC, the carrier shall carry the goods to the port of discharge on the agreed or customary or geographically direct route. Therefore, if the route of carriage has been agreed upon between the carrier

37. *See* §1, Ch. 4 of Part II.

and the shipper, the ship shall follow the agreed route; if no route has been agreed upon, the ship shall follow the customary route between the port of loading and the port of discharge; if there is no agreed route nor customary route, the ship shall sail in the geographically direct route, i.e., the shortest route between the port of loading and the port of discharge on the condition that the safety of carriage will be ensured.

346. Reasonable deviation from the required route is allowed and shall not be deemed to be a breach of law. Deviation for the purpose of saving or attempting to save life or property at sea is deemed as reasonable, so is any other reasonable deviation, e.g., a deviation for the common safety or interests of the ship and the cargo or made in compliance with any governmental order or instruction (paragraph 2, Article 49, MC).

Under Chinese law, deviation is limited to the geographical sense only, in contrast to the Anglo-American law in which deviation may cover material breach of contract, e.g., unauthorized or illegal stowage of cargo on open deck.

D. Delivery of Goods Within Agreed Time

347. Paragraph 1 of Article 50 of MC provides that delay in delivery occurs when the goods have not been delivered at the designated port of discharge with the time expressly agreed upon. Thus, where time of delivery is expressly agreed upon between the carrier and the shipper, the carrier is obliged to deliver the goods within this expressly agreed time. Failure to deliver the goods with the expressly agreed time constitutes delay in delivery. The agreed time of delivery should be in express form and thus cannot be presumed.

348. Noticeably, in accordance with paragraph 1 of Article 50 of MC, where no time of delivery has been expressly agreed upon, no delay in delivery shall occur, even if the carrier fails to deliver the goods within the time which it would be reasonable to require of a diligent carrier, having regard to the circumstances of the case. Under the Hamburg Rules, however, such a case also constitutes delay in delivery. The approach of agreed time was adopted in MC mainly for two reasons. First, the meaning of a 'reasonable' time and 'diligent' carrier is uncertain and too vague and may easily cause disputes. Second, before the Hamburg Rules would be widely accepted, full adoption of the scope of delay in delivery from the Hamburg Rules would put on the Chinese carriers a heavier burden than under the Hague-Visby Rules. Also noticeably, Article 21 of the Rotterdam Rules adopted almost the same approach as Article 50 of MC and provides that delay in delivery occurs when the goods are not delivered at the place of destination provided for in the contract of carriage within the time agreed. The only difference is that the Rotterdam Rules does not contain the word 'expressly' before the words 'time agreed'.

It was anticipated by the draftsmen of MC that most shippers would negotiate time of delivery with the carriers in consideration of adoption of the single criterion of agreed time. In shipping practice after the coming into force of MC, however, shippers seldom did so, as a result of which unreasonable results may occur, e.g., where there is a long delay during voyage due to ship's unseaworthiness or even unreasonable deviation, the shipper or consignee is not entitled to claim for pure economic losses against the carrier due to lack of expressly agreed time of delivery.

Article 811 in Chapter XIX 'Contracts of Carriage' of Book Three of CC provides that the carrier shall carry cargoes to the agreed place within agreed time or reasonable time. However, this provision applies to the domestic carriage of goods only and does not override paragraph 1 of Article 50 of MC in international carriage of goods by sea, because the provisions of MC as special law have priority over those of CC as basic law.

349. As regards the carrier's liability for delay in delivery, paragraph 2 of Article 50 of MC provides: 'The carrier shall be liable for the loss of or damage to the goods caused by delay in delivery due to the fault of the carrier, except those arising or resulting from causes for which the carrier is not liable as provided for in the relevant articles of this Chapter.' Paragraph 3 further provides: 'The carrier shall be liable for the economic losses caused by delay in delivery of the goods due to the fault of the carrier, even if no loss of or damage to the goods had actually occurred unless such economic losses has occurred from causes for which the carrier is not liable as provided for in the relevant articles of this Chapter.'

However, the exemptions of liability provided for in Article 51 do not literally cover the economic losses caused by delay in delivery. This is an oversight made by the draftsmen of MC in forming this article by reference to Article 4(2) of the Hague-Visby Rules that do not contain the concept of delay in delivery. Nevertheless, these exemptions should cover delay in delivery and this is the case in admiralty practice in China as a matter of construction of Article 51 of MC.

The economic losses referred to above include, *inter alia,* the loss of market, extra import tax or port disbursements levied on the goods due to the late arrival thereof, or the consignee's liability for breach of contract of sale to an end-user.

Paragraph 3 of Article 50 provides that the person entitled to make a claim for the loss of goods may treat the goods as lost when the carrier has not delivered the goods within sixty days from the expiry of the time for delivery expressly agreed upon.

§7. Rights of Carrier

I. Claim for Freight, Dead Freight and Other Expenses

A. *Claim for Freight*

350. Freight is the reward for the carrier's transport service and payment thereof is the main obligation of the shipper.

The shipper shall pay freight to the carrier as agreed upon (paragraph 1, Article 69, MC). The amount of freight or calculation thereof, time, place and method of payment are all subject to agreement between the carrier and the shipper. In liner shipping, the rate of freight is normally fixed in the tariff of the carrier, liner conference or the shipper. Sometime, the freight is collected on a lump sum basis.

The carrier and the shipper can reach an agreement that the freight shall be paid by the consignee. However, such an agreement shall be stated in a bill of lading, sea waybill (SWB) or other transport document (paragraph 2, Article 69, MC). Otherwise, the consignee other than the shipper is not obliged to pay the freight.

351. In shipping practice, freight can be divided into prepaid freight and freight to be collected in accordance with the time of payment.

Prepaid freight, or the so-called advance freight, shall be paid by the time when the bill of lading marked 'freight prepaid' is issued, unless the carrier and the shipper have agreed otherwise. It need be mentioned that, unlike the traditional non-returnable nature of the prepaid freight under the English common law, Article 835 of CC provides that where the cargo is lost during carriage due to force majeure and the freight has not been paid, the carrier cannot claim for freight; if the freight has already been paid, the shipper can demand return thereof. Under Chinese law, therefore, prepaid freight is returnable in the case of loss of goods during carriage due to force majeure or otherwise. However, if the loss of goods was due to the cause for which the shipper is responsible, the carrier is entitled to claim for loss of freight after reduction of the costs saved.

Freight to be collected, or freight to collect, or freight payable at destination, means freight to be paid by the consignee before delivery of goods, unless the carrier and the shipper have agreed otherwise. Statement of freight to be collected in a bill of lading or other transport document is deemed as a statement that freight is to be paid by the consignee as required by paragraph 2 of Article 69 MC. If the consignee fails to pay, the shipper is not discharged from the obligation to pay by virtue of Article 523 of CC stipulating that, where parties have agreed that a third party shall fulfil obligation to the creditor and the third party fails to fulfil or has not fulfilled as agreed, the debtor shall bear liability for breach of contract.

B. Claim for Dead Freight

352. Dead freight means the expenses to be paid by the shipper where the quantity of cargo supplied by him is less than that agreed upon between the carrier and the shipper as compensation for the loss of freight suffered by the carrier. Therefore, the amount of dead freight shall be calculated on the basis of the undercharged freight after deduction of the costs saved and the freight which the carrier has earned for the carriage of substituted goods, if any.

C. Claim for Other Expenses

353. Other expenses to be paid to the carrier include, *inter alia*, contribution in general average on cargo, demurrage, container detention fees and necessary expenses which the carrier has paid for the cargo in advance.

Demurrage seldom occurs under a bill of lading, because, unlike a voyage charter party, it is exceptional that a bill of lading contains a demurrage clause. However, demurrage may occur as a consequence of the incorporation of a voyage charter into the bill of lading issued hereunder in pursuance of an incorporation clause contained in the bill.

Container detention fees may occur where the shipper or consignee fails to return the containers supplied by the carrier after expiration of a grace period. Normally, the rate of container detention fees are contained in the tariff of a liner shipping company or agreed upon between the carrier and the shipper or consignee.

II. Lien on Goods

A. *Definition of Lien on Goods*

354. Under Chinese law, lien means possessory lien in the sense of the Anglo-American law.

As a type of security for the fulfilment of debt, Article 447 of CC provides that, where a debtor fails to pay off its due debt, the creditor may exercise a lien on the moveable of the debtor and in the lawful possession of the creditor, and has the right to seek preferred payments from such moveable. As a statutory right of the creditor under a contract, lien can be enforced only on the moveable that is in the lawful possession of the creditor in accordance with a contract. The creditor may obtain compensation by way of conversion of the moveable into money or with priority from the proceeds of private sale or sale by auction of the moveable.

355. As provided for in Article 87 of MC, where the freight, contribution in general average, demurrage to be paid to the carrier and other necessary charges paid by the carrier on behalf of the owners of the goods as well as other charges to be paid to the carrier have not be paid in full, nor has appropriate security been given, the carrier may exercise lien on the goods of the debtor to a reasonable extent.

By virtue of Article 87 of MC and Article 447 of CC, the exercise of the carrier's lien on the goods under a contract of international carriage of goods by sea shall meet the following conditions:

- the freight or any other expenses to be paid to the carrier under the said contract have not been paid or not been paid in full;
- no appropriate security has been provided by the debtor or on his behalf;
- the goods are owned by the debtor and in the possession of the carrier under the contract;
- the value of the goods under lien shall be equivalent to the amount of the principal claim, interests thereon and the estimated reasonable costs for the enforcement of lien.

B. Enforcement of Lien on Goods

356. By virtue of paragraph 1 of Article 88 of MC, where the goods under lien have not been taken delivery of within sixty days from the next day of the ship's arrival at the port of discharge by the consignee either after the payment of the expenses giving rise to the lien or provision of a security for the payment thereof, the carrier may apply to a court of law for an award on selling the goods by auction; where the goods are perishable or the expenses for keeping such goods will exceed their value, the carrier may apply for an earlier sale by auction.

The word 'may' in paragraph 1 of Article 88 of MC means that an application to the court of law for sale by auction is not a must, but is a choice of the carrier in his enforcement of the lien. The carrier may choose other means of enforcement of lien as provided for in Article 454 of CC, i.e., conversion of the goods under lien into money by negotiating with the debtor, or seeking preferred payments from the proceeds of the sale of goods by auction by an auctioneer entrusted by the carrier or private sale of the goods under lien, provided that when the goods under lien is converted into money or sold off, its market price shall be referred to.

357. Where the carrier chooses the enforcement of lien by filing an application with a maritime court for an order on selling the goods by auction, the detailed procedures thereof are provided for in Chapter III 'Security for Maritime Claims' of SMPL which are similar to those of arrest of a ship.

The carrier shall file such an application with the maritime court in the place where the goods are located, if the application is filed before litigation, or with the maritime court having entertained the case of dispute, if filed during litigation (Article 13).

The application shall be in writing and indicate the items of maritime claims, reasons of application, the goods to be sold by auction and be attached with supporting documents (Article 15).

After receipt of the application, the maritime court shall examine the application and make an award either granting or rejecting the sale within seven days. If any party raises objection to the award, it may apply to the maritime court for reconsideration within five days from the receipt of the award. The maritime court shall make the decision of reconsideration. During the reconsideration, execution of the award shall not be discontinued (Article 48).

The sale of the goods by auction shall be executed by an auction organization consisting of a court martial designated and the auctioneers appointed by the court, or solely by the auctioneers appointed by the court (paragraph 1, Article 49).

Other procedures shall refer to those of sale of ship by auction contained in Chapter III of SMPL.[38]

Noticeably, a maritime court often entrusts an internet operator to sell the goods by auction on its internet nowadays.

358. As provided for in paragraph 2 of Article 88 of MC, the proceeds from the sale by auction of the goods shall be used to pay off the expenses for the storage

38. *See* §9, Ch. 14 of Part II.

and sale of the goods, the freight and other related charges to be paid to the carrier. If the proceeds fall short of such expenses, the carrier is entitled to claim the difference from the shipper, whereas any amount in surplus shall be refunded to the shipper. If there is no way to make the refund and the surplus has not been claimed within one year after the sale by auction, it shall go to the state treasury.

III. Immunities of Liability of Carrier

A. *General Immunities of Liability of Carrier*

359. The immunities, or exemptions or exoneration as synonym, of liability of the carrier for the loss of or damage to goods are provided for in Article 51 of MC. The carrier shall not be liable for the loss of or damage to the goods occurred during the period of carrier's responsibility arising or resulting from any of the following causes:

- fault of the master, other crewmembers, pilot or servant of the carrier in the navigation or management of the ship;
- fire, unless caused by the actual fault of the carrier;
- act of God and perils, dangers and accidents of the sea or other navigable waters;
- war or armed conflict;
- act of the government or competent authorities, quarantine restrictions or seizure under legal process;
- strikes, stoppages or restraint of labour;
- saving or attempting to save life or property at sea;
- act of the shipper, owner of the goods or their agents;
- nature or inherent vice of the goods;
- inadequacy of packing or insufficiency or illegibility of marks;
- latent defect of the ship not discoverable by due diligence;
- any other cause arising without the fault of the carrier or his servant or agent.

The carrier who is entitled to exoneration from the liability for compensation shall bear the burden of proof, with the exception of the case of fire.

360. Four points need be mentioned as regards the provisions of Article 51 of MC cited *supra*.

First, the above twelve specific items of immunities are in essence in conformity with the catalogue of seventeen items contained in Article 4(2) of the Hague-Visby Rules, although two or more items contained in the Rules are emerged into one in Article 51 of MC. Some expressions in the Rules are modified in Article 51 of MC in order to meet with the Chinese legal culture. No difference in coverage between them has been speculated upon by the draftsmen of MC.

Second, Article 51 of MC provides literally that the immunities of liability are applicable to loss of or damage to goods. Nevertheless, as a matter of construction, they shall also apply to the economic losses resulting from delay in delivery of goods, even if no physical loss or damage occurs due to the reason explained in §6 *supra*.

Third, the loss of or damage to goods is specifically mentioned to have occurred during the period of the carrier's responsibility. However, as a matter of construction, the loss of or damage to the goods subject to the immunities of liability shall include those occurring after the expiration of the period of the carrier's responsibility as provided for in Article 46 of MC, if it resulted from one or more immunities during the period of responsibility.

Fourth, by virtue of paragraph 2 of Article 51 of MC cited *supra*, although it is clear that the burden of proving that loss of or damage to goods is caused by one or more immunities shall be borne by the carrier, the distribution of burdens of proof in cargo claims between the claimants and the carrier as a whole is still not clear enough. This is because neither MC nor CPC contains clear provisions in this respect. The basic rule of burden of proof contained in paragraph 1 of Article 64 of CPC *viz.* 'who alleges, who proves' is too vague. SMPL does not change such a situation at all. In admiralty practice in China, this problem can only be solved in accordance with the circumstances of a particular case.

The principle of presumption of fault on the part of the carrier contained in Article 5 'Basis of Liability' of the Hamburg Rules or in Article 17 'Basis of liability' of the Rotterdam Rules is not applicable in admiralty practice in China. However, it may be adopted when MC is revised in the near future.

B. Additional Immunities in Case of Live Animals or Deck Cargo

361. Articles 52 and 53 of MC provide additional immunities of liabilities of the carrier for loss of or damage to live animals and deck cargo respectively, in addition to the general immunities provided for in Article 51. The two articles are laid down by reference to Article 5(5) and Article 9 respectively of the Hamburg Rules.

By virtue of Article 52 of MC, the carrier shall not be liable for loss of or damage to live animals arising or resulting from the special risks inherent in the carriage thereof, provided that the carrier shall be bound to prove that he has fulfilled the special requirements of the shipper with regard to the carriage thereof and that the loss or damage has occurred due to the special risks inherent therein.

By virtue of paragraph 1 of Article 53 of MC, the carrier is entitled to carry the goods on deck only where an agreement of deck carriage has been concluded with the shipper, or such carriage complies with the custom of the trade, e.g., carriage of logs on the deck of a timber ship or carriage of containers on the deck of a container ship, or with the relevant law or administrative regulations, e.g., some kinds of dangerous goods are recommended to be stowed on deck by the IMO International Maritime Dangerous Goods Code (IMDG Code). In the case of authorized carriage of goods on deck, the carrier shall not be liable for loss of or damage to the goods caused by the special risks involved in such carriage by virtue of paragraph 2 of Article 53. Noticeably, it is not decided yet whether the carrier is entitled to stow the containerized goods or vehicles on the deck of non-container ship. In this regard, paragraph 1 of Article 25 'Deck cargo on ships' provides, *inter alia*, that the containers or vehicles may be carried on the deck of a ship if they are fit for deck carriage and the decks are specially fitted to carry such containers or vehicles.

IV. Limitation of Liability of Carrier

A. *Limit of Liability for Loss of or Damage to Goods*

362. Identical with the provisions contained in Article 4(5)(a), (b) & (c) of the Hague-Visby Rules as amended by its SDR Protocol of 1979, Article 56 of MC provides for the carrier's package or kilo limitation of liability for loss of or damage to the goods.

The carrier's liability for loss of or damage to the goods shall be limited to an amount equivalent to 666.67 SDR per package or other unit, or 2 SDR per kilogram of the gross weight of the goods lost or damaged, whichever is the higher, except where the nature and value of the goods have been declared by the shipper before shipment and inserted in the bill of lading, or where a higher amount has been agreed upon between the carrier and the shipper.

In the case that a container, pallet or similar article of transport is used to consolidate goods, the number of packages or other shipping units enumerated in the bill of lading other shipping document as packed in such article of transport shall be deemed to be the number of packages or shipping units. If not so enumerated, the goods in such article of transport shall be deemed to be one package or one shipping unit. In addition, if the article of transport is not owned or furnished by the carrier, such article of transport itself shall be deemed to be one package or one shipping unit in the calculation of limit.

B. *Limit of Liability for Economic Losses Resulting from Delay in Delivery*

363. As provided for in Article 57 of MC, the limit of liability of the carrier for the economic losses other than physical loss or damage to goods resulting from delay in delivery of goods as defined in Article 50 of MC shall be an amount equivalent to the freight payable for the goods so delayed.

Obviously, this limit is lower than that provided for in Article 6(1)(b) of the Hamburg Rules, i.e., two and half times of the freight of the goods delayed, but not exceeding the aggregate of freight of all the goods under a contract of carriage.

In practice, the limit provided for in Article 57 of MC proves too low. Sometimes, such a limit means symbolic compensation only.

In the case that loss of or damage to the goods has occurred concurrently with delay in delivery thereof, the limit of liability of the carrier shall be calculated as provided for in Article 56 of MC.

C. Loss of Right to Limit

364. Identical with the provisions contained in Article 4(5)(e) of the Hague-Visby Rules, by virtue of paragraph 1 of Article 59 of MC, the carrier shall lose the right to limit his liability for loss of or damage to or delay on delivery of the goods provided for in Article 56 or Article 57 of MC, if it proves the loss, damage or delay in delivery of the goods resulted from an act or omission of him done with the intent to cause such loss, damage or delay in delivery or recklessly and with knowledge that such loss, damage or delay would probably result.

§8. Responsibilities of Shipper

I. General Rule of Liability of Shipper

365. Like Article 12 of the Hamburg Rules, paragraph 1 of Article 70 of MC provides that the shipper shall not liable for the loss sustained by the carrier or the actual carrier, or for damage sustained by the ship, unless such loss or damage was caused by the fault or neglect of the shipper, his servants or agents. In this regard, the shipper shall be responsible for the fault or neglect of an independent contractor entrusted by the shipper.

Therefore, the rule of fault liability is adopted by MC concerning the shipper's liability. However, Chapter IV of MC provides in various articles the main obligations of the shipper and his liability in the case of failure in fulfilling thereof as introduced *infra*. The liability provided for in these articles is not conditional upon the fault of the shipper, his servant or agent or independent contractor and therefore the shipper shall bear strict liability.

366. Paragraph 2 of Article 70 of MC further provides that the servant or agent of the shipper shall not be liable for loss sustained by the carrier or the actual carrier, or for damage sustained by the ship, unless the loss or damage was caused by fault the servant or agent of the shipper.

Literally, the servant or agent of the shipper shall be held liable for the loss or damage suffered by the carrier or the actual carrier due to his fault, even if the fault is committed within the scope of his employment or agency. However, it is fully doubtful that this provision shall be implemented as a deviation of the general principle of vicarious liability or *respondent superior* as mentioned in §1 of Chapter 4 of Part II *supra* to the effect that claims for such loss or damage caused by the fault of the servant or agent of the shipper, if committed within the scope of employment or agency, shall be made against the shipper, unless the act of the servant or agent is illegal in nature.

II. Main Obligations of Shipper

A. *Proper Packing and Guarantee of Accuracy of Goods Particulars*

367. As required by paragraph 1 of Article 66 of MC, the shipper shall have the goods properly packed and shall guarantee the accuracy of the description, mark, number of packages or pieces, weight or quantity of the goods at the time of shipment. The shipper shall indemnify the carrier against any loss resulting from inadequacy of packing or inaccuracies in the abovementioned information.

Where the goods have not been properly packed, the carrier may refuse to carry (paragraph 2, Article 827, CC).

The liability of the shipper to the carrier for any loss resulting from inadequacy of packing or inaccuracies in the abovementioned information is a strict liability. However, the carrier's right to indemnification as provided for in paragraph 1 of Article 66 of MC shall not affect the obligations of the carrier under the contract of carriage of goods towards those other than the shipper (paragraph 2, Article 66, MC).

B. *Performance of Transport Formalities and Provision of Documents*

368. The shipper shall perform all necessary formalities at the port, customs including quarantine and inspection or other competent authorities with respect to the shipment of the goods and shall furnish to the carrier all the relevant documents concerning the procedures which the shipper has gone through. The shipper shall be liable for any damage to the interests of the carrier resulting from the inadequacy or inaccuracy or delay in delivery of such documents (Article 67, MC). Similar provisions are contained in Article 826 of CC.

The formalities of customs declaration and quarantine or inspection of goods necessary for the shipment of exported goods are provided for in the *Customs Law of 1987* as latest amended on 4 November 2017, the *Imported and Exported Commodity Inspection Law of 1989* as latest amended on 29 April 2021 and the *Law on Entry-Exit Live Animals and Plants Quarantine of 1991* as amended on 27 August 2009. Competent authorities in charge of quarantine and inspection of imported and exported goods are the customs.

The liability of the shipper to the carrier for any damage to the interests of the carrier resulting from the inadequacy or inaccuracy or delay in delivery of such documents is a strict liability.

C. *Shipment of Dangerous Goods as Required*

369. Requirements for the shipment of dangerous goods are provided for in Article 68 of MC.

At the time of shipment of dangerous goods, the shipper shall, in compliance with the regulations governing the carriage of such goods, have them properly packed, distinctly marked and labelled and notify the carrier in writing of their proper description, nature and the precautions to be taken.

In the shipper fails to notify the carrier or notified him inaccurately and the dangerous goods have been loaded onboard without the carrier's knowledge of the nature of the dangerous goods and his consent to carry, the carrier may have the goods landed, destroyed or rendered innocuous when and where circumstances so require, without compensation, even if the goods have not become an actual dangerous to the ship, the crew and other persons onboard or to other goods. In such a case, the shipper shall be liable to the carrier for any loss, damage or expenses, if any, resulting from such shipment. The liability of the shipper is a strict liability.

Where the dangerous goods have been loaded onboard with the carrier's knowledge of the nature of the dangerous goods and his consent to carry, he may still have such goods landed, destroyed or rendered innocuous without compensation, but only when they become an actual dangerous to the ship, the crew and other persons onboard or to other goods, even if the shipper has no fault in the packing, marking and labelling of the dangerous goods and notification of their proper description, nature and the precautions to be taken. However, such a provision shall not cause prejudice to the contribution in general average, i.e., where the carrier has the goods landed or takes other measures in the case the goods becomes an actual danger common to the ship and all the goods carried onboard, the carrier is obliged to contribute with the cargo interests in general average of the loss of or damage to the dangerous goods resulting from such measures.

Obviously, the law imposes heavy responsibility on the shipper with respect to shipment of dangerous goods. This is because such shipment may seriously cause prejudice to maritime safety and even cause marine pollution.

D. Payment of Freight and Other Expenses

370. As mentioned in §7 *supra*, the shipper shall pay the freight to the carrier as agreed, unless an agreement has been reached between the carrier and the shipper that the freight shall be paid by the consignee and noted in bill of lading or other transport document. However, if the consignee fails to pay the freight, the shipper is still obliged to pay.

The shipper shall also pay to the carrier the dead freight, contribution in general average on the goods, demurrage, necessary expenses paid by the carrier on behalf the shipper as well as other expenses to be paid to the carrier by the shipper under the contract of carriage of goods by sea (Article 87, MC).

§9. NON-CONTRACTUAL CLAIMS

I. Non-contractual Claim Against Carrier

A. *Choice Between Contractual Claim and Non-contractual Claim*

371. Before the enactment of the *Contract Law* on 15 March 1999, it was arguable that a party to a contract was entitled to claim against the other party founded in tort. Article 122 of the *Contract Law* allowed a party to a contract to choose between the claim founded in contract and the claim founded in tort by providing that, where breach of contract by one party to a contract causes loss of life of or personal injury or loss of proprietary rights to the other party, the other party who has suffered loss is entitled to require at his choice the offending party to bear liability for breach of contract by virtue of this Law or bear tortuous liability by virtue of other law. The said choice between contractual claim and claim in tort is called competition between contractual claim and claim in tort under Chinese civil law theory.

Article 186 of CC contains similar provisions, i.e., where one party to a contract suffers damage to his personal or property interests due to the breach of contract of the other party, he may choose to require the other party to bear liability for breach of contract or liability in tort.

372. By virtue of paragraph 1 of Article 1165 and Article 1166 of CC, any person who infringes on other people's civil rights and interests through his fault shall assume tort liability. In addition, any person infringes on other people's civil rights and interests and statutory provision specifies that he shall assume the liability in tort, such a provision shall govern, whether such a person is at fault or not. Such a liability is called tortuous liability.

Four requirements should be met for tortuous liability, *viz.* illegal act or omission, fault or intent, loss or damage and causation between the act or omission and the loss or damage. On the other hand, by virtue of Article 577 of CC, a party to a contract shall bear liability where he commits breach of contract or fails to fulfil other obligations. This liability is called contractual liability for which three requirements should be met, *viz.* breach of contract or failure in fulfilling other obligations, loss or damage suffered by the other party and causation between the breach or failure and the loss or damage.

Obviously, the common requirements for tortuous and contractual liability are not difficult to meet under a contract of carriage of goods by sea. Thus, the said principle of competition between contractual claim and claim in tort may have a wide scope of application between the carrier as one party and the shipper as the other to a contract of carriage of goods by sea.

373. Where the claimant and the respondent are not parties to a contract, claim can only be founded in tort and no contractual claim shall occur. Therefore, the shipper, consignee or holder of bill of lading can only make claim founded in tort against the actual carrier, as the claimant and the actual carrier have no contractual relations. Strictly speaking, the consignee or holder of bill of lading other than the shipper is not a party to a contract of carriage of goods by sea and thus can only make claim founded in tort against the carrier and *vice versa*. In admiralty practice, however, a lawful holder of bill of lading is often deemed as a party to a contract of carriage of goods by sea evidenced by the bill and may make a choice between contractual claim and claim in tort against the carrier by virtue of the said principle of competition. For example, in a case of carrier's delivery of goods without production of bill of lading, by virtue of Article 3 of the *Provisions on Certain issues of application of Law in the Trial of Cases of Delivery of Goods without Original Bills of Lading* promulgated by SPC, the lawful holder of bill of lading may claim against the carrier either founded in breach of contract or in tort for loss resulting from such delivery.

B. Application of Immunities and Defence to Non-contractual Claims Against Carrier

374. By virtue of paragraph 1 of Article 58 of MC, the immunities and limitation of liability and other defences available to the carrier under Chapter IV of MC shall apply to any legal action brought against the carrier in respect of loss of or damage to or delay in delivery of the goods covered by the contract of carriage of goods by sea, whether the claimant is a party to the contract or not, or whether action is founded in contract or in tort. As a result, there will be no or only slight difference between contractual liability and tortuous liability as the claimant may choose to make against the carrier.

Therefore, the carrier can avail of the immunities and limitation of liability and other defences provided for in Articles 51, 56 and 57, etc., of MC in any claim against him made by the shipper, even if the claim is founded in tort, or in any claim against him made by the consignee or other third party than the shipper founded in contract or in tort, provided that the claim is for loss of or damage to or delay in delivery of the goods covered by the contract of carriage of goods by sea.

II. Claims Against Carrier's Servant or Agent, Actual Carrier or His Servant or Agent

A. Claims Against Carrier's Servant or Agent

375. As provided for in paragraph 2 of Article 58 of MC, the immunities and limitation of liability and other defences available to the carrier under Chapter IV of MC shall also apply if the action is brought against the carrier's servant or agent, provided that the servant or agent proves that his action was within the scope of his employment or agency.

The servant or agent of the carrier shall lose his right to limit his liability for loss of or damage to or delay on delivery of the goods, if it proves the loss, damage or delay in delivery of the goods resulted from an act or omission of him done with the intent to cause such loss, damage or delay in delivery or recklessly and with knowledge that such loss, damage or delay would probably result.

The provision of paragraph 2 of Article 58 of MC is incorporated from paragraph 2 of Article 4*bis* of the Hague-Visby Rules and paragraph 2 of Article 7 of the Hamburg Rules, and is a reflection of 'Himalaya clause'.

However, by virtue of the general principle of vicarious liability or *respondent superior* as mentioned in §6 and §8 *supra*, where, due to the fault of the carrier's servant or agent, the shipper or consignee suffers loss of or damage to the goods, the claimant cannot make claim against the carrier's servant or agent, but against the carrier only, if the servant or agent proves that his act or omission was within the scope of his employment or agency, unless his action is illegal. For example, where, as instructed by the carrier, the agent delivered the goods to a third person without production of bill of lading and thus the provision of Article 71 of MC is violated and consequently the holder of bill of lading suffers loss, the latter is entitled to claim against the carrier and/or his agent, even if the agent proves that his act was done in the carrier's name and within the scope of agency. In such a case, the carrier and the agent shall bear joint and several liability to the holder for his loss, if the claimant claims against both the carrier and the agent.

Where an act committed by the carrier's servant or agent is not within the scope of his employment or agency, the servant or agent shall be personally liable to a third person for loss or damage arising therefrom. In such a case, the carrier shall not be held liable. In addition, the servant or agent cannot avail of the immunities and limitation of liability and other defences available to the carrier under Chapter IV of MC by virtue of paragraph 2 of Article 58 thereof in such a case.

376. Modern 'Himalaya clause' contained in some forms of bill of lading or charter parties intends to make the immunities and limitation of liability and other defences that the carrier is entitled to avail of also available to stevedores and other independent contractors, besides carrier's servants or agents. However, diverse judgments are made by the courts of law in different countries concerning the effectiveness of this clause. Independent contractors are expressly not allowed to avail of the immunities and defences available to the carrier in paragraph 2 of Article 4*bis* of the Hague-Visby Rules. The Hamburg Rules do not contain the limitation that the servant or agent of the carrier should not be an independent contractor, but the meaning of the deletion of this limitation is not very clear. Quite possibly, an independent contractor entrusted by the carrier is within the scope of actual carrier who is entitled to avail of the immunities and limitation of liability and other defences which the carrier is entitled to avail.

In admiralty practice in China, the stevedores or port operators are not construed as servants or agents of the carrier nor actual carriers and are not entitled to avail of the immunities and limitation of liability and other defences available to the carrier under Chapter IV of MC.

B. Claims Against Actual Carrier

377. Unless the contract provides to the contrary, the carrier is at liberty to entrust the performance of carriage of goods by sea or part thereof to an actual carrier as defined in Article 42 of MC, i.e., the person to whom the performance of carriage of goods, or of part of the carriage, has been entrusted by the carrier, and includes any other person to whom such performance has been entrusted under a sub-contract. Where so entrusted, as a rule, the carrier remains responsible for the entire carriage performed by the actual carrier and for the acts or omissions of the actual carrier and of his servant and agent acting within the scope of his employment or agency (paragraph 1, Article 60, MC). However, as an exception of this rule, where a contract of carriage by sea provides explicitly that a specified part of the carriage covered by the said contract is to be performed by a named person other than the carrier, the contract may also provide that the carrier is not liable for loss, damage or delay in delivery caused by an occurrence which takes place while the goods are in the charge of the actual carrier during such part of the carriage (paragraph 2 of Article 60 of MC).

All the provisions contained in Chapter IV of MC governing the responsibility of the carrier also apply to the actual carrier for the carriage performed by him (Article 61, MC). Such provisions include those of the carrier's obligations, liabilities, immunities and defence with regard to loss of or damage to or delay in delivery of the goods. However, a special agreement concluded between the carrier and the shipper, if any, under which the carrier assumes obligations not imposed by Chapter IV of MC or waives his rights conferred by Chapter IV of MC shall affect the actual carrier only if agreed to by him expressly and in writing. On the other hand, whether or not the actual carrier has so agreed, the carrier nevertheless remains bound by the additional obligations or waivers of rights arising from such a special agreement (Article 62, MC).

378. By virtue of Article 61 of MC, where an action with regard to loss of or damage to or delay in delivery of the goods caused by an occurrence that takes place while the goods are in his charge is brought against the actual carrier, he is entitled to avail of the immunities and limitation of liability and other defences available to the carrier.

The actual carrier shall lose his right to limit liability for the loss of or damage to or delay in delivery of the goods, if it proves the loss, damage or delay in delivery of the goods resulted from an act or omission of him done with the intent to cause such loss, damage or delay in delivery or recklessly and with knowledge that such loss, damage or delay would probably result.

379. Where and to the extent that both the carrier and the actual carrier are liable, i.e., the actual carrier is liable due to the fault of him, his servants or agent which cannot be exempted and the carrier is liable by virtue of paragraph 1 of Article 60 of MC, then their liability shall be joint and several. However, any right of recourse as between the carrier and the actual carrier shall not be prejudiced (Article 65, MC).

C. *Claims Against Actual Carrier's Servant or Agent*

380. By virtue of paragraph 2 of Article 58 of MC, the servant or agent of the actual carrier has the same legal status as that of the servant or agent of the carrier.

Therefore, where a claim for loss of or damage to or delay in delivery of the goods is made against the servant or agent of the actual carrier whose act is within the scope of his employment or agency, the servant or agent is entitled to avail of the immunities and limitation of liability and other defence available to the carrier.

The servant or agent of the actual carrier shall lose his right to limit liability for the loss of or damage to or delay in delivery of the goods, if it proves the loss, damage or delay in delivery of the goods resulted from an act or omission of him done with the intent to cause such loss, damage or delay in delivery or recklessly and with knowledge that such loss, damage or delay would probably result.

381. Like the case of the servant or agent of the carrier, the general principle of vicarious liability or *respondent superior* as mentioned in §1 of Chapter 4 of Part II *supra* applies to the servant or agent of the actual carrier.

D. *Aggregate Amount Recoverable*

382. As provided for in Article 64 of MC, where a claim for loss of or damage to or delay in delivery of the goods is made separately against the carrier, the actual carrier and their servants or agents, the aggregate of the amounts recoverable shall not exceed the limit of liability available to the carrier provided for in Article 56 or 57 of MC, unless one of them loses his right to limit liability by virtue of Article 59 of MC.

§10. Non-negotiable SWBs

I. Definition and Functions

A. *Definition of SWB*

383. A SWB is a non-negotiable document and marked as such which serves as an evidence of a contract of carriage of goods by sea and the taking over or loading of the goods by the carrier and based on which the carrier undertakes to deliver the goods to the named consignee.

B. *Functions of SWB*

384. As compared with a bill of lading, a SWB serves as an evidence of a contract of carriage of goods by sea and the taking over or loading of the goods by the carrier. However, being a non-negotiable document, a SWB lacks negotiability and only the named consignee in the SWB is entitled to take delivery of the goods, whereas an order bill of lading may be negotiated with special endorsement or endorsement in blank and a bearer bill of lading is negotiable without endorsement by virtue of Article 79 of MC.

The lack of negotiability is an obvious shortcoming of SWB as compared with bill of lading and limits the use of SWB normally to where the buyer of goods does not intend to re-sell the goods *in transitu* by documentary sale.

385. Unlike a bill of lading, a SWB is not a document based on which the carrier undertakes to deliver the goods against surrendering the same. Consequently, the named consignee in a SWB does not need to surrender the SWB to take delivery of the goods from the carrier, but only produces his identity as such. Obviously, therefore, a SWB has the advantage of enabling expeditious delivery of goods. This advantage helps to solve the widespread problem of delivery of goods without production of bill of lading due to its arrival at the hands of the consignee later than the arrival of the goods at the port of discharge. No doubt, the modern shipping world needs the full play of this advantage, especially in the carriage of liquefied goods, in short sea transport and in container transport. This is especially the case in China as a significant part of international trade is with Japan, South Korea and other neighbouring coastal countries in which a voyage only needs a short time, whereas the circulation of bills of lading cannot follow the speed of cargo movement in many cases.

386. SWBs are not often used in international shipping now in China. This seems also the case in many other shipping countries. Possibly, this is mainly because of the question of application of the law on carriage of goods by sea to SWBs as discussed below, besides its lack of negotiability.

II. Application of Law to SWBs

387. The law on carriage of goods by sea now prevailing in the world is mainly based upon bills of lading and The Hague or Hague-Visby Rules. It is arguable whether the law is adaptable to SWBs. Mainly, two opinions exist in this respect.

One opinion is that The Hague or Hague-Visby Rules shall not apply to SWBs on the ground the Rules apply to contracts of carriage covered by bills of lading or any similar documents of title by virtue of Article 1(b) thereof and a SWB is not a bill of lading or similar document of title.

The other opinion is that the Hague or Hague-Visby Rules shall apply to SWBs in ordinary commercial shipment because, by virtue of Article 6 of the Rules, the Rules are not applicable only where a special agreement has been entered into between the carrier and the shipper, provided that no bill of lading has been or shall be issued and the terms agreed shall be embodied in non-negotiable receipt marked as such, no ordinary commercial shipment is involved, and the special agreement is reasonably justified by the character or condition of the property to be concerned or the circumstances, terms and conditions under which the carriage is to be performed.

Anyhow, one thing is sure, i.e., the provisions contained in The Hague or Hague-Visby Rules specifically relating to bill of lading are not adaptable to SWBs.

388. MC contains no specific provisions as to SWBs. Same as Article 18 of the Hamburg Rules, Article 80 of Section 4 'Transport Documents' of MC provides that, where a carrier has issued a document other than a bill of lading as evidence of the receipt of the goods to be carried, such a document is prima facie evidence of the conclusion of the contract of carriage of goods by sea and the taking over by the carrier of the goods as described therein and that such a document shall not be negotiable. A SWB may be deemed as a document referred in Article 80 of MC. In addition, a contract of carriage by goods by sea is defined in Article 41 as a contract under which the carrier, against payment of freight, undertakes to carry by sea the goods contracted for shipment by the shipper from one port to another. Thus, a contract of carriage to which Chapter IV of MC applies is not limited to that covered by a bill of lading or any similar document of title.

Therefore, it may be concluded that the provisions of Chapter IV of MC shall apply in the case of a SWB, except those specifically relating to bill of lading.

389. The *CMI Uniform Rules on Sea Waybills of 1990* does not have any binding effect of law and therefore cannot fully solve the problem of application of law on carriage of goods by sea to SWBs. The Rules shall apply only when adopted by a contract which is not covered by a bill of lading or similar document of title, whether the contract is in writing or not (Article 1).

To make widespread use of SWBs, solution of the problem of application of law on carriage of goods by sea seems a precondition. This should be done at international level. The Rotterdam Rules which provides transport documents in general, without indication of bill of lading or SWB, may solve this problem, if the Rules come into effect.

III. Main Contents of SWB

390. A SWB is normally marked 'non-negotiable'. Similar to a bill of lading, a SWB normally contains the following particulars:

- the description of the goods, mark, number of packages or pieces, weight or quantity of goods;
- the name and principal place of business of the carrier;
- the name of the ship;
- the name of the shipper and of the consignee;
- the port of loading and discharge;
- the date and place of issue;
- the payment of freight;
- the signature of the carrier or a person acting on his behalf.

IV. Rights and Obligations of Carrier, Shipper and Consignee

A. *Rights and Obligations of Carrier and Shipper*

391. The provisions of Chapter IV of MC governing the rights and obligations of the carrier and the shipper shall apply where a contract of carriage of goods by sea is evidenced by a SWB, except those specifically relating to bill of lading.

B. *Rights and Obligations of Consignee*

392. Unlike the case of a bill of lading in which, the relations between the carrier and the holder of bill of lading with respect to their rights and obligations shall be defined by the clauses of the bill of lading as provided for in paragraph 1 of Article 78 of MC, MC contains no provision regarding the rights and obligations of the consignee named in a SWB or not under a bill of lading.

The provisions of Chapter VI of MC relating to the consignee not under a bill of lading are mainly contained in section 5 'Delivery of Goods'. Article 81 provides that, unless a notice of loss or damage is given in writing by the consignee to the carrier at the time of delivery of goods by the carrier to the consignee, such delivery shall be deemed to be prima facie evidence of the delivery of goods by the carrier as described in the transport document and of the apparent good order and condition of such goods. Article 86 provides that if the goods were not taken delivery of at the port of discharge or if the consignee has delayed or refused the delivery of the goods, the master may discharge the goods into warehouses or other appropriate places, and any expenses or risks arising therefrom shall be borne by the consignee.

CC provides in Article 830 that the consignee has an obligation to take delivery of goods timely after receiving the carrier's notice of the arrival of the goods. Article 831 further provides that the consignee has the obligation to inspect the goods when taking delivery of the goods.

393. The *CMI Uniform Rules on Sea Waybills of 1990* adopted in Article 3 the principle of agency to the effect that the shipper concludes the contract of carriage evidenced by a SWB not only on his own behalf, but also as the agent for and on behalf of the consignee, as a result of which the consignee becomes a party to the contract of carriage and thus his rights and obligations shall be determined in accordance with the SWB. In fact, the Rules provides in Article 3(ii) that they shall apply if, and only if, it is necessary by the law applicable to the contract of carriage so as to enable the consignee to sue and be sued thereon, and the consignee shall be under no greater liability than he would have been had the contract of carriage been covered by a bill of lading or similar document of title.

However, it is fully doubtful that, under Chinese law, the shipper can be deemed as has concluded a contract of carriage with the carrier not only in his own name, but also on behalf of the consignee as an agent at the same time.

§11. ELECTRONIC BILL OF LADING

I. Definition and Functions of Electronic Bill of Lading

A. *Definition of Electronic Bill of Lading*

394. An electronic bill of lading means the data relating to contract of carriage of goods by sea that are transmitted electronically.

As a paperless document, an electronic bill of lading consists of the data contained in traditional paper bill of lading which are formatted and interchanged by EDI or other modern technology of the computer communication network connecting the shipper, carrier, consignee and other various parties concerned in carriage of goods by sea in accordance with specified rules.

B. *Functions of Electronic Bill of Lading*

395. An electronic bill of lading retains the functions of a paper bill of lading as an evidence of contract of carriage of goods by sea and the taking over or loading of the goods by the carrier and based upon which the carrier undertakes to deliver to goods to the consignee.

Unlike a SWB, an electronic bill of lading also retains the negotiability of a paper bill of lading by means of transfer of the right of control and transfer as mentioned *infra* and can thus overcome the shortcoming of a SWB. On the other hand, an electronic bill of lading is transmitted very fast and thus enables expeditious delivery of goods at port of discharge or other destination and can thus overcome the shortcoming of a paper bill of lading and effectively avoid delivery of goods without production of bill of lading.

Therefore, along with the development of modern technology in international electronic commerce, electronic bills of lading have great future, especially along with the application of blockchain technology.

At the present stage, electronic bills of lading are not widely used yet in shipping practice due to the technical and financial problems as well as legal matters as mentioned *infra*.

II. Transmission of Electronic Bill of Lading

396. By virtue of the *CMI Rules for Electronic Bills of Lading of 1990*, a typical process of transmission of an electronic bill of lading may be summarized as follows:

- The shipper books a cargo space of a ship by sending a booking message to the carrier.

- The carrier shall send a message confirming his acceptance of booking and indicating the terms and conditions of contract of carriage, and the contract of carriage is concluded once the shipper accepts these terms and conditions by electronic message.
- The carrier or his agent shall, upon receipt of the goods delivered by the shipper for carriage, send a receipt message indicating the name of the shipper, particulars of the goods, date and place of the receipt, reference to the carrier's terms and conditions of carriage as well as a private key for subsequent transmission.
- The shipper shall confirm the receipt message to the carrier, upon which the shipper becomes the holder of the right of control and transfer who, as against the carrier, may claim delivery of the goods, nominate the consignee or substituted consignee, transfer the right of control and transfer to another party, and instruct the carrier on other respect concerning the goods in accordance with the terms and condition of the contract of carriage as if he were the holder of a paper bill of lading.
- Upon demand of the shipper, the carrier shall update the receipt message with the date and place of shipment as soon as the goods have been loaded onboard and shall copy it to the bank in accordance with the electronic address nominated by the shipper.
- After settlement of exchange with the shipper, the bank shall notify the carrier thereof by a message and consequently obtain the right of control and transfer.
- After payment of cargo price, the bank shall transfer the right of control and transfer to the consignee and notify the carrier thereof by a message.
- The carrier shall send a message to the consignee confirming his possession of the goods and indicating the particulars thereof as well the carrying ship to be confirmed by the consignee.
- Before the ship's arrival at the port of discharge, the carrier shall send a message to his agent at that port indicating the ship, the goods carried onboard and the name of consignees to whom the agent shall send a message of arrival of the goods.
- Upon receipt of the message of arrival, the consignee shall obtain a delivery order or delivery message from the carrier's agent upon production of his proper identification.

The aforementioned process of transmission of an electronic bill of lading is centred around the carrier. Other electronic bill of lading system like Bolero and essDOCS are all centred around the system managers. However, centralization has the shortcoming of causing the concern about the safety of transport data and thus may cause difficulty of being relied by the merchants, banks and other parties concerned in the transaction. It seems clear that the application of blockchain electronic bill of lading can realize decentralization and may become an effective means of electronization of bills of lading.

III. Legal Matters Concerning Electronic Bills of Lading

A. *Introduction*

397. To make widespread use of electronic bills of lading, solution of the matter of application of law and other legal matters is as important as the technical and financial concerns.

Great efforts have been made both at international and national level in the shaping of rules of electronic commerce. One achievement is the adoption of the *UNCITRAL Model Law on Electronic Commerce of 1996* with additional Article 5*bis* as adopted in 1998. Another remarkable achievement is the adoption of the Rotterdam Rules containing detailed provisions of electronic transport record mainly in Chapter 3 'Electronic transport records' and Chapter 8 'Transport documents and electronic transport records'.

As regards electronic bills of lading, the *CMI Rules for Electronic Bills of Lading of 1990* were adopted in order to solve the matter of application of law and other legal matters. However, the Rules do not have the effect of law and shall apply only when the parties so agree (Article 1). Besides, the *ICC Uniform Customs and Practice for Documentary Credits* (UCP 600), especially the *UCP600 Supplement for Electronic Presentation* (eUCP) recognizes electronic bills of lading as acceptable transport documents.

It is sure that paper transport documents including bills of lading will be gradually replaced by the paperless electronic transport documents. Nevertheless, there is still a long way to go before electronic bills of lading or other electronic transport documents are widely used in the maritime transport.

398. In China, great importance is attached in the development of electronic commerce.

China has the *Law on Electronic Signature* adopted on 28 August 2004 and latest amended on 23 April 2019, and the *Law of Electronic Commerce* adopted on 31 August 2018. In addition, several regulations have been adopted in order to facilitate the application of electronic documents. Paragraph 3 of Article 469 of CC recognizes the effect of being in written form of electronic contracts. Paragraph 1 of Article 491 and Article 492 stipulate the time and place of electronic contracts.

However, commercial rules of law governing electronic bills of lading or other electronic transport documents are still needed. It can be anticipated that rules concerning electronic transport record to be shaped by reference to those contained in the *Rotterdam Rules* will be contained in MC after revision in the near future.

B. *Application of Law to Electronic Bills of Lading*

399. Similar to the case of SWBs, it is doubtful that the law on carriage of goods by sea now prevailing in the world based upon the paper bills of lading and The Hague or the Hague-Visby Rules is fully adaptable to electronic bills of lading, because an electronic bill of lading is not deemed as a bill of lading in The Hague or the Hague-Visby Rules. This seems also the case in the Hamburg Rules, although

Article 14(3) provides that the signature on a bill of lading may be made by any electronic means, if not consistent with the law of the country where the bill of lading is issued.

400. By virtue of Article 6 of the *CMI Rules for Electronic Bills of Lading of 1990*, the international convention or national law that would have been compulsorily applicable if a paper bill of lading had been issued shall apply to the case of electronic bill of lading. However, the enforceability of this provision itself is doubtful.

401. Under MC, electronic data are not deemed as having the effect of written document in Article 43. Although it is not decided yet, it seems doubtful that an electronic bill of lading is a bill of lading defined in Article 71 or a document other than a bill of lading referred to in Article 80. Therefore, it seems doubtful that Chapter IV of MC applies to electronic bills of lading, although electronic data are recognized as being in written form in Article 469 of CC.

C. Rules of Transmission of Electronic Bills of Lading

402. In the use of electronic bill of lading, the contents relating to a contract of carriage of goods by sea are transformed into electronic messages and one or more electronic messages are combined into a unit of dispatch and transmitted from one computer to another. Therefore, one legal matter concerned is the rules of transmission shared by all electronic commerce.

In this respect, the United Nations has adopted two rules *viz.* the *United Nations Rules for Electronic Data Interchange for Administration, Commerce and Transport*, known as 'UN/EDIFACT', and the *Uniform Rules of Conduct for Interchange of Trade Data by Teletransmission*, known as 'UNCID'. The two Rules are adopted in the *CMI Rules for Electronic Bills of Lading of 1990* on non-compulsory basis.

Among the technical matters, the secrecy and safety of electronic messages in transmission is of significant importance, because an electronic message shall have function equivalence to a paper bill of lading. Thus, private key is used and is defined in Article 2 of the *CMI Rules for Electronic Bills of Lading* as 'any technically appropriate form, such as a combination of numbers and/or letters, which the parties may agree for securing the authenticity and integrity of transmission'. Article 8 of the Rules further provides that a private key is unique to each successive holder of the right of control and transfer.

D. Terms and Conditions of Contract of Carriage

403. It is unreasonable in economic sense to transmit all the clauses of a paper bill of lading electronically. One solution is a reference in an electronic bill of lading to the terms and conditions of contract of carriage formulated by the carrier and readily available to shippers.

By virtue of Article 5 of the *CMI Rules for Electronic Bills of Lading*, these terms and conditions shall form part of the contract of carriage.

E. Equivalence of Electronic Data to Written Form

404. Function equivalence of an electronic document to a paper document is a basic requirement of electronic commerce. In this respect, Article 11 of the *CMI Rules for Electronic Bills of Lading* provides that the carrier and the shipper and all subsequent parties concerned agree that requirement of written contract or evidence thereof is satisfied by the transmitted and confirmed electronic data residing on computer data storage media displayable in human language on a video screen or as printed out by a computer.

It is doubtful that a written form of contract or evidence thereof shall be subject to the agreement of the parties thereto under Chinese law. Instead, what is a written contract or evidence thereof is an issue of statutory provision. As mentioned *supra*, electronic data are recognized as being in a written form by Article 469 of CC.

Chapter 7. Pilotage

§1. Introduction

I. Concept of Pilotage

405. Pilotage of a ship is a special kind of professional service provided by a pilot who pilots over a ship during her getting or leaving or shifting berth, or sailing in or off port areas, rivers, straits or other water areas where her master is not familiar with the waterways, navigational aids, port instalments or other natural conditions as well as regulations or provisions regarding safety of navigation prevailing in such waters. In China, a ship's pilot is a person who holds an effective certificate of competency of a pilot and is employed by a pilot station to render his service.

A pilot commands the ship under his pilotage or acts as a nautical adviser to the shipmaster. He renders his service either on board the ship under pilotage or on board the piloting boat leading the ship under pilotage in the case the pilot is unable to board the ship due to wind, wave or other exceptional reasons.

Since the founding of the People's Republic in 1949, China has been maintaining the provision of pilotage services in all its open ports, whether located along the sea coastline or the main navigable rivers. In every open seaport or river port, there is a pilot station or branch rendering pilotage services for ships in or off their respective ports.

II. Competent Authorities

406. The administration on pilotage in China is a function of MOT. MOT promulgates administrative provisions regarding the provision of pilotage services in seaports, the Yangtze River and other navigable rivers. MOT also promulgates the rates of pilotage fees together with the National Development and Reform Commission.

The provision of pilotage services in and off port areas is the function and responsibility of port authorities as required by the *Port Law*. Now, the pilotage services in and off port areas are provided by the pilot stations established by the local governmental organs responsible for port or traffic. The Yangtze River Pilotage Center provides the pilotage services along the Yangtze River.

The training and certificating of pilots, delimitation of pilotage area including pilotage anchorages as well as the matters of safety of pilotage including investigation into maritime accidents occurred during pilotage and imposition of disciplinary sanctions on faulty pilots are within the jurisdiction of MSA by virtue of MTSL or the *Regulations Governing Administration on Traffic Safety in Rivers*.

III. Qualification for Pilot

407. A pilot should hold a certificate of competency issued by MSA as provided for in the *Measures Regarding Administration on Pilots* promulgated by MOT on 13 February 2008 and amended on 24 December 2013.

Pilots are divided into four grades in China. Application for qualification for any grade of pilot shall meet the following conditions: holding a crewmember's service book, meeting the health inspection requirements for a deck officer, having gone through the required training and MSA's exams and assessment, having the required experience of serving onboard and good safety record.

§2. Statutory Provisions

I. Applicable Laws

408. Pilotage is governed by MTSL and MC as well as the following administrative statutes:

- The *Provisions Regarding Administration on Ship's Pilotage* (hereinafter referred to as 'Pilotage Administration Provisions'), promulgated by the former MOC on 30 November 2001 and amended on 25 August 2021 by MOT.
- The *Measures Regarding Administration on Pilots*, promulgated by MOT on 13 February 2008 and amended on 24 December 2013.
- *The Regulations Governing Administration on Traffic Safety in Rivers*, promulgated by the State Council on 28 June 2002.

II. Compulsory Pilotage

409. Traditionally, pilotage has twofold functions in law, *viz.* a reflection of the sovereignty of the coastal State and the necessity for the safety of ships and port. In the modern time, however, the first function is weakened or even disappeared. Nevertheless, Article 1 of the Pilotage Administration Provisions still refers to safeguarding the State sovereignty by imposing compulsory pilotage on foreign ships.

As provided for in Article 30 of MTSL and Article 9 of the Pilotage Administration Provisions, the following ships shall apply for pilotage when navigating, berthing or shifting berths in the designated pilotage areas at sea:

- ships of foreign nationality, unless exempted by MOT after approval of the State Council;
- nuclear ships, ships carrying radioactive substances or very large crude oil carriers with DWT of more than 100,000 tons;
- bulk liquefied gas carriers or bulk dangerous chemical carriers which may cause danger to the port safety;

- ships of which the length, width and height are near the limits for the relevant waterway navigation conditions as may be published by MSA for respective ports.

As provided for in Article 19 of the *Regulations Governing Administration on Traffic Safety in Rivers*, the following ships shall apply for pilotage when navigating in the Chinese rivers:

- ships of foreign nationality;
- seagoing power-driven ships with gross tonnage more than 1,000 tons, unless the master has navigated seagoing ship of the same kind in the same river not more than two months ago;
- ships navigating in waters with restricted navigation conditions;
- passenger ships or ships carrying dangerous goods as stipulated by MOT.

As regards the other ships flying Chinese flag, pilotage is non-compulsory and is up to the master to decide whether pilotage service shall be applied for in consideration of safety of the ship, even if the ship is engaged in international shipping. Where pilotage is applied for on non-compulsory basis, the pilot station or centre shall provide pilotage services.

§3. Duties of Pilot and Master of Ship under Pilotage

I. Duties of Pilot

410. By virtue of the Pilotage Administration Provisions, a pilot has the following duties:

- after boarding on the ship under pilotage, the pilot shall introduce the pilotage plan to the master (Article 26);
- the pilot shall conduct pilotage with due care and timely report the movement of the ship under pilotage to MSA; the pilot shall report maritime accident, pollution accident or action in violation of regulations he has discovered to MSA (Article 29);
- where a traffic accident occurs to the ship under pilotage, the pilot shall take effective measures to mitigate loss or damage, report to the pilotage station or centre and MSA soonest, and accept, cooperate with or assist in investigation (Article 31);
- the pilot shall board the ship in the designated water area, pilot the ship from the designated place of commencement of pilotage to the designated place of destination of pilotage, and shall leave the ship under pilotage after handover of command of the ship to the master or the successive pilot and confirmation of safety by both parties (Article 34);
- the pilot and the master shall accurately fill in the pilotage voucher after completion of pilotage (Article 39).

In addition, by virtue of Article 30 of the Pilotage Administration Provisions, a pilot may refuse, suspend or finish piloting and timely report to the pilot station or centre and MSA under the following circumstances: adverse weather or sea conditions; unseaworthiness of the ship to be piloted or under pilotage; the waterway or berth conditions not meeting the safety requirements for the ship's navigating, berthing or operation; not feeling well and being unable to continue piloting the ship; other causes unfit for pilotage. However, the pilot shall expressly notify the master of the ship before he makes such a decision, and make appropriate arrangement for the safety of the ship including piloting the ship to a place where she will be safe and will not cause prejudice to the normal navigation, berthing or anchoring, and operation of other ships.

II. Duties of Master of Ship under Pilotage

411. By virtue of Article 33 of the Pilotage Administration Provisions, the master of the ship under pilotage shall comply with the following requirements:

- the master shall provide equipment for the pilot's safe and convenient boarding and leaving the ship, take necessary measure to ensure the pilot's safe boarding and leaving the ship, as required by the SOLAS Convention; by virtue of paragraph 2 of Article 31 of MTSL, the master shall ensure that the ship has equipment for embarkation and disembarkation as required and the safety of the pilot during his embarkation and disembarkation well as onboard;
- the master shall provide convenience to and cooperate with the pilot in conducting pilotage;
- the master shall answer the pilot's inquiries and adopt the pilot's pilotage orders unless such orders may cause danger to the ship's safety;
- the master shall appoint a deck officer to take his position before leaving the bridge and advise the pilot of the same, and shall return back soonest;
- when the master finds a pilotage order given by the pilot may cause threat to the ship's safety, he may require the pilot to change the order and, when necessary, require the pilotage station or centre to change the pilot and shall report to MSA timely.

In addition, Article 26 of the Pilotage Administration Provisions provides that the master shall introduce the ship's manoeuvrability and other information relating to the pilotage to the pilot.

It is important to note that paragraph 3 of Article 31 of MTSL and Article 39 of MC provide that the master is not discharged from his duty in the command, management and navigation of the ship while under pilotage, whether the pilotage is compulsory or not. Thus, the master shall take care of the safety of the ship's navigation while under pilotage, but shall not unreasonably interfere with the pilot's service, although he may raise reasonable advices and requirements for the sake of safety of the ship's navigation or even change the pilot's orders when necessary.

§4. Liability of Pilot

I. Civil Liability

412. Under Chinese law, on the ground that the master of the ship under pilotage is not discharged from his statutory duty in the management and navigation of the ship with the presence of a pilot onboard as provided for in Article 39 of MC and paragraph 3 of Article 31 of MTSL, where a maritime accident occurs due to the fault of a pilot during pilotage causing loss of or damage to the ship under pilotage or liability of her owners to third parties, neither the pilot nor the pilotage station or centre which employed the faulty pilot nor the port authority responsible for the provision of pilotage service in or off the port area shall bear any civil liability for such loss, damage or liability to any third parties. In this regard, the fault committed by the pilot shall be deemed as committed by the master of the ship under pilotage. Consequently, the shipowners or other persons who are responsible for the acts or omissions of the mater shall be responsible for such loss, damage or liability to any third parties.[39]

By virtue of Articles 22, 23 and 24 of the Pilotage Administration Provisions, a pilot station or centre shall timely arrange a pilot or pilots who hold valid certificate upon receiving pilotage application, make pilotage plan where the length, width, draft or height above water surface of the ship to be piloted are near the limits for navigation in the relevant waterway, and make reasonable plan of the use of tugs based upon the circumstances of the ship, navigation conditions and the requirements for the use of tugs. However, the pilot station or centre shall not bear any civil liability for loss of or damage to the ship under pilotage or loss or damage suffered by a third party due to failure of the pilot station or centre in performing any of the above duties, on the same ground that the master of the ship is not discharged from his statutory duty in the management and navigation of the ship with the presence of a pilot on board. This may imply that the master of the ship has the right to raise objection to the pilotage plan or the plan of use of tugs in order to ensure safety.

II. Disciplinary Liability

413. A pilot may bear disciplinary liability in the case of an accident due to his fault committed during pilotage in the light of the circumstances of violation of MTSL, the *Regulations Governing Administration on Traffic Safety in Rivers*, the Pilotage Administration Provisions or other maritime safety regulations.

The disciplinary liability which shall be imposed by MSA includes warning, withholding or revocation of certificate of competency and fines.

Where a maritime accident occurs during pilotage, the pilot concerned shall submit a pilotage accident report and accept the investigation of MSA within whose jurisdiction the pilotage and the accident took place. Disciplinary liability shall be

39. Judgment by Dalian Maritime Court in the case of M.V. 'Ai Tai' in 1993.

imposed on the pilot by virtue of the result of investigation. Disciplinary liability in the form of fines may also be imposed on the pilot station or centre by MSA if it fails to fulfil its duties.

Like the case of a shipmaster, if the pilot does not accept the disciplinary sanction imposed on him, he may apply to the superior MSA's office for reconsideration in accordance with the *Administrative Reconsideration Law* adopted on 29 April 1999 and latest amended on 1 September 2017. He may also file an administrative lawsuit directly with a court of law against MSA which has imposed on him the disciplinary sanction in accordance with the *Administrative Litigation Law* adopted on 4 April 1989 and latest amended on 27 June 2017.

III. Criminal Liability

414. Also like the case of a shipmaster, criminal liability of the pilot for his fault during pilotage causing a maritime accident and the consequential loss or damage shall be imposed by court of law in accordance with the *Criminal Code* and the *Criminal Procedure Code*.

Chapter 8. Towage and Pushing Contract

§1. Introduction

I. Concept of Towage and Pushing

415. Towage and pushing is a special kind of water-borne operation.

In China, towage is understood to mean any movement in which a tugboat or other vessel called 'tug' tows a barge or other object such as a platform, floating crane or vessel without power or otherwise not self-movable called 'towed object' which moves by means of the power provided by a tug via towline and/or towing gear. In accordance with the way the tug and the towed object are connected, towage is divided into two forms: (a) the tug moves ahead of the towed object; (b) the tug and the towed object are connected together side by side.

Pushing means the movement of a barge or other object not self-movable as pushed in its rear by a tugboat or other vessel.

Obviously, towage and pushing share the common feature of provision of power by a tug for the movement of other vessel or object, although they have differences in physical sense. This is why towage, in its broad sense, covers pushing in Chinese law.

In this chapter, towage covers pushing unless otherwise indicated.

A convoy consists of at least one tug and one towed object. In many cases, a convoy in inland navigation especially in the Yangtze River consists of one tug and two or more barges with a total loading capacity of more than 10,000 mt of cargo. Sometimes, two tugs are used in a convoy.

416. Towage services are widely used in China. The main areas of towage services are: (a) towage of barge or barges for the carriage of goods in inland navigation or seaport area; (b) tug's assistance in ship's manoeuvre of berthing or buoying in port; (c) towage of a platform, floating crane or other waterborne object without power; (d) towage in salvage operations. Traditionally in the Yangtze River, towage was the main form of carriage of cargo and huge amount of coal, ore, oil and other bulk cargoes were carried through towage, especially from Shanghai, Nanjing, Nantong or other big ports in the lower reaches to other places in the upper reaches or tributaries thereof. Now, more and more self-movable vessels of which many are called self-movable barges are used in the Yangtze River and other inland navigation.

In China, many inland water transport companies have their own fleet of tugs and barges. In every seaport, there is one or two companies called 'tug and barge company' which provide towage services. The three professional salvage companies based in Yantai, Shanghai and Guangzhou respectively and China Ocean Engineering Corporation are the main companies that provide services of ocean towage.

II. Towage Contract

A. *Definition and Contents of Towage Contract*

417. A towage contract is a contract concluded between the owner or operator of a tug called 'towing party' and the owner of the towed object or other interest called 'towed party' by which the towing party provides service of towage of the towed object from one place to another at sea, in port area or in inland waters and the towed party pays the agreed expenses of towage.

A contract of sea towage is defined in Article 155 of MC as 'a contract whereby the towing party undertakes to tow an object by sea with a tug from one place to another and the towed party pays the towage expenses'.

The towing party may, besides tug-owners, be an operator of a tug upon a contract of tug operation or charterers of a tug under a charterparty who provides towage services for a third party.

418. A towage contract concluded for the purpose of a salvage operation is classified as a salvage contract and is not taken as a contract of towage in law. Where the owners or operator of a tug towing a barge or barges owned or operated by him carries goods by sea or in inland navigation from one port or place to another, such an operation is deemed as carriage of goods and is not taken as towage in law (Article 164, MC).

419. As provided for in Article 156 of MC, a contract of sea towage shall be made in writing and its contents shall conclude:

- the name and address of the towing party;
- the name and address of the towed party;
- the name and main particulars of the tug;
- the description and main particulars of the towed object;
- the place of commencement of towage and destination;
- the date of commencement of towage;
- the towage expenses and the way of payment thereof;
- the other related matters.

The other related matters include, *inter alia*, seaworthiness of the tug and the towworthiness of the towed object, cancelling date, expected date of arrival, substitute of tug, crew on board the vessel to be towed, safe port, lien on the towed object, deviation, salvage, termination of contract, arbitration or jurisdiction and application of law.

B. *Forms of Towage Contract*

420. A contract of towage in many cases is concluded on the basis of a standard form thereof as agreed upon between the two parties.

Two main forms of towage contract are used in China, i.e., the towage contract form on lump sum basis coded as 'CHINATOW' and formulated by the former China Ocean Engineering Services Company Ltd. which is now China Ocean Engineering Corporation and the towage contract form on daily hire basis formulated by the former China Towage Company.

Other towage contract forms that are often used in international towage and occasionally used in China include, *inter alia*, the form of international ocean towage agreement, coded as 'TOWHIRE', jointly recommended by International Salvage Union (ISU), European Tugowners Association (ETA) and BIMCO.

Where a contract of towage based upon a standard form is concluded, the statutory provisions of Articles 496, 497 and 498 of CC governing the use of form clauses shall apply.

C. Termination and Alteration of Towage Contract

421. Termination and alteration of a towage contract is subject to the provisions governing termination and alteration of a contract contained in Book Three 'Contracts' of CC. Special provisions are contained in MC regarding termination or alteration of a contract of towage due to force majeure or other causes not attributable to the fault of either party, the main contents of which are as follows:

- if before the commencement of towage service, the towage contract cannot be performed due to force majeure or other causes not attributable to the fault of either party, either party may terminate the contract and neither party shall be liable towards the other, and the towage expenses already paid by the towed party shall be returned by the towing party, unless otherwise agreed upon in the towage contract (Article 158, MC);
- if after the commencement of towage service, the performance of towage contract cannot be continued due to force majeure or other causes not attributable to the fault of either party, either party may terminate the contract and neither party shall be liable towards the other (Article 159, MC), and towage expenses shall be paid according to the ratio of the distance already towed to the whole distance of the voyage, unless otherwise agreed upon in the towage contract;
- where the towed object cannot reach its destination due to force majeure or other causes not attributable to the fault of either party, unless the towage contract provides otherwise, the towing party may deliver the towed object to the towed party or its agent at a place near the destination or at a safe port or an anchorage chosen by the master of the tug, and the towage contract shall be deemed as have been fulfilled (Article 160, MC).

§2. Applicable Laws

422. A contract of towage by sea is governed by Chapter VII 'Contract of Sea Towage' of MC which applies to contracts of both international towage and domestic towage by sea but does not apply to contracts of towage in inland waters.

Towage services rendered by tugs in assisting ships' manoeuvre in berthing or buoying within port area are excluded from the scope of application of this chapter for the main reasons that such services occur too frequently to be regulated by the complicated rules contained in this chapter and that the rendering of such services are under the command of the assisted ships unlike in normal towages.

There is no special law or regulation governing towage in inland navigation which is thus governed by Book Three 'Contracts' of CC only.

Book Three 'Contracts' of CC also applies a contract of sea towage to the extent of no repugnance to Chapter VII of MC.

There is no international treaty concerning contracts of towage at sea.

§3. Obligations under Towage Contract

I. Obligations of Towing party

423. Paragraph 1 of Article 157 of MC provides that the towing party shall, before and at the beginning of the towage, exercise due diligence to make the tug seaworthy and tow-worthy, properly man the tug and equip it with gears and tow-lines, and to provide all other necessary supplies and appliances for the intended voyage.

Other obligations of the towing party shall be decided by the terms of the contract of towage and general provisions contained in Book Three 'Contracts' of CC. The other contractual obligations include, *inter alia*, being responsible for the command of the convoy during towage, salving the towed object the persons and cargo on board a towed vessel in distress, performing the towage with reasonable dispatch and without unjustifiable deviation.

II. Obligations of Towed Party

424. As provided for in paragraph 2 of Article 157 of MC, the towed party shall, before and at the beginning of the towage, make all necessary preparations for the towage, exercise due diligence to make the towed object tow-worthy, and provide certificate of tow-worthiness and other documents issued by the relevant survey and inspection organization. The said certificate and other documents are issued by a ship's classification society such as CCS in most cases in China.

Another main statutory obligation of the towed party is to pay the towage expenses and other expenses such as demurrage as agreed upon by the parties. By virtue of Article 161 of MC, where the towed party fails to pay the towage expenses or other reasonable expenses as agreed upon, the towing party shall have a lien on the towed object. Towage expenses are calculated either on lump sum basis or daily hire of the tug. In the case of lump sum basis, other expenses such as demurrage are often agreed upon by the parties.

Other obligations of the towed party shall be decided by the terms of the towage contract and general provisions contained in Book Three 'Contracts' of CC. The other obligations include, *inter alia*, obedience to the command of the master of the tug during towage, undertaking the safety of the port of commencement of towage, port of destination and port of call, and taking delivery of the towed object without delay at destination.

§4. Liability and Limitation of Liability

I. Liability Between Contractual Parties

425. The liability of one party under a contract of towage to the other shall be determined by the terms of the contract and the applicable law.

A party may incur contractual liability due to its breach of contract or statutory obligations. It may also incur tort liability to the other party due to its tortuous act or omission not covered by the contract and statutory provisions. In addition, by the application of the rule of competition between contractual liability and tort liability as adopted in Article 186 of CC, a party to the contract of towage may incur tort liability due to its breach of contract or statutory obligations, if the other party so chooses to make claim against it.[40]

426. MC adopted the rule of fault liability under a contract of sea towage. As provided for in paragraph 1 of Article 162, if loss or damage suffered by the towing party or the towed party was caused by the fault of the other party in the course of sea towage, the party at fault shall be liable for loss or damage; where loss or damage was caused by the faults of both parties, they shall be responsible for loss or damage in proportion to the extent of their respective faults.

Nevertheless, as an exception of this statutory rule as provided for in paragraph 2 of Article 162 of MC, the towing party shall not be liable where it proves that the loss or damage suffered by the towed party was due to the fault of the master or other crewmembers of the tug, the pilot or other servant or agent of the towing party in the navigation or management of the tug or the fault of the tug in saving or attempting to save life or property at sea.

427. Noticeably, the above provisions of liability between the parties under a contract of sea towage contained Article 162 of MC shall apply only if there is no provision or no different provision in this regard in the contract. This provision leaves the parties to negotiate their respective liability and was laid down by reference to the corresponding legislations of several other jurisdictions and in consideration of the diversity of provisions of liability in various standard forms of towage contract.

40. For details concerning the rule of competition between contractual liability and tort liability, *see* §9, Ch. 6 of this part.

II. Liability Towards Third Party

428. As provided for in Article 163 of MC, if death of or personal injury to a third party or loss of or damage to property of a third party occurred during the sea towage due to the fault of towing party or of the towed party or of both, they shall be liable jointly and severally to that third party. Therefore, the third party may raise claim against either the towing party or the towed party or both of them for full compensation for its loss or damage, regardless of which party was at fault or, in a case both the parties were at fault, what the proportion to the extent of their respective faults will be.

The underlying reason of this protective provision is that, in the course of towage, the tug and the towed object are so closely physically connected that they move as an integrity and consequently it may be very difficult for a third party to prove which party has fault or what the proportion to the extent of their respective faults will be in the case both parties are at fault, let alone the determination of fault may be subject to the terms of the towage contract to which the third party is not a party.

429. However, where a party has paid compensation for the loss or damage suffered by a third party for which it is not liable as between the two parties or in an amount exceeding the proportion for which it is liable, it shall have the right of recourse against the other party, unless otherwise provided for in the towage contract.

III. Limitation of Liability

A. *Statutory Provisions*

430. No special provisions are contained in MC or its by-laws regarding the limitation of liability between the parties under a contract of towage or towards a third party.

Thus, the limitation of liability under a contract of towage shall be determined by virtue of the general provisions of Chapter XI 'Limitation of Liability for Maritime Claims' of MC and the *Provisions Regarding the Limitation of Liability for Ships with a Gross Tonnage not Exceeding 300 Tons and Those Engaging in Transport Services between the Ports of China* promulgated by the former MOC on 1 January 1994 as empowered by paragraph 2 of Article 210 of MC.[41]

B. *Limitation of Liability to Other Contractual Party*

431. By virtue of these statutory provisions governing limitation of liability, as between the towing party and the towed party, the limit of liability of the towing

41. For details, *see* §8, Ch. 4 of Part II.

party shall be calculated in accordance with the gross tonnage of the tug and that of the towed party shall be calculated in accordance with the gross tonnage of the towed object.

However, problem occurs where the towed object is not a ship with gross tonnage. Under the current legal regime of limitation of liability for maritime claims, the only criterion for calculating the limits of liability is the gross tonnage of the ship involved, except the case of loss of life of passengers carried on board a passenger ship. Thus, the current statutory provisions applicable to ships with gross tonnage cannot offer limitation of liability to such a towed party. Therefore, it seems advisable to adopt a new criterion in law for the case in which the towed object is not a ship with gross tonnage, e.g., the value of the towed object.

In addition, there are arguments as to whether limitation of liability applies as between the parties to a contract of towage.

C. *Limitation of Liability to Third Party*

432. As regards limitation of liability for death or personal injury, or loss of or damage to property suffered by a third party, it is not decided whether the basis of calculation of the limit shall be the gross tonnage of the tug or the towed ship or the aggregate gross tonnage of both.

It seems advisable that, in correspondence with the joint and several liability of the contractual parties towards a third party, the limit of liability of either or both parties towards a third party shall be calculated on the basis of the aggregate gross tonnage of the tug and the towed ship, no matter the death or personal injury, or loss of or damage to property suffered by the third party was caused by the tug or the towed ship or both. Another opinion is that the limit of liability shall be calculated on the basis of the gross tonnage of the tug or the towed ship that caused the death or personal injury or loss or damage, no matter which party is claimed against. In such a case, however, it is not always easy to prove whether the loss or damage was caused by the tug or the towed ship or, if fault is to be taken into consideration, which party was at fault, especially where the third party is to bear the burden of proof.

The problem arising from the case in which the towed object is not a ship with gross tonnage as mentioned *supra* also exists in the calculation of the limit of liability towards a third party.

D. *Loss of Right to Limit*

433. The right of one party under a towage contract to limit its liability towards the other party, or the right of one or both parties to the contract to limit liability towards a third party shall be lost, if it proves that death or personal injury, or loss or damage, resulted from an act or omission of the party or parties concerned done with the intent to cause such death or personal injury, loss or damage, or recklessly and with knowledge that such death or personal injury, or loss or damage, would probably result (Article 209, MC).

Chapter 9. Salvage at Sea

§1. Definitions

434. Salvage at sea is deemed as a special legal regime of maritime law in China. Traditionally, where a salvor renders salvage service that makes or assists a ship, cargo on board the ship or other property at sea in distress out of danger, he shall be entitled to payment, known as 'salvage remuneration' or 'salvage reward', from the owners of the property salved.

Thus, salvage at sea can be defined as services for the purpose of salving a ship, cargo on board her or other recognized property in danger at sea or other navigable waters and rendered on a voluntary basis in the sense of being attributable neither to pre-existing contractual or statutory duty owed to the owner of the salved property, nor to the interest of self-preservation.

435. The law of several civil law countries divides such services into two kinds, *viz.* salvage and assistance. Salvage means services rendered to a ship in such a state of danger that her master and other crewmembers no longer have the control over her, no matter whether they are still onboard or have left the ship. Assistance means services rendered to a ship in danger, but still under the control of her master and other crewmembers.[42]

The difference between salvage and assistance may only be important in determining the reward to be paid to the salvor. Basically, the salvor may be entitled to a higher reward in the case of salvage than that in the case of assistance, where all the other relevant factors are the same.

Under Chinese law, salvage embodies assistance.

436. Salvage at sea in its broad sense can be divided into two kinds in the light of the object of salvage, i.e., salvage of life and salvage of property. In narrow sense, however, salvage means salvage of property only. This is because the kernel of the statutory provisions on salvage at sea is the reward for salvage of property. Saving life in danger is an obligation provided for both in domestic law and in international treaties and therefore is not rendered on a voluntary basis, as a result of which reward for salvage of life at sea is denied in principle.[43] This is why the maritime law of some countries stipulates salvage of property at sea only.

The provisions governing salvage at sea contained in Chapter IX 'Salvage at Sea' in MC do not cover salvage of life, except the obligation of saving life in danger and the right of the salvor of life to a reasonable share with the salvor of property in the salvage payment where salvage of life and that of property occur in the same salvage operations.

42. Si, Y. & Hu, Z. *e.a.*, *Maritime Law*, Beijing, 2023, 265.
43. Article 174 of MC provides that every master is bound, so far as he can do so without serious danger to his ship and persons on board, to render assistance to any person in danger of being lost at sea. Duty of master of a ship to render assistance to any person at high seas in danger of being lost is contained in Article 98 of UNLOS.

437. Salvage services may be rendered by either professional salvage companies, ships navigating nearby or other salvors.

In China, there are three professional salvage companies and three professional rescue bureaus all of which are under China Rescue and Salvage of MOT, i.e., Yantai Salvage and Beihai Rescue Bureau in the north, Shanghai Salvage and Donghai Rescue Bureau in the middle, and Guangzhou Salvage and Nanhai Rescue Bureau in the South. Each salvage company has established salvage stations and each rescue bureau has established rescue bases in several big ports within its responsible water area. The three salvage companies are quasi-commercial companies, whereas the three rescue bureaus are basically funded by the government and provide public service for the search and rescue of life at sea.

The State administration on salvage at sea rests with MOT. MSA's head office and its subordinate organs are responsible for the organization, cooperation and other administrative affairs of salvage, search and rescue at sea. China Rescue and Salvage is responsible for the administrative affairs of the three salvage companies and the three rescue bureaus.

§2. Applicable Laws

I. International Treaties

438. On 29 December 1993, China ratified the *International Convention on Salvage*, known as '1989 Salvage Convention', signed in London on 28 April 1989 and came into force on 14 July 1996.

Reservations were made on Article 30(1)(a), (b) and (d) of this Convention, as a result of which the Convention does not apply in China where the salvage operation takes place in inland waters and all the ships involved are of inland navigation or no ship in involved, or the property involved is maritime cultural property of prehistoric, archaeological or historic interest and is situated on the sea-bed.

Another international treaty that China has ratified relating to salvage at sea is the 'SAR', signed in Hamburg on 27 April 1979. This Convention deals such matters of search and rescue of life at sea as the organization, cooperation among the related States, preparatory measures, working procedures of search and rescue and ship position reporting system. It embodies the important rule to the effect that each contracting State shall allow salvors of other contracting States to have an immediate access to or transit in its territorial water or land for the purpose of search and rescue of human lives in distress.

II. Domestic Legislation

439. Chapter IX 'Salvage at Sea' of MC governs salvage at sea. The provisions of this chapter are basically a reproduction of the 1989 Salvage Convention.

Noticeably, when MC was adopted, the 1989 Salvage Convention had not come into force yet, and the prevailing international treaty at that time was the *International Convention for the Unification of Certain Rules of Law Relating to Assistance and Salvage at Sea*, known as '1910 Salvage Convention', signed in Brussels on 23 September 1910 and entered into force on 1 March 1913. The draftsmen of MC realized that the 1910 Salvage Convention was partly out of date, and the 1989 Salvage Convention represented the tendency of international legislation in this regard. When MC came into force on 1 July 1993, China became *ex facto* the first country to implement the 1989 Salvage Convention as a result of adopting most of its substantial provisions in MC.

440. Article 171 of MC provides that the provisions of this chapter shall apply to salvage operations rendered at sea or any other navigable waters adjacent thereto to ships or other property in distress.

Within the meaning of this scope of application, a ship is defined in Article 172 of MC as any ship referred to in Article 3 of MC and any other ship or craft that has been involved in a salvage operation not used for military or public service purposes. By virtue of this definition, in the case of salvage between or among ships, MC shall apply where one of the ships involved, whether she is the salving ship or the salved ship, is a ship defined in Article 3 of MC, i.e., seagoing ship or other mobile unit excluding a ship or craft to be used for military or public services purpose and a small vessel of less than 20 tons gross tonnage, while the other ship or ships involved can be either a ship defined in Article 3 of MC or any vessel other than those used for military or public service purpose and thus include inland vessel and small seagoing vessel of less than 20 tons gross tonnage, regardless of where the salvage occurs. However, MC does not apply to salvage service rendered to an inland vessel or a small seagoing vessel of less than 20 tons gross tonnage by the salvor who has not used a salving ship within the definition of ship contained in Article 3 of MC. MC also does not apply to a salvage between two inland vessels, between two small seagoing vessels of less than 20 tons gross tonnage, or between an inland vessel and a small seagoing vessel of less than 20 tons gross tonnage. If a ship used for military or public services purpose is involved, MC shall not apply.

441. Property is defined in Article 172 of MC as any property not permanently and intentionally attached to the shoreline and includes freight at risk.

By virtue of this definition, a grounded, abandoned or even sunken ship, cargo remaining on board a ship or floating at sea, floating warehouse or dockyard and any other property not permanently and intentionally attached to the shoreline, whether on board a ship or at sea, can be an object of salvage at sea. However, as provided for in Article 173, MC does not apply to salvage services rendered to fixed or floating platforms or mobile offshore drilling units on location and engaged in the exploration, exploitation or production of sea-bed mineral resources. This is because salvage thereof usually needs professional skills and equipment.

442. Chapter IX of MC applies to a salvage operation between sister ships, i.e., salvage operation carried out by and for a ship of the same owners (Article 191).

In addition, Article 192 provides that with respect to the salvage operations performed or controlled by the relevant competent authorities of the State, the salvors shall be entitled to avail themselves of the rights and remedies provided for in Chapter IX in respect of the salvage operations.

In admiralty practice, it is commonly recognized that MSA or its subordinate offices, the administrations on fishing vessels and fishing ports and other related governmental authorities are not entitled to salvage reward as a result of salvage of property at sea because they are obliged to render salvage service or to organize, coordinate and control salvage operations. However, such governmental authorities do not include the three professional salvage companies and three professional rescue bureaus mentioned in §1 of this chapter *supra*.

443. In most of the salvage cases, salvage services are rendered in accordance with a salvage contract concluded between the salvor and the salved party. Therefore, the general rules and provisions governing contract contained in Book Three 'Contracts' of CC regarding, *inter alia*, the conclusion, effect, performance, termination of rights and obligations, and breach of contract, are applicable as provisions of basic law to the salvage contract to the extent they are not repugnant to Chapter IX of MC.

§3. SALVAGE CONTRACT

I. Conclusion of Salvage Contract

444. By virtue of Article 175 of MC, a contract for salvage operation at sea is deemed as concluded when an agreement has been reached between the salvor and the salved party regarding the salvage operation to be undertaken by the salvor.

The master of a ship in distress has the authority to conclude a contract for salvage operation on behalf of the shipowners; the master of a ship in distress or her owners have the authority to conclude a contract for salvage operation on behalf of the owners of the cargo and other properties onboard (paragraph 2, Article 175, MC). Thus, a salvage contract concluded by the master of a salved ship shall be binding upon the owners of the salved ship, and a salvage contract concluded by the master or owners of a salved ship shall be binding upon the owners of the cargo or other salved properties on board the ship.

445. A salvage contract is usually concluded on the basis of a standard form of salvage contract in order to expedite the conclusion thereof.

The standard form widely used in the world is known as Lloyd's Open Form (LOF), first published in 1908 and with its latest version in 2020. By use of this form, any dispute arising from a salvage contract shall be referred to arbitration in the Lloyd's in London unless the contract provides otherwise.

The form of salvage contract formulated by CMAC in 1994 and amended in 2022, known as 'Beijing Form 2022', is also used in China. The disputes arising from this form shall be referred to arbitration in CMAC, unless the contract provides otherwise.

II. Modification or Annulment of Salvage Contract

446. A salvage contract is concluded where a ship or other property to be salved is in danger and is normally concluded at the time of urgency. Thus, two possibilities may exist in the case of salvage. One is the salvor may possibly take advantage of the precarious position of the salved party to try to put inequitable terms in the contract. The other is, due to lack of proper and physical anticipation of the extent of danger to the ship or other property, the difficulties of, and the time and costs needed for the salvage operation, the amount of payment agreed upon in the contract to the salvor may possibly prove too high or too low in contrast with the actual difficulties in salvage operation, the actual time used and costs spent by the salvor. Therefore, where these circumstances occur, the agreement as to the amount of salvage payment or other conditions of the salvage contract need be modified or even annulled in order to attain an equitable result of law.

It is thus expressly provided for in Article 176 of MC that a salvage contract may be modified by judgment of a court of law which has entertained the lawsuit brought by either party, or by an award of the arbitration organ to which the dispute has been referred for arbitration upon the agreement of the parties, where the contract has been entered into under undue influence or the influence of danger and its terms are obviously inequitable, or the payment under the contract is in an excessive degree too large or too low for the services actually rendered.

447. Noticeably, Article 176 of MC does not stipulate that a court of law or arbitration organ can annul a salvage contract in accordance with the circumstances of the case upon application of a party or parties.

In this respect, where no foreign element in concerned, Article 147 to Article 151 of CC shall apply enabling a court of law or arbitration organ to annul a salvage contract upon application of any party to the contract under one of the following circumstances: (a) the contract was concluded due to serious misunderstanding; (b) the contract was concluded due to the fraud of one party and being contrary to the other party's true intention; (c) the contract was concluded due to the fraud of a third party and being contrary to one party's true intention while the other party knew or should have known the fraud; (d) the contract was concluded due to coerce of one party or a third party resulting in the other party to conclude the contract in a situation such as critical state of distress or lack of judgment ability resulting in obvious inequity at the time of conclusion of the contract. By virtue of Article 152 of CC, the party entitled to apply for annulling the contract shall exercise his right within one year dating from the day on which he knows or should have known the reason for annulment, or from the day on which the act of coerce stopped, or within ninety days from the day on which he knows or should have known the serious misunderstanding, but not later than five years from the date of conclusions of the contract.

Where foreign element is related in a salvage operation, by virtue of Article 7 of the 1989 Salvage Convention to which China is a party, however, a court of law or arbitration organization cannot only modify, but also annul a salvage contract under either of the two situations as provided for in Article 176 of MC.

III. Obligations of Parties to Salvage Contract

A. *Obligations of Salvor*

448. As provided for in Article 177 of MC, the salvor has the following statutory obligations towards the salved party during the salvage operation:

- to carry out the salvage operation with due care;
- to exercise due care to prevent or minimize the pollution damage to the environment;
- to seek the assistance of other salvors where reasonably necessary;
- to accept the reasonable request of the salved to seek the participation in the salvage operation of other salvors, provided that if the request is not well-founded, the amount of payment due to the original salvor shall not be affected.

B. *Obligations of Salved*

449. As provided for in Article 178 of MC, the salved party has the following statutory obligations towards the salvor during the salvage operation:

- to cooperate fully with the salvor;
- to exercise due care to prevent or minimize the pollution damage to the environment;
- to promptly accept the request of the salvor to take delivery of the ship or property salved when such ship or property has been brought to a place of safety.

§4. Salvage Payment

450. Salvage payment as defined in Article 172 of MC embodies salvage reward, salvage remuneration and special compensation each of which is discussed below.

I. Salvage Reward

A. *Definition*

451. Salvage reward or reward as referred to in MC is the payment that the salvor is entitled to for his salvage services rendered to a ship or other recognized property with useful result in the meaning that all or part of the value of property is successfully salved.

B. Principle of 'No Cure, No Pay'

452. Traditionally, the determination of salvage reward adheres to the principle of 'no cure, no pay'. This principle was adopted in the 1910 Salvage Convention and remains in the 1989 Salvage Convention with respect to salvage services rendered to a ship or other property. The principle is also universally followed by national legislations.

In China, this principle is reflected in Article 179 of MC which stipulates: 'Where the salvage operation rendered to the ship or other property has had a useful result, the salvor shall be entitled to a reward. Except as otherwise provided for in Art. 182 of this Code or by other laws or the salvage contract, the salvor shall not be entitled to any payment if the salvage operation has had no useful result.' Noticeably, Article 182 of CC is the provision of special compensation same as Article 14 of the 1989 Salvage Convention.

C. Fixing of Salvage Reward

453. As provided for in Article 180 of MC, salvage reward shall be fixed with a view to encouraging salvage operations, taking into full account the following criteria:

– the value of the ship and other property salved;
– the skill and efforts of the salvor in preventing or minimizing the pollution damage to the environment;
– the measure of success obtained by the salvor;
– the nature and extent of the danger;
– the skill and efforts of the salvor in salving the ship, other property and life;
– the time used and expenses and losses incurred by the salvor;
– the risk of liability and other risks run by the salvor or his equipment;
– the promptness of the salvage service rendered by the salvor;
– the availability and use of ships or other equipment intended for salvage operation;
– the state of readiness and efficiency of the salvor's equipment and the value thereof.

454. The amount of salvage reward shall not exceed the value of the ship and other property salved which is defined in Article 181 of MC as 'the assessed value of the ship and other property salved or the proceeds of the sale thereof, after deduction of the relevant taxes and customs dues, quarantine expenses, inspection charges as well as expenses incurred in connection with the discharge, storage, assessment of the value and the sale thereof'. The salved personal belongings of the crew and cabin luggage of the passengers are not included in the value of the property salved and are thus exempted from the payment of salvage reward.

455. Where two or more salvors took part in the same salvage operation, the total salvage reward shall still be fixed by virtue of the above criteria contained in Article 180 of MC and shall also not exceed the value of the ship and other property salved.

The salvage reward shall be distributed between or among the salvors by agreement. Where no such agreement is reached, the dispute may be brought before a maritime court with jurisdiction for a judgment or be referred to arbitration if an arbitration agreement has been reached. The distribution shall be made in accordance with the above criteria contained in Article 180 with respect to each salvor (Article 184, MC).

456. The salvage reward shall be paid by the owners of the ship or other property salved. Where both the ship and other property are salved, the shipowners and owners of the property salved shall pay salvage reward in accordance with their respective proportion that the salved values of the ship and other property bear to the total salved value (Article 183, MC). Therefore, they shall not bear joint and several liability for the payment of salvage reward.

D. Denial of Salvage Reward in Full or in Part

457. As introduced in §1 *supra*, salvage reward is based upon the salvage services that the salvor rendered voluntarily and, if the salvage services rendered are attributable either to any pre-existing contractual or statutory duty owed to the owners of the salved property or to the interest of self-preservation of the salvor, the salvor is not entitled to salvage reward.

Thus, under the following circumstances, the salvor of a ship or other property cannot claim salvage reward against the owners of the ship or other property salved, or the reward shall be deprived partly:

- where salvage is rendered by a tugboat or other towing vessel to the towed vessel or other towed object, the owners of the tugboat or other towing vessel shall not be entitled to salvage reward, unless the salvage is in the nature of special service beyond the performance of the contractual obligation (Article 186, MC);
- the master and other crewmembers shall not be entitled to salvage reward for their salvage rendered to the ship they are serving on, because they have the duty under the articles of employment to salve the ship in case of danger and such salvage is also to the interests of their self-preservation;
- a pilot shall not be entitled to salvage reward for his salvage rendered to the ship under his pilotage, especially where her danger is caused by his fault, unless the salvage is in the nature of special service beyond the performance of his duty as a pilot and is not to the interest of his self-preservation;
- a passenger on a ship in danger shall not be entitled to salvage reward for his salvage rendered thereto, because the salvage is to the interest of his or her self-preservation and he or she has a duty to obey the orders of the master with respect to the management of ship including salvage, unless his or her performance is beyond his or her self-preservation and obedience to the orders of the master;

- where salvage is rendered by a colliding ship to another after collision, the salving ship shall not be entitled to salvage reward, because Article 166 of MC provides that the master of each of the ships in collision is bound, so far as he can do so without serious danger to his ship and persons onboard, to render assistance to the other ship and persons onboard after a collision and, if the salving ship is at fault in the collision, salvage to another is to her own interests in the sense that the extent of damage and her liability to another ship will be minimized;
- the salvage operation is carried out in spite of the express and reasonable refusal by the master of the ship in distress, the owners of the ship in question and the owners of other property (Article 186, MC);
- where salvage operation has become necessary or more difficult due to the fault of the salvor or where the salvor has committed fraud or other dishonest conduct, the salvor shall be deprived of the whole or part of the salvage reward payable to him (Article 187, MC).

II. Salvage Remuneration

458. The word 'remuneration' only appears in Article 185 of MC which reads: 'The salvor of human life may not demand any remuneration from those whose lives are saved, but is entitled to a fair share of the payment awarded to the salvor for salving the ship or other property or for preventing or minimizing the pollution damage to the environment'. Thus, salvage remuneration can be understood to be the payment to the salvor for his salvage of human lives.

As introduced in §1, salvage of human life at sea is an obligation of both humanism and public law. Article 174 of MC specifically provides: 'Every master is bound, so far as he can do so without serious danger to his ship and persons on board, to render assistance to any person in danger of being lost at sea.'

By virtue of Article 185 of MC cited *supra*, the salvor of human life shall not be entitled to salvage reward per se. In fact, remuneration in terms of a fair share of the salvage reward shall be paid by the owners of the ship and other property salved, because the skills and efforts of the salvor in salving life in the same salvage operation is a factor to be taken into account in fixing the salvage reward as provided for in Article 180 of MC. In other words, where salvage of property and that of human life take place in the same operation, the amount of salvage reward shall be higher than the case of salvage of property only. For the purpose of equity, the remuneration may also be in terms of a fair share of the special compensation paid by the shipowners to the salvor as mentioned *infra*.

III. Special Compensation

A. *Definition*

459. By virtue of paragraph 1 of Article 182 of MC, special compensation can be described as salvage payment by the owners of a ship in distress to the salvor who has carried out salvage operation where the ship by herself or the goods carried onboard threatened pollution damage to the environment and who has failed to earn a salvage reward to cover his costs.

Therefore, to claim for special compensation, two conditions shall be met *viz.* first, the salvor has carried out salvage operation in respect of a ship that by herself or her goods threatened pollution damage to the environment, regardless of whether the salvage has had any useful result in preventing or minimizing pollution damage to the environment; second, the salvor has failed to earn a salvage reward to cover his costs due to lack of useful result in the salvage of property or the useful result having been not sufficient enough.

Remarkably, the statutory provision of special compensation has broken through the traditional principle of 'no cure, no pay' in law with a view to prevention or minimization of damage to the marine environment. In other words, the new principle of 'no cure, some pay' is added.

Noticeably, by virtue of Article 14 of the 1989 Salvage Convention, special compensation shall be awarded to the salvor where he has carried salvage operation in respect of a ship that by herself or her goods threatened 'damage to the environment' which is defined in Article 1(d) of as 'substantial physical damage to human health or to marine life or resources in coastal or inland waters or areas adjacent thereto, caused by pollution, contamination, fire, explosion or similar major incidents'. By contrast, 'damage to the environment' is broader than 'pollution damage to the environment' stipulated in Article 182 of MC. On the other hand, the 1989 Salvage Convention limits the damage to the environment to 'substantial' physical damage to human health or to marine life or resources 'in coastal or inland waters or areas adjacent thereto', whereas Article 182 of MC does not contain the restrictive word 'substantial' and the term 'in coastal or inland waters or areas adjacent thereto'.

460. Special compensation shall be paid by the shipowners, regardless whether the salvage operation is carried out in respect of her or her goods or both and who shall be responsible for the threat of damage to the environment as between the shipowners and other party. However, if the shipowners shall not be responsible for the threat of such damage, his right of recourse against any other party including the owners of the goods who shall be responsible therefor shall not be prejudiced (paragraph 6, Article 182, MC). In practice, the shipowners' liability for special compensation is covered by P&I insurance.

B. Amount of Special Compensation

461. The amount of special compensation depends upon whether the salvage operation has had useful result in the prevention or minimization of damage to the environment.

Thus, where the salvage has had no useful result, the amount of special compensation shall be equivalent to the salvor's expenses, *viz.* 100% of the salvor's expenses (paragraph 1, Article 182, MC). Where the salvor has prevented or minimized pollution damage to the environment, the amount of special compensation may be increased by an amount up to a maximum of 30% of the expenses incurred by the salvor. In addition, the court of law which or the arbitration organ has entertained the case of disputes may, if it deems fair and just and taking into consideration the provisions of paragraph 1 of Article 180 of MC, render a judgment or an award further increasing the amount of special compensation, but in no event shall the total increase be more than 100% of the expenses incurred by the salvor (paragraph 2, Article 182, MC). Thus, the amount of special compensation shall be in the range between 100% of the salvor's expenses and 200% thereof in accordance with the circumstances of the case.

462. The said salvor's expenses are defined in paragraph 3 of Article 182 of MC as 'the salvor's out-of-pocket expenses reasonably incurred in the salvage operation and the reasonable expenses for the equipment and personnel actually used on the salvage operation'.

In determining the salvor's expenses, the last three factors in fixing salvage reward contained in paragraph 1 of Article 180 of MC as cited *supra* shall be taken into consideration.

463. Under all circumstances, the amount of special compensation shall be paid only if the amount of special compensation is greater than the salvage reward recoverable by the salvor from the owners of the ship and/or her goods and the amount to be paid shall be the difference between the amount of special compensation and that of salvage reward. That is, if the amount of salvage reward is equivalent to or higher than that of special compensation, no special compensation shall be paid; if the amount of salvage reward is lower than that of special compensation, the amount of special compensation to be paid shall be the difference between the two.

C. Denial of Special Compensation in Full or in Part

464. If the salvor has been negligent and has thereby failed to prevent or minimize the pollution damage to the environment, the salvor may be totally or partly deprived of the right to special compensation (paragraph 5, Article 182, MC).

IV. Securities for Salvage Payment and Payment on Account

A. Security for Salvage Payment

465. As provided for in paragraph 1 of Article 188 of MC, after the completion of salvage operation, the salved party shall provide satisfactory security for the potential salvage payments as demanded by the salvor.

Noticeably, the owners of the salved ship are not obliged to provide security for the share of the salvage reward to be borne by the owners of goods carried onboard. However, he shall make best endeavours to cause the owners of goods salved to provide satisfactory security for the share of the reward to be borne by the latter before the delivery of goods (paragraph 2, Article 188, MC). If there are other properties such as bunkers onboard provided by a time or bareboat charterers, the owners of the salved ship are also not obliged to provide security for the share of the salvage reward to be borne by the owners of such other properties

466. Where no satisfactory security has been provided with respect to the ship or other property salved as demanded by the salvor, the ship or other property salved shall not be removed from the port or place of first arrival after the completion of salvage operation without his consent (paragraph 3, Article 188, MC). In other words, the salvor shall have possessory lien on the ship or other property salved under such circumstances, provided that the salved ship or other property is in his possession.

Article 190 of MC further provides that, if the salved party has neither made the payment nor provided satisfactory security for the ship and other property salved in ninety days after completion of the salvage, the salvor may apply to a court of law for an order of forced sale by auction. If the ship or other property salved cannot be kept or properly kept, or the storage charge to be incurred may exceed its value, the salvor may apply for an earlier forced sale by auction. The proceeds of the sale shall, after deduction of the expenses incurred for the storage and sale, be used for the salvage payment. Surplus, if any, shall be returned to the salved party. If there is no way to return the surplus and the surplus has not been claimed in one year of the forced sale, the same shall go to the State treasury. In case of any deficiency, the salvor has the right of recourse against the salved party.

B. Payment on Account

467. The maritime court or the arbitration organ handling the salvor's claim for salvage payment may decide or make an award ordering the salved party to pay on account an appropriate amount to the salvor in light of the specific circumstances and under fair and just terms (Article 189, MC).

§5. Reward of Crew

468. There is no express statutory provision in Chinese law governing the right of master and other crewmembers in the distribution of salvage reward, except Article 139 of section 2 'Time Charter Party' of Chapter VI of MC which reads: 'Should the ship be engaged in salvage operation during the charter period, the charterer shall be entitled to half of the amount of the payment for salvage operation after deducting therefrom the salvage expenses, compensation for damage, the portion due to the crewmembers and other relevant costs.' There is no reported case in China concerning salvage reward of master and other crewmembers.

469. It is understood, however, where a master and other crewmembers took part in the salvage operation rendered to another ship or other property salved, they shall be entitled to a reasonable portion of the salvage reward which the shipowners are entitled to, unless the crewmembers are those employed on board a professional salvage ship.

The amount of reward that the crewmembers are entitled to shall be decided in accordance with the circumstances of a case. For examples, where the salvage is rendered wholly or mainly by the crewmembers, they shall be entitled to the full or most part of the reward; where the salvage is mainly due to the use of the ship or her equipment, the shipowners of the salving ship shall be entitled to the most part of the reward in the distribution thereof.

§6. Liability and Limitation of Liability of Salvor

I. Liability of Salvor

470. As provided for in Article 177 of MC, when carrying out salvage operation, the salvor is obliged to carry out the operation with due care and to exercise due care to prevent and minimize pollution damage to the environment. Otherwise, the salvor shall be liable for loss of or damage to the salved ship or other property, other salving ship, if any, and loss of life or personal injury, loss or damage as well as damage to the environment suffered by a third party resulting from the fault on the part of the salvor.

Therefore, due to the fault of the salvor, his servants or agents within the scope of their employment or agency committed during salvage operation, the salvor may not only be deprived of the whole or part of the salvage payment to him in accordance with Article 187 of MC, but also may incur contractual liability for loss of or damage to the salved ship or other property or tortuous liability for loss of or damage to the environment or other property than the salved one or loss of life or personal injury suffered by third parties.

II. Limitation of Liability of Salvor

471. Before the adoption and coming into force of LLMC, under the 1957 CLC, a salvor was not entitled to avail of limitation of liability, nor was his servants or agents so entitled.

After the remarkable case of M/V ‘Tojo Maru’[44] in which the salvor was held liable for the damage to the salved ship due to the fault of his employee during salvage operation without any limitation of liability, the international community realized that limitation of liability should be available to the salvor and his servants or agents. Consequently, salvor, his servants or agents and the liability insurer of the salvor are listed as persons who can avail of statutory limitation of liability in LLMC. The corresponding provisions of this Convention are incorporated in Chapter XI ‘Limitation of Liability for Maritime Claims’ of MC.

44. *See* Lloyd’s Rep. [1971] 1 p. 341.

472. The limit of liability available to the salvor, his servants or agents or liability insurer is provided for in paragraph (5) of Article 210 of MC. Where a salvor rendered salvage services from a salving ship, the limit of liability shall be calculated according to the gross tonnage of salving ship, Where a salvor rendered salvage services not from a salving ship or solely on the salved ship, the limit of liability shall be calculated according to gross tonnage of 1,500 tons. Other provisions in Chapter XI of MC concerning limitation of liability for maritime claims shall also apply to the case of limitation of liability of the salvor, his servants or agents or his liability insurer.[45]

§7. Employed Salvage Service

I. Definition

473. Employed salvage service is a kind of salvage services in which the salvage reward is not based upon the principle of 'no cure, no pay', but is calculated in accordance with the time, manpower and equipment actually used by the salvor, regardless whether the salvage is finally successful or not.

The rate of salvage payment and other conditions of salvage shall be agreed upon by the salvor and the salved party. Sometimes, a contract of employed salvage provides that, if the salvage has useful result finally or within a certain time limit, an additional payment shall be made by the salved party to the salvor. Due to the increasing ratio of salvage reward to the value of salved ships or properties and the high amount of special compensation in practice as a result of implementation of Chapter IX of MC or the 1989 Salvage Convention, the shipowners, hull insurers and even P&I clubs may prefer employed salvage service in more and more cases in order to foresee and control the salvage payments.

Unlike the salvage operation based upon the principle of 'no cure, no pay', sometimes the salvage operation is under the command of the salved party under an employment salvage contract.

II. Statutory Provisions

474. Traditional maritime law covered employed salvage services. In the modern time, however, this kind of salvage services is not deemed in the academic circle as salvage at sea, but as a kind of ordinary maritime services and thus shall not be regulated by the provisions of salvage at sea in maritime law.

In China, MC does not exclude application of Chapter IX to employed salvage service. Article 179 of MC provides: 'Where the salvage operations rendered to the distressed ship and other property have had a useful result, the salvor shall be entitled to a reward. Except as otherwise provided for by Article 182 of this Code or by other laws or the salvage contract, the salvor shall not be entitled to the payment if the salvage operations have had no useful result.'

45. For details, *see* Ch. 4 of Part II.

Therefore, employed salvage services are within the scope of the exception of Article 169 of MC, i.e., otherwise provided for by the salvage contract. Thus, Chapter IX of MC shall apply to employed salvage services except for those provisions reflecting to the principle of 'no cure, no pay', e.g., Article 180 stipulating the factors for fixing salvage reward, Article 183 stipulating that the salvage reward shall be paid by the owners of the salved ship and other property in accordance with the respective proportions which the salved values of the ship and other property bear to the total salved value. Noticeably, this was confirmed by the judgment of SPC in the case of retrial of M/T 'Archangelos Gabriel' in 2016.

475. The person responsible for the salvage payment, the amount or rate of salvage payment and other issues relating thereto in an employed salvage service are subject to Book Three 'Contracts' and Book One 'General Provisions' of CC.

§8. Wrecks Removal

I. Concepts

476. In the *WRC of 2007*, wreck is widely defined as a sunken or stranded ship, or any part of a sunken or stranded ship, including any object that is or has been on board such a ship, or any object that is lost at sea from a ship and that is stranded, sunken or adrift at sea, or a ship that is about, or may reasonably be expected, to sink or to strand, where effective measures to assist the ship or any property in danger are not already being taken, following upon a maritime casualty (Article 1(4)); removal is defined as any form of prevention, mitigation or elimination of the hazard created by a wreck (Article 1(7)). Removal is a general technical word and can be in various forms. Under Chinese law and regulations, the forms of removal of wreck include raising, removal, destruction or otherwise rendering harmless of a wreck.

477. In practice, it may be difficult to draw a line between salvage and wreck removal. Roughly speaking, a wreck means a ship, goods or other property at sea, whether sunken or drifting, in such a seriously damaged condition that it will have no remaining value or have only little remaining value after removal thereof. Thus, removal will have no or only little useful result in the sense of salved value of the wreck. Therefore, the mainly difference between salvage and wreck removal may lie in the extent of damage suffered by the ship, goods or other property at sea. In other words, wreck removal is for or mainly for the purpose of elimination of danger to or hindrance of the safety of navigation, other maritime activities or marine resources, while the purpose or main purpose of salvage is also for the saving of the remaining value of the salved property. In determining whether a contract is a salvage contract and a contract of wreck removal, the intentions of the parties thereto and the contexts of contract, etc., shall also be considered.

II. Statutory Provisions

A. Administration on Wreck Removal

478. Normally, wreck removal directly or closely concerns the public interests of safety at sea and the protection of marine environment. Wreck removal is in the first place a matter of administrative law that especially deals with compulsory wreck removal.

Noticeably, China is a party to the *WRC of 2007*, but this Convention does not play an important rule with respect to wreck removal. This is because this Convention applies to the exclusive economic zone of a State party only, but does not apply to the inner waters and territorial sea of a State party, whereas most wreck removal takes place the inner waters and territorial sea of a State party. In fact, this Convention plays a role of modal law instead of direct application.

In China, MTSL governs wreck removal at sea and the *Regulations Governing Administration on Traffic Safety in Rivers* governs wreck removal in inland waters. By virtue of Articles 51 and 106 of MTSL, where a sunken, drifting or stranded ship or other object may affect the safety of navigation, the owners, operator or manager thereof shall remove the object within a deadline set by MSA, failing which MSA shall have the right to take measures to compulsorily remove the object at the expenses of its owners, operator or manager. Similarly, by virtue of Articles 42 and 75 of the *Regulations Governing Administration on Traffic Safety in Rivers*, where a sunken, drifting or stranded ship or other object may affect the safety of navigation, the owners or manager thereof shall remove the object within a deadline set by MSA, failing which MSA shall have the right to take measures to compulsorily remove the object at the expenses of its owners or manager.

Where immediate wreck removal is needed, MSA can organize the removal in time at the expenses of its owners, operator or manager.

In addition, the owners, operator or manager of a wreck shall report the wreck to MSA and apply to the governmental navigation service centre responsible for the water area where the wreck is located for marking the wreck before removal. MSA is responsible for determining whether a wreck affects the safety of navigation and, if yes, issuing necessary notice to mariners or navigational warning accordingly. Wreck removal operation is subject to the approval and under the supervision of MSA, whether the operation is based upon the removal within a deadline set by MSA, compulsory removal, immediate removal or voluntary removal. Before wreck removal operation begins, a permit for underwater operation shall be obtained from MSA.

As regards the removal of sunken ships, the State Council promulgated the *Provisions on the Administration on Removal on Sunken Ships* on 7 September 1957 and the *Provisions on the Administration on the Participation of Foreign Wrecking Companies in Removal of Sunken Ships in Chinese Coastal Waters* on 12 July 1992. These provisions are seldom applied in practice, as their contents are basically out of date.

B. Contractual Issues of Wreck Removal

479. Wreck removal is based upon a contract concluded between a salvage and wreck removal company and the owners or manager of the wreck, except in the case of compulsory removal or immediate removal organized by MSA in which MSA appoints or entrusts a salvage and wreck removal company to remove the wreck.

The contractual terms are subject to the agreement between the parties thereto and the provisions of Book Three 'Contracts' and Book One 'General Provisions' of CC.

A wreck removal contract normally contains, *inter alia*, the following provisions: date and place of conclusion, name and address of the contractor and the owners or other interested party of the wreck, subject-matter of removal, kind and period of service, place of delivery or disposal of the removed wreck, expenses of wreck removal and method of payment, extra costs and other related expenses, liability for breach of contract and liability to third persons, penalty or liquidated damages, security for payment of expenses of wreck removal, Himalaya clause, lien on removed wreck, resolution of disputes.

Chapter 10. General Average

§1. HISTORICAL INTRODUCTION

480. The rules concerning general average initialled as G/A or G.A. are among the oldest ones in the area of maritime law. In the early times, the terms used were 'common average' or 'gross average'. The term 'general average' was first officially used in 1721 in the *Code of Rotterdam.*

The origin of general average may be traced back to the ancient *Lex Rhodia* in the fourth century B.C., in which the principle of contribution of the cargo jettisoned for the purpose of lightening cargo load was established. During the Middle Ages, all parties concerned with a maritime adventure, *viz.* the ship, her master and other crewmembers, the merchants and the cargo, were considered as one community. Based upon these ancient traditions, the subsequent *Consulat de la Mer* or *Lex Consolato*, compiled in the fourteenth century in Barcelona, and the *Lex Oléron*, compiled in the twelfth century, contained more specific rules regarding general average. In these customary laws, before cargo carried on board a ship was jettisoned or a ship was beached, consent of the merchants who sailed with the ship must be given. Later, when the merchants no longer sailed with the ship, the master was authorized to act on behalf of the merchants. After consultation with the officers of the ship, the master would be acting on his own initiative and responsibility in taking such measures.

Later, the necessity to work out clear rules concerning general average became adamant. These rules were laid down in the *French Ordonnance de la Marine* in 1681. In 1877, the first version of the YAR was adopted based upon the *York Rules* of 1864, which led to the beginning of universal adherence to the YAR in the area of general average.

§2. DEFINITION AND CHARACTERISTICS OF GENERAL AVERAGE

I. Definition of General Average

481. The prevailing YAR of 2016 do not contain a definition of general average but provide that 'there is a general average act when, and only when, any extraordinary sacrifice or expenditure is intentionally and reasonably made or incurred for the common safety for the purpose of preserving from peril the property involved in a common maritime adventure'.

By reference to same provision contained in the YAR of 1974, MC defines general average in Article 193 as 'the extraordinary sacrifice or expenditure intentionally and reasonably made or incurred for the common safety for the purpose of preserving from peril the ship, cargo or other property involved in a common maritime adventure'. General average shall be contributed by the shipowners, cargo owners and other interested parties who have benefited from the measures taken for this purpose.

482. General average is in contrast to particular average initialled as P/A or P.A., which is understood as loss of or damage to ship, her cargo or other property onboard or expenses other than general average sacrifices or expenditures and shall be borne either by the party who suffered them or the party who is liable therefor.

II. Characteristics of General Average

483. By virtue of the definition contained in Article 193 of MC cited *supra*, there are four important characteristics of general average as follows, as recognized in the area of maritime law in China.

A. *Real and Common Danger*

484. Common danger to the ship, her cargo and other property onboard should really exist instead of being only imagined or speculated, although it does not need be immediate. Common danger means that it will inevitably cause total loss of the ship, her cargo and other property onboard sooner or later, if no measure or measures known as general average act were taken for the common safety for the purpose of preserving them from the danger. A typical example of other property onboard is the bunkers supplied by the charterers under a time or bareboat charter party. Another example of other property is the freight to be earned by the charterers of a ship who as the carrier have concluded a contract of carriage of goods with shipper or as the disponent owners have concluded a sub-charter with sub-charterers.

B. *Intentional and Reasonable Measures for Common Safety*

485. Intentional measures mean that they were be taken by the carrier, master or cargo interests voluntarily on his or their own initiatives instead of being ordered or imposed upon him or them by an official authority or other persons with knowledge that the measures would cause sacrifices of the ship, cargo and/or other property onboard or expenditures. Reasonable measures mean that the sacrifices and expenditures caused thereby shall be limited to the minimum extent necessitated for the common safety for the purpose of preserving the ship, her cargo and/or other property onboard from danger. In this regard, common safety means that the taking of the measures is for the common benefit of the owners of the ship, her cargo and other property onboard. Common benefit distinguishes general average from particular average.

486. In practice, general average measures are mainly in the following forms in modern time:

- assisting a ship in getting out of grounding by use of a professional salvage tug or tugs or other ship;

- towing a ship in an uncontrolled state to a safe port or place by a professional salvage tug or tugs or other ship;
- extinguishing fire on board by a salvor;
- overloading the ship's engines to be out of grounding by herself which gives rise to breakdown or damage to her machinery;
- voluntarily stranding the ship by her master in order to avoid her sinking or to extinguish fire on board.

Therefore, general average measures are taken by salvors in most general average cases in modern times. This is why salvage reward the salvor is entitled to where the salvage of the ship and/or cargo has useful result was in most cases allowed in general average expenditure under the YAR in its version of 1994 and earlier versions.

In early times, general average measures were often in the forms of jettison of cargo on board, cutting away wreck, using cargo or vessel's materials or stores as bunkers. Historically, the general average rules originated from jettison of cargo in the time of sailing vessels. In modern times, the taking of these measures seldom appears.

C. Extraordinary Sacrifices and Expenditures

487. Extraordinary sacrifices and expenditures mean that they shall not be considered as normal ones during the course of an ordinary voyage. Where expenditures such as port disbursement at the port of discharge would inevitably incur even if no such measures were taken, they shall not be admitted as general average.

In addition, sacrifices and expenditures should be the immediate result of the general average measures. In this respect, paragraph 2 of Article 193 of MC expressly provides that loss or damage sustained by the ship or cargo through delay, whether during the voyage or subsequently, such as demurrage and loss of market as well as other indirect losses shall not be admitted as general average.

D. Useful Result

488. Useful result means that the total loss of the ship, her cargo and other property onboard is successfully avoided. However, it is not requisite that both the ship and her cargo together with other property, if any, be preserved. Where all the ship, her cargo and other property onboard became a total loss, no party benefited from the measures to contribute in the sacrifices and expenditures. Where either the ship or her cargo still becomes total loss, there is still useful result.

III. General Average and Fault

489. In China, it is arguable whether there is general average in the case the danger common to the ship, her cargo and other property onboard is the result of fault committed by one party giving rise to his liability by virtue of a contract of carriage of goods by sea or a charter party or the applicable law.

From the definition of general average contained in Article 193 of MC cited *supra*, the cause of common danger in irrelevant to the constitution of general average. However, it may affect the contribution in general average. That is, if one party shall be responsible for the cause of danger, the other party or parties may refuse to contribute in general average, or may make recourse against the responsible party if the other party or parties have already contributed in general average. In this sense, therefore, the contribution in general average is largely dependent upon the liability regime under the law of carriage of goods by sea as discussed in Chapter 5 and Chapter 6 of this part *supra*.

490. In practice, it often occurs that, where the cause of danger common to the ship, cargo and other property onboard is not obvious, the party who is in most cases the shipowners and has incurred extraordinary sacrifices and/or expenditures caused by measures taken internationally and reasonably for the common benefit of all the owners of the properties in danger may seek contribution in these sacrifices and/or expenditures from other parties who have benefited from the measures, even if the danger was possibly caused by the fault on his part for which he is responsible under the circumstances of the case.

In view of such a situation, it is provided for in Rule D of the YAR of 2016 and Article 197 of MC that the rights to contribution in general average shall not be affected, though the event which gave rise to the sacrifice or expenditure may have been due to the fault of one of the parties to the adventure; however, this shall not prejudice any remedies or defences which may be open against or to that party in respect of such fault.

491. On the other hand, the duty of the carrier to contribute in general average of any party to the adventure will not be affected by the rules of exemption of liability provided for in Article 51 of MC, or in Article 4(2) and (3) of the *Hague-Visby Rules*. Neither the carrier nor the cargo interests will be able to avail themselves of exemptions of liability in order not to contribute in the general average. The reason for this is that the general average principles are founded on the services that are rendered in favour of the community of the ship, her cargo and other property onboard by one of them for the common benefit. Contribution in general average per se is not a matter of liability, but may be deemed as a special legal regime based upon the concept of equity.

§3. Applicable Laws

492. The rules concerning general average are contained in Chapter X 'General Average' of MC, including the definition and scope of general average, onus of proof, amount of sacrifices and expenditures of general average, contributory value of general average, and general average security. The main provisions of this chapter are incorporated from the YAR of 1974. However, the provisions of Chapter X of MC prove too simple as compared with the very complicated contents of general average.

493. By virtue of Article 203, the adjustment of general average shall be governed by the average adjustment rules agreed upon in the relevant contract or, in the absence of such an agreement in the contract, the relevant provisions of Chapter X of MC shall apply. Therefore, the provisions contained in Chapter X of MC are not compulsorily applicable. In other words, where the average adjustment rules agreed upon between the parties contain provisions which are not contained in or contrary to the provisions of Chapter X of MC, the average adjustment rules shall prevail.

In practice, almost all the bills of lading and charter parties contain general average clause indicating that general average shall be adjusted in accordance with the *YAR*. Thus, Chapter X of MC proves not very useful except Article 203.

§4. General Average Adjustment

I. Concept of General Average Adjustment

494. General average adjustment means the settlement of general average normally done by a professional institution or persons called general average adjusters or average adjusters in accordance with the average adjustment rules agreed upon between the parties. The main tasks of general average adjustment are to determine the amount of sacrifices and expenditures, the contributory value and the contributory amount of general average of the owners of the ship, her cargo and other property respectively.

In China, the professional institution handling general average is a sub-division of CCPIT.

495. General average adjusters are non-governmental. Thus, their conclusions of general average adjustment normally in the form of general average statement have no compulsory binding effect, but for the parties concerned to voluntarily accept it and contribute in general average in accordance with it. Any party who does not accept it may file a lawsuit with a court of law with jurisdiction or refer the dispute to arbitration in accordance with the arbitration agreement concluded between the parties.

Occasionally, disputes concerning general average are directly brought to a court of law for judgment or referred to an arbitration organization for award.[46] In such a case, the court or arbitration organization may appoint average adjusters to make general average adjustment.

II. General Average Adjustment Rules

A. *York-Antwerp Rules*

496. The YAR are used worldwide in general average adjustments.

After the first version of the YAR was adopted in 1877, the Rules were revised in 1890, 1924, 1950, 1974, 1994, 2004 and 2016. Since the establishment of CMI in

46. For details, *see* §7 of this chapter.

1897, the revisions were organized by CMI. Noticeably, the YAR are not an international treaty. However, for more than a century, the role it has been playing in the area of general average adjustment is not less important than an international treaty in other areas in maritime law. The latest YAR of *2016* consist of the rule of interpretation, the rule paramount, the lettered rules from A to G and the numbered rules from I to XXIII.

B. Beijing Rules

497. In China, CCPIT promulgated its *Temporary Rules on General Average of 1975*, known as 'Beijing Adjustment Rules of 1975' or 'Beijing Rules of 1975'. These Rules were annulled by the *General Average Adjustment Rules of 2022*, known as 'Beijing Adjustment Rules of 2022', promulgated by CCPIT on 31 August 2022.

The Beijing Adjustment Rules of 2022 include a preface stipulating the purpose of the Rules and eight rules the titles of which are respectively scope of general average, principle of adjustment, calculation of the amount of losses, contribution in general average, interests, general average security, time limit of general average adjustment and supplementary provisions.

Objectively speaking, the Beijing Rules of 1975 had and the Beijing Adjustment Rules of 2022 have an obvious shortcoming, i.e., their provisions aiming at simplifying general average adjustment prove to be too simple to handle the complicated matters of general average adjustment. In addition, the Beijing Rules of 1975 had another shortcoming, i.e., the Rules set forth the power of the adjusters to determine whether the losses have been caused by fault on one party to the contract of carriage of goods by sea for which he cannot be exempted from liability, a power obviously the adjusters should not have. In practice, due to these reasons, the Beijing Rules of 1975 are seldom applied. Instead, general averages are adjusted in CCPIT in accordance with the YAR as agreed between the parties in most cases.

§5. General Average Sacrifices and Expenditures

I. General Average Sacrifices

A. Ship

498. The calculation of the amount of general average sacrifice of a ship is provided for in paragraph (1) of Article 198 of MC dependent upon whether damage to her has been repaired or not, or whether she has become total loss or not.

499. Where damage to a ship has been repaired, the amount of general average sacrifice shall be calculated on the basis of the repair costs actually paid from which a reasonable deduction in respect of 'new for old' shall be made.

The repair costs to be allowed in general average are limited to those of damage to the ship in the nature of general average sacrifice *viz.* damage to her as directly caused by general average measures. To be allowed in general average, therefore, deduction of repair costs of damage to the ship in the nature of particular average shall be made from the total repair costs.

Theoretically, deduction in respect of 'new for old' means, where new materials have replaced the old ones during repair, the increased value due to use of new materials replacing the old damaged ones shall be deducted from the repair costs allowed in general average in order to be in conformity with the principle of *restitutio in integrum*. Reasonable deduction requires the deduction to be made in accordance with the circumstances of the case, especially the age of the ship's hull, machinery or equipment that was repaired or replaced. In this respect, more specific provisions are contained in Rule XIII of the YAR of 2016. As a rule, deduction of 'new for old' in terms of the amount of repair costs shall be made only with respect to permanent repair, but not in the case of temporary repair.

500. Where the ship has not been repaired after sacrifice, the amount of general average sacrifice shall be the reasonable depreciation in value arising from the damage to her in the nature of such sacrifice calculated on the basis of the reasonable reduced value of the ship after the sacrifice, but not exceeding the estimated repair costs. In the estimation of the repair costs, deduction of 'new for old' shall be taken into consideration.

501. Where a ship has sustained an actual total loss or the estimated repair costs will exceed her value after being repaired, the amount to be allowed in general average shall be the difference between the estimated sound value of her before the general average accident occurred after deducting therefrom the estimated costs of repairing the damage to her that is not general average sacrifice and the estimated actual value of her in her damaged state. Where the damaged ship is sold, her estimated actual value in her damaged state may be measured by the net proceeds of sale.

B. Cargo

502. The calculation of the amount of general average sacrifice of cargo is provided for in paragraph (2) of Article 198 of MC dependent upon whether the cargo has been lost or damaged.

Where the cargo has been lost as a result of general average measures, the amount of general average sacrifice shall be calculated on the basis of the value of cargo at the time of shipment plus insurance and freight, *viz.* the CIF value thereof, less the freight that would have been incurred but for the sacrifice, should it arrive at destination in sound condition without the occurrence of the general average accident.

Where the cargo has been damaged as a result of general average measures and sold after the accident, but before an agreement had been reached between the parties as to the extent of the damage, the amount of general average sacrifice shall be calculated on the basis of the difference between the CIF value of the cargo and the net proceeds of sale of the damaged cargo.

In addition, by virtue of Article 200 of MC, where the description of cargo was undeclared or wrongfully declared by the shipper before shipment under the contract of carriage by sea, sacrifice of such cargo shall not be allowed in general average; where the value of cargo improperly declared by the shipper before shipment is lower than its actual value, the amount of sacrifice of such cargo allowed in general average shall be calculated on the basis of the declared value.

C. *Freight*

503. By virtue of paragraph (3) of Article 198 of MC, the amount of general average sacrifice of freight shall be calculated on the basis of the freight lost owing to the general average sacrifice of cargo, less the operating costs of the ship that ought to be paid in order to earn such freight, but need not be paid because of the sacrifice.

Traditionally, general average sacrifice of freight applies to freight to be collected only, as freight prepaid is not returnable even if the cargo is lost during the voyage under English common law. However, by virtue of Article 835 of CC, the prepaid freight is also returnable if the cargo is lost during the voyage. Thus, general average sacrifice of freight also applies to the prepaid freight under Chinese law.

II. General Average Expenditures

A. *Expenses at Port of Refuge*

504. Where a ship in a damaged condition in consequence of maritime accident during the voyage entered a port or place of refuge or returned to her port or place of loading to effect repairs necessary for the safe prosecution of the voyage *viz.* for the common benefit of the owners of ship, her cargo and other property, then the port charges, the wages and maintenance of the master and other crewmembers incurred and the fuel and stores consumed during the extra period of detention in such port or place as well as the loss or damages and charges arising from the discharge, storage, reloading and handling of the cargo, fuel, stores and other property onboard in order to have the repairs effected shall be admitted as general average (Article 194, MC).

B. *Wages and Maintenance of Crew and Other Expenses for and from Port of Refuge*

505. Where, after a maritime accident, a ship entered a port or place of refuge or returned to her port or place of loading to effect repairs necessary for the safe prosecution of the voyage, besides the expenditures incurred at the port of refuge, the port charges, the wages and maintenance of the master and other crewmembers incurred and the fuel and stores consumed during the extra period of detention for the port of refuge in the nature of extraordinary expenditures shall also be allowed in general average under MC. However, MC does not provide whether such expenses incurred during the extra period of leaving such port or place shall be admitted as general average. Theoretically, such expenses shall be so admitted.

C. Substituted Expenses

506. Any extraordinary expenditure incurred in place of another expenditure or expenditures that would have been allowed in general average shall be deemed as general average, but the amount of such expenditure incurred shall not be in excess of the general average expenditure or expenditures avoided (Article 195, MC).

For example, in the case of repair of damage to ship in the nature of general average sacrifice, the expenses paid for the overtime of the repairers during repair shall be allowed in general average, since these expenses have avoided part of the port charges, the wages and maintenance of the master and other crewmembers and the fuel and stores that would have been incurred or consumed during the period of repair and allowed in general average. However, in such a case, the amount of the expenses paid for the overtime during repair to be allowed in general average shall be limited to that of the expenses avoided by the overtime.

D. Salvage Reward

507. Salvage operation carried out by a salvor is in many cases a general average measure. Chapter X of MC does not mention salvage reward. Therefore, salvage reward shall be allowed in general average if and only if it is within the definition of general average contained in Article 183 mentioned *supra*.

Salvage reward paid by the owners of ship and/or cargo is allowed in general average under the YAR of 1994 and in the earlier versions. However, salvage reward is not allowed in general average anymore under the YAR of 2004 in order to simplify general average adjustment. The reason is that salvage reward is contributed among the owners of the salved properties on the basis of the salved value of their respective property in proportion to the total salved value and, therefore, there is no need or great need to be contributed for the second time in the general average. The YAR of 2016 took a compromised approach and provide in Rule VI 'Salvage Remuneration' that salvage reward is allowed in general average only under the following circumstances: (i) there is a subsequent accident or other circumstances resulting in loss or damage to property during the voyage that results in significant differences between salved and contributory values; (ii) there are significant general average sacrifices; (iii) salved values are manifestly incorrect and there is a significantly incorrect apportionment of salvage expenses; (iv) any of the parties to the salvage has paid a significant proportion of salvage due from another party; (v) a significant proportion of the parties have satisfied the salvage claim on substantially different terms, no regard being had to interest, currency correction or legal costs of either the salvor or the contributing interest.

It need be mentioned that the special compensation paid by the shipowners in accordance with Article 182 of MC or Article 14 of the 1989 Salvage Convention or any other provision similar in substance such as SCOPIC shall not be allowed in general average in accordance with Chapter X of MC or the YAR of 2016. This is because the special compensation is paid by the shipowners where the salvor carried out salvage operation in respect of a ship or cargo threatened pollution damage to the environment under MC or damage to the environment under the 1989 Salvage Convention, but the salvage operation had no useful result or obvious useful result in the salvage of the ship and/or her cargo giving rise to salvage reward. Thus, the payment of special compensation was not incurred for the common safety for the purpose of preserving from danger the ship and her cargo involved in a common maritime adventure. On the other hand, the salvage reward paid for the salvage of the ship and/or her cargo with useful result has been fixed by taking into consideration of the skills and efforts of the salvor in preventing or minimizing the pollution damage to the environment. Nevertheless, such reward shall be allowed in general average in full under Chapter X of MC or paragraph (c) of Rule VI of the YAR of 2016, provided that the salvage operation carried out by the salvor is in nature a general average measure.

III. Interests and Commissions

508. By virtue of Article 201 of MC, interests shall be allowed on general average sacrifices and expenditures paid on account and commissions shall be allowed on the general average expenditures paid on account, except those for the wages and maintenance of the master and other crewmembers and fuel and stores consumed.

Under the Beijing Adjustment Rules of 2022, the rate of interests is fixed at 7% annually. Paragraph (b) of Rule XXI 'Interest on Losses Allowed in General Average' of the YAR of 2016 provides that the rate for calculating interest accruing during each calendar year shall be the month London Inter-Bank Offered Rate (ICE LIBOR) for the currency in which the adjustment is prepared, as announced on the first banking day of that calendar year, increased by four percentage points and that if the adjustment is prepared in a currency for which no ICE LIBOR is announced, the rate shall be the twelve-month US Dollar ICE LIBOR, increased by four percentage points. No commission on the general average expenditures is provided for in both the Beijing Adjustment Rules of 2022 and the YAR of 2016.

§6. Contributory Values

I. Concept

509. Contributory values of general average mean the respective value of the ship, her cargo and other property onboard which have been benefited from the general average measures in proportion to which contribution in general average shall be made by the owners of the ship, the cargo and other property onboard.

Calculation of the contributory values of general average is provided for in Article 199 of MC.

510. General average sacrifices and expenditures shall be contributed by the contributing interests, *viz.* the owners of the ship, her cargo and other property onboard and consequently shall be benefited themselves from the general average measures giving rise to them.

Therefore, the contributory values of general average consist of three parts, *viz.* the values of the ship, her cargo and other property onboard respectively preserved from the common danger due to the general average measures, the general average sacrifices of the ship, her cargo and other property onboard, and the general average expenditures incurred by the owners of the ship, her cargo and/or other property onboard.

II. Calculation of Contributory Values

A. Ship

511. The contributory value of ship shall be calculated on the basis of either her value in sound condition at the time and place of the termination of voyage, should the general average accident had not occurred, less the amount of damage to her that does not come under general average sacrifice, or her actual net value at the time and place of the termination of the voyage plus the amount of damage to her that comes under general average sacrifice (Article 199(1), MC).

B. Cargo

512. The contributory value of cargo shall be calculated on the basis of either its CIF value less the amount of damage to it that does not come under general average sacrifice and the freight at the risk of the carrier, or the net proceeds of sale where the cargo was sold before its arrival at the destination plus the amount of its general average sacrifice (Article 199(2), MC).

Passengers' luggage and personal effects shall not contribute in general average mainly because of their limited number and value.

In addition, by virtue of Article 200 of MC, where the description of cargo was undeclared or wrongfully declared by the shipper before shipment under the contract of carriage by sea, the cargo shall contribute in general average; where its value improperly declared is lower than its actual value, the contributory value of such cargo shall be calculated on the basis of its actual value.

C. Freight

513. The contributory value of freight shall be calculated on the basis of the amount of freight at the risk of the carrier and subsequently earned at the termination of the voyage less the expenses incurred for the prosecution of voyage after the general average accident in order to earn the freight, plus the amount of the general average sacrifice of freight.

§7. PROCEDURES

I. Declaration of General Average

514. Normally, after the taking of general average measures, the master or shipowners declare the general average in writing to the owners of cargo carried on board stating the time, place and nature of the accident, the measures taken, the sacrifices and expenditures incurred, and requiring the cargo owners to provide security before or at the time of taking delivery of goods for their contribution in general average.

In accordance with the Beijing Adjustment Rules of 2022, general averages shall be declared within forty-eight hours after the first arrival of the ship at a port if the accident occurred at sea, or within forty-eight hours after the accident occurred in a port.

II. General Average Security

515. General average security is provided in most cases by the owners of cargo as demanded by the shipowners to secure the cargo's contribution in general average. Occasionally, general average security is provided by the shipowners as demanded by the owners of cargo. Sometimes, where the security is provided by the cargo owners, a counter-security is provided by the shipowners as demanded. If the cargo owners fail to provide general average security as demanded, the shipowners may exercise lien on cargo.

516. Article 202 of MC provides that a contributory party shall provide security for general average contribution at the request of other party having interest therein; where the security has been provided in the form of cash deposit, the deposit shall be put in a bank by an average adjuster in the name of a trustee; the provision, use and refund of the deposit shall not prejudice the ultimate liability of the contributing parties.

The statutory provisions contained in Chapter VI 'Maritime Securities' of SMPL apply to general average security.[47]

47. For details, *see* Ch. 14 of Part II.

517. General average securities are normally in the form of cash deposit, letter of general average guarantee issued by cargo insurer or average bond concluded between the shipowners and the cargo owners.

Where the cargo onboard is discharged from ship at the port of refuge for the purpose of repair of damage to the ship and is carried to the port of destination by another ship, normally an agreement called 'non-separation agreement' shall be concluded between the shipowners and the cargo owners to the effect that contribution in general average between them shall not be affected by the transhipment of cargo.

III. Onus of Proof and Time Limit for Submission to Adjustment

A. *Onus of Proof*

518. By virtue of Article 196 of MC, the onus of proof shall be upon the party claiming for general average contribution to show that the sacrifices or expenditures shall be properly allowable in general average. Same provision is contained in paragraph 1 of Rule E of the YAR of 2016.

B. *Time Limit for Submission to Adjustment*

519. The party claiming for general average contribution from other party or parties shall give a notice to the agreed average adjuster to this effect together with supporting documents within a certain time limit provided for in the agreed general average adjustment rules.

In this respect, paragraph 2 of Rule E of the YAR of 2016 provides that all parties to the common maritime adventure shall, as soon as possible, supply particulars of value in respect of their contributory interest and, if claiming in general average, shall give notice in writing to the average adjuster of the loss or expense in respect of which they claim contribution, and supply evidence in support thereof. By virtue of the Beijing Adjustment Rules of 2022, supporting documents in relation to general average accident and losses shall be submitted as soon as possible after the related parties have received them and all these documents shall be submitted not later than one year after the termination of voyage.

520. Paragraph 3 of Rule E of the YAR of 2016 further provides that, failing notification, or if any party does not supply particulars in support of a notified claim, within twelve months of the termination of the common maritime adventure or payment of the expense, the average adjuster shall be at liberty to estimate the extent of the allowance on the basis of the information available to the adjuster, and that particulars of value shall be provided within twelve months of the termination of the common maritime adventure, failing which the average adjuster shall be at liberty to estimate the contributory value on the same basis. It further provides that such estimates shall be communicated to the party in question in writing and that estimates may only be challenged within two months of receipt of the communication and only on the ground that they are manifestly incorrect. By virtue of the Beijing Adjustment Rules of 2022, where a party or parties failed to supply the required documents within the stipulated time limit, the adjusters may estimate the contributed amount or the contributory value on the basis of the materials available to them, and no objection to such estimation can be raised unless new materials prove that the estimation is incorrect.

IV. Judicial Procedure in General Average Case

521. SMPL in section 2 'Provisions on the Trial of General Average Cases' of Chapter VIII 'Trials Procedures' contains the provisions governing special procedures in the trial of general average cases as follows:

- Disputes arising from general average may be submitted to adjustment by an average adjustment organ as agreed upon between the parties concerned or a party concerned may directly file a lawsuit with a maritime court; in the case of disputes arising from general average that have not been adjusted, the maritime court may appoint an average adjustment organ for adjustment (Article 88).
- The adjustment statement made by an average adjustment organ either appointed by the parties concerned as agreed or by the maritime court shall be taken as the basis of deciding liabilities for contribution in general average between the parties concerned, if the parties concerned have no objection to the statement; where any party raises objection, the maritime court shall decide whether the statement shall be adopted (Article 89).
- Where a maritime accident gave rise to both general average sacrifices and expenditures and loss or damage not in the nature of general average, any party concerned may, not affected by the litigation procedures regarding the lawsuit that has been filed for claim for general average, file a lawsuit for the claim for such loss or damage against the other party who is responsible for it (Article 90); where a lawsuit for the claim for loss or damage not in the nature of general average has been filed with a maritime court having entertained the lawsuit for the claim for general average arising from the same accident, the maritime court may merge the two lawsuits in trial (Article 91).
- The trial of a general average case shall be finalized within one year, except there is special circumstance necessitating an extension, in which case the extension is subject to the approval of the president of the maritime court (Article 92).

Other procedures in the trial of a general average case shall follow those provided for in SMPL and CPC.

Chapter 11. Marine Insurance

§1. General Introduction

I. Introduction to Marine Insurance Industry in China

522. It is common practice in modern time that, in order to protect oneself against the exposure to the adverse financial consequences resulting from loss of or damage to ships or cargoes, extra expenses or liabilities in maritime adventure, the shipowners and the cargo owners take out proper insurance covers.

523. In China, the many domestic insurance companies are operating marine insurances. Among the biggest ones are PICC Property & Casualty Company Limited (known as 'PICC P&C') within the People's Insurance Company (Group) of China Limited (known as 'PICC'), China Pacific Property Insurance Company within China Pacific Insurance (Group) Co., Ltd. (known as 'CPIC'), Ping An Property & Casualty Insurance Company of China, Ltd. (known as 'Ping An Property & Casualty') within Pin An Insurance (Group) Company of China (known as 'Ping An'), China Continent Property & Casualty Insurance Company Ltd. within China Reinsurance (Group) Corporation.

The former name of PICC was the People's Insurance Company of China set up in 1949 and was the only insurance company in China for decades. In the area of marine insurance, PICC P&C offers hull insurance, marine cargo transport insurance and marine liability insurance.

China Shipowners' Mutual Assurance Association (known as 'CPI') was established in 1984 and offers shipowners' protection and indemnity insurance to its members. COSCO Shipping Captive Insurance Co., Ltd. was set up in 2017 and operates hull insurance and shipowners' liability insurance for the ships and shipowners within COSCO SHIPPING.

524. The setting up of an insurance company in China is subject to the approval of the State Administration of Financial Supervision and Administration established on the basis of the former China Banking and Insurance Regulatory Commission on 18 May 2023.

Setting up of an insurance company shall meet the general requirements of a legal person stipulated in the *Company Law*. Besides, IL contains detailed additional requirements for the setting up of an insurance company and provisions governing the business operation thereof. By virtue of Article 69 of IL, an insurance company shall meet the requirement of the minimum amount of registered capital of CNY 200 million or a higher minimum amount as the State Administration of Financial Supervision and Administration may adjust in accordance with the business scope and operation scale of the insurance company concerned. Where the setting up of an insurance company is approved by the State Administration of Financial Supervision and Administration taking into account the needs of the insurance industry development and fair competition, a licence for engaging in the insurance business shall be issued.

The setting up of branches of an insurance company also needs licences. Noticeably, the branches of an insurance company do not have the status of legal entity and their civil liabilities shall be borne by mother company (Article 74, IL).

The business operation of an insurance company is subject to the supervision and control of the State Administration of Financial Supervision and Administration in accordance with IL and the related administrative regulations. Matters such as change of name, registered capital or places of business, adjustment of business scope, split or merger of an insurance company are subject to approval by the State Administration of Financial Supervision and Administration. Serious violation of laws and administrative regulations by an insurance company may cause the licence to be revoked by the State Administration of Financial Supervision and Administration, as a result of which the said company shall be dissolved according to law.

II. Applicable Laws

525. Marine insurance is mainly provided for in Chapter XII 'Contract of Marine Insurance' of MC. This chapter is applicable to the insurance of hull, cargo, income from the operation of ship, including freight, charter hire and passengers' fare, crew's wages and other remuneration, liability to third persons, and other property that may sustain loss or damage from a maritime peril and the liability and expenses arising therefrom as well as reinsurance of these subject matters of marine insurance (Article 218, MC).

IL applies to all kinds of insurance including marine insurance. However, the provisions of Chapter XII of MC have priority over those contained in IL to the extent of repugnancy and the latter shall apply to marine insurance where Chapter XII of MC does not contain provision (Article 184, IL).

A contract of marine insurance is also subject to the provisions of Sub-Book One 'General Provisions' of Book Three 'Contracts' of CC to the extent they are not repugnant to those of MC and IL.

Besides, SPC promulgated judicial interpretations in the area of marine insurance, i.e., the *Provisions on Certain Issues in the Trial of Cases of Disputes over Marine Insurance* on 23 November 2006 and judicial interpretations in the area of insurance generally, i.e., the *Interpretations on Certain Issues regarding Application of Insurance Law of the People's Republic of China* on 14 September 2009 and 6 May 2013. These judicial interpretations shall have the effect of law. The application of the first judicial interpretations has priority over the second judicial interpretations.

III. Marine Insurance Contract

A. Definition and Characteristics of Marine Insurance Contract

526. A marine insurance contract is defined in paragraph 1 of Article 216 of MC as 'a contract whereby the insurer undertakes as agreed to indemnify the loss of the subject matter insured and the liability of the insured caused by perils covered by the insurance against the payment of an insurance premium by the insured'.

Noticeably, the parties to a marine insurance contract are the insurer and the insured under Chapter XI of MC, but the parties to an insurance contract are the insurer and the applicant under IL, although the applicant may be the insured entitled to the insurance indemnity paid by the insurer. In the marine insurance practice, however, the parties to a marine insurance contract often appear to be the insurer and the applicant. Therefore, the expression of 'the insured' contained in Chapter XI of MC means the applicant or both the applicant and the insured except where the insurance indemnity to be paid to the insured is concerned.

527. A marine insurance contract has the nature of a contract of indemnity, upon speculation and of adhesion.

As a contract of indemnity, the principle of indemnity is the most fundamental or paramount principle of marine insurance by which the insurer is obliged to compensate for the loss of or damage to the subject matter insured or for the liability of the insured to a third party arising from perils insured against.

As a contract upon speculation, the amount of premium the insurer is entitled to is not the same as that of indemnity the insurer is obliged to pay for the loss of or damage to the subject matter or the liability of the insured to a third party insured. Therefore, a contract of marine insurance has to some extent the nature of gambling. However, in order to avoid that the insurance industry is to be one of pure gambling industry, the principle of insurable interest is adopted in IL. An insurable interest is defined in Article 12 of IL as 'an interest recognized by law that the insurance applicant or the insured has over the subject matter insured'. This Article further provides that the insured of property insurance shall have an insurable interest over the subject matter insured at the time of occurrence of an insurance accident.

As a contract of adhesion, the insurance clauses drafted by the insurer and contained in an insurance policy form part of the insurance contract subject to the rules of law governing the form clauses or form contract contained in Articles 17 and 19 of IL and Articles 496, 407 and 498 of CC as discussed *infra*.

B. Contents of Marine Insurance Contract

528. By virtue of Article 217 of MC, the contents of a marine insurance contract mainly include the name of the insurer, name of the insured, subject matter insured, insured value, insured amount, perils insured against and perils excepted, duration of insurance coverage and insurance premium.

529. As provided for in Article 219 of MC, the insured value of the subject matter insured shall be agreed upon between the insurer and the insured.

Where the insured value has been agreed upon and indicated in the insurance policy, the policy is called a valued policy. Where no insured value has been agreed upon, i.e., in the case of an unvalued policy, the insured value shall be fixed as follows:

- the insured value of a ship shall be the total value of her hull, machinery, equipment, fuel, stores, gear, provisions and fresh water onboard, as well as the insurance premium when the insurance liability commences;
- the insured value of cargo shall be the aggregate of the invoice value of the cargo or the actual value of the non-trade commodity at the place of shipment, plus freight and insurance premium, i.e., the CIF value when the insurance liability commences;
- the insured value of freight shall be the aggregate of the total amount of the freight payable to the carrier plus the insurance premium when the insurance liability commences;
- the insured value of other subject matter shall be the aggregate of the actual value thereof plus the insurance premium when the insurance liability commences.

530. The insured amount or the sum insured of the subject matter shall also be agreed upon between the insurer and the insured. The insured amount shall not exceed the insured value. Otherwise, i.e., in the case of over-insurance, the portion in excess shall be null and void (Article 220, MC). The insured amount means the maximum measure of indemnity or payment of the insurance benefit to be paid by the insurer (Article 18, IL).

531. The perils covered by marine insurance mean any maritime perils as agreed upon between the insurer and the insured, including perils occurring in rivers or on land that are related to a maritime adventure (paragraph 2, Article 216, MC).

532. Where an insurance contract contains clauses on liability exemptions of the insurer, the insurer shall at the time of conclusions of the contract make indication in the insurance application form, insurance policy or other insurance certificate which is sufficient to bring to the insurance applicant's attention, and expressly explain the contents of these clauses to the insurance applicant in writing or verbally, failing which such clauses shall not have binding force (Article 17, IL).

C. Conclusion of Marine Insurance Contract

533. An insurance contract shall be concluded upon the insurer's agreement to insure based upon the applicant's demand for insurance (Article 13, IL). A contract of marine insurance is concluded when the terms and conditions of the insurance are agreed upon between the insurer and the insured after the insured has put forth an offer for insurance and the insurer has agreed to accept it (Article 221, MC). The basic provisions contained in Sub-Book One 'General Provisions' of Book Three 'Contracts' of CC governing the conclusion of a contract apply to the conclusion of a contract of marine insurance.

In many cases, the insurer authorizes its insurance agent to conclude a contract of marine insurance, issue policy, conduct survey on ship or cargo insured, handle insurance claim on its behalf. On the other hand, an insurance broker often negotiates an insurance contract with the insurer or insurance agent for and on behalf of the insured.

534. As a matter of the principle of good faith, the insured has the statutory obligation of disclosure before the insurance contract is concluded.

By virtue of Article 222 of MC, before a contract of marine insurance, is concluded, the insured shall truthfully inform the insurer of the material circumstances that the insured has or ought to have knowledge of in its ordinary business practice, and that may have a bearing on the insurer in deciding the insurance premium or whether it agrees to insure or not. However, the insured need not inform the insurer of the facts that the insurer has or ought to have knowledge of in its ordinary business practice if the insurer did not make an enquiry about them. Therefore, the duty of disclosure adopted in MC is the so-called duty of 'unlimited disclosure'. In contrast, the duty of disclosure of the applicant provided for in IL is the so-called duty of 'disclosure upon inquiry' because paragraph 1 of Article 16 provides that the applicant shall truthfully inform the insurer of the circumstances concerning the subject matter and the insured upon inquiry.

As provided for in Article 223 of MC, the legal consequence on the marine insurance contract arising from the failure of the insured to truthfully inform the insurer of the material circumstances depends upon whether such failure is due to the intentional act of the insured or not. In details, if the failure is due to the intentional act of the insured, the insurer has the right to terminate the contract without refunding the insurance premium already paid and shall not be liable for any loss arising from the perils insured against before the contract is thus terminated. If the failure is not due to the intentional act of the insured, the insurer has the right to terminate the contract or to demand a corresponding increase in the insurance premium but shall, in case the contract is thus terminated, be liable for the loss of or damage to the subject matter insured arising from the perils insured against that had occurred prior to the termination of the contract, except where the material circumstances uninformed or wrongly informed of had an impact on the occurrence of such perils.

In addition, where the insured was aware or ought to be aware that the subject matter insured had suffered loss or damage due to the incidence of a peril insured against when the contract was concluded, the insurer shall not be liable for indemnification but shall have the right to the insurance premium. On the other hand, where the insurer was aware or ought to be aware that the occurrence of loss or damage of the subject matter insured due to a peril insured against was impossible, the insured shall have the right to recover the insurance premium already paid (Article 224, MC).

D. Assignment and Modification of Marine Insurance Contract

535. A contract of marine insurance is assignable. However, the conditions of assignment of a marine insurance contract for the carriage of goods by sea and that of hull insurance contract are different under Chinese law.

In the case of marine insurance for the carriage of goods by sea, a contract may be assigned by the insured by endorsement of the policy or otherwise without the consent of the insurer. Where the contract is assigned, the insured and the assignee shall be jointly and severally liable for the payment of the insurance premium, if the premium remains unpaid up to the time of assignment (Article 229, MC).

In the case of hull insurance, however, consent of the insurer shall be obtained where the insurance contract is assigned in consequence of the transfer of ownership of the ship insured (Article 230, MC). Otherwise, the insurer may terminate the contract. This is because different shipowners may expose different risks on a ship.

536. A contract of marine insurance contract may be modified by agreement between the insurer and the applicant or the insured.

In this respect, Article 20 of IL provides that, within the period of validity of an insurance contract, the applicant and the insurer may modify the relevant contents of insurance contract upon agreement through negotiation; where an insurance contract is modified, the insurer shall make notes or attach a slip on the original insurance policy or other insurance certificate, or the applicant and the insurer shall make an agreement in writing on such modification.

E. Termination of Marine Insurance Contract

537. Under the following circumstances, the insurer may legally terminate a marine insurance contract:

- the insured has violated the provisions of its duty of disclosure contained in Article 222 of MC, and the insurer terminates the contract by virtue of Article 223 of MC, as discussed *supra*;
- in the absence of the insurer's consent, the ownership of the insured ship is transferred, in which case the contract shall be terminated from the time of transfer or, where the transfer takes place during the voyage, from the time the voyage ends (Article 230, MC);
- the insured has not complied with its warranty as discussed *infra*, and the insurer terminates the contract by virtue of Article 235 of MC stipulating that the insured shall notify the insurer in writing immediately of its non-compliance with the warranty under the contract, in which case the insurer may, upon receipt of the notice, terminate the contract or demand an amendment to the terms and conditions of the insurance coverage or demand for an increase in the insurance premium;
- where no insurance accident happens, the insured or beneficiary lies about the occurrence of an accident and claims for indemnity, in which case the insurer may terminate the contract without any insurance liability and without refunding the insurance premium already paid; or where the insured intentionally causes an insurance accident, in which case the insurer may terminate the contract without any insurance liability and without refunding the insurance premium already paid (Article 27, IL);
- the applicant or the insured has failed to fulfil the responsibility in ensuring the safety of the subject matter insured as agreed, in which case the insurer may terminate the contract or demand for increase in the insurance premium (Article 51, IL);

- within the validity period of an insurance contract, the degree of danger of the subject matter insured significantly increases, in which case the insurer may terminate the contract or demand for increase in the insurance premium as agreed in the contract; where the contract is terminated, the insurer shall refund the insurance premium already paid to the applicant after deducting the receivable part from the day of commencement of insurance liability to the day of termination of contract (Article 52, IL);
- where partial loss of the subject matter insured occurs, unless otherwise provided for in the contract, the insurer may terminate the contract subject to fifteen days' notice thereof to the insured, in which case the insurer shall refund to the insured the insurance premium on the undamaged part of the subject matter insured after deducting the part receivable for the period from the date of the commencement of insurance liability to the date on which the contract is terminated (Article 58, IL);
- by virtue of Article 5 of the *Provisions on Certain Issues in the Trial of Cases of Disputes over Marine Insurance* promulgated by SPC on 23 November 2006, where the insured fails to pay the insurance premium to the insurer as agreed, the insurer may terminate the contract before the commencement of insurance liability, unless the insurer has issued the insurance certificates. However, the insurer may not terminate the contract after the commencement of insurance liability on the ground that the insured fails to pay the insurance premium, but is entitled to claim for the unpaid insurance premium.

538. Under the following circumstances, the insured may legally terminate a marine insurance contract:

- Prior to the commencement of the insurance liability, the insured may demand the termination subject to payment of the handling fees to the insurer, in which case the insurer shall refund the insurance premium already paid (Article 226, MC).
- Where partial loss of the subject matter insured occurs, the applicant may terminate the contract within thirty days after the insurer has made indemnity (Article 58, IL).

539. A contract of marine insurance may provide that the contract may be terminated by the insurer or the insured after the commencement of the insurance liability of the insurer.

Where the contract so provides and the insurer thus terminates the contract, the insurance premium not expired from the day of termination to the day of expiration of the period of insurance shall be refunded to the insured; if the insured demands the termination of contract, the insurer has the right to the premium payable from the day of commencement of the insurance liability to the day of termination of the contract but shall refund the remaining portion thereof (Article 227, MC). However, the insured may not demand termination of the contract of cargo insurance or hull voyage insurance after commencement of the insurance liability (Article 228, MC).

Where the insurer and the insured have not agreed in the contract that the contract may be terminated after commencement of the insurance liability of the insurer, neither the insurer nor the insured may terminate the contract (Article 227, MC). In this respect, the general provision of termination of contract by agreement contained in Article 562 of CC does not apply to the contracts of marine insurance, except the cases provided for in Articles 227 and 228 of MC *supra*.

F. Warranties and Effect of Breach

540. Chinese law including IL does not have the concept of warranty, let alone any provision of the effect of breach of warranties. The exception is the principled provision concerning the insured's breach of warranties under a marine insurance contract contained in Article 235 of MC stipulating: 'The insured shall notify the insurer in writing immediately where the insured has not complied with the warranties under the contract. The insurer may, upon receipt of the notice, terminate the contract or demand an amendment to the terms and conditions of the insurance coverage or an increase in the premium.' However, MC does not define warranty, nor does it contain specific provision concerning warranties in hull or marine cargo insurance. Article 235 of MC was drafted by reference to the provisions concerning warranty contained in the UK *Marine Insurance Act of 1906*, but does not contain detailed provisions in consideration of the arguments already existing even in the UK during the time of drafting of MC as regards the severe result of breach of warranty thereunder. The warranties in hull or marine cargo insurance are to be agreed upon between the insurer and the insured.

The *Provisions on Certain Issues in the Trial of Cases of Disputes over Marine Insurance* promulgated by SPC on 23 November 2006 contains provisions additional to Article 235 of MC concerning the effect of breach of warranties. If the insured failed to notify the insurer in writing immediately of its breach of warranty agreed upon in the contract, the insurer may terminate the contract from the day of breach of warranty (Article 6). If the insurer still paid insurance indemnity after receipt of the notice from the insured in writing of its breach of warranty, the insurer cannot terminate the contract on the ground of such breach of warranty (Article 7). Where, after receipt of the notice from the insured in writing of its breach of warranty, the insurer fails to reach an agreement with the insured as to the amendments to the coverage conditions, increase in premiums and other issues, the contract shall be deemed as have been terminated from the day of breach of warranty (Article 8).

In admiralty practice, the maritime courts and courts of appeals in China adopt strict interpretations of the contractual provisions with respect to warranty.

541. The following provisions concerning warranty are contained in the PICC P&C Ocean Hull Clauses of 2009:

- Unless previously agreed to by the insurer in writing, the insurance shall terminate automatically at the time of change of the classification society of the insured vessel, or change, cancellation or withdrawal of her class therein, or change in the ownership or flag, assignment or transfer to new management, being chartered out

on bareboat basis or requisitioned for title or use of the vessel, provided that, if the insured vessel has cargo onboard or is at sea, the termination shall, if required, be deferred until her arrival at next port, final port of discharge or port of destination.
- Where the cargo, voyage, trading limit, towage, salvage or date of commencing voyage is in violation of the provisions in the policy, the insurance shall remain in force only upon prompt notice to the insurer when the insured becomes aware of the same and agrees to payment of an additional premium if required; otherwise the insurance shall be terminated automatically.
- Unless the insurer agrees in advance and the insured agrees to the amended conditions of insurance and pays the required additional premium, the insurer shall not be responsible for the losses and liability resulting from towage or salvage service undertaken by the insured vessel, cargo loading or discharging operation at sea from or into another vessel other than a harbour or inshore craft including approaching, lying alongside and leaving, or the insured vessel's sailing with the intention of being broken up or sold for breaking up.

542. The provisions contained in the PICC P&C Marine Cargo Clauses of 2009 are less specific in this respect. The Clauses only provide that, in the case of change of voyage or any omission or error in the name of the cargo, vessel or voyage, the insurance shall remain in force only upon prompt notice to the insurer when the insured becomes aware of the same and payment of an additional premium if required.

IV. Insurance Policy and Clauses

A. *Insurance Policy or Other Certificate*

543. An insurance policy is a certificate or evidence of the conclusion and contents of insurance contract.

In practice in China, an insurance contract is not always evidenced by an insurance policy, but may be evidenced by a cover note issued by the insurer, an insurance application form signed by the insurer, a slip normally used in the case where an insurance contract is concluded through an insurance broker, a receipt of insurance premium issued by the insurer, or an insurance certificate or combined insurance certificate issued by the insurer or its insurance agent. The issuance of an insurance policy is not a must, although in most cases of marine insurance, policies are issued by the insurers or their insurance agents. Upon agreement by both parties, the insurance contract may be evidenced by other forms than a policy or be concluded in writing in other forms (Article 13, IL).

However, Article 221 of MC provides that, after the conclusion of a marine insurance contract, the insurer shall issue to the insured an insurance policy or other certificate of insurance in time and the contents of the contract shall be contained therein.

544. Like other insurances, marine insurance has various kinds of policies.

In terms of the number of the subject matters insured, insurance policies can be divided into single policy, collective policy and open policy.

In terms of whether the insured value is agreed upon or not, insurance policies can be divided into valued policy and unvalued policy.

In terms of the duration of insurance, policies can be divided into voyage policy, time policy or combined policy.

An insurance policy or other insurance certificate is the most important document which the insured should submit to the insurer in its claim for insurance indemnity.

B. Insurance Clauses

545. Insurance clauses are contained either at the back page of an insurance policy or exists separately. The clauses are formulated by insurances companies in advance for the purpose of repeated use and form an important part of the contents of an insurance contract.

As the insurance clauses are formulated by the insurer in advance for repeated use and not subject to negotiation with the insured in the conclusion of contract, these clauses are within the category of form clauses in the meaning of paragraph 1 of Article 496 of CC. Thus, the provisions governing the legal effects of form clauses contained in Articles 17 and 19 of IL and Articles 496, 497 and 498 of CC shall apply. Consequently, by virtue of paragraph 1 of Article 496 of CC, the insurer is obliged to follow the principle of fairness in determining the rights and obligations of the insurer and the insured, to require the insured to pay attention to the provisions concerning the exemptions and limitation of liability,[48] and to make explanation of the clauses if required by the insured. By virtue of Article 497 of CC, any provision of such clauses that increases the obligations or eliminates the main rights of the insured shall be null and void. Article 19 of IL also provides that the following clauses contained in an insurance contract based upon the form clauses provided by the insurer shall be null and void: (a) eliminating the obligations of the insurer to be assumed by virtue of law or increasing the obligations of the applicant or insured; (b) eliminating the rights of the applicant, insured or beneficiary to be enjoyed by virtue of law. As regards the interpretation of such clauses, by virtue of Article 498 of CC, the rule of *contra profererem* shall be applied, i.e., where a clause, word or phrase may have two interpretations, it shall be interpreted unfavourable to the insurer. Where any provision of such clauses is repugnant to that of non-form clauses, the latter shall have priority.

48. Article 17 of IL provides that where form clauses provided by the insurer are used in the conclusion of an insurance contract, the application form provided by the insurer shall be attached with the form clauses and the insurer shall explain the contents of contract to the applicant; where an insurance contract contains clauses on liability exemption of the insurer, the insurer shall at the time of conclusions of the contract make indication in the insurance application form, insurance policy or other insurance certificate which is sufficient to bring to the insurance applicant's attention, and expressly explain the contents of those clauses to the insurance applicant in writing or verbally, failing which such clauses shall not have binding force.

546. Various insurance clauses mainly formulated by PICC P&C and approved by the former China Banking and Insurance Regulatory Commission are used in the insurance market in China over the years. In marine insurance, the following are the main clauses:

- Hull Clauses of 2009 with additional War and Strike Clauses applicable to the insurance of vessels engaging in international transport.
- Coastal & Inland Vessel Clauses of 2009 with various additional clauses applicable to the insurance of vessels engaging in domestic coastal and inland transport.
- Inland Vessel Clauses of 2009 with various additional clauses applicable to the insurance of vessels engaging in inland navigation.
- Shipowners' Protection & Indemnity Clauses of 2009 applicable to the insurance of liability of owners of vessels engaging in international transport.
- Vessel Construction Clauses of 2009 applicable to the insurance of vessels under construction.
- Marine Cargo Clauses of 2009 with various additional clauses applicable to the insurance of cargo in international maritime trade.
- Waterway Cargo Clauses of 2009 with various additional clauses applicable to the insurance of cargo in domestic waterway transport.

In this chapter, among the various clauses listed above, only the Hull Clauses of 2009 with additional War & Strike Clauses, the Marine Cargo Clauses of 2009 with various additional clauses and the Shipowners' Protection & Indemnity Clauses of 2009 are discussed. The Coastal & Inland Vessel Clauses of 2009, the Inland Vessel Clauses of 2009 and the Waterway Cargo Clauses of 2009 with various additional clauses are discussed in Chapter 3 of Part III *infra*. The clauses of cargo insurances in other modes of transport are discussed in other corresponding chapters in Part III *infra*.

§2. Hull Insurance

I. Kinds of Insurance

A. *Voyage Insurance*

547. Under a voyage insurance contract or policy, the ship is covered for a particular and fixed voyage against the perils described in the insurance contract or policy as agreed upon between the insurer and the insured, *viz*. the owners, bareboat charterers or operator of a ship, as the case may be.

Chinese law does not define the voyage or the time of commencement and that of termination of the voyage, but leaves the insurer and the insured to agree. Under the PICC P&C Hull Clauses of 2009, the voyage in a voyage insurance policy means the one described in the policy. Where the ship is not loaded with cargo, the voyage shall commence when she casts off lines or weighs up anchor at the port of departure and end when she lets go anchor or ties up at the port of destination. Where the ship is loaded with cargo, the voyage shall commence when loading operation starts and end when discharge operation completes, but shall not exceed thirty days dating from the midnight of the day of her arrival at the port of destination.

B. Time Insurance

548. Under a time insurance contract or policy, the ship is covered for a fixed duration against the perils described in the insurance contract or policy as agreed upon between the insurer and the insured.

Likewise, Chinese law does not limit the duration of coverage, but leaves the insurer and the insured to agree. Under the PICC P&C Hull Clauses of 2009, the duration of coverage in the case of a time policy shall not exceed one year. The time of commencement and that of termination shall be described in the policy.

C. Combined Voyage/Time Policy

549. Combined voyage/time policy is not a statutory concept under Chinese law, but is used in the hull insurance subject to agreement between the insurer and the insured. The purpose of a combined policy is to avoid the disadvantage of a time policy, i.e., when the agreed duration, normally twelve months, expires, the policy automatically comes to the end, while the insured vessel is often still at sea and has to complete a voyage. A combined policy enables the insured to have its ship covered until her completion of voyage after the expiration of the agreed duration. The insured is normally required to pay extra insurance premium for such extension period of time.

Under the PICC P&C Hull Clause of 2009, in the case of a time policy, if the ship is still on her voyage, in distress or at the port of refuge or port of call when the agreed duration expires, the coverage shall be extended until she arrives at the port of destination, provided that the insured notifies the insurer in advance thereof and pays additional daily insurance premium in proportion. In such a case, if the ship suffers total loss during the time of extension, an insurance premium for a period of six months shall be paid by the insured.

II. Scope of Cover

550. By virtue of paragraph (1) of Article 219 of MC, hull insurance covers the hull, machinery, equipment, bunkers, stores, gears, provisions and fresh water of the ship insured. Under the PICC P&C Hull Clauses of 2009, the insurance covers hull, lifeboats, machinery, equipment, instruments, gears, bunkers and stores.

The hull insurance coverage includes three main forms, i.e., total loss cover, all risks cover and mixed cover.

A. Total Loss Cover

551. This insurance covers the total loss of the ship insured including actual total loss and constructive total loss as mentioned *infra* caused by any of the following perils:

- earthquake, volcanic eruption, lightning or other natural calamity;
- grounding, collision, contact with any fixed or floating object or other object (allision), or other perils of the sea;
- fire or explosion;
- violent theft by persons outside the ship or piracy;
- jettison;
- breakdown of or accident to nuclear installation or reactor;
- accident in loading, discharging or shifting of cargo or fuel;
- latent defect in machinery or hull of the ship;
- wrongful act wilfully committed by the master or other crewmembers to the prejudice of the insured's interests;
- negligence of the master, other crewmembers or pilot, repairer or charterers;
- act of any governmental authority to prevent or minimize pollution resulting from damage to the ship caused by peril insured against.

Noticeably, the coverage of the last five categories of perils listed *supra* is conditional upon that the total loss resulting therefrom has not caused by want of due diligence on the part of the insured, owners or manager of the ship insured.

B. All Risks Cover

552. This insurance covers the total loss or partial loss of or damage to the insured ship arising from the perils insured against under the total loss cover and also the liabilities for and expenses of collision, general average and salvage, and sue and labour.

553. The provision of collision liability is called 'Running Down Clause' (RDC). Under the PICC P&C Hull Clauses of 2009, the insurance of collision liability covers the legal liabilities of the insured as a consequence of the insured ship coming into collision or contact with any other vessel or any object, fixed or floating or otherwise. Thus, this RDC covers 4/4 of the collision liability instead of 3/4 in some other countries and allision liability.

However, this RDC does not cover any liability resulting from collision or allision of the insured ship in respect of:

- loss of life of, personal injury to or illness of any person whether onboard or ashore;
- cargo or other property onboard, or engagement of, the insured ship;
- removal or disposal of obstruction, wrecks, cargo or any other things whatsoever;

- pollution or contamination of any property or thing whatsoever including the cost of preventive measures and cleaning operations, except pollution or contamination of the other vessel with which the insured ship is in collision or property on such other vessel;
- indirect expenses arising from delay to, or loss of use of, any object fixed or floating or otherwise.

554. The insurance of general average and salvage covers the insured ship's proportion of contribution in the general average or salvage reward not in the nature of general average. Special compensation as provided for in Article 182 of MC or Article 14 of the *International Convention on Salvage of 1989* is normally not covered under this clause, but is covered under the protection and indemnity insurance as discussed in §5 *infra*.

Noticeably, under the PICC P&C Hull Clauses of 2009, in the case of general average sacrifice of the insured ship, the insured may recover such loss or damage in full without first obtaining contribution in general average from other parties. After the payment for such loss or damage, the insurer has the right of subrogation to claim against other interests for contribution in general average.

Under these Clauses, the general average shall be adjusted in accordance with the relative contract of carriage and/or governing law or customs. Where the contract of carriage does not so provide, the general average shall be adjusted in accordance with the *Beijing Rules*[49] or other similar rules. In practice, where general average is adjusted in accordance with the YAR as in most cases, general average is covered under this insurance.

It is expressly provided for in the PICC P&C Hull Clauses of 2009 that, where all the contributing interests are owned by the insured, or where the insured ship sails in ballast and there are no other contributing interests, the provisions of the *Beijing Rules* except Rules 5,[50] or similar adjustment rules, if expressly agreed upon, shall apply as if the interests were owned by different persons. The voyage for this purpose of adjustment shall be deemed to be from the port or place of departure until the arrival of the ship at the first port thereafter other than a port of refuge or a port of call for bunkering. If, at any such intermediate port or place, there is abandonment of the adventure originally contemplated, the voyage shall thereupon be deemed terminated.

555. Under the sue and labour clause, where there is loss of or damage to the insured ship from a peril insured against, or where she is in immediate danger from such a peril, and as a result, reasonable expenses are incurred by the insured in order to avert or minimize a loss that would be recoverable under this insurance, the insurer shall be liable for the expenses so incurred by the insured. However, this clause shall not apply to general average or salvage reward or other expenditures provided for in other clauses.

49. *See* §4, Ch. 10 of Part II.
50. Interests and commission. *See* §5, Ch. 10 of Part II.

C. Mixed Cover

556. On some occasions in the practice of hull insurance in China, a mixed cover is agreed upon between the insurer and the insured. For example, especially in the past, the insurance covers total loss, partial loss arising from stranding or grounding, liability of collision or allision, salvage, general average and war and strike risks as discussed *infra* as agreed in the hull insurance contract.

III. Exclusions

557. Under the PICCP&C Hull Clauses of 2009, loss, damage, liabilities and expenses resulting from the following causes shall be excluded under both the total loss cover and the all risks cover:

- unseaworthiness of the insured ship, including not being properly manned, equipped or loaded, provided that the insured knew or should have known of such unseaworthiness when the ship was sent to the sea;
- negligence or intentional act of the insured or its representative;
- ordinary wear and tear, rust, corrosion, rottenness or insufficient upkeep, or defect in material that the insured should have discovered with due diligence, or replacement of or repair to any part in unsound condition;
- war, civil war, revolution, rebellion or civil strife or hostile act arising therefrom;
- capture, seizure, arrest, detainment, confiscation or blockage;
- various war weapons including mines, torpedoes, bombs, atomic bombs, hydrogen bombs or nuclear weapons;
- strikes, lock-outs or other similar events;
- civil commotions, riots or other similar events;
- malicious acts committed by any person with political intentions.

558. By virtue of Article 244 of MC, unless otherwise agreed upon in the insurance contract, the hull insurer shall not be liable for loss of or damage to the insured ship arising from her unseaworthiness at the time of commencement of the voyage, unless under a time policy the insured had no knowledge thereof, or from wear and tear or corrosion of the ship.

The provisions of Article 244 of MC are not compulsorily applicable and therefore the insurer and the insured are allowed to agree as to the exclusions of the insurer in a hull insurance contract. Thus, the exclusions contained in the PICC P&C Hull Clauses of 2009 above shall have full effect, provided that they are agreed upon between the insurer and the insured.

In addition, by virtue of Article 242 of MC the insurer's liability for loss of or damage to the insured ship caused by intentional act of the insured shall also be excluded.

IV. Hull War and Strike Clauses

A. *Scope of Cover*

559. Under the PICC P&C War & Strike Clauses of 2009, this insurance covers the total or partial loss of the insured ship, collision liability, contribution in general average and salvage reward as well as sue and labour resulting from any of the following causes:

- war, civil war, revolution, rebellion or civil strife or hostile act arising therefrom;
- capture, seizure, arrest, detainment, confiscation or blockage, provided that such claims shall not be accepted before expiry of six months from the date of occurrence of such peril;
- various war weapons including mines, torpedoes, bombs;
- strikes, lock-outs or other similar events;
- civil commotions, riots or other similar events;
- malicious acts committed by any person with political intentions.

B. *Exclusions*

560. Under the PICC P&C War & Strike Clauses of 2009, this insurance does not cover the loss of or damage to the insured ship, liabilities or expenses resulting from:

- explosions of atomic bombs, hydrogen bombs or nuclear weapons;
- capture, seizure, arrest, detainment, confiscation of the insured vessel as taken or ordered by the government or local authorities of the State of the ship's flag or registry;
- requisition, requisition for title or sale of the insured ship;
- war broken between or among the permanent members of the Security Council of the United Nations, whether declared or not.

§3. Ocean Marine Cargo Insurance

I. Kinds of Insurance

A. *Voyage Insurance*

561. A voyage insurance of marine cargo covers the cargo in maritime transport on a particular voyage as agreed upon between the insurer and the insured and indicated in the insurance policy. It is common that such an insurance contract contains a 'warehouse to warehouse clause' to the effect that the insurance also covers the risks on land at both ends of the voyage.

The PICC P&C Marine Cargo Clauses of 2009 contain a 'warehouse to warehouse clause', i.e., 'This insurance attaches from the time the cargo hereby insured leaves the warehouse or place of storage named in the Policy for the commencement of the transit and continues in force in the ordinary course of transit including sea, land and inland waterway transits and transit in lighter until the insured cargo is delivered to the consignee's final warehouse or place of storage at the destination named in the Policy or to any other place used by the insured for allocation or distribution of the cargo or for storage other than in the ordinary course of transit. This insurance shall, however, be limited to sixty (60) days after completion of discharge of the insured cargo from the seagoing vessel at the final port of discharge before it reaches the abovementioned warehouse or place of storage. If prior to the expiry of the above mentioned sixty (60) days, the insured cargo is to be forwarded to a destination other than that named in the Policy, this insurance shall terminate at the commencement of such transit.'

562. Chinese law does not contain provision concerning the time of commencement and that of termination of the voyage. Therefore, the parties are free to negotiate.

The PICC P&C Marine Cargo Clauses of 2009 does not contain a separate 'extended cover' clause. However, the 'termination of contract of carriage' clause covers the situation where, owing to delay, deviation, forced discharge, reshipment or transhipment beyond the control of the insured or any change or termination of contract of carriage arising from the exercise of a liberty granted to the carrier under the contract of carriage, the insured cargo arrives at a port or place other than the destination named in the policy, subject to immediate notice being given to the insurer by the insured and an additional insurance premium being paid, if required, this insurance shall remain in force. Under such circumstances, if the insured cargo is sold at port or place other than the destination named in the policy, the insurance shall terminate on delivery of the cargo sold, but in no event shall this insurance extend beyond sixty days after completion of discharge of the insured cargo from the seagoing ship at the port of discharge; if the insured cargo is to be forwarded to the original destination named in the policy or any other destination, this insurance shall terminate in accordance with the 'warehouse to warehouse' clause.

B. *Time Insurance*

563. A time insurance of marine cargo covers the cargo for an agreed period of time between one fixed moment and the other. However, since the duration of carriage of marine cargo is dependent upon the sea carrier and the cargo owners are difficult or even impossible to determine exactly how long the cargo will be at risk, time insurance of marine cargo is rarely used in practice, except where no carriage is foreseen in the near future and the cargo need be stored in a warehouse ashore in port or onboard for a long time. In such a case, however, the time insurance of cargo is not marine cargo insurance in essence anymore, but is an ordinary property insurance.

C. *Open and Floating Policy*

564. By virtue of Article 231 of MC, the insured may conclude an open cover with the insurer for the cargo to be shipped or received in batches within a given period and the open cover shall be evidenced by an open policy to be issued by the insurer.

Thus, an open policy is a certificate of an open cover under which all the marine cargo to be shipped or received in batches during a fixed period of time shall be automatically covered as agreed upon between the insurer and the insured, whenever the cargo is at risk during the fixed period of time, subject to possibly the agreed geographical limits. Besides the period of time, an open marine cargo insurance contract or an open policy contains the description or types of cargo insured, scope of cover, the maximum insured amount for each cargo or each place (locality clause) and payment of insurance premiums.

Combining the advantages of voyage insurance and those of time insurance, this type of insurance has the benefit of saving expenses of both the insurer and the insured. Besides, it can effectively avoid any omission of cargo insurance by the insured. It also benefits the insurer, since it can bring out steady insurance premium incomes during a long period of time. This is why it is common in China that professional traders and the insurers conclude this type of marine cargo insurance contracts.

565. Under an open cover or policy of marine cargo, when any cargo covered is loaded on board a ship, the insured shall notify the insurer immediately on learning that the cargo insured under open cover has been shipped or arrived of the name of the carrying ship, voyage, value of the cargo and the insured amount (Article 233, MC). However, any omission of, delay in or mistakes of such notification by the insured shall not prejudice the effect of insurance, provided that it is not committed by the insured intentionally.

The insurer shall, upon request of the insured, issue policies or other insurance certificates separately for the cargo shipped in batches in accordance with an open cover. Where the contents of such insurance certificates differ from those of the open cover, the formers shall prevail (Article 232, MC).

566. Open policy was developed from floating policy and has replaced the latter on the whole in the practice of marine cargo insurance. Floating policies are now mainly used in the cargo warehousing insurance. The characteristics of a floating policy are that the subject matters insured can be increased or decreased and it contains no specific insured amount, but the maximum limit of the insurer's liability only.

II. Scope of Cover

567. Chinese law does not contain any provision concerning the scope of cover in marine cargo insurance, but is up to the insurer and the insured to negotiate.

Marine cargo insurance coverage includes principal risks and additional risks. Under the PICC P&C Marine Cargo Clauses of 2009, the principal risks include three conditions *viz.* free from particular average (F.P.A.), with average (W.A.) and all risks. Various additional risks are covered under the various PICC P&C clauses of 2009.

Additional risks cannot be insured against independently of the principal risks and include three types in the practice in China *viz.* ordinary or general additional risks, special additional risks and peculiar additional risks which are mainly the war and strike risks. Ordinary additional risks are covered under the conditions of all risks and therefore can be insured against under the conditions of either F.P.A. or W.A. upon agreement between the insurer and the insured.

A. *Free from Particular Average*

568. This insurance covers:

- the actual total loss or constructive total loss of the whole insured cargo caused in the course of carriage by natural calamities including heavy weather, lightning, tsunami, earthquake and flood;
- the total or partial loss of the insured cargo caused by accidents of the carrying ship being grounded, stranded, sunk, in collision with other vessel or floating ice or other objects, fire or explosion;
- the partial loss of the insured cargo caused by natural calamities including heavy weather, lightning, tsunami, etc., where the carrying ship has suffered accident of being grounded, stranded, sunk or burnt, irrespective of whether the event or events took place before or after such accidents;
- the partial or total loss of the insured cargo consequent upon falling of entire package or packages into sea during loading, transhipment or discharge;
- the reasonable costs incurred by the insured in salvaging the insured cargo, averting or minimizing loss of the insured cargo recoverable under the insurance, i.e., the sue and labour expenses, provided that such costs shall not exceed the insured amount of the cargo so saved;
- the losses caused by discharge of the insured cargo at a port of refuge following a sea peril encountered by the means of transport as well as special charges arising from discharge, warehousing and forwarding of the cargo at an intermediate port of call or refuge;
- the general average sacrifice and contribution in general average and salvage payment;
- such proportion of losses sustained by the shipowners/carrier as is to be reimbursed by the cargo owners under the Both to Blame Collision Clause in the contract of carriage.

B. With Average

569. Aside from the risks covered under F.P.A. condition as introduced *supra*, this insurance also covers the partial loss of the insured cargo caused by natural calamities including heavy weather, lightning, tsunami, earthquake and/or flood.

C. All Risks

570. Aside from the risks covered under the F.P.A. and W.A. conditions as introduced *supra*, this insurance also covers total or partial loss of the insured cargo arising from external causes in the course of carriage.

D. Ordinary Additional Risks

571. Upon agreement between the insurer and the insured, the ordinary additional risks cover loss of the insured cargo, whether total or partial, arising from:

- theft, pilferage and non-delivery (T.P.N.D.);
- fresh water and/or rain damage (F.W.R.D);
- shortage;
- intermixture and contamination;
- leakage;
- clash and breakage;
- taint of odour;
- sweat and heating;
- hook damage;
- breakage of packing;
- rust.

E. Special Additional Risks

572. Upon agreement between the insurer and the insured, the loss of or damage to the insured cargo, expenses or liabilities is covered by the following clauses:

- Import Duty Clause which covers the insured's contingent interest on import customs duty arising from the insured goods arriving at the port of destination damaged by a peril insured against, but full import duty had been levied and paid thereon as if the goods had arrived sound, provided that claims payable hereunder shall not exceed an agreed percentage of the insured value on the damage portion of the insured goods.
- On Deck Clause which extends to cover the risks of jettison and/or washing overboard of the insured goods shipped on deck additional to the risks covered by the Marine Cargo Clauses.

- Rejection Clause which covers the loss arising from rejection and/or condemnation at the port of entry by the government of the country of import or its relevant authorities on the basis of the insured value of the goods so rejected or condemned, or the cost of return freight to the country of export or the additional freight to other destination in the event of any embargo or prohibition being declared by the importing country after the insured goods left the port of shipment named in the policy not exceeding the insured value of the goods so rejected.
- Aflatoxin Clause which covers the loss arising from rejection or confiscation of the insured goods or the alteration of original purpose of the insured goods for which they are intended is compulsorily altered by reason of the existence of the aflatoxin to any extent exceeding the limit sanctioned by the importing country as evidenced by the inspection by the local health authorities at the port or place of import, to the extent of the insured value of the portion so rejected or confiscated or the loss arising from the alteration of the original purpose for which the goods are intended.
- Failure to Deliver Clause which covers the total loss of the insured goods in case the insured goods, once loaded onboard a seagoing ship, fail to be delivered at destination within six months of scheduled arrived date from whatever cause, excluding loss or damage recoverable under the Ocean Marine Cargo Clauses and the Ocean Marine War Risks Clauses.
- Perishable Goods Clause which covers the loss of market or loss, damage or deterioration of the insured cargo arising from delay whether caused a peril insured against or otherwise.

F. Peculiar Additional Risks

573. Under the PICC P&C Ocean Marine Cargo War Risks Clauses of 2009, the insurance of war risks on cargo within the duration of insurance which is in principle limited to the period of the cargo being on board the carrying ship, unless otherwise agreed upon to cover the war risks while the insured cargo is on land, covers the following loss of or damage to the insured cargo, expenses or liabilities:

- the loss or damage directly caused by war, warlike operation, hostile act, armed conflict or piracy;
- the loss or damage caused by capture, seizure, arrest, restraint or detainment consequently upon the above acts;
- the loss or damage caused by various conventional weapons including mines, torpedoes and bombs;
- the general average sacrifice or contribution in general average and salvage reward occurred within the above scope of the cover.

574. Under this insurance, the insurer shall not be liable for loss, damage or expenses caused by nuclear or heat energy weapons used due to hostile act, or any claim caused by loss or frustration of the insured voyage due to seizure or detainment by rulers or armed group. The transhipment expenses and other losses caused by the loss or frustration of the insured voyage shall be covered under the conditions of 'Additional Expenses – War Risks'.

575. Under the PICC P&C Strike Clauses of 2009, the insurance of strike risks on cargo covers the losses directly caused by the acts of strikers, locked-out workmen or persons taking part in the labour disturbances, riots or civil commotions or malicious acts of any person, and general average sacrifice or contribution in general average or salvage reward arising from the above acts.

The insurer shall not be liable for any loss or damage to the insured goods occurred in the strike due to insufficiency of labour or failure to perform duties in due course, including loss or damage to the insured refrigerated goods due to stoppage of work of refrigerator as a result of insufficiency of power or fuel.

576. Other peculiar additional risks are covered under the PICC P&C Special Insurance Clauses of Carriage of Imported Containerized Goods of 2009, the PICC P&C Insurance Liability Extension Clauses of Imported Marine Cargo during Domestic Transhipment of 2009, the PICC P&C Customs Inspection Clauses of 2009, the PICC P&C Port Terminal Inspection Clauses of 2009, or the PICC P&C Seller's Interest Insurance Clauses of 2009.

III. Exclusions

577. Under the PICC P&C Marine Cargo Clauses of 2009, the insurance of principal risks covered under the conditions of F.P.A., W.A. or all risks does not cover:

- the loss or damage caused by the intentional act or fault of the insured;
- the loss or damage falling under the liability of the consignor;
- the loss or damage arising from the interior quality or shortage of the insured cargo prior to the attachment of this insurance;
- the loss or damage arising from the normal loss, inherent vice or nature of the insured goods, loss of market and/or delay in carriage and any expenses arising therefrom;
- the risks and liabilities covered and excluded by the PICC P&C Ocean Marine Cargo War Risks Clauses and the PICC P&C Strike Clauses.

578. The ordinary or special additional risks clauses may include their respective exclusions. The peculiar additional risks clauses include their respective exclusions.

By virtue of Articles 242 and 243 of MC applicable to various marine insurances, the insurer shall not be liable for loss of or damage to the insured cargo caused by the intentional act of the insured, delay in the voyage or in the delivery of cargo or change of market, fair wear and tear, inherent vice or nature of the cargo, or improper packing. However, these statutory exclusions are not compulsorily applicable. Instead, the insurer and the insured are allowed to agree as to the exclusions of the insurer in the marine cargo insurance contract.

IV. Special Marine Cargo Insurance Clauses

579. PICC P&C also formulated several special marine cargo insurance clauses *viz.* the Roll-on/Roll-off Ship Cargo Insurance Clauses of 2009 applicable to the insurance of motor vehicles and the goods thereon during carriage by roll-on/roll-off ships in costal trade or inland navigation, the Marine Refrigerated Cargo Insurance Clauses of 2009, the Marine Tung in Bulk Insurance Clauses of 2009, and the Logistic Cargo Insurance Clauses of 2009.

§4. Settlement and Indemnity in Marine Insurance

I. Notification of Insurance Accident

580. When a marine insurance accident occurs, the insured has the statutory obligation to notify the insurer immediately thereof.

By virtue of Article 236 of MC, the insured shall notify the insurer immediately upon the occurrence of the peril insured against. IL also provides in Article 21 that, at the time of being aware of the occurrence of an insurance accident, the insurance applicant, insured or beneficiary shall timely notify the insurer, and that if the insurance applicant, insured or beneficiary fails to do so intentionally or due to gross negligence which makes it difficult to determine the nature, cause, degree of damage, etc., of the insurance incident, the insurer shall not be liable for paying the indemnity or insurance money for the undeterminable part, unless the insurer has known or should have known the incident in a timely manner through any other channel.

Under the PICC P&C Hull Clauses of 2009, the insured shall, within forty-eight hours after being aware of any accident or loss of or damage to the insured ship, give notice to the insurer or the nearest insurance agent if the ship is abroad.

The PICC P&C Marine Cargo Clauses of 2009 do not contain provision concerning the insured's obligation of timely notifying the insurer of the occurrence of an insurance accident and, therefore, the statutory provisions contained in Article 236 of MC and Article 21 of IL shall apply. However, the Clauses provide that the insured shall give immediate notice to the insurer when the cargo owners' actual responsibility under the Both to Blame Collision Clause in the contract of affreightment becomes known.

II. Obligation of Insured to Mitigate Loss

581. The insured has the statutory obligation to take measures to avoid or minimize loss. By virtue of Article 236 of MC, upon the occurrence of the peril insured against, the insured shall take necessary and reasonable measures to avoid or minimize the loss and, where special instructions for the adoption of reasonable measures to avoid or minimize loss are received from the insurer, the insured shall act according to such instructions, otherwise the insurer shall not be liable for the exaggerated loss caused by the insured's breach thereof.

Under the PICC P&C Hull Clauses of 2009, the insured shall take all reasonable measures for the purpose of averting or minimizing the loss or damage that would be coverable under the insurance. The insured shall obtain agreement of the insurer in determining the liabilities and expenses in respect of the insured ship. Under the PICC P&C Marine Cargo Clauses of 2009, the insured shall, and the insurer may, take all reasonable measures to averting or minimizing the loss or damage that would be coverable under the insurance. The taking of such measures by the insured or the insurer shall not be deemed as waiver or acceptance of abandonment of the insured ship or otherwise prejudice the rights of either party.

III. Obligation of Insured to Take Protective Measures

582. Under the PICC P&C Marine Cargo Clauses of 2009, the insured has the obligation to take protective measures in the event of any damage to the insured cargo.

The insured shall take delivery of the insured cargo after the cargo has been carried to the port or place of destination. If any loss of or damage to the insured cargo is found, the insured shall immediately apply for survey to the surveying and/or settling agent stipulated in the policy. If the insured cargo is found short in entire package or packages or to show apparent traces of damage, the insured shall obtain from the carrier, bailee or relevant authorities (customs and port authorities, etc.) certificate of loss or damage and/or shortage memo. Should the carrier, bailee or relevant authorities be responsible for such loss, damage or shortage, the insured shall lodge a claim against them in writing and, if necessary, obtain their confirmation of an extension of the time limit for such a claim.

Under the PICC P&C Hull Clauses of 2009, where a third party is liable for the loss of or damage to the insured ship, the insured shall lodge a claim against the third party. Where the third party fails to make compensation, the insured shall take necessary measures to protect the time limit for litigation.

If the insured fails to take these protective measures and such failure prejudices the exercise of the insurer's right of recourse against any responsible third party based upon its right of subrogation, such failure shall constitute the fault of the insured referred to in Article 253 of MC which provides that, where the insured waives its right of claim against the third person without the consent of the insurer or the insurer is unable to exercise the right of recourse due to the fault of the insured, the insurer may make a corresponding reduction from the amount of indemnity.

IV. Burden of Proof

583. After the occurrence of a peril insured against and before the payment of insurance indemnity, the insurer may demand the insured to submit evidence and materials relating to the determination of the nature of the peril and the extent of loss or damage (Article 251, MC). Thus, when so demanded, the insured has the burden of proof showing that the loss of or damage to the subject matter or its liability to a third party is covered by the insurance and the exact amount of such a loss or damage or liability. Where the insurer considers that the relevant proofs and materials provided by the insurance applicant, insured or beneficiary are incomplete in accordance with the provisions of the insurance contract, it shall notify the applicant, insured or beneficiary to submit additional ones (Article 22, IL).

The PICC P&C Hull Clauses of 2009 provide expressly that at the time of claim for indemnity against the insurer, the insured shall submit the original policy, harbour master's visa, logbook, engine room book, accident report, statutory survey certificates, ship's operation certificate, certificates of the master and other crewmembers, cargo record, reconciliation statement or award of court of law relating to the responsibility for accident, list of damages and other documents and materials which the insured can provide and relate to the determination of the nature, causes and extent of damage, etc.

The PICC P&C Marine Cargo Clauses of 2009 provide expressly that the documents accompanying any claim against the insurer shall include the original policy, bill of lading, invoice, packing list, tally sheet, weight memo, certificate of loss or damage and/or shortage memo, survey report, statement of claim. If any third party's liability is involved, the documents relating to pursuing recovery from such a party shall also be included.

The insured shall provide these proofs and materials truthfully. If, after the occurrence of an insurance accident, the insurance applicant, insured or beneficiary forges or alters the relevant proofs, materials or other evidence so as to provide false ones accounting for the causes of accident or to overstate losses, the insurer shall bear no liability over indemnity or payment of the insurance benefit for the part falsified (Article 27, IL).

584. Unless otherwise agreed upon between the insurer and the insured in the insurance contract or provided for in law, the insured shall bear the time and expenses in collecting the related evidence in order to fulfil its burden of proof.

In this respect, the PICC P&C Hull Clauses of 2009 provides that in no case shall any sum be allowed under the insurance either by way of remuneration of the insured for time and labour taken to obtain and supply information or documents or in respect of the commission or charges of any manager, agent, managing or agency company or the like, appointed by or on behalf of the insured to perform such a service, unless the insurer's agreement has been obtained.

By virtue of Article 64 of IL, however, necessary and reasonable expenses paid by the insurer and the insured for the purpose of investigating and determining the nature, causes of the insurance accident and extent of damage to the subject matter insured shall be borne by the insurer. For example, the expenses paid to the CCS or other classification society or other surveyors for the survey on damage to the insured ship for such a purpose as authorized by the insurer or the insured shall thus be borne by the insurer. In addition, in the case of liability insurance, where the insured is brought to arbitration or legal proceedings due to an insurance accident in which damage or loss is caused to a third party by the insured, the insurer shall bear the arbitration charges or court costs as well as other necessary and reasonable expenses paid by the insured, unless the contract contains provisions to the contrary (Article 66, IL).

V. Total or Partial Loss

A. Total Loss

585. Total loss of a ship in hull insurance or of cargo in marine cargo insurance includes actual total loss and constructive total loss. Both actual total loss and constructive total loss are covered by the coverage of total loss in hull or marine cargo insurance.

586. Actual total loss of a ship or cargo means that the insured ship or cargo is lost or is so seriously damaged that it is completely deprived of its original structure and usage or the insured is deprived of the possession thereof after the occurrence of a peril insured against (Article 245, MC).

Under the PICC P&C Hull Clauses of 2009, actual total loss means that the insured ship is completely destroyed or so seriously damaged that her original condition cannot be restored, or the insured is unavoidably to be deprived of the possession thereof.

Missing of the insured ship is deemed as actual total loss, i.e., where the insured ship fails to arrive at her destination within a reasonable time from the place where she was last heard of, and, unless the insurance contract provides otherwise, she remains unheard of upon the expiry of two months (Article 248, MC). Similarly, a ship which is unheard of upon the expiry of two months from the scheduled date of her arrival at destination shall be deemed to be actual total loss under the PICC P&C Hull Clauses of 2009.

587. As provided for in paragraph 1 of Article 246 of MC, constructive total loss of a ship means that total loss of the insured ship is considered to be unavoidable after the occurrence of a peril insured against, or the expenses necessary for avoiding the occurrence of actual total loss would exceed the insured value. The concept of constructive total loss of a ship under the PICC P&C Hull Clauses of 2009 is slightly different. Under these Clauses, the insured ship shall be deemed as constructive total loss where total loss of the insured ship appears to be unavoidable, or the amount of any or all of the expenses to restore, repair and salvage the damaged ship shall exceed the insured value.

As provided for in paragraph 2 of Article 246 of MC, constructive total loss of cargo means that total loss of the insured cargo is considered to be unavoidable after the occurrence of a peril insured against, or the expenses to be incurred for avoiding the total loss plus that for forwarding the cargo to its destination would exceed its insured value. The definition of constructive total loss of cargo contained in the PICC P&C Marine Cargo Clauses of 2009 is more specific and refers to the situation that actual total loss appears to be unavoidable or the cost to be incurred in recovering or reconditioning the cargo together with the forwarding cost to the destination named in the policy would exceed its value on arrival at such destination.

B. Partial Loss

588. Partial loss is defined in Article 247 of MC as any loss other than actual total loss or constructive total loss. Partial loss includes particular average loss and general average loss.

Where, during the period of insurance, two or more perils insured against occur and the aggregate amount of damages resulting therefrom exceeds the insured amount, the insurer shall still be liable for the damage to the insured ship or cargo. However, if total loss of the insured ship or cargo occurs after partial loss has occurred and the partial loss has not been repaired, the insurer shall be liable for the total loss only (Article 239, MC).

589. In the case of partial loss, the following provisions are contained in the PICC P&C Hull Clauses of 2009:

- The claims shall be payable without deduction of 'new for old'.
- In no case shall a claim be admitted in respect of derusting or painting the ship's bottom, unless directly related to repairs of plating damaged by an insured peril.
- Where the insured ship is put into drydock for repairs for the owners' own account necessary for making the ship seaworthy and/or routine drydocking concurrently with repairs covered by the insurance, the cost of entering and leaving the dock and the dock dues for the time spent therein shall be divided equally. However, where it is necessary to place the ship in drydock for repair of damage covered by the insurance, the insurer's liability for the cost of docking shall not be deducted, should the insured has surveys or other work carried out while the ship is in dock, provided that the time for the work for the insured's account is not prolonged in dock or the cost of docking is not in any way increased.

No specific provision concerning indemnity of partial loss of cargo is contained in the PICC P&C Marine Cargo Clauses of 2009.

VI. Payment and Measurement of Indemnity

A. Time of Payment of Indemnity

590. The insurer shall indemnify the insured promptly after the loss or damage from a peril insured against has occurred (Article 237, MC).

Besides the rule of prompt payment of indemnity provided in Article 237 of MC, detailed provisions thereof are contained in IL.

By virtue of Article 23 of IL, the insurer shall, after receiving claims for indemnity from the insured or beneficiary, come to determination timely or, where the situation is complicated, within thirty days unless otherwise agreed upon in the insurance contract. The insurer shall notify the insured or beneficiary of such determination. In the case of insurance liability, the insurer shall execute the liability of indemnity within ten days after reaching an agreement over indemnity with the insured; if the insurance contract has stipulations on the insured amount and the period for indemnity, the insurer shall execute the liability of indemnity as agreed upon in the contract. If the insurer fails to execute the liability as above, the insurer shall indemnify the insured for losses therefrom apart from paying the insurance indemnity. In this regard, no organization or person shall illegally interfere with the execution of the insurer to pay insurance indemnity or restrict the right of the insured or beneficiary to receive the insurance indemnity.

After the insurer makes determination by virtue of Article 23 of IL in the case not falling under the insurance liability, the insurer is required to issue a notice of refusal with reasons thereof to indemnify to the insured within three days from the date of determination (Article 24, IL). If the insurer is unable to determine the amount of indemnity within sixty days from the date on which the request for indemnity as well as relevant proofs and materials are received, it shall make advance payment in an amount that can be determined by the proofs and materials already available; after determining eventually the amount of indemnity, the insurer shall pay the corresponding difference (Article 25, IL).

B. *Measurement of Indemnity*

591. As a rule, the insurer's indemnity for the total or partial loss of the insured ship or cargo from the peril insured against shall be limited to the agreed insured amount.

Where the insured amount is lower than the insured value, i.e., in the case of under insurance, the insurer shall indemnify in the proportion that the insured amount bears to the insured value in the case of partial loss (Article 238, MC). Where the insured amount exceeds the insured value, i.e., in the case of over-insurance, the portion in excess shall be null and void by virtue of Article 220 of MC and the insurer's indemnity shall still be limited to the insured amount.

It is worthy of noting that, under the PICC P&C Hull Clauses of 2009 and the PICC P&C Marine Cargo Clauses of 2009 the insured shall abandon to the insurer the damaged insured ship or cargo and all its rights and title pertaining thereto to the insurer in the case a constructive total loss is claimed for. The insurer shall pay indemnity in the insured amount, whether the abandonment is accepted or not. Where the insurer accepts the abandonment, the damaged insured ship or cargo shall be owned by the insurer and the insurer may bear the shipowner's liability.

592. The insurer's liabilities under the RDC, the general average or salvage clause and/or the sue and labour clause are additional to its liability for total or partial loss of the insured ship or cargo. Besides the indemnity for the total or partial loss of the insured ship or cargo, the insurer shall indemnify the insured for its liabilities and/or expenses under these additional clauses. Thus, it is not rare in practice that the aggregate of the insurer's liabilities arising from one insurance accident may exceed the insured amount.

593. The insurer shall indemnify the insured for its liability under the RDC including the legal costs, additional to the indemnity for the total or partial loss of the insured ship, if any, but shall not exceed the insured amount in respect of each separate occurrence.

Under the PICC P&C Hull Clauses of 2009, where the insured ship is in collision with another ship and both ships are to blame, unless the liability of one or both ships are limited by virtue of the applicable law, the indemnity shall be calculated on the principle of cross-liability. This principle also applies to the case of allision.

The PICC P&C Hull Clauses of 2009 contains a Sister Ship Clause to the effect that where the insured ship comes into collision with another ship owned by the insured or under the same management, the insurer shall be liable as if the other ship were owned by a third party or not under the same management.

594. Similarly, the insurer shall indemnify the insured for its liability under the general average or salvage clause, additional to its indemnity for the total or partial loss of the insured ship or cargo, if any, but shall not exceed the insured amount of the ship or cargo. In this respect, by virtue of Article 241 of MC, where the insured amount is lower than the contributory value in general average, the insurer shall be liable for the general average contribution in proportion that the insured amount bears to the contributory value.

The provisions contained in the PICC P&C Hull Clauses of 2009 are different, i.e., where the insured amount is less than the contributory amount in respect of general average, then the insurer is only liable to pay in proportion that the insured amount bears to the contributory amount. Similarly, under these Clauses, where the insured amount is less than the amount of salvage reward that the insured of ship is liable for payment to the salvor, the insurer is only liable to pay in proportion that the insured amount bears to the amount of salvage reward.

Under the Sister Ship Clause contained in the PICC P&C Hull Clauses of 2009, where the insured ship receives salvage service from another ship owned by the insured or under the same management, the insurer shall be liable as if the other ship were owned by a third party or not under the same management.

595. The measurement of indemnity for the sue and labour expenses are provided for in Article 240 of MC by virtue of which the insurer shall pay, in addition to the indemnity to be paid with regard to the subject matter insured, the necessary and reasonable expenses incurred by the insured for avoiding or minimizing the loss recoverable under the insurance contract, the reasonable expenses for survey and assessment of the value for the purpose of ascertaining the nature and extent of the peril insured against and the expenses incurred for acting on the special instructions of the insurer. The payment of sue and labour expenses shall be limited to that equivalent to the insured amount of the insured ship or cargo. Where the insured amount is lower than the insured value, the insurer shall be liable for the expenses in proportion that the insured amount bears to the insured value, unless the contract provides otherwise.

The PICC P&C Hull Clauses of 2009 and the PICC P&C Marine Cargo Clauses of 2009 also provide that the insurer's liability under the sue and labour clause shall not exceed an amount equal to the sum insured in respect of the ship or cargo.

596. Noticeably, MC contains peculiar provision in Article 255 concerning the indemnity of the insurer by virtue of which after the occurrence of a peril insured against, the insurer is entitled to waive its right to the subject matter insured and pay the insured the insured amount in full to relieve itself of the liability with respect to the subject matter insured. By way of such payment before the extent of loss of or damage to the insured ship is determined, in principle, the insurer is not obliged to pay under the sue and labour clause and its liability is finally limited to the insured amount. In the exercise of this right by virtue of this Article, however, the insurer shall notify the insured thereof within seven days from the day of the receipt of the notice from the insured regarding the indemnity and shall remain liable for the necessary and reasonable expenses already paid by the insured for avoiding or minimizing the loss or damage prior to its receipt of the said notice.

VII. Franchise/Deductible

597. Franchise or deductible is normally agreed upon between the insurer and the insured and stipulated in a marine insurance policy in order to avoid smallest claims and also to effectively avoid reckless act of the insured. As a consequence of the franchise or deductible, the insurer's administrative costs of handling small claims can be avoided or minimized.

Where a franchise is agreed upon between the insurer and the insured and stipulated in the policy, it means a certain amount shall be for the insured's own account. However, if the amount of damage to the insured subject matter exceeds the amount of franchise, the insured shall be entitled to recover the damage in full from the insurer.

Where a deductible is agreed upon and stipulated in the policy, the amount of deductible is always for the insured's own account, even if the amount of damage to the insured subject matter exceeds the amount thereof. Consequently, the insured is only able to recover from the insurer the amount of damage in excess of the deductible in any case.

598. Chinese law does not contain any specific provision concerning franchise or deductible in marine insurance. The circumstances in which a franchise or deductible will be applied and the amount thereof are subject to the agreement between the insurer and the insured.

Under the PICC P&C Hull Clauses of 2009, an agreed deductible shall apply to the indemnity for partial loss of the insured ship caused by perils insured against for each separate accident or occurrence excluding claims under the circumstances of collision liability, salvage, general average, and sue and labour. In the application of deductible, claims for damages caused by heavy weather occurring during a single sea passage between two successive ports shall be treated as being due to one accident. Deductible shall not apply to claim for total loss of the insured ship or the reasonable expenses of inspecting the bottom of the ship after grounding, if incurred specially for that purpose.

The PICC P&C Marine Cargo Clauses of 2009 contain no provision concerning franchise or deductible. Therefore, franchise or deductible is up to the agreement between the insurer and the insured on a case by case basis.

In the business of marine insurance, a higher franchise or deductible normally means a lower insurance premium.

VIII. Right to Subject Matter and Right of Subrogation

A. Right to Subject Matter

599. Except for the case stipulated in Article 256 of MC as mentioned *supra*, where a total loss occurs to the subject matter insured, and the insured amount is paid in full; the insurer shall acquire the full right to the subject matter insured. However, in the case of under-insurance, the insurer shall acquire the right to the subject matter insured in proportion to the insured amount bears to the insured value (Article 256, MC).

B. Right of Subrogation

600. Where loss of or damage to the subject matter insured is caused wholly or partly by a third person, the insurer acquires the right of claim against the third party after payment of indemnity to the insured. Such a right is called the right of subrogation. Thus, by paragraph 1 of Article 252 of MC, where the loss of or damage to the subject matter insured within the insurance coverage is caused by a third person, the right of the insured to demand compensation from the third person shall be subrogated automatically to the insurer from the time of payment of the indemnity. However, the insurer's right of subrogation against a third party shall be exercised within the amount of indemnity (Article 60, IL). Thus, in the case of under-insurance, the exercise of the insurer's right of subrogation does not affect the right of claim of the insured against the third party for compensation for that part of loss or damage not indemnified by the insurer.

Noticeably, where the insurer exercises its right of subrogation against a third person, the insurer shall simultaneously bear the corresponding liability to the third person in the case of collision of ships in which both ships are to blame.

601. Noticeably, under Chinese law, the insurer claims against such a third person in its own name instead of the name of the insured in the exercise of the right of subrogation. The insured has the obligation to assist the insurer in the exercise of the right. As provided for in paragraph 2 of Article 252 of MC, the insured shall furnish the insurer with the necessary documents and information that comes to its knowledge and shall endeavour to assist the insurer in pursuing recovery from the third person.

602. As regards the insurer's right of subrogation, Articles 253 and 254 of MC need be mentioned.

By virtue of Article 253 of MC, where the insured waives wholly or partly its right of claim against a third person without the consent of the insurer, or the insurer is unable to exercise the right of recourse against the third person due to the fault of the insured, the insurer may make a corresponding reduction in the amount of indemnity. In this regard, paragraph 2 of Article 61 of IL provides that if, after the insurer has paid indemnity to the insured, the insured forfeits the claim against a third party, such an act is invalid.

By virtue of paragraph 1 of Article 253 of MC, where a certain amount has already been paid by a third person to the insured, the insurer may make a corresponding reduction in the payment of indemnity of such amount. By virtue of paragraph 2 of Article 253, where the compensation obtained by the insurer from a third person exceeds the amount of indemnity paid by the insurer, the part in excess shall be returned to the insured.

IX. Abandonment

603. Abandonment means that, in the case of constructive total loss of the insured ship or other property, the insured unilaterally demands indemnity of the insured amount from the insurer and transfers its ownership and all its rights, interests, obligations and liabilities in the insured ship or other property to the insurer. Abandonment of the insured ship or other property to the insurer is a precondition for the insured to obtain indemnity on the basis of total loss. Abandonment is executed by sending a notice thereof to the insurer.

By virtue of Articles 249 and 250 of MC, where the insured ship or cargo has become a constructive total loss and the insured demands indemnity from the insurer on the basis of a total loss, the insured ship or cargo shall be abandoned to the insurer. The abandonment shall not be attached with any condition. The insurer may accept the abandonment or choose not to, but shall inform the insured of its decision whether to accept the abandonment within reasonable time. Once the abandonment is accepted by the insurer, it shall not be withdrawn.

Where the insurer has accepted the abandonment, all the rights, obligations and liabilities relating to the insured property abandoned are transferred to the insurer. Therefore, by accepting the abandonment of the insured ship or cargo, the insurer becomes the owners of the ship or cargo against the payment of the insured amount to the insured. As the owners of the ship or cargo, the insurer may be obliged to take measures such as removing the wreck by virtue of MTSL.

Where the insurer does not accept the abandonment in the case of constructive total loss of the insured ship or cargo, the insurer shall still indemnify the insured with the insured amount. In such a case, the insured remains the owners of the insured ship or cargo and the insurer does not bear the obligations and liabilities as the owners of the ship or cargo, nor does it enjoy any right and interest of the owners in the ship or cargo other than its right of subrogation.

On the other hand, the insured is not obliged to send a notice of abandonment to the insurer in the case of constructive total loss unless the insured demands indemnity of the insured amount from the insurer. Instead, it may still choose to have the insured ship or cargo repaired and demand indemnity from the insurer up to the insured amount.

§5. Protection and Indemnity Insurance

I. Introduction

604. The protection and indemnity insurance, or P&I insurance in short, is a popular name of mutual insurance of maritime liabilities operated mainly by the mutual protection and indemnity associations called P&I clubs. However, some commercial insurance companies like PICC P&C also operate the P&I insurance in China.

The P&I insurance has a long history over one century. The first shipowners mutual protection society was established on 1 May 1855 in Britain which began to insure its members' liability for personal injuries or loss of life and the one-fourth collision liability not covered by the RDC in hull insurance. In 1873, the first shipowners mutual indemnity society was established and began to insure its members' liability for loss of or damage to cargo. At present, there are dozens of shipowners mutual insurance associations in operation in the world market and the major ones have joined the International Group of P&I Clubs forming a pool for reinsurance purposes as well as giving attention to the issues of general concern to its members.

605. Traditionally, protection meant insurance of liability for personal injuries or loss of life and the one-fourth collision liability not covered by the RDC in hull insurance, while indemnity meant insurance of liability for loss of or damage to cargo. Gradually, a P&I club began to cover both these two kinds of risks and extended the scope of insurance to cover other risks of liability of its members. It is now difficult to say what risks under the title of protection are and what risks under indemnity are. However, the risks covered by the P&I insurance remain basically those not covered by the hull insurance in the commercial insurance market.

606. A P&I club is formed by its members and is a mutual insurance association. Therefore, the purpose of a P&I club is the mutual insurance against liabilities, losses, expenses and costs incurred by its members in direct connection with the operation of the entered ships. As a result of the homogeneity of risks faced by its members, a club operates on a mutual basis where risks are placed in the same portfolio by use of the premiums in the name of calls paid by its members into a common fund in accordance with the degree of exposure to risks out of which the losses incurred by its members are indemnified. The operation of a club is not for the purpose of making profit. Being mutual, in theory, the members mutually insure their liabilities among them. In other words, the members of a club share each other's liabilities. However, a member shall not be liable to other members or to third parties for the liabilities of a club in particular claims.

Normally, a P&I club consists of the general meeting of all its members, board of directors and management. A club has a network of correspondents providing various technical and commercial services to its members.

607. All members shall pay an annual advance call before the beginning of insurance liability as annual contribution to the club. Each member is rated for its advanced call in accordance with the risks it wishes to cover, the deductibles chosen, and the individual risk exposure it represents. The advance call is the result of this basic rate including the member's share of expenditures for the running of the club and for reinsurance premiums multiplied by the member's tonnage of ships entered for the club's financial year or 'policy year'. After a financial year ends, a balance is struck between the income derived from the advance calls of all the members and the expenditure for claims paid and outstanding and management, reinsurance and representatives' fees. The excess expenditure over income is collected from members by one or more supplementary calls in proportion to their advance calls. If the income exceeds the expenditure, a return is made on the same basis. After the financial year of the club, therefore, the members may be required to pay supplementary call to the club in order to make up a deficit of the club in the past financial year.

Theoretically speaking, the rate of calls paid to a club is lower than that of the insurance premiums paid to a commercial insurance company in the market due to the non-profitable nature of the club. In addition, a P&I club provides various services to its members, issues letters of undertakings for the purpose of release from the arrest of its entered ships, and cover unlimited liabilities except the oil pollution liability.

608. Traditionally, the membership of a shipowners P&I association, as its name stands, was open to owners of ships only. Now, besides shipowners, the membership is also open to the operators and charterers of ships and even to those of floating structures, except in several professional P&I associations such as the Charterers Mutual Insurance Association.

As statistics show, more than 95% of the ocean merchant ships in the world have entered the various P&I clubs.

609. In China, the P&I insurance began in 1965 when the Shanghai Branch of PICC began to cover the P&I risks of two ships of the China-Poland Shipping Company by reference to the Rules of the West of England P&I Association. In 1973, PICC began to cover oil pollution liability of ocean tankers. In 1978, PICC adopted its P&I clauses. Noticeably, unlike a P&I club, PICC covers P&I insurance not on the mutual insurance basis.

CPI was established in 1984. Its members are mainly the Chinese shipping companies.

CPI covers P&I insurance of many Chinese ships. Some Chinese ships have entered the P&I clubs in other countries. The Chinese insurance companies cover the P&I insurance of a small proportion of the Chinese ships.

Like a few shipowners P&I clubs, CPI also offers to cover hull insurance of its entered ships in accordance with Rule 5 'Hull & Machinery Risks Covered' and other provisions of its Rules of 2023/2024. The conditions of hull insurance are very similar to those under the PICC P&C Hull Clauses of 2009.

II. Ordinary Risks Covered and Exclusions

610. Each P&I club has its own Rules providing the scope and conditions of insurance. The risks covered by the various P&I clubs share a lot of similarities.

A. *Risks Covered by CPI and Exclusions*

611. Under the CPI Rules of 2023/2024, the following losses, liabilities and expenses incurred by its members are covered as ordinary risks:

- injury to, illness and death of the seamen on board the entered ships;
- injury to, illness and death of persons other than the seamen on board the entered ships and liability to passengers;
- repatriation and substitute expenses of the seamen on board the entered ships;
- loss of or damage to personal effects of the seamen or any other persons on board the entered ships;
- shipwreck unemployment indemnity;[51]
- liability arising under certain indemnities and contracts;[52]
- collision liability not covered under hull insurance;
- loss of or damage to property;[53]
- diversion expenses;[54]
- stowaways and refugees;
- life salvage;[55]

51. Liability to compensate any seaman for the loss of his employment caused in consequence of the actual or constructive total loss of an entered ship, where the wages or compensation are payable under statutory or other legal obligation or under the terms of any crew agreement or other contract of service or employment if and to the extent that those terms have previously been approved by the Managers in writing.
52. Liability, costs and expenses arising under the terms of an indemnity or contract given or made by or on behalf of the Member relating to facilities or services provided or to be provided to or in connection with an entered ship.
53. Liability to pay damages or compensation for any loss of or damage to any property (including infringement of rights) whether on land or water and whether fixed or moveable.
54. The net loss to a Member (over and above the expenses as would have been incurred but for the diversion) in respect of the cost of provisions, stores, fuel, insurance, wages, seamen allowance and port charges during a diversion of an entered ship incurred solely for the purpose of saving life at sea or for the purpose of securing treatment for an injured or sick person or while awaiting a substitute for such person or for the purpose of landing stowaways or refugees, but only if and to the extent that they are not recoverable from any third party.
55. Sums legally due to third parties by reason of the fact that they have saved or attempted to save the life of any person on or from an entered ship but only if and to the extent that such payments are not recoverable under the Hull Policies or the Hull Certificates of the entered ship or from cargo owners or underwriters.

- pollution risks with a limitation of USD 1 billion in each event;
- towage liability;
- wreck liabilities;
- quarantine expenses;
- cargo liability;
- property on entered ship, i.e., liability of a Member for loss of or damage to any containers, equipment, fuel or other property on board the entered ships;
- unrecoverable general average contributions;
- ship's proportion of general average;
- fines;
- special compensation to salvors;
- enquiry expenses;[56]
- expenses incidental to the operation of the entered ships;
- sue and labour and legal costs;
- expenses incurred by direction of the Association.

612. The following are the normal exclusions of a P&I insurance by which the P&I insurance normally shall not cover the losses, liabilities or expenses:

- exclusion of sums insurable under the hull insurance;
- exclusion of war risks;
- exclusion of nuclear risks;
- exclusion of damage to an entered ship, loss of hire, etc.;
- exclusion of certain liabilities, costs and expenses of salvage ships, drilling ships, dredgers and others, specialist operation, diving, etc.;
- double insurance;
- imprudent trading including contraband, blockade running, unlawful trade, imprudent or hazardous operations;
- paperless trading, unless approved by the club;
- failure in maintaining the ship's class and conforming to the statutory requirements, unless decided to compensate by the board of directors of a club.

B. Risks Covered and Exclusions under the PICC P&I Clauses of 2009

613. The scope of coverage and exclusions under the PICC P&C Shipowners Protection & Indemnity Clauses of 2009 are quite similar to those under the CPI Rules of 2023–2024 as introduced *supra.*

56. Costs and expenses incurred by a Member in defending himself or in protecting his interests before a formal enquiry into the loss of or into a casualty involving the entered ship but only to the extent that such costs and expenses were incurred with prior approval of the Managers and on such conditions as the Managers may determine.

III. Additional Risks

614. In the international market, the risks additional to the ordinary risks are often covered in the P&I insurance subject to individual agreement between a club and its members and to the payment of additional calls.

The examples of such additional risks are listed below. Some P&I clubs also cover liabilities arising from oil exploitation, fishing vessels, small vessels, loss of charter hires, confiscation of ships and shipbuilding, etc., as the case may be.

A. Freight, Demurrage and Defence (F.D.&D.)

615. This insurance shall cover, in accordance with the Rules of a P&I club involved or agreement between the club and its members:

- the freight the member is entitled to under a contract of affreightment;
- the demurrage the member is entitled to mainly under a voyage charter party;
- the member's reasonable costs for necessary legal assistance and the member's liability for recoverable costs in relation to disputes that are directly connected with the operation of an entered ship or insured ship and that are in respect of the carriage of goods or passengers, charterparties, loss of or damage to or delay to the ship, general average, salvage and towage, insurance contracts in respect of the ship, personal injuries or loss of life, etc.

B. P&I War Risks and Special P&I War Risks

616. The P&I war risks insurance covers the war risks, especially at the time of war when the premium of war risks insurance in the insurance market is very high. Such risks are the same as or similar to those additional to the hull insurance covered by the insurance market.

The special P&I war risks insurance covers only the liability of the owners of an entered ship arising from the risks of war not covered by the ordinary P&I insurance. Sometimes, the P&I war risks insurance also covers the special P&I war risks.

C. Through Transport P&I Insurance

617. This insurance covers the losses or liabilities in respect of container through transport.

The Through Transport Mutual Insurance Association Limited known as 'TT Club' is a professional P&I club that covers the losses or liabilities in respect of container through transport. Its members include the various parties concerned in this area, e.g., the shipowners and charterers, container terminals and yards, MTOs, international container trailer or warehouse operators. The insurance of the war risks on land (WROL) involved in through transport is subject to the agreement between the club and its members.

D. Charterers P&I Insurance

618. Along with the increase in number of the charterers of ships and in their liabilities, the P&I clubs began to recruit charterers as members and thus to covers the charterers' losses and liabilities. In addition, the Charterers Mutual Insurance Association is a professional P&I club that covers charterers' losses and liabilities.

The charterers P&I insurance mainly covers:

- the liability of the carrier for loss of or damage to the goods;
- the liability for personal injury or loss of life occurred during the operation of loading and discharging of goods;
- the liability to the shipowners arising from the nomination of unsafe ports or berths;
- the liability arising from the provision of wrongful transport documents.

Chapter 12. Collisions

§1. Definitions

619. Collision, or collision of ships, is defined in paragraph 1 of Article 165 of Chapter VIII 'Collision of Ships' of MC as 'an accident arising from the touching of ships at sea or other navigable waters adjacent thereto'. Paragraph 2 of this Article provides: 'Ships referred to in the preceding paragraph shall include those non-military or non-public service ships or craft that collide with the ships mentioned in Article 3 of this Code.'

Therefore, to come within the scope of collision under MC, there must be a physical touching between two or more ships. Furthermore, at least one of the colliding ships must be a ship defined in Article 3 of MC, i.e., a seagoing ship or other mobile unit, excluding a ship or craft to be used for military or public services purpose and a small vessel of less than 20 tons gross tonnage. The other colliding ship or ships can be any ship or ships other than those used for military or public service purpose and thus include inland vessels and small vessels of less than 20 tons gross tonnage.

The touching parts of the colliding ships are not limited to their hulls, but include their anchors or anchor chains, lines and other appurtenances.

620. It often occurs that when navigating in river, canal, port area or other narrow waterway, due to her high speed in excess of the statutory limit, a ship causes damage to another smaller vessel, property onboard the other vessel or even death of or personal injury to persons on board the other vessel by her wave, whether the other vessel is underway, mooring or at anchor. Such a situation is called wave damage. Due to bad seamanship such as navigating too close to others or her nonobservance of navigation regulations, a ship may cause another ship going stranding or colliding with a third ship in order to avoid collision with her and as a result the other ship or the third ship or property onboard suffers damage.

Such wave damage or other indirect collision of ships is not a collision of ships *sensu strictu* on the ground that there is no physical touching between the ships. However, except this physical feature, the indirect collision has no difference in legal nature with collision between ships. Therefore, the legal rules dealing with collision of ships apply to the indirect collisions of ships. In this respect, Article 170 of MC expressly provides that where a ship has caused damage to another ship and persons, goods or other property on board that ship, either by the execution or non-execution of a manoeuvre or by the non-observance of navigation regulations, even if no collision has actually occurred, the provisions of Chapter VIII of MC shall apply. Article 13 of the 1910 Collision Convention contains same provisions.

621. Where a ship collides with a structure or installation at sea, in a port or other navigable water including wharf, breakwater, landing stage, buoy, floating crane, bridge, ship's lock, navigational aid and other facility, whether floating or fixed, or even with submerged object such as wreck, such a collision is called 'allision'. An allision is not a collision of ships within the meaning of MC, although it shares with a collision of ships the legal nature of maritime tort. However, allision is normally within the meaning of collision of ship under hull insurance.

§2. APPLICABLE LAWS

I. International Treaties

622. The international treaties regarding or in connection with collision of ships are introduced in Chapter 2 of Part I. It needs to be mentioned that China is a party to the *International Convention for the Unification of Certain Rules of Law with Respect to Collisions between Vessels*, signed in Brussels on 23 September 1910, known as '1910 Collision Convention'.

II. National Laws

623. Chapter VIII 'Collision of Ships' of MC deals with collision of ships. This chapter is in fact a reproduction of the 1910 Collision Convention and covers collision of seagoing ships and collision between a seagoing ship and an inland vessel, but does not apply to collision between inland vessels, as introduced in §1 of this chapter *supra*.

The rules governing tortuous liability contained in Book Seven 'Tortuous Liability' of CC are applicable as provisions of basic law to a collision of ships to the extent they are not repugnant to Chapter VIII of MC.

Besides, SPC promulgated in 1995 the *Provisions for the Trial of Cases of Compensation for Damages to Property in Ship's Collision or Allision* as amended on 23 December 2020, known as 'Collision Compensation Provisions' and hereinafter referred to as 'CCP', stipulating the scope of compensation for and calculation of the damages occurred in collision or allision of ships. In 2008, SPC promulgated the *Provisions on Certain Issues for the Trial of Cases of Ship's Collision* governing some legal issues regarding the trial of cases of ship's collisions.

624. As regards procedural matters, SMPL contains in section 1 of Chapter VIII the special provisions concerning the procedures of trial of collision cases. The provisions of CPC, the SMPL Interpretations and CPC Interpretations adopted by SPC shall also apply to the trial of ship's collision cases to the extent they are not repugnant to SMPL.

§3. LIABILITY

I. Liability of Colliding Ships

625. Where a ship's collision is caused by the fault of one of the colliding ships, i.e., only one ship is to blame, the one in fault shall be liable for the losses suffered by the other ship and for the losses suffered by a third party, if any (Article 168, MC).

626. Where the colliding ships are all at fault, i.e., both or all are to blame, each shall be liable in proportion to the extent of her fault. If the respective faults are equal in proportion or it is impossible to determine the extent of the proportion of respective faults, the liability of the colliding ships shall be apportioned equally (paragraph 1, Article 169, MC).

Where damage is caused to the property of a third party including, *inter alia*, the goods, passengers' luggage carried on board either colliding ship, the properties on water or ashore, the liability of any of the colliding ships shall not exceed the proportion she shall bear (paragraph 2, Article 169, MC). Therefore, the colliding ships shall not bear joint and several liabilities for the damages to properties of third persons, although both or all are at fault (paragraph 2, Article 169, MC). The civil law rule of joint and several liability in the case of loss or damage suffered by a third party and caused by joint faults of two or more parties contained in Article 1168 of CC shall not apply. However, where the colliding ships at fault have caused death of or personal injury to a third person including the master and crewmembers onboard, they shall be jointly and severally liable therefor (paragraph 3, Article 169, MC). If, as a result of the bearing of joint and several liability of one colliding ship, a ship has paid an amount of compensation in excess of the proportion to the extent of her fault, she shall have the right of recourse against the other colliding ship or ships at fault.

627. Same as in civil law countries, there is no in rem action in China and thus a ship being an object cannot be taken as a defendant in a case of ship's collision. By virtue of Article 3 of the *Provisions on Certain Issues for the Trial of Cases of Ship's Collision* promulgated by SPC in 2008, therefore, the ship's collision liability shall be borne by the registered owners of the ship, unless the ship is under a bareboat charter and the bareboat charter is duly registered by virtue of law in which case the bareboat charterers shall be liable.

628. The faults committed by a colliding ship or ships in most collision cases prove to be non-observation of COLREGs, local regulations for the prevention of collisions of ships or other navigation rules, or non-execution of good seamanship. In exceptional cases, collisions are caused by ship's unseaworthiness, e.g., the master or duty officer of a colliding ship is not properly manned, or breakdown of the ship's engine or other equipment as a result of failure of the shipowners, bareboat charterers or manager to exercise of due diligence to the make the ship seaworthy.

It need be mentioned that in the determination of fault in collision cases, the traditional rules which were or are prevailing in a few countries, including the rule of presumption of fault in the case of violation of regulations for the prevention of collisions at sea,[57] the last opportunity rule or the rule of last clear chance,[58] or the rule of alternative danger in the case of measures taken by one ship in the agony of the moment of collision that prove wrong afterwards,[59] are not applicable under Chinese law.

57. The Pennsylvanian rule under US common law. *See* Tetley, W., 'The Pennsylvanian Rule – An Anachronism? Judgement – An Error?' 1 *Journal of Maritime Law and Commerce*, 1982.
58. *See* Moguffie, K.C., *Collision as Sea*, 1961, 22.
59. *See* Huybrechts, M. *e.a.*, *Monograph of Belgian Transport Law*, 156.

II. Exemption of Liability of Colliding Ships

629. Article 167 of MC provides that neither of the colliding ships shall be liable to the other if the collision is caused by force majeure or other causes not attributable to the fault of either ship or if the cause thereof is left in doubt.

Correspondingly, Article 2 of the 1910 Collision Convention provides that if the collision is accidental, caused by force majeure, or the cause of collision is left in doubt, the damages are borne by those who have suffered them.

Force majeure is defined in paragraph 2 of Article 180 of CC as 'an objective situation that cannot be foreseen, avoided and overcome'. As compared with the concept of act of God in Anglo-American law, the scope of force majeure is much wider and covers act of God and situations caused by human elements that cannot be foreseen, avoided and overcome such as war, hostility or act of government.

Other causes not attributable to the fault of either ship means each of the colliding ships has no fault in the collision and thus the collision is accidental as between or among the colliding ships. It covers a collision wholly caused by the fault of a third party.

The cause of collision is left in doubt means that the real cause of collision remains unclear, especially where neither ship can prove any contributory fault on other ship or ships.

630. Where a collision is covered by Article 167 of MC, each colliding ship shall not be liable for any loss or damage suffered by the other colliding ship or ships. As a result, each shall bear her own loss or damage.

In addition, under such circumstances, a third party who has suffered loss of or damage to his property or death or personal injury cannot claim against any colliding ship, except the case of oil pollution damage or other damage to the marine environments resulting from the collision for which the owners of colliding ship causing the damage to marine environment shall bear strict liability, unless the liability can be exempted by virtue of Articles 90 and 92 of MEPL, paragraphs 2 and 3 of Article 3 of 1992 CLC or Article 3 of 2001 Bunker Convention, as the case may be.[60]

§4. Damages

I. Basic Principles

631. The following principles under Chinese law governing the determination of scope and calculation of damages under tortuous liability apply to the cases of collision of ships.

60. For details, *see* Ch. 13 of Part II.

A. *Principle of* Restitutio in Integrum

632. By virtue of this principle, compensation for damages shall make the party who suffered loss or damage due to the tortuous act of the other in such an economic or financial situation as it was before the occurrence of the tortuous act. The compensation shall ensure *restitutio in integrum* as much as possible (Article 2, CCP).

B. *Principle of Direct Causation*

633. By virtue of this principle, only the loss or damage that are directly caused by the tortuous act and can be reasonable foreseeable shall be recoverable. Thus, the claimant is entitled to claim compensation for proprietary loss caused by ship's collision or allision, expenses and loss consequently upon ship's collision or allision, reasonable expenses and loss incurred in order to avoid or mitigate losses as well as loss of expected profit, provided that they are the direct result of the collision or allision and could be reasonably foreseen by the owners or bareboat charterers of the ship at fault in collision or allision (paragraph 1, Article 1, CCP).

C. *Principle of Obligation to Mitigate*

634. By virtue of this principle, the party who suffered loss or damage has the correlative duty to mitigate the loss or damage; otherwise, any loss or damage, or exaggerated loss or damage resulting from failure in the fulfilment of its duty to mitigate shall not be recoverable (paragraph 2, Article 1, CCP).

Noticeably, there is no principle of obligation to mitigate in tortuous liability in the civil law theory in China. Instead, what is described is the principle of offsetting faults to the effect that, if the party who suffered loss or damage had fault causing exaggeration of loss or damage, the other party's liability may be reduced by virtue of Article 1173 of CC. However, there is no substantial difference between the two principles.

II. Scope and Calculation of Damages

A. *Loss of or Damage to Ship*

635. By virtue of Article 3(1) of CCP, the compensation for total loss of a ship shall include: (a) loss of ship's value; (b) bunkers, stores, spare parts, provisions or, in the case of a fishing vessel, fishing apparatus and nets, etc., that are not included in the ship's value; and (c) crew's wages, repatriation expenses and other reasonable expenses.

The loss of ship's value shall be calculated on the basis of the market price of a similar ship at the time and place of collision, or, in the absence of such a market price, of the market price of a similar ship at the port of her registry, or of the average price of market prices of similar ships in other places. Where there is no such market price, it shall be calculated on the basis of her original building or purchase price after deduction of depreciation at the rate of 4–10% annually. If no value remains after such a deduction, the scrap value shall be the loss of ship's value. Where the ship has scrap value after her removal, it shall be deducted from her value (Article 8, CCP).

636. By virtue of Article 3(2) of CCP, compensation for damage to a ship shall include reasonable temporary repair expenses, permanent repair expenses, auxiliary expenses and maintenance expenses, provided that the ship's repair shall be conducted in a nearest place, unless the claimant can prove that repair in another place can reduce loss, save expenses or has other reasonable reasons. Where the ship can continue operation after temporary repair, the claimant is obliged to have her repaired temporarily.

The auxiliary expenses mentioned above means the reasonable expenses for the repair including but not limited to the expenses necessary for docking, discharge and disposal of oil sewage, port disbursements, pilotage and berthing charges. Maintenance expenses means the expenses of daily consumption of the ship and her master and other crewmembers including bunkers, stores, fresh water, provisions and crew's wages (Article 16, CCP).

Where the repair of damage to a ship caused by collision is conducted simultaneously with the repair conducted for ensuring the ship's seaworthiness, necessitated by other accident or with ship's regular inspection and repair, the compensation shall be limited to the expenses and loss necessitated by the repair of damage to the ship caused by the collision by virtue of the principle of direct causation.

637. By virtue of Article 3(3) of CCP, compensation for loss of or damage to a ship shall also include: (a) reasonable salvage charges, expenses of survey, re-floating or removal of sunken ship and expenses of laying mark of sunken ship; (b) towage charges, loss of hire or freight in the voyage concerned; (c) reasonable loss of use of a ship; and (d) other reasonable expenses.

Loss of hire shall be limited to the amount of off-hire under a time charterparty resulting from collision after deduction of the expenses which can be saved; loss of freight resulting from loss of cargo shall be the amount of freight not paid after deduction of the expenses which can be saved (Article 11, CCP).

As provided for in Article 10 of CCP, calculation of loss of use of a ship shall be limited to the reasonable period of time necessary for finding a substituted ship in the case of loss of a ship not exceeding two months, or to the period of time of repair in the case of damage to a ship including the reasonable time for liaison, lying in dock and survey. In the case of a fishing vessel, deduction of the period in which fishing should be stopped shall be made from the above period of time and the period of time in the calculation of loss of ship is limited to one normal fishing period.

Loss of use of a ship other than a fishing vessel shall normally be calculated on the basis of the average net profit during two voyages before and after collision respectively. Where no such an average net profit can be referred to, the calculation shall be made in accordance with the average net profit in the corresponding voyages.

Loss of use of a fishing vessel shall be calculated on the basis of the average net profit during the fishing period at the time of the year in the past three years, or of the average net profit of fishing vessels of the same kind during the fishing period at the time of the year in which the collision occurred.

B. Loss of or Damage to Property on Board

638. Compensation for loss of or damage to the property onboard shall include: (a) depreciation in value arising from loss or damage; (b) reasonable repair or handling expenses; (c) reasonable salvage charges, expenses of re-floating and removal, contribution in general average; and (d) other reasonable expenses (Article 4, CCP).

639. As provided for in Article 9 of CCP, loss of or damage to the property onboard shall be calculated as follows:

- the total loss of cargo shall be calculated on the basis of its actual value, i.e., her CIF value, after deduction of expenses which can be saved;
- the damage to cargo shall be calculated on the basis of the necessary repair expenses or its actual value after deduction of its scrap value and expenses which can be saved;
- the loss arising from delay in delivery within the agreed time between the carrier and the shipper due to ship's collision shall be calculated on the basis of the difference between the market value at the port of discharge and the actual value of the cargo delayed plus the expected profit not exceeding 10% of the its actual value;
- the fishes onboard shall be calculated on the basis of their actual value to be determined by reference to the market value at the time and place of collision after deduction of the expenses which can be saved;
- the fishing apparatus and nets shall be calculated on the basis of their purchase price or costs of construction after deduction of depreciation and scrap value, but their sorts and quantity shall be determined in accordance with those necessitated for fishing operation in the voyage concerned after deduction of the remaining quantity onboard, provided that any of the sorts or quantity beyond the scope stipulated or permitted by the fishing administration shall not be recoverable;
- the loss of passengers' baggage or articles including cabin baggage on board the carrying ship shall be dealt with in accordance with Chapter V 'Contracts of Carriage of Passengers at Sea' of MC; the loss of passengers' baggage on board the other colliding ship may be dealt with by reference to the provisions concerning compensation for loss of or damage to passengers' baggage under a contract of carriage of passengers at sea;
- the loss of personal belongings of the master or other crewmembers shall be compensated for to an appropriate extent;

- the loss of currencies, gold, silvers, pearls, negotiable securities and other valuables in the custody of the carrier as agreed in writing between the carrier and the passengers shall be dealt with in accordance with Chapter V of MC; the loss of currencies, gold, silvers, peals, negotiable securities and other valuables which the master, other crewmembers and passengers carry by themselves shall not be recoverable;
- the loss of other properties onboard shall be calculated on the basis of their actual values.

C. Loss of or Damage to Installations Caused by Ship's Allision

640. An installation means a fixed or movable structure including fixed platform, berth, bridge, cable or pipeline under, on or above waters (Article 16, CCP).

The compensation for loss of or damage to an installation caused by ship's allision shall include: (a) the total loss of or repair expenses of damage to an installation; and (b) the reasonable loss of income due to its being unable to be used in normal way before the completion of repair (Article 5, CCP).

By virtue of Article 12 of the CCP, calculation of loss of use of an installation shall be limited to the period of time when its use was actually stopped after deduction of the time needed for regular inspection and repair.

The total loss of an installation shall be calculated on the basis of its reconstruction expenses, whereas damage thereto shall be calculated on the basis of the expenses of repair. Deduction shall be made of depreciation in accordance with its service life.

The loss of use of an installation shall be the amount of actual decrease in net income calculated on the basis of the average net profit during the three months before its use was stopped after deduction of the income of partial use thereof, if any.

D. Loss of or Damage to Property of Third Party

641. By virtue of Article 6 of CCP, the loss of or damage to property of a third party shall be compensated for and its calculation depends on the nature of the property concerned.

E. Interests

642. By virtue of Article 7 of CCP, the interests on the recoverable loss shall be compensated for.

As provided for in Article 13, the interests on the loss of ship's value shall be calculated from the date when calculation of the loss of use is stopped to the due date indicated in the judgment or conciliation statement issued by a court of law; the interests on other loss or expenses shall be calculated from the date of occurrence thereof to the due date indicated in the judgment or conciliation statement. The interest rate shall be that prevailing at the same period of time regarding the corresponding loss or expenses.

§5. Procedures

I. Investigation of Collision Accident

643. By virtue of MTSL, the competent authority for the investigation of a collision accident is MSA or, in the case of collision between fishing vessels, the administration on fishing vessels and fishing port, except the case of extraordinary serious accident in which the investigation shall be organized by the State Council or the governmental department authorized by the State Council. The competent authority shall ascertain the facts and causes of accident and determine the responsibilities for the accident (Article 83, MTSL).

Where a collision occurs, the colliding ships shall respectively submit a written accident report and relative materials to the competent authority, accept its investigation and handling of the accident. During the investigation, the parties involved in the accident and the relevant personnel shall give truthful accounts of the circumstances at the scene of the accident and other relevant information to the competent authority.

II. Special Provisions for Trial of Collision Cases

644. The disputes arising from a collision of ships are subject to the jurisdiction of a maritime court. The litigation of a collision case is governed by SMPL and the SMPL Interpretations. CPC and the CPC Interpretations shall apply to the extent that their provisions are not repugnant to those of SMPL and the SMPL Interpretations.

SMPL contains in section 1 of Chapter VIII the special provisions governing the trial of collision cases as follows:

A. Submission of Maritime Accident Investigation Form

645. The plaintiff shall at the time of filing a lawsuit, and the defendant shall at the time of filing pleadings, fill in the Maritime Accident Investigation Form respectively (Article 82, SMPL).

This form shall contain, *inter alia*, the particulars of the colliding ships including the name, tonnage, dimension, year of being built, material of hull, engine power, speed of each colliding ship as well as the name and address of the owners and operator, port of registry of each colliding ship; time, place and the surrounding circumstances of the collision; course of the collision in detail including the speeds and courses of the ships, lookouts onboard, measures taken during the course of collision; faults and responsibilities; damages suffered by the ships. Supporting documents such as the original or abstracts of the sea charts, deck and engine logbooks, telegraph records used during the course of collision shall be attached to the Form.

A party involved is estopped from reversing his statement in this form, unless he has new evidence that, due to sufficient reasons, he was unable to submit during the period of submission of evidence provided for in Article 84 of SMPL (Article 85, SMPL).

B. *Non-service of Supporting Documents*

646. The service by the maritime court of the plaintiff's writ of lawsuit on the defendant or of the defendant's pleadings on the plaintiff shall not contain the supporting documents attached to the writ of lawsuit and the pleadings respectively (Article 83, SMPL).

C. *Period of Submission of Evidence*

647. The parties involved shall fulfil their respective burden of proof before the court hearing or the first court hearing. After fulfilment of the burden of proof and submission of the statement thereof, a party is entitled to have an access to the evidential materials concerning the facts of the collision in the maritime court (Article 84, SMPL).

D. *Survey on and Evaluation of Ships*

648. In handling a collision case, survey on and evaluation of damages to the colliding ships are almost inevitable.

As provided for in Article 86 of SMPL, such surveys and evaluations shall be conducted by the organs or individual persons authorized by the State or qualified therefor. Otherwise, any conclusion made by any organ or individual person not authorized by the state or qualified therefor shall not be adopted by maritime courts, unless accepted by both parties. The organs thus authorized by the State currently in China include, *inter alia*, CCS or organs of survey on fishing vessels under the administration on fishing vessels and fishing ports. Qualified individual persons include those holding certificates of competency of ship surveyors or evaluators.

Normally, where a colliding ship is abroad, a conclusion of ship survey or evaluation made by a foreign ship classification society as a member of the International Association of Classification Societies known as 'IACS' will be adopted by a maritime court in China. However, it is not sure whether a conclusion in this respect made by a so-called classification society of convenience shall be adopted.

E. Time Limit of Trial Finalization

649. The trial of a collision case in a maritime court shall be finalized within one year from the date of entertainment thereof by the court. Extension of the limit due to special circumstances shall be subject to approval of the president of the maritime court concerned (Article 87, SMPL).

Chapter 13. Marine Pollution

§1. Applicable Laws

I. International Treaties

650. In the area of marine environmental protection and oil pollution liability, as mentioned in §1 of Chapter 2 of Part I, China has ratified 1992 CLC, 2001 Bunker Convention, Intervention Convention, LDC, MARPOL 73/78 and UNCLOS.

China became the largest oil import country in the world in 2013. China has ratified 1992 Fund Convention, but this Convention applies in Hong Kong only. However, by virtue of Article 66 of MEPL[61] and Article 56 of the Ships Pollution Regulations,[62] the Ministry of Finance and MOT jointly promulgated the *Administrative Provisions on Levying and Use of Ship's Oil Pollution Compensation Fund* on 11 May 2012 which came into force as of 1 July 2012 and by which the Chinese domestic Ship's Oil Pollution Compensation Fund was established. Same as the International Oil Pollution Compensation Fund (IOPC Fund) under 1992 Fund Convention, the Ship's Oil Pollution Compensation Fund follows the principle that shipowners and cargo owners shall jointly bear the risks of pollution damage from ships.

By virtue of Article 97 of MEPL, if any of the above or other international treaties regarding marine environmental protection ratified or acceded to by China contain different provisions from those contained in the laws or regulations of China in this respect, the provisions of such international treaties shall apply with priority, except the provisions on which China has announced reservations.

II. National Laws

651. Environmental protection is one of the State's fundamental policies in China. China emphasizes the legislation and implementation of laws in the area of environmental protection, especially in the area of marine environmental protection.

61. Article 66 of MEPL provides: 'The State improves and implement the regime of civil liability for oil pollution damage from ships. Following the principle that shipowners and cargo owners shall jointly bear the risks of liability for pollution damage from ships, the regime of ship's oil pollution insurance and the regime of oil pollution compensation fund shall be established. The detailed provisions for implementing the regime of ship's oil pollution insurance and the regime of oil pollution compensation fund shall be promulgated by the State Council.'
62. Article 56 of the *Ships Pollution Regulations* provides: 'The cargo owners who receive cargo of permanent oily substances carried by sea within the waters of jurisdiction of the People's Republic of China or their agents shall pay contributions to the ship's oil pollution compensation fund. The detailed provisions on the levying, use and administration of the ship's oil pollution compensation fund shall be promulgated by the financial department under the State Council together with the transport department under the State Council. The State shall establish an administrative commission to be responsible for the compensations to be made by the ship's oil pollution compensation fund and other affairs. The administrative commission of the ship's oil pollution compensation fund shall consist of the related administrative organs and the main cargo owners who pay contributions to the ship's oil pollution compensation fund.'

Besides MEPL and the Ships Pollution Regulations as mentioned in §1 of Chapter 2 of Part I, the following are the laws and regulations regarding or in connection with marine environmental protection:

- the *Environmental Protection Law,* hereinafter referred to as 'EPL', adopted by the Standing Committee of NPC on 26 December 1989 and latest amended on 24 April 2014;
- the *Regulations on the Environmental Protection in Offshore Oil Exploration & Exploitation,* hereinafter referred to as 'Offshore Oil E&E Regulation', promulgated by the State Council on 29 December 1983;
- the *Regulations on the Control over Dumping of Wastes in the Ocean*, hereinafter referred to as 'Ocean Dumping Reg.', promulgated by the State Council on 6 March 1985 and latest amended on 1 March 2017;
- the *Regulations on the Prevention of Pollution Damage to Environment by Ship Scraping*, hereinafter referred to as 'Ship Scraping Regulations', promulgated by the State Council on 18 May 1988 and latest amended on 1 March 2017;
- the *Regulations on the Prevention of Pollution Damage to Marine Environment by Coastal Construction Project*, promulgated by the State Council in 25 June 1990 and amended on 25 September 2007 and latest amended on 19 March 2018;
- the *Regulations on the Prevention of Pollution Damage to Marine Environment by Land-sourced Pollutants*, promulgated by the State Council in 22 June 1990.

652. MEPL applies to the internal seas, territorial seas, contiguous zones, exclusive economic zones and continental shelves of China as well as other sea areas within the jurisdiction of China. Navigation, exploration, exploitation, production, tour, scientific research and other activities within the sea areas within the jurisdiction of China, or any organization or individual engaged in activities in coastal land area which impact marine environment, shall comply with MEPL. MEPL also applies to the pollution of the sea areas within the jurisdiction of China caused beyond the sea areas within the jurisdiction of China (Article 2, MEPL).

MEPL as a special law shall have priority over EPL as a basic law. Where MEPL does not contain provision, EPL shall apply to the matters of marine environmental protection.

The above Regulations are promulgated by the State Council mainly for the purpose of implementation of MEPL in different and specific aspects. As administrative regulations, by virtue of Article 88 of the *Law on Legislation*, the contents thereof shall not be repugnant to MEPL. Otherwise, they shall be of no effect.

§2. Concepts and Definitions

653. The following concepts and definitions are adopted in the applicable laws, regulations and international conventions:

- 'Environment' means the total body of all natural elements and artificially transformed natural elements affecting human existence and development.

- 'Pollution damage to marine environment' means any direct or indirect introduction of substances or energy into the marine environment which results in deleterious effects such as harm to marine living resources, hazards to human health, hindrance to fishing and other legitimate activities at sea, impairment of useful quality of sea water and degradation of environmental quality.
- 'Ocean functional division' means division of the leading functions of utilization of the ocean and the scope of utilization in the light of the natural and social attributes of the ocean as well as natural resources and specific conditions of the environment.
- 'Oil' means any kind of oil and its refined products, unless otherwise provided for.
- 'Oil mixture' means any mixture containing oil.
- 'Discharge' means an activity of draining pollutants into the sea including pumping, spilling, releasing, gushing and pouring.
- 'Dumping' means disposal of wastes or other harmful substances into the sea from ships, airborne vehicles, platforms or other means of transport, including the abandonment of ships, airborne vehicles, platforms and other floating apparatus.
- 'Fishing areas' means spawning grounds, feeding grounds, wintering grounds and migration channels of fishes and shrimps as well as aquacultural grounds of fishes, shrimps, shellfishes and aquatic plants.
- 'Land-based pollution sources' means places, facilities, etc., which discharge pollutants to the sea areas from land and causes or may cause marine environmental pollution.
- 'Land-sourced pollutants' means pollutants discharged from land-based pollution sources.
- 'Coastal land area' means the land area which connects directly with the coastline, or in which pollutants are directly or indirectly discharged into the ocean via pipelines, ditches or facilities, or related activities are conducted.

§3. Supervision and Administration on Marine Environment

I. Competent Authorities Concerned

654. By virtue of Article 5 of MEPL and Article 7 of EPL, the following authorities are concerned in the supervision and administration on marine environment with respective powers and responsibilities:

- the environmental protection department under the State Council, i.e., the Ministry of Ecology and Environment (MEE) shall, as the authority responsible for the uniform supervision and administration on the environmental protection of the State, exercise directive function, function of coordination and supervision on the marine environmental protection in the whole State, be in charge of the environmental protection against marine pollution damage caused by land-sourced pollutants and coastal construction projects in the whole State. MEE is also be responsible for the supervision and administration on the ocean environment, for the organization of investigations and monitoring of and surveillance over the marine environment, and in charge of the environmental protection against marine pollution damage caused by the offshore oil exploration and exploitation and by the dumping of wastes into the sea;

- the state administrative department of maritime affairs, i.e., MSA shall be responsible for the environmental protection against marine pollution damage from ships other than military ships in the waters of the port areas under its jurisdiction, by ships other than fishing ships or ships other than used for military service purposes in the waters outside the port areas, for the investigation and handling of pollution incidents caused thereby, including the inspection on board foreign ships navigating, lying or operating within waters within the jurisdiction of China and handling of pollution incidents caused thereby, provided that where a ship's pollution incident causes damage to fishery, the State fisheries administrative department shall also take part in the investigation and handling of the incident;
- the State fisheries administrative department, i.e., the Fisheries Administration under the Ministry of Agriculture and Rural Affairs shall be responsible for the environmental protection against marine pollution damage from ships other than military ships in the waters of the fishing port areas, from fishing vessels in the waters outside the port areas, for the ecological protection in the fishery waters, and for the investigation and handling of the fishery pollution incidents other than those within the responsibility of MSA;
- the environmental protection department of the armed forces shall be responsible for the environmental protection against marine pollution damage from military ships and for the investigation and handling of the pollution incidents caused thereby;
- the environmental protection departments of the coastal local governments shall exercise their functions in the marine environmental protection as specified by the respective coastal provinces, autonomous regions or municipalities directly under the central government.

II. Basic Marine Environmental Protection Regimes

655. The Chinese government has established and implements the system of control on the total discharge volume of pollutants into the key sea areas, determines the quotas of the total discharge volume of the main pollutants into the sea and distributes the respective volume of discharge thereof (Article 3, MEPL).

656. The State has adopted the system of ocean functional divisions. Utilization of sea areas shall be in conformity with such divisions. The State has formulated the State marine environmental protection plan and regional marine environmental protection plan for the key sea areas in accordance with such divisions (Articles 6 and 7, MEPL).

657. The State has formulated the State quality standards of marine environment on the basis of the situation of marine environment quality, the State economy and technical conditions. Local governments have formulated regional quality standards of marine environment with respect to the items for which the State quality standards have not provided (Article 9, MEPL).

658. The State has established and maintains the information system of surveillance over marine environment that shall be made public (Articles 15 and 16, MEPL).

659. The State has established the State emergency plan for serious marine pollution accidents as necessitated by the prevention of marine environmental pollution. MEE and MSA have established respectively the emergency plan for serious oil spills in the offshore oil exploration and exploitation and that for serious oil spill from ships. A coastal company or other entity that may cause serious marine pollution accidents has established emergency plan for such accidents. Where serious marine pollution accident occurs, measures shall be taken in accordance with corresponding emergency plan to avoid or minimize danger (Article 18, MEPL).

660. Any individual or entity which discharges or dumps pollutants directly into the sea shall pay discharge or dumping expenses as stipulated by the State. The expenses shall only be used for the administration of marine environmental pollution (Article 11, MEPL).

Where discharge of pollutants exceeds the specified standards, or task of decreasing the discharge of pollutants has not been accomplished within specified period of time, or serious marine environmental pollution has been caused, measures shall be taken by the responsible individual or entity within limited period of time (Article 12, MEPL).

In the case of incident which may cause pollution damage to the marine environment, the individual or entity which caused the incident shall immediately take effective measures to control and eliminate such pollution, and shall notify the individuals and entities which may sustain the pollution damage and report the matter to the marine environmental protection authorities for investigation and settlement. Where coastal or offshore sea area suffers serious pollution, the local governments in that area are obliged to take effective measures to eliminate or mitigate the pollution damage (Article 17, MEPL).

§4. Prevention of Marine Pollution from Ships

I. Compliance with Laws and Regulations

661. As required by paragraph 1 of Article 26 of MEPL and Article 4 of Ships Pollution Regulations, no ship may discharge oils, oil mixtures, wastes, garbage and other harmful substances into the sea areas in violation thereof within the jurisdiction of China.

Where MARPOL 73/78 is applicable, its provisions concerning the discharge of pollutants by ships shall be complied with.

In addition, ships shall comply with the provisions of law and regulations governing maritime traffic safety for the prevention of marine environmental pollution caused by collision, grounding, fire, explosion and so on (Article 65, MEPL).

II. Equipment, Facilities and Documents

662. As required by Article 64 of MEPL, ships shall be fitted with appropriate anti-pollution equipment and facilities. Where a ship carries goods in the nature of pollution danger, she shall have the capability in her structure and equipment of preventing or mitigating marine environmental pollution to be caused by the goods.

Details of the anti-pollution equipment and facilities are provided for in MARPOL 73/78 and Ships Pollution Regulations, where they are applicable respectively.

An oil tanker shall be fitted with the corresponding emergency equipment for the spill of oil (paragraph 2, Article 69, MEPL).

663. Engagement in accepting pollutants, wastes or garbage from ships, cleaning or washing ship's holds shall have appropriate capacity of acceptance and disposal (paragraph 2, Article 62, MEPL). A port, wharf, loading and discharge terminal, ship yard for the shipbuilding or ship repair shall be fitted with the required equipment and facilities sufficient for acceptance and disposal of pollutants and wastes from ships, and shall maintain them in good conditions (Article 69, MEPL).

664. Ships shall have on board the required certificates and documents of prevention of marine environmental pollution and shall make true record of activities involving discharge and operation of pollutants (Article 63, MEPL). The technical certificates and documents in this respect are provided for in MARPOL 73/78 where applicable.

An oil tanker shall have emergency plan for the spill of oil (paragraph 2, Article 69, MEPL).

As required by the *Implementing Provisions on Liability Insurance for Oil Pollution Damage from Ships* promulgated by MOT on 19 August 2010 and amended 31 August 2013, the owners of any ships navigating in the sea areas within the jurisdiction of China carrying oil as cargo, or ships carrying cargo other than oil with a gross tonnage of more than 1,000 tons, shall maintain the insurance or corresponding financial security to cover the liability for oil pollution damage. Such ships are required to hold valid certificates attesting the liability insurance or other financial security. In details:

- the ships carrying persistent oil as cargo shall hold the Certificate of Insurance or Other Financial Security for Civil Liability against Oil Pollution Damage;
- the ships with a gross tonnage of more than 1,000 tons carrying non-persistent oil as cargo shall hold the Certificate of Insurance or Other Financial Security for Civil Liability against Bunker Oil Pollution Damage or the Certificate of Insurance or Other Financial Security for Civil Liability against Non-persistent Oil Pollution Damage;

- the ships with a gross tonnage of less than 1,000 tons carrying non-persistent oil as cargo shall hold the Certificate of Insurance or Other Financial Security for Civil Liability against Non-persistent Oil Pollution Damage;
- the ships with a gross tonnage of more than 1,000 tons carrying cargo other than oil shall hold the Certificate of Insurance or Other Financial Security for Civil Liability against Bunker Oil Pollution Damage.

III. Carriage of Goods in Nature of Pollution Danger

665. Where a ship carries goods in the nature of pollution danger, besides her capability in her structure and equipment of preventing or mitigating marine environmental pollution to be caused by the goods as required by Article 63 of MEPL, the carrier, owners of goods or their agents shall declare to MSA in advance. Such a ship can enter a port, stop for transit, load or discharge goods only after approval by MSA (Article 67, MEPL).

The documents of carriage, packing, marks of such goods and the limit of quantity thereof shall meet the relevant requirements. In the loading or discharge operation of oil, poisonous or harmful substances, both the ship and the shore side shall comply with the rules of safety operation for the prevention of pollution (Article 68, MEPL).

IV. Operations Subject to Approval

666. By virtue of Article 70 of MEPL, the following operations are subject to approval in advance by the competent authorities:

- use of ship's incinerator within port water area;
- washing or cleaning ship's hold, dispelling gas, discharging ballast water, accepting residual oil or oily sewage, eradicating rust or painting at the side of a ship;
- use of chemical oil-eliminating liquids by a ship, wharf or facility;
- washing ship's deck contaminated with pollutants, noxious or harmful substances;
- ship's lighterage operation of liquid goods in bulk in the nature of pollution danger;
- scraping on water, salvage, repair, building of a ship or other ship's construction on or under water.

V. Ship Scraping

667. In the construction of ship scraping factory, environmental protection shall be taken into consideration and approval shall be obtained from the environmental protection authority of local government (Articles 5 and 6, Ship Scraping Regulations).

668. Ship scraping operations shall be under the supervision of the environmental protection authority which has the power to inspect the scraping operations, to require a scraping factory to provide information and documents, to order a scraping factory to take measures for the prevention or control of pollution in the case of pollution incident, and to impose fines on violation of the EPL and regulations.

669. A ship scraping factory shall be fitted with equipment and facilities for the acceptance or disposal of residual oil, oily sewage and wastes and with other required facilities. Approval by the environmental protection authority shall be obtained before scraping operation takes place (Article 10, Ship Scraping Regulations).

The Ship Scraping Regulations also contains detailed provisions governing the ship scraping activities. For examples, a scraping factory shall before scraping dispel inflammable, explosive and noxious or harmful substances, close sea valves, seal up pipelines through which oily sewage may spill, carry garbage, residual oil, slop oil, oily sewage and other wastes to shore for concentrated disposal (Article 11); effective measures shall be taken during scraping in water for the prevention of spill of oil and other floating substances (Article 12); discharge of ballast water or hold washing water shall comply with the applicable State or local standards (Article 13); scraped ship's parts and wastes with pollutants are prohibited to be deposited in water (Article 14).

VI. Preventive and Minimization Measures

670. If a ship is involved in a marine accident that has caused or is likely to cause serious pollution damage to the marine environment, MSA shall have the power to compulsorily take action to avoid or minimize the pollution damage (paragraph 1, Article 71, MEPL).

By virtue of paragraph 2 of Article 71 of MEPL and the Intervention Convention, where a ship or facility at sea is involved in a marine accident in the high seas has caused serious pollution damage to the sea areas within the jurisdiction of China or has the threat of such pollution damage, MSA shall have the power to take necessary measures appropriate to the pollution damage which has actually caused or may cause.

VII. Surveillance on Marine Pollution

671. Every ship is obliged to exercise surveillance on marine pollution and to immediately report marine pollution incident or violation of law on marine environmental protection which she has discovered to the nearest competent authority. Every civil aircraft shall, on discovering any incident of pollutant discharge at sea or marine pollution incident, also immediately report the matter to the nearest air traffic control which shall immediately pass the information to the competent authorities in marine environment supervision and administration (Article 72, MEPL).

§5. Prevention of Marine Pollution from Land-Based Sources

I. Responsibility of the State or Local Governments

672. It is the responsibility of the environmental protection authority and water administration authority of a province, autonomous region or municipality directly under the central government to strengthen their control over rivers that empty into the sea in accordance with the *Law on the Prevention & Disposal of Water Pollution* to prevent them from being polluted and to ensure the quality of the water in the estuaries (Article 31, MEPL).

The governments of coastal municipalities have the responsibilities to establish and improve the pipelines and networks of water discharge, to construct factories or other facilities for the concentrated disposal of sewages in the cities (Article 40, MEPL).

The State shall take necessary measures to prevent, minimize and control marine environmental pollution damage from or though atmospheric layer (Article 41, MEPL).

II. Control on Discharge of Pollutants into Sea

673. The discharge of land-sourced pollutants into the sea shall be in strict compliance with the standards and the relevant regulations promulgated by the State or local governments (Article 29, MEPL).

The choice of outlets for discharging pollutants shall be made in accordance with the functional division of the ocean and the related provisions and subject to the approval by the environmental protection authority in the local governments. No outlet for discharging pollutants shall be allowed within the marine sanctuaries, important fishery water areas, seashore scenic and tourist areas (Article 30, MEPL).

Any entity which discharges land-sourced pollutants shall report to the environmental protection authority concerned the facilities for the discharge and disposal of such pollutants, kinds, volume and density of pollutants in the normal discharge thereof (Article 32, MEPL).

674. Discharge of waste water containing oil, acid liquid, lye, extremely noxious waste liquid, high-level or medium-level radioactive matters into the sea is prohibited. Discharge of waste water containing low-level radioactive matters into the sea is strictly limited and, where really necessary, shall be carried out in strict compliance with the State provisions concerning radioactive protection. Discharge of waste water containing organic matters or heavy mental which is not easy to be diluted into the sea is strictly controlled (Article 33, MEPL).

No medical sewage, domestic sewage or industrial waste water carrying infectious pathogens may be discharged into the sea before it is properly treated to meet the State standards for discharge thereof (Article 34, MEPL).

Discharge of industrial waste water and domestic sewage containing organic and nutrient matters into bays, semi-closed seas and other sea areas with low capacities of self-purification shall be strictly controlled (Article 35, MEPL).

At the time of discharge of heated waste water into the sea, measures shall be taken to ensure that the water temperature in the adjacent fishery areas is kept within the State's water quality standards in order to avoid damage to the aquatic resources by heat pollution (Article 36, MEPL).

III. Other Use or Disposal of Pollutants

675. The use of chemical pesticides in coastal farmlands or forests shall conform to the State's provisions and standards for the safe use of pesticides (Article 36, MEPL).

Discarding, piling up or disposing tailings, slag, cinders, garbage and other solid wastes on the beaches shall be conducted in accordance with the *Law on the Prevention and Disposal of Environmental Pollution from Solid Wastes* (Article 38, MEPL).

Transfer of dangerous wastes via the inner waters or territorial sea of China is prohibited, and transfer via other sea areas within the jurisdiction of China is subject to the consent in writing by the administrative agency concerned under MEE (Article 39, MEPL).

§6. Prevention of Marine Pollution from Construction Projects

I. Prevention of Marine Pollution from Coastal Construction Projects

676. Coastal construction projects include, *inter alia*, the construction of harbours, terminals, water conservancy facilities on the coastline, tidal power stations in estuaries and factories or other facilities on land near the coastline.

Coastal construction projects which may pollute the marine environment and impact the seashore scene shall be prohibited within marine sanctuaries, important fishery water areas, seashore scenic and tourist areas or other areas in which the environment needs special protection (paragraph 2, Article 42, MEPL).

Construction of chemical factories or other industrial projects which may pollute the marine environment seriously and which lack effective treatment measures of such pollution shall be prohibited (Article 45, MEPL).

677. As required by paragraph 1 of Article 42 of MEPL, building or rebuilding of coastal construction projects shall conform to the State's provisions concerning environmental protection with respect to construction projects. The capitals needed for the prevention and treatment of pollution shall be embodied into the investment plan thereof. Before construction, an Environmental Impact Statement shall be submitted to the environmental protection authority concerned for approval (Article 43, MEPL).

Facilities for the environmental protection in a coastal construction project shall be designed, built and put into operation simultaneously with the design, building and operation of the principal part of the project. Where the said facilities for the environmental protection have not been approved of by the environmental protection authority concerned, the project cannot be put into operation (Article 44, MEPL).

In the building of a coastal construction project, effective measures shall be taken for the protection of aquatic resources (Article 46, MEPL).

II. Prevention of Marine Pollution from Ocean Construction Projects

A. *General Requirements*

678. As required by Article 47 of MEPL, the ocean construction projects mainly in offshore oil exploration and exploitation shall conform to the functional division of the ocean, marine environmental protection plan and the State's environmental protection standards. Before a project takes place, a Marine Environmental Impact Statement shall be submitted to the ocean administrative authority concerned for approval. The project is subject to the supervision of the environmental protection authority concerned.

Like the case of coastal construction project, facilities for the environmental protection in an ocean construction project shall be designed, built and put into operation simultaneously with the design, building and operation of the principal part of the project. Where the said facilities for the environmental protection have not been approved of by the ocean administrative authority concerned, the project cannot be put into operation (Article 44, MEPL).

Use of materials containing radioactive substances exceeding the relevant standards or easy to dissolve noxious or harmful substances is prohibited in the projects (Article 49, MEPL).

Where a project involves explosive operations, effective measures shall be taken to protect aquatic resources (paragraph 1, Article 50, MEPL).

B. *Special Requirements for Oil Exploration and Exploitation*

679. As required by Article 7 of the Offshore Oil E&E Regulations, fixed or movable platforms shall be fitted with various equipment and facilities for the prevention of pollution. The equipment shall be approved of by CCS and valid certificates shall be obtained.

Offshore oil pipelines and oil-storage installations[63] shall always be kept in good condition as required for the prevention of seepage, leakage and corrosion, so as to prevent oil leakage accidents (Article 14, Offshore Oil E&E Regulations).

A platform shall also have the required Oil Record Book which shall record, *inter alia*, the operation of the above equipment and facilities, discharge of oily sewage, disposal and discharge of other wastes, accidents of oil spill or leakage, blowouts and treatment thereof (Articles 10 and 18, Offshore Oil E&E Regulations).

---

63. Normally in the form of floating production storage and offloading (FPSO).

The operators of offshore oil exploration and exploitation shall maintain valid insurance or other financial security for civil liability against oil pollution damage (Article 9, Offshore Oil E&E Regulations).

Effective measures shall be taken to avoid accident of oil spill during oil exploration and exploitation and transport of oil (paragraph 2, Article 50, MEPL).

An oil spill emergency plan shall be submitted to the administrative agency concerned under the MEE for approval (Article 54, MEPL).

680. Oily sewage and oil mixtures from drilling ships or platforms or oil extraction platforms can be discharged into the sea only when they meet the standards for discharge after treatment. Residual or slop oil shall be recovered instead of being discharged into the sea. When it is discharged after recovery treatment, the oil content shall not exceed the standards set by the State (Article 51, MEPL).

Drilling ships or platforms, oil extraction platforms and their related facilities at sea shall not dispose industrial wastes into the sea. Disposal of other industrial wastes shall not cause marine environmental pollution (Article 52, MEPL).

Testing of wells shall ensure that the gas and oil be thoroughly flared and the oil and oil mixtures shall not be discharged into the sea (Article 53, MEPL).

681. In the case of accident of oil spill or leakage, measures shall be taken immediately to control, minimize or eliminate pollution. Once serious oil pollution accident such as blowout, spill or leakage of large volume of oil occurs, the entity concerned shall immediately report it to the competent authority, take effective measures to control and eliminate oil pollution, and accept the investigation and handling of the case by the authority (Article 16, Offshore Oil E&E Regulations).

§7. Prevention of Marine Pollution by Dumping of Wastes

I. Responsibility of MEE

682. MEE formulates the standards for the dumping of wastes into the sea in the light of their toxicity, contents of harmful elements and the impacts upon the marine environment, decide the types of wastes, and make a list of wastes which can be dumped into the sea. Such a list is subject to the approval by the State Council (Article 56, MEPL).

MEE shall designate the dumping areas in accordance with the principles of being scientific, rational, safe and economical and shall be submitted to the State Council for approval (paragraph 1, Article 57, MEPL; Article 5, Ocean Dumping Regulations). Temporary dumping areas shall be subject to approval by the administrative agency concerned under MEE (paragraph 1, Article 57, MEPL).

MEE shall exercise supervision and administration on the utilization of the dumping areas, organize the environmental surveillance on such areas and shall close any area when finding it no longer suitable for waste dumping (Article 58, MEPL; Article 16, Ocean Dumping Regulations).

II. Dumping Permit

683. Dumping permit regime is adopted in MEPL and the Ocean Dumping Regulations as the main means of governmental control on the dumping of wastes into the sea.

Thus, any entity, ship, aircraft, platform or other means of transport may dump any kind of waste into the sea areas within the jurisdiction of China only after a dumping permit has been granted by the administrative agency concerned under MEE upon written application therefor (Article 55, MEPL; Article 6, Ocean Dumping Regulations).

A dumping permit shall indicate the dumping entity, period of validity, quantity and type of wastes as well as the method for dumping. The issuing authority may change or withdraw the permit in accordance with the changes in ecological environment and the development in science and technology (Article 10, Ocean Dumping Regulations).

684. An entity which has obtained a permit for dumping wastes shall dump wastes at the designated place, within the designated time limit and in accordance with the conditions specified in the permit (Article 59, MEPL). The only exemption is that, where for emergency or rescue purposes, a ship may dump wastes with no regard to the terms and areas as specified in the permit. In such a case, however, the ship shall try to avoid or reduce pollution damage and report to the competent authority as soon as possible. The waste pumping entity and beneficiaries of the emergency or rescue act shall make compensation for the pollution damage thus caused (Article 15, Ocean Dumping Regulations).

685. Wastes to be dumped shall be verified by the approving authority after their loading. Wastes to be dumped by means of ships shall be supervised and verified by MSA organ at the port of departure (Article 59, MEPL).

Where the wastes to be dumped are found to be not inconsistent with the dumping permit, the competent authority shall order to stop loading of wastes or disallow the departure of a ship. Serious violation may cause suspension or withdrawal of the permit (Article 12, Ocean Dumping Regulations).

In addition, an entity which has obtained a permit for dumping wastes shall make detailed record of such operation and present a written report to the approving authority thereafter. A ship which has finished dumping shall present a written report to MSA at the port of departure (Article 60, MEPL).

III. Other Matters of Control on Dumping of Wastes

686. Dumping of wastes coming from outside the territory of China into the sea areas within the jurisdiction of China is prohibited (Article 55, MEPL).

Burning wastes at sea and disposal of radioactive wastes or other radioactive substances is prohibited (Article 61, MEPL).

687. The competent authorities shall monitor and supervise the dumping activities. If needed, an authority may also send agents to supervise on board a ship. The dumping entity shall offer facilitation for these functionaries (Article 13, Ocean Dumping Regulations).

§8. Liability for Marine Pollution

I. Civil Liability for Marine Pollution Damage

A. Where 1992 CLC Applicable

688. The 1992 CLC governs the civil liability for the pollution damage caused by persistent hydrocarbon mineral oil in bulk from ships only and is not concerned with the pollution damage to marine environment caused by other pollutants. It has its specified scope of application with regard to the ship, oil and geographical limit.

By virtue of Article 1, a ship means any seagoing ship and sea-borne craft of any type whatsoever constructed or adapted for the carriage of oil in bulk as cargo, provided that a ship capable of carrying oil and other cargoes shall be regarded as a ship only when it is actually carrying oil in bulk as cargo and during any voyage following such carriage unless it is proved that it has no residues of such carriage of oil in bulk aboard; oil means any persistent hydrocarbon mineral oil such as crude oil, fuel oil, heavy diesel oil and lubricating oil, whether carried on board a ship as cargo or in the bunkers of such a ship.

As provided for in Article 2, 1992 CLC shall apply exclusively to the pollution damage caused in the territory, including the territorial sea, of a contracting State and in its exclusive economic zone established in accordance with international law, or, if a contracting state has not established such a zone, in an area beyond and adjacent to its territorial sea determined in accordance with international law and extending not more than 200 nautical miles from the baselines from which the breadth of its territorial sea is measured, and to preventive measures, wherever taken, to prevent or minimize such damage.

Pollution damage is defined in paragraph 6 of Article 1 of this Convention as loss or damage caused outside the ship by contamination resulting from the escape or discharge of oil from the ship, wherever such escape or discharge may occur, provided that compensation for impairment of the environment other than loss of profit from such impairment shall be limited to costs of reasonable measures of reinstatement actually undertaken or to be undertaken, and the costs of preventive measures and further loss or damage caused by preventive measures.

Preventive measures mean reasonable measures taken after the occurrence of oil pollution incident by any person, including the shipowners, the master and crew of the ship, in order to prevent or minimize pollution damage. Incident means any occurrence, or series of occurrences having the same origin, which causes pollution damage or creates a grave and imminent threat of causing such damage.

Noticeably, by virtue of paragraph 1 of Article 268 of Chapter XIV 'Application of Law in Relation to Foreign-related Matters' of MC, an international treaty concluded or acceded to by China shall be applicable only to matters with foreign elements. By virtue of this principle, the 1992 CLC is not applicable to a domestic oil tanker carrying persistent hydrocarbon mineral oil as cargo in bulk, because the matter of oil pollution from her is not normally foreign-related. However, the Ships Pollution Regulations provides in Article 54 that the limit of liability for pollution damage from a ship carrying persistent hydrocarbon mineral oil in bulk shall be determined in accordance with the relevant international treaty or treaties concluded or acceded to by China. Therefore, the limit of liability provided for in the 1992 CLC shall be applicable to the above domestic oil tankers, regardless of lack of foreign elements in a particular case, in order to ensure sufficient or adequate compensation for oil pollution damage. Nevertheless, it seems clear that other provisions of the 1992 CLC than the limit of liability shall still not be applicable due to lack of foreign elements.

689. In order to facilitate the liability insurance or other financial security for oil pollution damage, Article 3 of the 1992 CLC provides that the person who shall be liable for any pollution damage caused by the ship as a result of an incident is the owner of ship only at the time of an incident, or, where the incident consists of a series of occurrences, at the time of the first such occurrence.

The shipowner mean the registered owner of the ship, or, in the case of no registry, the person who owns the ship, or, in the case a ship is State-owned and is operated by a company registered as the operator of the ship, the ship operator.

It is emphasized that no claim for compensation for pollution damage may be made against the servants or agents of the shipowner or the members of the crew, the pilot or any other person who, without being a member of the crew, performs services for the ship, any charterers, manager or operator of the ship, any person performing salvage operations with the consent of the shipowner or on the instructions of a competent public authority, or servants or agents, or any person taking preventive measures, unless the damage resulted from their personal act or omission, committed with the intent to cause such damage, or recklessly and with knowledge that such damage would probably result.

690. When an incident involving two or more ships occurs and pollution damage results therefrom, the owners of all the ships concerned, unless exonerated under Article 3, shall be jointly and severally liable for all such damage that is not reasonably separable (Article 4).

691. The 1992 CLC has adopted the rule of strict liability for oil pollution damage.

By virtue of Article 3, the shipowner shall be liable for oil pollution damage, unless it proves that the damage:

- resulted from an act of war, hostilities, civil war, insurrection, or a natural phenomenon of an exceptional, inevitable and irresistible character;

- was wholly caused by an act or omission done with intent to cause damage by a third party;
- was wholly caused by the negligence or other wrongful act of any government or other authority responsible for the maintenance of lights or other navigational aids in the exercise of that function; or
- resulted wholly or partially either from an act or omission done with intent to cause damage by the person who suffered the damage or from the negligence of that person, in which case the shipowner may be exonerated wholly or partially from his liability to that person.

In any other cases, the owner of the ship from which oil was escaped or discharged and caused pollution damage or created a grave and imminent threat of causing such damage shall be liable for the pollution damage, whether the owner, the master or other crewmembers, other servant or agent has committed contributory fault or not.

However, the provision of the 1992 CLC shall not prejudice any right of recourse of the shipowner against a third party who caused the pollution damage wholly or partially. For example, if Ship A is 100% to blame in a ship's collision due to her fault in the navigation and the collision causes leakage of oil carried on board Ship B, the owner of Ship B shall be solely liable to the innocent third parties who suffer oil pollution damage caused by the oil leakage, but shall have the right of recourse against the owner of Ship A.

Noticeably, however, SPC issued judgments for the retrial of a series of four cases of M/V 'CMA CGM Florida' from September to November 2019 in which SPC reversed the judgments of the Ningbo Maritime Court in the first instance and the judgments of the High People's Court of Zhejiang Province in the second instance and decided that the claimants who suffered oil pollution damage may claim such damage against the owner of a colliding ship in the ship's collision case from which no oil escaped in proportion to the degree of fault committed by her in the collision. Therefore, the claimants who suffered oil pollution damage may choose to claim the full amount of damages against the owner of a colliding ship from which oil escaped, or to claim the damages against the owners of both colliding ships in proportion to the degree of fault committed by them respectively. Nevertheless, these SPC judgments remain arguable in China.

692. By virtue of Article 5 of the 1992 CLC as amended in 2000, the owner of a ship shall be entitled to limit his liability in respect of any one incident to an aggregate amount of 4.51 million SDR for a ship not exceeding 5,000 gross tonnage, and for a ship with a gross tonnage in excess thereof, but not exceeding 140,000 gross tonnage, 4.51 million SDR plus 631 SDR for each additional gross tonne, and for a ship over 140,000 gross tonnage, 89.77 million SDR.

The ship's gross tonnage is calculated in accordance with the tonnage measurement regulations contained in Annex I of the *International Convention on Tonnage Measurement of Ships of 1969*.

693. The shipowner shall not be entitled to limit his liability, if it is proved that the pollution damage resulted from his personal act or omission, committed with the intent to cause such damage, or recklessly and with knowledge that such damage would probably result.

694. For the purpose of availing himself of the benefit of limitation, the owners shall constitute a fund for the total sum representing the limit of his liability with the court of law or other competent authority of any one of the contracting States in which an action is brought under Article 9 or, if no action has been brought, with any court of law or other competent authority in any one of the contracting States in which an action can be brought under Article 9 of the 1992 CLC. The fund can be constituted either by depositing the sum or by producing a bank guarantee or other guarantee acceptable under the legislation of the contracting State where the fund is constituted and considered to be adequate by the court or other competent authority.

In China, a limitation fund shall be constituted with the maritime court having jurisdiction over the case. So far as a letter of guarantee is concerned, a maritime court only accepts one issued by a Chinese bank, Chinese insurance company or CPI and does not accept one issued by a foreign bank, foreign insurance company or a foreign P&I club unless agreed to by the claimants.

Such a fund may be constituted even if the owners are not entitled to limit his liability, but its constitution shall in that case not prejudice the rights of any claimant against the owners.

695. Compulsory insurance or other financial security of civil liability for oil pollution damage is adopted in Article 7 of the 1992 CLC with respect to a ship registered in a contracting State carrying more than 2,000 mt of oil.

In practice, such liability is normally covered by a shipowners' P&I club.[64]

Thus, each of such ships shall carry a Certificate of Insurance or Other Financial Security in Respect of Civil Liability for Oil Pollution Damage attesting that insurance or other financial security is in force in accordance with the provisions of the 1992 CLC. Without such a certificate, each contracting State shall not allow the ship to operate, whether the ship is engaged in international trade or domestic trade.

A ship not registered in a contracting State is not subject to the compulsory insurance or other financial security by virtue of Article 7 of the 1992 CLC. However, when such a ship enters a port in a contracting State, she shall also carry such a certificate, as a result of which her owners are *ex facto* bound by the 1992 CLC in this respect.

The certificate shall be issued or certified by the appropriate authority of the State of the ship's registry, if she is registered in a contracting State, or, with respect to a ship not registered in a contracting State, may be issued or certified by the appropriate authority of any contracting State. A certificate issued or certified by the authority of a contracting State shall be accepted by other contracting States and shall be regarded by other contracting States as having the same force as a certificate issued or certified by them, even if issued or certified in respect of a ship not

64. *See* §5, Ch. 11 of Part II.

registered in a contracting State. Such a certificate for a tanker flying the Chinese flag is issued by MSA at the port of her registry.

The certificate is subject to inspection by the appropriate authority of contracting State when the ship enters its port.

696. As an exception, a State-owned ship is not subject to the compulsory insurance or other financial security. However, such a ship shall carry a certificate issued by the appropriate authority of the State of the ship's registry attesting that she is State-owned and the State shall bear civil liability for oil pollution damage as required by the 1992 CLC.

697. In order to ensure the effectiveness of compulsory insurance or other financial security, the 1992 CLC adopted the regime of direct action against the liability insurer or financial guarantor, by virtue of which a claimant may file a lawsuit directly against the insurer who covers the civil liability for oil pollution damage of the shipowners or against the person who provides other financial security thereof.

In such a case, the defendant may, even if the shipowner is not entitled to limit his liability, avail himself of the limits of liability prescribed in Article 5 of the 1992 CLC. Where the defendant proves that the pollution damage was caused by the wilful misconduct of the shipowner, the liability of the liability insurer or financial guarantor shall be discharged.

698. Article 9 of the 1992 CLC contains provisions regarding procedural matters.

The principle of territorial jurisdiction is adopted to the effect that, where an incident has caused pollution damage in the territory, including the territorial sea and the exclusive economic zone, of one or more contracting States or preventive measures have been taken to prevent or minimize pollution damage therein, the litigations for compensation may only be brought in the courts of law of any such contracting State or States which shall ensure that their courts have jurisdiction over such legal actions.[65] Reasonable notice of any such action shall be given to the defendant.

The time limit for claim with regard to compensation for oil pollution damage is three years counting from the day on which the pollution occurred, but shall not exceed six years counting from the day on which the incident causing the pollution occurred.

A judgment made by a court of law of a contracting State shall, if enforceable in that State, be recognized and enforced in any other contracting States, unless the judgment is obtained by fraud, or reasonable notice of action or justifiable chance for presentation of case was not given to the defendant.

---

65. Such actions are subject to the exclusive jurisdiction of the maritime courts of China by virtue of Art. 7(2) of SMPL which provides that a compensation action in respect of discharge, leakage or dumping of oil or other harmful substances shall be subject to the jurisdiction of the maritime court of the place where the pollution or damage occurred or the preventive measures have been taken.

B. Where 2001 Bunker Convention Applicable

699. The 2001 Bunker Convention governs the civil liability for pollution damage caused by bunker oil from ships other than persistent hydrocarbon mineral oil in bulk in the bunkers of a ship within the scope of application of the 1992 CLC.

The 2001 Bunker Convention has its specified scope of application with regard to the ship, oil and geographical limit.

By virtue of Article 1, a ship means any seagoing ship and sea-borne craft of any type whatsoever; bunker oil means any hydrocarbon mineral oil, including lubricating oil, used or intended to be used for the operation or propulsion of the ship, and any residues of such oil. Article 2 provides the same geographical scope of application as provided for in Article 2 of the 1992 CLC, i.e., it shall apply exclusively to the pollution damage caused in the territory, including the territorial sea, of a contracting State and in its exclusive economic zone, and to preventive measures, wherever taken, to prevent or minimize such damage.

The definitions of pollution damage, incident and preventive measures contained in Article 1 of the 2001 Bunker Convention are the same as those contained in Article 2 of the 1992 CLC.

700. Same as Article 3 of the 1992 CLC, Article 3 of the 2001 Bunker Convention provides that the person who shall be liable for any pollution damage caused by the ship as a result of an incident is the owner of the ship at the time of an incident, or, where the incident consists of a series of occurrences, at the time of the first such occurrence. Noticeably, unlike Article 1 of the 1992 CLC which defines the shipowner as the registered owner of the ship, or, in the case of no registry, the person who owns the ship, or, in the case a ship is State-owned and is operated by a company registered as the operator of the ship, the ship operator, Article 1 of the 2001 Bunker Convention provides that the shipowner means the owner, including the registered owner, bareboat charterer, manager and operator of the ship. Therefore, the bareboat charterer, manager and operator of a ship are also deemed as the shipowner in the 2001 Bunker Convention.

701. Same as Article 4 of the 1992 CLC, Article 5 of the 2001 Bunker Convention provides that when an incident involving two or more ships occurs and pollution damage results therefrom, the owners of all the ships concerned, unless exonerated under Article 3, shall be jointly and severally liable for all such damage that is not reasonably separable. In addition, where more than one person among the registered owner, bareboat charterer, manager and operator of a ship is liable, their liability shall be joint and several.

702. Same as Article 3 of the 1992 CLC, Article 3 of the 2001 Bunker Convention has adopted the rule of strict liability of the shipowner for bunker oil pollution damage.

703. Unlike Article 5 of the 1992 CLC, the 2001 Bunker Convention does not provide particular limitation of liability of the shipowner for bunker oil pollution damage. Instead, Article 6 of the 2001 Bunker Convention provides that nothing in this Convention shall affect the right of the shipowner and the person or persons providing insurance or other financial security to limit liability under any applicable national or international regime, such as the *Convention on Limitation of Liability for Maritime Claims, 1976* as amended. Thus, the limitation of liability of the shipowner for such damage shall be determined in accordance with the provisions of Chapter XI of MC in China.[66]

Same as in the case of the 1992 CLC, for the purpose of availing himself of the benefit of limitation, the owner shall constitute a fund for the total sum representing the limit of his liability with the maritime court having jurisdiction.

704. Compulsory insurance or other financial security of civil liability for oil pollution damage is adopted in Article 7 with respect to a ship having a gross tonnage greater than 1,000 registered in a contracting State carrying more than 1,000 mt of oil. Each of such ships shall carry a Certificate of Insurance or Other Financial Security in Respect of Civil Liability for Bunker Oil Pollution Damage attesting that insurance or other financial security is in force in accordance with the provisions of the 2001 Bunker Convention. In order to ensure the effectiveness of compulsory insurance or other financial security, the 2001 Bunker Convention also adopted the regime of direct action against the liability insurer or financial guarantor, by virtue of which a claimant may file a lawsuit directly against the insurer who covers the civil liability for bunker oil pollution damage of the shipowner or against the person who provides other financial security thereof. A judgment made by a court of a contracting State shall, if enforceable in that State, be recognized and enforced in any other contracting States, unless the judgment is obtained by fraud, or reasonable notice of action or justifiable chance for presentation of case was not given to the defendant.

C. Where Both 1992 CLC and 2001 Bunker Convention Inapplicable

705. Where the pollution damage to the marine environment is not within the scope of application of both the 1992 CLC and the 2001 Bunker Convention, e.g., the pollution damage caused by pollutants other than oil, by non-persistent oil or oil not in bulk as cargo, or by bunker oil without foreign elements, the civil liability for such damage shall be determined by virtue of MEPL and the Ships Pollution Regulations.

706. The civil liability shall be imposed on the party who has resulted in the pollution damage to the marine environment from a ship, unless the liability shall be exempted by virtue of Articles 89 and 91 of MEPL or Articles 50 and 51 of the Ships Pollution Regulations as mentioned *infra*. Such a party is called the 'responsible party' in Article 90 of MEPL or Article 50 of the Ships Pollution Regulations. By virtue of the *Provisions on Certain Issues in Respect of Trial of Cases of Disputes on Compensation for Oil Pollution Damage from Ships* promulgated by SPC

66. *See* Ch. 4 of Part II.

on 4 May 2011, the 'responsible party' shall be the owners of the ship from which oil was discharged or escaped in a case of pollution from a ship.

707. Same as the 1992 CLC, MEPL and the Ships Pollution Regulations have adopted the rule of strict liability for the pollution damage to the marine environment from a ship, whatever the source of such pollution is.

By virtue of Article 92 of MEPL or Article 51 of the Ships Pollution Regulations, the liability for the pollution damage to the marine environment from a ship shall be exempted, if the pollution damage cannot be avoided, despite prompt and reasonable measures taken, and when the pollution damage is caused by:

- act of war;
- irresistible natural calamity;
- negligence or other wrongful act in the exercise of the functions of competent authorities responsible for the lighthouses or other navigational aids.

Paragraph 1 of Article 90 of MEPL or Article 50 of the Ships Pollution Regulations further provides that, in the case of pollution damage to the marine environment resulting entirely from the intentional or wrongful act of a third party, that party shall be liable for compensation.

Therefore, the liability for the pollution damage to the marine environment from a ship shall be exempted upon two conditions. First, the damage is caused either by one of the three circumstances specified above or entirely by the intentional or wrongful act of a third party. Second, the responsible party has taken prompt and reasonable measures in order to avoid or minimize the damage.

Where the pollution damage is not entirely caused by the intentional or wrongful act of a third party, but partly by such an act and partly by another cause not within the category of exemptions specified above, the responsible party shall still be liable for the damage, but the right of the defendant to pursue recourse against that the third party shall not be prejudiced.

Noticeably, there exists difference in the exemptions of liability between paragraphs 3 and 4 of Article 3 of the 1992 CLC or paragraphs 3 and 4 of Article 3 of the 2001 Bunker Convention and Articles 90 and 92 of MEPL or Articles 50 and 51 of the Ships Pollution Regulations.

First, where the damage is caused entirely by the fault or negligence of a third party, the responsible party shall be exempted from liability under MEPL or the Ships Pollution Regulations, but shall not exempted from liability under the 1992 CLC or the 2001 Bunker Convention.

Second, the exemption of liability due to negligence or other wrongful act in the exercise of the functions of competent authorities responsible for lighthouses or other navigational aids is limited to that in the maintenance of lighthouses or other navigational aids only under the 1992 CLC or the 2001 Bunker Convention, but there is no such restriction under MEPL or the Ships Pollution Regulations.

Third, paragraph 4 of Article 3 of the 1992 CLC or the 2001 Bunker Convention stipulates that if the shipowner proves that the pollution damage resulted wholly or partially either from an act or omission done with intent to cause damage by the person who suffered the damage or from the negligence of that person, the shipowner may be exonerated wholly or partially from liability to such person, but MEPL or the Ships Pollution Regulations do not contain such a provision.

In addition, sub-paragraph (a) of paragraph 3 of Article 3 of the 1992 CLC or the 2001 Bunker Convention covers 'act of war, hostilities, civil war, insurrection or a natural phenomenon of an exceptional, inevitable and irresistible character', but paragraphs 1 and 2 of Article 92 of MEPL or paragraphs 1 and 2 of Article 51 of the Ships Pollution Regulations only covers 'act of war' and 'irresistible natural calamity'. However, there is no material difference between the two as a matter of construction.

In the light of the rule of strict liability, the burden of proving exemption of liability as specified in Articles 90 and 92 of MEPL or Articles 50 and 51 of the Ships Pollution Regulations is on the responsible party.

708. Where the pollution damage to the marine environment is caused by the pollutants from a ship, the limitation of liability of the responsible party for such damage shall be determined in accordance with the provisions of Chapter XI of MC.[67]

In a case of the pollution damage to the marine environment not caused by pollutants from a ship, the responsible party shall not avail of any limitation of liability.

709. With regard to the procedural matters of civil liability for the pollution damage to the marine environment, the legal actions of claims for such damage caused by ships, production or operation at sea, ship scraping or repair are subject to the exclusive jurisdiction of maritime courts (Articles 3 and 7(2), SMPL). Any other legal action shall be subject to the jurisdiction of the court of law in the place where the tortuous act was committed or the defendant has its domicile (Article 29, CPC).

Like the case of the 1992 CLC or the 2001 Bunker Convention, the time limit for claim with regard to the compensation for the oil pollution damage caused by a ship is three years counting from the day on which the pollution occurred, but shall not exceed six years counting from the day on which the incident causing the pollution occurred. In any other case of damage to the marine environment, the time limit shall be three years counting from the day on which the claimant has learnt or should have learnt the occurrence of damage by virtue of Article 188 of CC.

D. Governmental Authority as Claimant

710. In China, the ocean resources such an ocean ecological resources and ocean aquatic resources are owned by the State. As provided for in paragraph 2 of Article 89 of MEPL, where the ocean ecological environment, ocean aquatic resources or ocean protection zone established in accordance with Articles 21 and 22 of MEPL is damaged and thus the State suffers such damage, the authority authorized by

67. *See* Ch. 4 of Part II.

MEPL to exercise supervision and administration over marine environmental protection shall represent the State to make claim against the responsible party for compensation for such damage. In particular, the State Oceanic Administration (SOA) or agencies under the Ministry of Natural Resources shall claim for damage to the ocean ecological environment or ocean protection zone on behalf of the State, and the administration authorities or agencies under the Ministry of Agriculture and Rural Affairs shall claim for damage to the ocean aquatic resources on behalf of the State.

II. Disciplinary Liability

A. *Disciplinary Liability Imposed on Violators*

711. Chapter IX of MEPL specifies the various violations thereof in which the supervision and administration authorities on marine environmental protection may impose disciplinary liabilities on the violators.

For example, by virtue of Article 73 of MEPL, the authorities may impose disciplinary liabilities on the violators in the following cases:

- discharge into the sea of pollutants or other substances which are prohibited to discharge;
- discharge into the sea of pollutants, not in accordance with MEPL or discharge exceeding the specified standards;
- dumping into the sea of wastes without dumping permit;
- failure to take immediate measures in the case of marine pollution incidents.

Besides, Chapter VIII of the Ships Pollution Regulations specifies the various violations thereof in which MSA may impose disciplinary liabilities on the violators. The disciplinary liabilities can be in the form of being ordered to stop violation or to take remedy measures within a definite time, warning and/or fines.

712. In the case of imposition of disciplinary liabilities, the *Administrative Litigation Law* and the *Administrative Reconsideration Law* shall apply.

B. *Disciplinary Liability Imposed on Personnel of Supervision and Administration*

713. By virtue of Article 94 of MEPL, disciplinary liability shall be imposed on the personnel of the supervision and administration authorities who have neglected their duties, abused their powers or practised favouritism and embezzlement if the pollution damage has been caused to the marine environment, thereby.

III. Criminal Liability

714. Where a violation of MEPL results in pollution damage to the marine environment and causes heavy losses to the public or private property or deaths of or injuries to persons, those who are responsible shall be investigated for criminal liability (paragraph 3, Article 91, MEPL). Where a violation of the Ships Pollution Regulations, other laws or regulations causes serious pollution to the marine environment, those who are responsible shall be investigated for criminal liability mainly by virtue of Article 338 of the *Criminal Code*, which provides: 'Discharge, dumping or disposal of radioactive wastes, infectious pathogens wastes, toxic substances or other hazardous wastes in violation of State regulations, causing serious pollution to the environment, shall be sanctioned with imprisonment for less than three years or criminal detention and concurrently or separately with a fine; where the consequence is particularly serious, it shall be sanctioned with imprisonment from three to seven years and concurrently with a fine.'

If the personnel of the supervision and administration authorities provided for in MEPL commit a crime, they shall be investigated for criminal liabilities.

Investigation for criminal liabilities shall be done in accordance with the *Criminal Code* and the *Criminal Procedure Code* by the judicial organs.

Chapter 14. Arrest of Ships

§1. Applicable Laws

I. International Treaties

715. As introduced in Chapter 2 of Part I supra, China is not a party to the International Convention for the Unification of Certain Rules relating to the Arrest of Se-going Ships signed in Brussels on 10 May 1952, and the International Convention on Arrest of Ships signed on 12 March 1999. However, reference was made in the shaping of Chapter III of SMPL to the International Convention on Arrest of Ships of 1999.

II. National Laws

716. The arrest of ships is governed by both basic law and special law in China. The arrest of a ship is subject to the provisions contained in Chapter III 'Preservation for Maritime Claims' of SMPL. The arrest of a ship as a compulsory measure of property preservation taken before or during litigation is also subject to the provisions contained in Articles 103 to 108 of CPC. However, the provisions of SMPL as a special law shall have priority over those of CPC as a basic law to the extent of repugnancy.

§2. Judicial Procedure for Arrest of Ship Before or During Litigation

I. Competent Court

717. The arrest of a ship arising from a maritime claim either before or during litigation is subject to the exclusive jurisdiction of a maritime court. Such jurisdiction is not subject to any agreement of jurisdiction or arbitration between the parties (Article 14, SMPL).

By virtue of Article 13 of SMPL, an application for the arrest of a ship before litigation by a maritime claimant shall be filed with the maritime court of the place where the ship to be arrested is located. The maritime court executing the arrest shall have jurisdiction over the disputes arising from the maritime claim that has given rise to the arrest. Thus, as provided for in Article 19 of SMPL, after execution of the arrest, where litigation or arbitration procedure has not started with respect to the related maritime disputes, any party concerned may file a lawsuit with respect to the maritime claim with the maritime court that has executed the arrest or another maritime court having jurisdiction over the maritime disputes, unless there exists an agreement of litigation jurisdiction or arbitration between the parties.

Where an application for the arrest of a ship arising from a maritime claim is made either by the plaintiff or the defendant after litigation has started but before a final and effective judgment is made, such an application shall be filed with the maritime court that has entertained or is hearing the case.

By virtue of Article 28 of AL and Article 289 of CPC, if an application for the arrest of a ship is made during maritime arbitration, such an application shall be filed with the arbitration commission, which shall deliver the application to the maritime court of the place where the ship to be arrested is located or the respondent has residence for decision and execution.

718. Where an application for the arrest of a ship is made for the purpose of the enforcement of an effective judgment or arbitration award, such an application shall be filed with the maritime court of the place where the ship to be arrested is located or the losing party has residence, unless there is no maritime court in such a place, in which case the application shall be filed with the intermediate court of law in such a place (Article 11, SMPL).

II. Application Conditions

719. An application for the arrest of a ship shall meet the following conditions:

- The applicant is a claimant of one of the maritime claims listed in Article 21 of SMPL as cited *infra*.
- The maritime court with which the application has been filed has jurisdiction over the arrest of a ship as stated *supra*.
- The ship is subject to arrest as stated *infra*.
- Where the maritime court so required, the applicant has paid the statutory application fee to the court and provided a counter-security as stated *infra*.

III. Application Procedure

720. By virtue of Article 14 of SMPL, a maritime claimant applying for the arrest of a ship either before or during maritime litigation shall file an application in writing with the maritime court having jurisdiction over the arrest as stated *supra*. The application shall be attached with supporting evidence and indicate the items of the maritime claim concerned, the reasons for application, the ship to be arrested, and the amount of security demanded.

IV. Award and Execution

721. Having accepted the application for the arrest of a ship, the maritime court shall make an award within forty-eight hours, either granting the application if the conditions for the arrest are met or rejecting the application if the conditions for the arrest are not met (paragraph 1, Article 17, SMPL).

Where the arrest of a ship is granted in the award, the president of the maritime court shall issue an order of arrest that shall be executed immediately by a judge or court martial who shall board the ship to declare the arrest before the master of the ship, serving the award and arrest order on him who is required to sign the receipt of service, and attaching the arrest order in a conspicuous place on the bridge or elsewhere on board the ship.

At the same time, the maritime court shall send a notice to MSA and the border control (immigration) of the place where the ship under arrest is located for assistance in the execution of the arrest order. The notice shall indicate the contents of the required assistance. MSA and the border control so required are obliged to render assistance (Article 26, SMPL). Normally, MSA is required not to allow the ship to sail and the border control is required to send two officials to board the ship under arrest who shall guard the ship and prevent the ship from escaping.

After the execution of the arrest order, any movement of the ship under arrest is subject to the approval of the maritime court. As an exception, however, upon consent of the maritime claimant, the maritime court may allow the ship under arrest to continue her operation, provided that she cannot be disposed of and no mortgage can be established on her (Article 27, SMPL). Such a situation is called 'live arrest' in admiralty practice in China and is applicable to the Chinese ships engaged in the domestic shipping only.

Where any party has objection to the award made by the maritime court either granting or rejecting the arrest of a ship, it may apply to the maritime court for reconsideration within five days after the receipt of the award. The maritime court shall make a decision of reconsideration within five days after the receipt of the application. During the period of reconsideration, execution of the award shall not be discontinued (paragraph 2, Article 17, SMPL).

§3. Ships Subject to Arrest

I. Definition of Ship

722. There is no definition of ship in SMPL. However, it is understandable that, since the arrest of a ship is a compulsory measure to secure maritime claims, any ship that may give to maritime claims shall be covered by SMPL, except ships or crafts to be used for military or public services purposes that are not subject to arrest as provided for in paragraph 3 of Article 23 of SMPL.

A small vessel of less than 20 tons of gross tonnage that is excluded from the scope of ship defined in Article 3 of MC may also give rise to maritime claims and therefore subject to arrest in accordance with SMPL.

723. The inland vessels shall be subject to the measures of property preservation by virtue of Articles 92 to 96 of CPC. If taken against a vessel, these measures include arrest thereof. Consequently, the inland vessels are also subject to arrest before or during litigation in accordance with CPC, as discussed in Chapter 3 of Part III *supra*.

II. Ships Subject to Arrest

724. The ships subject to arrest include the offending ships and other ships.

As provided for in paragraph 1 of Article 23 of SMPL, an offending ship may be arrested under one of the following circumstances:

- The owners of the offending ship are responsible for the maritime claim giving rise to the arrest and they remain the owners of this ship at the time of execution of arrest.
- The bareboat charterers of the offending ship are responsible for the maritime claim giving rise to the arrest and they remain the bareboat charterers or have become the owners of this ship at the time of execution of arrest.
- The maritime claim giving rise to the arrest arises from mortgage on a ship or right of the same nature to a ship.
- The maritime claim giving rise to the arrest arises from ownership or possession of a ship.
- The maritime claim giving rise to the arrest is secured by maritime lien.

By virtue of paragraph 2 of Article 23 of SMPL, a ship other than the offending ship may be arrested, if she is at the time of execution of arrest owned by the owners, bareboat or time or voyage charterers of the offending ship who are responsible for the maritime claim giving rise to the arrest, unless the maritime claim arises from the ownership or possession of a ship in which case only the offending ship may be arrested. Thus, a sister ship is subject to arrest conditionally.

§4. Maritime Claims

725. The scope of maritime claims that may give rise to the arrest of ships is comprehensive. As provided for in Article 21 of SMPL, a claimant of any of the following maritime claims may apply for the arrest of a ship:

- loss of or damage to property arising from ship's operation;
- loss of life or personal injury in direct connection with ship's operation;
- salvage at sea;
- damage or threatening of damage to the environment, coastline or the related interests caused by a ship; measures taken for the prevention, mitigation or elimination of such damage; compensation made for such damage; expenses of reasonable measures taken or to be taken for the reinstatement of environment; losses suffered or possibly to be suffered by a third party arising from such damage; and damage, expenses or loss similar in nature to those referred to in this item;
- expenses relating to the raising, elimination, recovering, destroying or making harmless of a sunken ship, wreck, grounding ship, abandoned ship, including the expenses relating to the raising, elimination, recovering, destroying or making harmless of objects remaining on or having been on board that ship, as well as the expenses relating to the maintenance of abandoned ship and her crew;

- agreement concerning the use or hire of a ship;
- agreement concerning the carriage of goods or passengers;
- loss of or damage to the goods carried on a ship including luggage and loss or damage relating thereto;
- general average;
- towage;
- pilotage;
- provision of materials or services for the ship's operation, management, maintenance or repair;
- ship's construction, rebuilding, repair, re-equipment or equipment;
- statutory charges and expenses concerning port, canal, berth, harbour and other waterways;
- crew's wages and other expenses including repatriation and social security expenses that should be paid for the master and other crewmembers;
- expenses paid for a ship or the shipowners;
- hull insurance premiums and P&I insurance calls that the shipowners or bareboat charterers should pay or a third person has paid for them;
- commissions, brokerage or agency fees relating to a ship that the shipowners or bareboat charterers should pay or a third person has paid for them;
- dispute arising from the ownership or possession of a ship;
- dispute between or among the part owners or joint owners of a ship relating to her use or benefit;
- ship mortgage or right of the same nature;
- dispute arising from a contract of sale and purchase of a ship.

The maritime claims listed above are exclusive. Thus, Article 22 of SMPL provides that no application for the arrest of a ship can be made if not based upon any of the maritime claims listed in Article 21, unless for the purpose of enforcement of a judgment, arbitration award or other legal document.

§5. Security and Counter-Security

I. Security

726. With respect to the arrest of a ship, a security is the one provided by the respondent or a third person on his behalf for the release of the ship from the arrest.

The security for this purpose may be provided either to the maritime court or to the maritime claimant (Article 74, SMPL). Its form and amount shall be agreed upon between the parties or decided by the maritime court if the parties failed to reach an agreement (Article 75, SMPL). As a general rule, a security should be valid and reliable in its form and sufficient as to its amount. Being valid and reliable, the security can be enforced later on. Being sufficient, a security shall fully cover the claim amount secured by it.

A security can be in the form of cash deposit, a letter of undertaking of a third person, mortgage or pledge established on property belonging to the respondent or a third person (paragraph 2, Article 73, SMPL).

The amount of security demanded by the maritime claimant shall be equivalent to the amount of credit including the principal amount and interests thereon together with the expenses of enforcement, but shall not exceed the value of the ship arrested (Article 76, SMPL). Where the amount of security provided as demanded by the claimant is too high, the claimant shall be liable for the loss suffered by the respondent resulting therefrom (Article 78, SMPL).

After provision of the security, the provider may apply to maritime court for ordering the decrease in the amount, change in its form or release of the security based upon reasonable reasons (Article 77, SMPL).

II. Counter-Security

727. With respect to the arrest of a ship, in contrast with the security provided by or for the respondent, a counter-security means the security provided by or for the maritime claimant in order to ensure the compensation for the loss suffered by the respondent or other interests if the application for the arrest proves wrongful afterwards.

A counter-security for this purpose shall be provided to the maritime court (Article 74, SMPL). Its form and amount shall be decided by the maritime court (Article 75, SMPL).

Like the security provided by or for the respondent, a counter-security can be in the form of cash deposit, a letter of undertaking of a third person, mortgage or pledge established on property belonging to the claimant or a third person (paragraph 2, Article 73, SMPL). After provision of the counter-security, the provider may also apply to maritime court for ordering the decrease, change or release of the security based upon reasonable reasons (Article 77, SMPL).

728. So far as the security and counter-security are concerned in admiralty practice, both parties and the maritime court are very careful in agreeing to or granting a security or counter-security in the form of a letter of undertaking provided by a third person for either the maritime claimant or the respondent. Normally, a letter of undertaking or the like issued by a foreign company, even if by a foreign bank, foreign insurance company or foreign P&I club, is not accepted by the Chinese party concerned or a maritime court due to the possible difficulties in enforcement thereof in the future. Therefore, it often occurs in practice that a foreign bank, foreign insurance company or foreign P&I club issues a counter-security in the form of a letter of undertaking to a Chinese bank, Chinese insurance company or CPI which then issues a letter of undertaking to the maritime court or the maritime claimant. A letter of undertaking or the like issued by a Chinese bank, Chinese insurance company or CPI will be accepted by the parties and maritime court. If it is issued by other Chinese company, its reliability will be carefully considered, depending upon the availability for future enforcement of properties of the provider and its reputation.

A letter of undertaking is a form of security provided for in Chapter XVI 'General Provisions' of Sub-book Four 'Real Rights for Security' of Book Two 'Real Rights' of CC and shall be governed by the relevant provisions contained in CC, provided that these provisions are not repugnant to those contained in SMPL.

§6. Subsequent Arrest of Same Ship

729. As provided for in Article 24 of SMPL, subsequent arrest of the same ship or re-arrest of the same ship due to the same maritime claim is prohibited in principle with the following exceptions:

- The respondent has not provided sufficient security.
- The person who has provided the security, whether he is the respondent or a third person, is possibly unable to fulfil all or part of his obligations under the security.
- Where, due to reasonable reasons, the maritime claimant has agreed to release the ship from the arrest or to return the security that had been provided, or could not prevent by way of reasonable measures the ship from being released or the security from being returned.

§7. Release of Ship from Arrest

730. A ship shall be released from the arrest under any of the following situations:

- The owners, charterers or operator of the ship under arrest or other person who is responsible for the maritime claim giving rise to the arrest has fulfilled his debt.
- The security demanded by the maritime claimant or decided by the maritime court that executed the arrest has been provided by or for the respondent (paragraph 1, Article 18, SMPL).
- Where the ship was arrested before litigation or arbitration, the maritime claimant failed to file a lawsuit with maritime court having jurisdiction over the maritime claim giving rise to the arrest or, where an arbitration agreement exists between the parties, failed to refer the dispute to arbitration, within thirty days from the date of execution of the arrest (paragraph 1, Article 28, paragraph 2, Article 18, SMPL).[68]
- The respondent has justifiable reasons for applying for the release of the ship from the arrest (paragraph 1, Article 18, SMPL).
- Other person or persons with interests raised objection to the arrest and the reasons for such objection are deemed as tenable by the maritime court that has executed the arrest (paragraph 3, Article 17, SMPL).

731. Noticeably, as regards the above fourth situation, the said justifiable reasons do not include the case in which the respondent provides evidence to the maritime court showing that he shall not be held responsible for the maritime claim giving rise to the arrest, because his responsibility can only be determined through litigation or arbitration, but shall include, *inter alia*, a case in which it is obvious

68. Where the maritime claimant files a lawsuit or refers to dispute to arbitration in accordance with arbitration agreement, or the arrest of ship is executed during litigation or arbitration as applied for, the arrest is not subject to the said time limit of thirty days (para. 2, Art. 28, SMPL).

that the application is wrongful, e.g., where the maritime claimant alleges in his application for the arrest that his claim is secured by maritime lien, but the ship under arrest is not the offending ship.

As the above fifth situation, a person with interests in most cases means the owners of the ship under arrest other than the respondent. Similarly, if it is obvious that the application for the arrest is wrongful based upon the reasons for his objection to the arrest that are supported by sufficient evidence provided by him, the maritime court shall release the ship from the arrest. For example, where the applicant alleges in his application for the arrest that the respondent is the owners of the ship and that its maritime claim arose from a voyage charter concluded between him and the respondent, a person other than the respondent proves he was the duly registered owners of the ship under arrest at the time of execution thereof and remains the registered owners, and thus his ship should not be arrested, then this reason for his objection shall be deemed as tenable by the maritime court, since a maritime claim arising from a voyage charter is commonly deemed as not secured by maritime lien under MC where it applies.

It seems the maritime court that executed the arrest may have a big discretion in determining whether these reasons for release of ship are tenable or not in the above fourth or fifth situation. However, it is sure that, if there is any doubt as to the tenability of the reasons that shall be finally determined through litigation or arbitration in the case of an existing arbitration agreement, the maritime court shall not order the release of the ship from arrest.

732. For the release of a ship from the arrest in any event, an award to this effect shall be made by the maritime court that executed the arrest and an order of release shall be issued by the president thereof. The two documents shall normally be served on the master of the ship under arrest. Execution thereof shall be done immediately. Where a notice of assistance in the execution of arrest has been sent to MSA and border control, the court shall notify them of the release.

§8. Remedies for Wrongful Arrest

I. Wrongful Arrest

733. By virtue of Article 20 of SMPL, where the application by the claimant for the maritime claim preservation including arrest of a ship before or during litigation proves wrongful, the claimant shall be liable for the losses suffered by the respondent or other persons with interests resulting therefrom. Similar provision is contained in Article 96 of CPC. However, Chinese law does not specify the conditions for the claimant's liability for losses resulting from wrongful application. Particularly, the law does not specify whether the liability is conditional upon the applicant's fault or intentional act in causing such losses.

In nature, the claimant's liability for the loss resulting from the wrongful application for the arrest of a ship is a tortuous liability. Thus, the provisions governing tortuous liability contained in Book Seven 'Tortuous Liability' of CC shall apply. Paragraph 1 of Article 1165 of CC provides: 'Any person who, through his own fault or intentional act, infringes on other people's civil rights and interests shall assume tortuous liability.' Thus, the claimant's liability for wrongful arrest is conditional upon the applicant's fault or intentional act in causing such losses.

Therefore, to constitute the claimant's liability for wrongful arrest of a ship, the following conditions shall be met:

- The application for arrest proves wrongful viz. the applicant does not have a maritime claim or his claim cannot give rise to the arrest of the ship.
- The respondent or other person with interests has suffered losses.
- The loss resulted directly from the applicant's wrongful application.
- The applicant had fault or intentional act in causing the wrongful application and the consequent losses.

In deciding whether the applicant had fault, it seems clear that, where he had prima facie evidence showing his application should be justified, the burden of proof showing wrongful application shall be on the party claiming such wrongful application.

II. Recoverable Losses

734. The recoverable losses shall include, *inter alia*, loss of use of the ship during the arrest, the expenses paid by the respondent or other person with interests during the arrest including the execution fees paid to the maritime court or the border control due on the respondent, and the liability of the respondent for third parties.

§9. Judicial Sale and Rules for Apportionment and Ranking

I. Conditions for Application for Judicial Sale by Auction

735. By virtue of Article 29 of SMPL, where a ship is arrested as applied for before litigation or arbitration, the maritime claimant can apply to the maritime court that executed the arrest for the sale by auction of the ship, provided that the following conditions are met:

- The period of arrest *viz.* thirty days from the date on which the arrested was executed has expired.
- No required security has been provided by or for the respondent.
- The ship is no longer suitable for further arrest.
- The claimant has filed a lawsuit with a maritime court having jurisdiction over the disputes giving rise to the arrest or referred the dispute to arbitration in accordance with arbitration agreement.

Where the arrest of ship was executed as applied for during litigation or arbitration, then the last condition for sale by auction shall be excluded.

In admiralty practice in China, the above third condition *viz.* unsuitability for further arrest is not strictly followed. In fact, where the other conditions are met, the sale by auction of the ship under arrest shall normally be granted by the maritime court as applied for.

II. Procedures of Sale by Auction

736. By virtue of section 2 of Chapter III of SMPL, the sale by auction of a ship under arrest shall adhere to the following procedures.

Where a ship is sold by auction for the compensation for debts in the procedure of enforcement of an effective judgment or arbitration award, reference shall be made to the procedures of the sale by auction (Article 43, SMPL).

A. Application and Security

737. The maritime claimant shall file with the maritime court that executed the arrest an application for the sale by auction of the ship under arrest. The application shall state that the reasons for the sale *viz.* the reasons stated *supra* are met.

Normally, where an effective judgment or arbitration award in favour of the claimant has not been delivered when it applies for the sale, the court shall order the claimant to provide a reliable and sufficient security in order to ensure the compensation for losses that the respondent or other persons with interests may possibly suffer if the sale proves wrongful later, if the counter-security for the arrest of the ship previously provided by or for the claimant does not sufficiently cover such a possible liability.

It occasionally occurs that after filing of the application, the claimant applies for discontinuance of the procedures of sale, regardless of whether an award granting the sale by the court has been made by the maritime court or not. In such a case, it is up to the maritime court to make an award whether discontinuance as applied for shall be granted or rejected. Where discontinuance is granted, the expenses already occurred in the preparation for the sale, if any, shall be borne by the claimant (Article 31, SMPL).

B. Acceptance of Application and Award for Sale by Auction

738. After the receipt of the application for the sale by auction of a ship under arrest, the maritime court shall make an award after examination of the application, either granting the sale where the conditions for such a sale are met or rejecting it where such conditions are not met. The award shall be served on the claimant and the respondent. The service on the respondent can be effected by service thereof on the master on board the ship under arrest.

Where any party has objection to the award, he may apply to the court for reconsideration within five days after the receipt thereof. The court shall make a decision of reconsideration within five days after the receipt of the application. During the period of reconsideration, the execution of the award shall be discontinued (paragraph 2, Article 30, SMPL).

C. *Notice of Sale by Auction*

739. Where the sale by auction of a ship under arrest is granted, the maritime court shall release a public notice thereof via newspapers or other new media not less than thirty days in advance (Article 32, SMPL). In the case of a foreign ship, such a notice shall be released via newspapers or other new media that are available abroad, e.g., the English newspaper of China Daily or the overseas version of People's Daily.

The public notice shall include the following contents:

- the name and nationality of the ship to be sold by auction;
- the reasons and grounds of law for the sale by auction;
- the organization of the auction committee;
- the time and place of sale by auction;
- the time and place of the exhibition of the ship to be sold by auction;
- the formalities required for participation in the sale by auction;
- the items relating to the registration of claims;
- other items that need be notified.

740. Meanwhile, the maritime court shall, thirty days before the sale by auction, notify the registration authority of the ship to be sold by auction, the claimants whose claims are secured by maritime liens, the mortgagee and owners of the ship who are known to the maritime court in writing or in such other appropriate manners to enable the court to confirm the receipt of the notice. The contents of notification shall include the name and nationality of the ship to be sold by auction, the reasons and grounds of law for the sale and the items relating to the registration of claims (Article 33, SMPL).

D. *Organization and Functions of Auction Committee*

741. The auction committee shall consist of court martial(s), registered auctioneer(s) and ship surveyor(s) designated by the maritime court in the total number of either three or five. The committee is responsible to and under the supervision of the maritime court. Its functions include:

- organizing the survey and evaluation of the ship to be sold by auction;
- accepting the registration of bidders;
- exhibiting the ship to be sold and providing the technical and other related materials for access by the bidders;
- organizing and presiding the auction;
- signing the fixture note of auction with the final buyer;
- going through the formalities of transfer of the ship after auction;

E. Conditions of Bidders

742. A bidder can be an individual person, an enterprise or other entity. A bidder shall enter registration during the stipulated period of time with the auction committee by submitting the certificate of identity of himself or of the legal representative of enterprise or other entity as well as the power of attorney in the case an attorney is appointed. A bidder shall pay a deposit at a certain figure as required by the auction committee (Article 35, SMPL).

F. Auction

743. Sale by auction shall be held in a public way in accordance with AUL in the presence of a notary public who shall supervise and notarize the auction. The bidder who offers the highest price shall be the purchaser and new owners of the ship. Nowadays, the sale of ship by auction often takes place on an internet platform entrusted by the auction committee.

Where two or more bidders collude maliciously with each other, the auction will be invalidated and they shall bear both civil liability and disciplinary liability. That is, the bidders shall bear the expenses occurred in the auction and compensate for the losses resulting therefrom and be imposed of a fine not less than 10%, but not exceeding 30%, of the highest price offered (Article 41, SMPL).

G. Delivery of Ship and Re-registration of Ownership

744. Having signed the fixture note of auction, the purchaser of the ship shall pay to the bank account nominated by the maritime court an amount of not less than 20% of the ship's sale price immediately and the rest of the price within seven days, unless otherwise agreed upon between the auction committee and the purchaser (Article 37, SMPL).

After the purchaser has paid the ship's price in full, the original shipowners shall deliver the ship to the purchaser within the period of time designated by the court in the place where the ship is lying in her *status quo*. The auction committee shall organize and supervise the delivery of the ship and shall issue the letter of confirmation of delivery of ship (paragraph 1, Article 38, SMPL).

Having taken delivery of the ship, the purchaser shall go through the registration of ship's ownership with the ship registration authority by submission of the letter of confirmation of delivery of ship and other documents. Meanwhile, the original shipowners shall go through the registration of cancellation of ship's ownership with her original registration authority. Where the original shipowners fail to go through such registration, the transfer of ownership of the ship shall not be affected (Article 40, SMPL). In such a case, MSA may register the ship based upon the application of the purchaser of the ship, the letter of confirmation of delivery of ship issued by the auction committee and other required documents for the new registration of ship's ownership and nationality.

H. Release of Ship and Public Notice

745. After delivery of the ship, the maritime court shall issue an order of release of the ship from the arrest (paragraph 2, Article 38, SMPL). Meanwhile, the court shall make public notice via newspaper or other news media indicating that the ship has been sold by auction and delivered to the purchaser (Article 39, SMPL).

III. Rules for Apportionment and Ranking

746. As introduced in §2 of Chapter 2 of Part II *supra*, in the distribution of proceeds of sale by auction of a ship defined in Article 3 of MC among the registered claimants, the general ranking of compensation shall be in the order of the legal costs and expenses referred to in Article 24 of MC, claims secured maritime lien, claims secured by possessory lien, claims secured by ship mortgage and other maritime claims.

Where two or more claims are secured by maritime lien, the ranking thereof shall be determined in accordance with Article 23 of MC. If there are two or more ship mortgages, the ranking thereof shall be determined in accordance with the dates of their respective registration as provided for in Article 19 of MC. Other claims shall be compensated for in proportion to their respective amounts.

747. In the case of a ship excluded from the scope of the ship defined in Article 3 of MC, also as introduced in §2 of Chapter 2 of Part II *supra*, in the distribution of proceeds of sale by auction of a ship among the registered claimants, the general ranking of compensation shall be in the order of the legal costs for enforcing the claim or claims and the expenses for preserving and selling the ship, the expenses for distribution of the proceeds of sale and other expenses incurred for the common interests of the claimants, claims secured by possessory lien, claims secured by ship mortgage and other claims.

If there are two or more claims secured by ship mortgage, the ranking thereof shall be determined in accordance with the time of their respective registration. If the mortgages registered at the same time, they shall be compensated for equally in proportion to their respectively amounts. Where one mortgage is registered and the other or others are not, the registered mortgage shall have priority over the one not registered, or, where both mortgages are not registered, they shall be compensated for equally in proportion to their respectively amounts, as provided for in Article 414 of CC. Other claims without security of mortgage or possessory lien shall rank equally in compensation and be compensated for in proportion to their respective amounts.

Chapter 15. Carriage of Passengers

§1. Introduction

I. Contract of Carriage of Passenger by Sea

748. Like the carriage of goods by sea, carriage of passenger by sea is based upon a contract *viz.* the contract of carriage of passenger by sea concluded by the carrier and the passenger which is defined in Article 107 of MC as 'a contract whereby the carrier undertakes to carry passenger and his or her luggage by sea from one port to another by a ship suitable for that purpose against the payment of fare by the passenger'.

749. The carrier and the passenger are the two parties to a contract of carriage of passenger by sea. As defined in Article 108 of MC, the carrier means 'the person by whom or in whose name a contract of carriage of passenger by sea has been entered into with the passenger' and the passenger means 'the person carried under a contract of carriage of passenger by sea' including 'a person supervising the carriage of goods aboard a ship covered by a contract of carriage of goods by sea with the consent of the carrier'.

750. The carriage of passenger's luggage is covered by a contract of carriage of passenger by sea.

Luggage means 'any article or vehicle carried by the carrier under the contract of carriage of passenger by sea, with the exception of live animal' (Article 108, MC). Luggage include cabin luggage and luggage other cabin luggage. Cabin luggage is defined as 'the luggage which the passenger has in his cabin or is otherwise in his possession, custody or control' (Article 108, MC). Luggage other than cabin luggage as termed in MC is also called 'checked luggage' in practice and is the luggage which the passenger hands over to the carrier or passenger transport terminal acting for the carrier, is loaded on board the ship by the carrier or the transport terminal, in the custody of the carrier during carriage by sea, discharged by the carrier or the transport terminal and taken delivery by the passenger at the port of disembarkation. A passenger is allowed to carry cabin luggage with a certain limit of weight free of charge. Where the weight of a passenger's luggage exceeds the limit, the excess luggage shall be the checked luggage and the passenger shall pay the fees of carriage thereof.

II. Passenger Ticket

751. A passenger ticket sold by the carrier, the passenger transport terminal or other agent of the carrier serves as an evidence that a contract of carriage of passenger by sea has been entered into (Article 110, MC). A contract of carriage of passenger by sea is concluded upon the delivery of the passenger ticket to the passenger by the carrier or his agent, unless the parties have agreed otherwise or there exists a practice to the contrary (Article 814, CC).

A passenger ticket used in domestic carriage normally contains, *inter alia*, the name of carrier, date and time and port of embarkation, port of disembarkation, cabin class and fare. Besides these items, a passenger ticked used in international carriage in China also contains the name of passenger, date of arrival at the port of disembarkation, conditions of carriage or information to the passengers, and application of law. A named passenger ticked is not transferable and can be used only by the named passenger, while an unnamed passenger ticket is transferable.

§2. Applicable Laws

I. International Treaties

752. As introduced in Chapter 2 of Part I *supra*, China has acceded to 1974 PAL and its SDR Protocol of 1976. Reservation was made on its application of the carrier's limitation of liability for loss of or personal injury to passengers and loss of or damage to luggage to the carriage by sea between the Chinese ports. China has not ratified the Protocol of 1990 to 1974 PAL or the Protocol of 2002 to 1974 PAL signed at London on 1 November 2002. Noticeably, 1974 PAL as amended by its Protocol of 2002 is called as 2002 PAL.

II. National Laws

753. Chapter V 'Contract of Carriage of Passenger by Sea' of MC which is basically a reproduction of 1974 PAL as amended by its SDR Protocol of 1976 governs the carriage of goods by sea, either international or domestic.

Besides, as introduced in Chapter 2 of Part I *supra*, the following statutes are also applicable to domestic carriage of passenger by sea:

- the *Regulations Governing Transport of Passengers by Waterways of 1995* as latest amended 2 January 2014;
- the *Provisions regarding the Limitation of Liability in the Carriage of Passengers between the Ports of the People's Republic of China of 1993*.

Section 1 'General Provisions' and section 2 'Contract of Carriage of Passengers' of Chapter XIX 'Contracts of Carriage' of Book Three 'Contracts' as basic law also apply to carriage of passengers of sea, both international and domestic, provided that the provisions are not repugnant to those of 1974 PAL as amended by its SDR Protocol of 1976 in the international carriage of passengers, Chapter V of MC and the *Provisions regarding the Limitation of Liability in the Carriage of Passengers between the Ports of the People's Republic of China* in both the international and domestic carriage of passengers.

754. The provisions of law regarding the carriage of passengers by sea are basically applicable compulsorily in order to protect the interests of the passengers. By virtue of Article 126 of MC, any of the following clauses contained in a contract of carriage of passenger by sea shall be null and void:

- a clause that exonerates the statutory responsibilities of the carrier with respect to the passenger;
- a clause that reduces the limitation of liability of the carrier as contained in Chapter V of MC;
- a clause that contains provisions contrary to those of Chapter V of MC concerning burden of proof;
- a clause that restricts the right of claim of the passenger.

§3. Obligations of Passenger

I. Payment of Fare and Holding Passenger Ticket

755. The passenger shall pay the fare and hold a valid ticket on boarding. A passenger ticket may be in an electronic form. Normally, a passenger may board the ship upon production of his or her identity card in the domestic carriage.

The fares or the margins of fares in the domestic carriage of passengers by sea in China may be fixed by the governmental organs and are thus not fully negotiable by the carriers and passengers. In other words, the carrier can fix the fares only within the stipulated margin.

Unless with the consent of the carrier, where a passenger travels without a ticket or with an invalid ticket, takes a higher class berth than booked or goes beyond the distance paid for, he or she shall pay for the fare or the excess fare as required. In addition, the carrier may charge an additional fare. Should any passenger refuse to pay, the carrier may refuse to carry the passenger or, if the passenger has already embarked, the master of the carrying ship is entitled to order the passenger to disembark at a suitable place and the carrier has the right of recourse against the passenger (Article 112, MC; Article 815, CC).

II. Not Taking Contraband or Dangerous Goods

756. As prohibited in Article 113 of MC and Article 818 of CC, no passenger may take on board as cabin luggage or pack in the checked luggage any contraband or any article of an inflammable, explosive, poisonous, corrosive or radioactive nature or other dangerous goods that would endanger the safety of life and property onboard. In the case of violation by a passenger, the carrier may refuse to carry, or if the passenger has already taken them on board or packed in the checked luggage, the carrier may have the contraband or dangerous goods discharged, destroyed or rendered innocuous at any time and at any place or sent over to appropriate authority without any liability for compensation. The passenger shall compensate for any loss or damage occurred as a result of his or her violation.

III. Notification of Loss of or Damage to Luggage

757. In the case of apparent damage to the luggage, the passenger shall notify the carrier or his servant or agent in writing of damage to the cabin luggage at the time of embarkation, or of damage to the checked luggage before or at the time of redelivery thereof, unless the damage has been jointly surveyed or inspected by the carrier and the passenger at the time of redelivery thereof in which case no notice is needed. Where the damage to the luggage is not apparent and is difficult for the passenger to discover at the time of disembarkation or of the redelivery thereof, or if the luggage is lost, the passenger shall notify the carrier or his servant or agent in writing within fifteen days from the next day of disembarkation of the passenger or of the redelivery of the luggage (Article 119, MC).

Where the passenger fails to send the notice as so required, it shall be presumed that the luggage has been received by the passenger undamaged, unless proof to the contrary is provided by the passenger.

§4. Obligations and Limitation of Liability of Carrier

I. Obligations of Carrier

758. As provided for in Chapter XIX of Book Three of CC, the carrier under a contract of carriage of passenger by sea has the following obligations:

- the carrier engaged in the public transport of passengers shall not refuse the ordinary or reasonable demand of transport of the passenger (Article 810, CC);
- the carrier shall strictly fulfil the obligations of safety carriage and timely inform the passenger of the precautions for safety carriage (Article 819, CC);
- the carrier shall begin the voyage at the time as indicated in the passenger ticket, carry the passenger to the agreed port of disembarkation within the agreed or reasonable time on the agreed or customary route (Articles 811, 812 and 810, CC); if there is any delay in the beginning of the voyage, the passenger is entitled to change the voyage or demand for repayment of fare;
- where the carrier changes the carrying ship at his own will and as a result the service standard is decreased, the carrier shall refund the fare as the passenger requires or reduce the fare; where the service standard is increased by the change of the carrying ship, the carrier is not entitled to increase the fare (Article 821, CC);
- in case of the passenger's emergent illness, childbirth or distress during carriage, the carrier shall render his utmost assistance (Article 822, CC).

II. Liability of Carrier

A. *Period of Carriage of Passenger or Luggage*

759. As provided for in Article 111 of MC, the period of carriage of passenger by sea commences from the time of embarkation of the passenger and terminates at the time of his disembarkation, including the period during which the passenger is carried by water from land to the ship or *vice versa*, if the cost of such carriage is included in the fare. However, the period of carriage does not include the time when the passenger is at a terminal or station or on a quay or in or on any other port installations. These excluded periods of carriage shall be the period of responsibility of the passenger transport terminal or port operator who shall be responsible by virtue of relevant law or regulations.

The period of carriage of passenger's cabin luggage shall be the same as that of the passenger. The period of carriage of passenger's checked luggage commences from the time when the carrier, his servant or agent receives it into his charge and terminates at the time when the carrier, his servant or agent redelivers it to the passenger.

B. *Liability for Death of or Personal Injury to Passenger or Loss or Damage to Luggage*

760. The carrier shall be liable for the death of or personal injury to the passenger or the loss of or damage to his or her luggage resulting from an accident occurred during the period of carriage as provided for in Article 111 of MC and caused by the fault of the carrier or his servant or agent committed within the scope of employment or agency (Article 114, MC).[69]

Therefore, unlike the case of international carriage of goods by sea as provided for in Article 51 of MC, the carrier cannot avail of the nautical fault, i.e., the fault of the master, other crewmembers, pilot or other servants of the carrier in the navigation or management of the ship. On the other hand, where the death of or personal injury to passenger or loss or damage to the passenger's luggage is not caused by any fault or intentional act or omission committed by the carrier or his servants or agents within the scope of employment or agency, the carrier shall not be held liable.

761. The provisions concerning burden of proof regarding the fault of the carrier or his servants or agents are complicated. In this regard, Article 114 of MC stipulates as follows:

- if the death of or personal injury to a passenger or loss of or damage to the passenger's cabin luggage occurred as a result of shipwreck, collision, stranding,

69. Death of a passenger covers the death of passenger occurred after his or her disembarkation, i.e., after termination of the period of carriage, but resulted from personal injury occurred during the period of carriage.

explosion, fire or defect of the ship, it shall be presumed that the carrier or his servants or agents have committed contributory fault, unless proof to the contrary has been given by the carrier or his servants or agents, i.e., in the case of ship's maritime accident, the rule of presumption of fault shall apply;
- as to any loss of or damage to the passenger's checked luggage, unless the carrier or his servants or agents proves to the contrary, it shall be presumed that the carrier or his servants or agents have committed contributory fault, no matter how the loss or damage was caused, i.e., the rule of presumption of fault shall also apply to the loss of or damage to the checked luggage;
- in other cases, the claimant shall bear the burden of proof regarding the fault of the carrier or his servants or agents.

C. *Exonerations of Liability*

762. By virtue of paragraph 1 of Article 115 of MC, where the carrier proves that the death of or personal injury to a passenger or the loss or damage to his or her luggage was caused by the fault of the passenger or the faults of the carrier and of the passenger jointly, the carrier's liability may be exonerated or appropriately mitigated. Paragraph 2 of this Article further provides that where the carrier proves that the death of or personal injury to a passenger or the loss or damage to his luggage was intentionally caused by the passenger, or the death or personal injury was due to his or her health condition, the carrier shall not be liable therefor. Clearly, two words are used in this Article *viz.* 'may' in paragraph 1 and 'shall' in paragraph 2. However, it seems the two words have the same meaning in favour of the carrier.

Noticeably, 1974 PAL leaves the question whether the carrier shall be liable for the death of or personal injury to the passenger or the loss of or damage to his luggage caused by the passenger's own fault or negligence to the solved by national legislation.[70] The above provision of paragraph 1 of Article 115 of MC provides an answer to this question.

In combination with the provisions of Article 114 of MC as stated *supra* by which the carrier shall be liable for the death of or personal injury to a passenger or loss of or damage to his luggage caused by fault of the carrier or his servants or agents, the regime of the carrier's liability under a contract of carriage of passenger by sea is the so-called complete fault liability.

763. Noticeably, Article 823 of CC provides that the carrier shall be liable for the death of or personal injury to a passenger occurred during carriage, unless the death or personal injury was caused by the passenger's health condition or the carrier proves that the death or personal injury was intentionally caused by the passenger or caused by the passenger's gross negligence. In other words, where the death

70. Article 6 of the *1974 PAL* provides: 'If the carrier proves that the death of or personal injury to a passenger or the loss of or damage to his luggage was caused or contributed to by the fault or neglect of the passenger, the court seized of the case may exonerate the carrier wholly or partly from his liability in accordance with the provisions of the law of that court.'

of or personal injury to a passenger was caused by the passenger's slight negligence, the carrier shall still be liable therefor. However, this liability rule does not apply to carriage of passenger by sea, because Article 823 of CC as the provisions of basic law is repugnant to the provisions of Article 115 of MC and thus the latter have priority, but shall apply to the carriage of passengers in inland navigation. For the same reason, the liability rule as regards the checked luggage adopted by Article 824 of CC does not apply to the carriage of passengers by sea either.[71]

764. The carrier shall not be liable for any loss of or damage to the monies, gold, silver, negotiable securities or other valuables of a passenger, unless the passenger has entrusted the carrier for their safe-keeping as agreed in which case the carrier can avail of his limitation of liability for loss of or damage to the checked luggage as stated *infra*, unless a higher limitation of liability has been agreed upon between the carrier and the passenger (Article 116, MC).

III. Limitation of Liability of Carrier

A. International Carriage by Sea

765. By virtue of paragraph 1 of Article 117 of MC, under a contract of international carriage of passenger, the limitation of liability of the carrier under each carriage of a passenger by sea is as follows:

- for death of or personal injury to the passenger, 46,666 SDR per passenger;
- for loss of or damage to the passenger's cabin luggage, 833 SDR per passenger;
- for loss of or damage to the passenger's vehicles including the luggage carried therein, 3,333 SDR per vehicle;
- for loss of or damage to other luggage, 1,200 SDR per passenger.

A higher limitation of liability than that set out in paragraph 1 of this Article may be agreed upon between the carrier and a passenger (paragraph 3, Article 117).

766. The carrier and a passenger may negotiate deductibles applicable to the compensation for loss of or damage to the passenger's luggage and, as a result, the agreed deductibles shall be deducted from the amount of compensation. However, the deductible with respect to the loss of or damage to the passenger's vehicles shall not exceed 117 SDR per vehicle and that with respect to the loss of or damage to other luggage shall not exceed 13 SDR per piece of luggage per passenger (paragraph 2, Article 117).

71. For details as to the provisions of Arts 823 and 824 of CC, *see* Ch. 3 of Part III.

B. Domestic Carriage by Sea

767. By virtue of paragraph 4 of Article 117 of MC, the limitation of liability of the carrier with respect to carriage of passengers by sea between the Chinese ports shall be fixed by the competent authority of transport and communications under the State Council and implemented after its being submitted to and approved by the State Council.

By virtue of this statutory provision, the *Provisions regarding the Limitation of Liability in the Carriage of Passengers between the Ports of the People's Republic of China* were adopted by the former Ministry of Communications (now MOT) and approved by the State Council and came into force as of 1 January 1994.

768. As provided for in paragraph 1 of Article 3 of this by-law, under a contract of domestic carriage of passenger between the Chinese ports, the limitation of liability of the carrier under each carriage of a passenger by sea is as follows:

- for death of or personal injury to the passenger, CNY 40,000 per passenger;
- for loss of or damage to the passenger's cabin luggage, CNY 800 per passenger;
- for loss of or damage to the passenger's vehicles including the luggage carried therein, CNY 3,200 per vehicle;
- for loss of or damage to other luggage, CNY 20 per kilogram thereof.

A higher limitation of liability than that set out in paragraph 1 of this Article may be agreed upon between the carrier and the passenger (paragraph 2, Article 3).

769. Currently, the limit of liability for death of or personal injury per passenger, i.e., CNY 40,000 is about USD 5,500, i.e., only about one-tenth of the limit applicable to international carriage as provided for in paragraph 1 of Article 117 of MC, let alone the latter is also low. The disaster of capsize of M/V. 'Da Shun' in Bohai Sea Strait in bad weather in 2,000 causing deaths of more than three hundred passengers proved the limit of CNY 40,000 was extremely too low. In that case, the compensation for loss of each life was settled by negotiation at a much higher figure. The limits of liability for the loss of or damage to luggage prove also too low. Expectedly, the limits applicable to the domestic carriage of passengers by sea shall be significantly increased when MC is revised in the near future.

IV. Loss of the Right to Limit

770. By virtue of paragraph 1 of Article 118 of MC, if it proves that the death of or personal injury to a passenger or the loss of or damage to his luggage resulted from an act or omission of the carrier done with the intent to cause such death or personal injury or loss or damage or recklessly and with knowledge that such death or personal injury or loss or damage would probably result, the carrier shall not invoke limitation of liability provided for in Articles 116 &117 or in the *Provisions regarding the Limitation of Liability in the Carriage of Passengers between the Ports of the People's Republic of China of 1994.*

§5. NON-CONTRACTUAL CLAIMS

I. Non-contractual Claims Against Carrier

771. As analysed in Chapter 6 of Part II *supra*, Article 186 of CC adopted the principle of competition between contractual claim and claim in tort by which where breach of contract by a party to contract caused loss of life or personal injury, or loss of or damage to property, the party who has suffered the loss or damage is entitled to require at his choice the offending party to bear liability for breach of contract or tortuous liability. This principle shall apply to a contract of carriage of passenger by sea.

772. Noticeably, unlike Chapter IV of MC with respect to a contract of carriage of goods by sea, Chapter V of MC does not contain express provisions to the effect that the immunities and limitation of liability and other defences available to the carrier under Chapter V shall apply to any legal action brought against him in respect of the death of or personal injury to a passenger or the loss of or damage to the passenger's luggage covered by the contract of carriage of passenger by sea, whether the claimant is a party to the contract or not, or whether the action is founded in contract or in tort. However, it is understandable that such a rule shall be implied under a contract of carriage of passenger by sea in consideration of the provisions of the whole Chapter, especially Article 124 stipulating that, with respect to the death of or personal injury to a passenger or the loss of or damage to the passenger's luggage, the aggregate of the amounts recoverable from the carrier, the actual carrier and their servants and agents shall not exceed the limits of liability provided for in Article 117 of MC.

II. Carrier's Servant or Agent

773. By virtue of Article 120 of MC, the immunities and limitation of liability and other defences available to the carrier under Articles 115, 116 and 117 of MC shall also apply if an action is brought against the carrier's servant or agent, provided that the defendant proves that his act or omission was within the scope of his employment or agency. Obviously, this statutory provision is a reflection of the Himalaya clause.

Where it proves that the death of or personal injury to a passenger or the loss of or damage to his luggage resulted from an act or omission of the carrier's servant or agent done with the intent to cause such death or personal injury or loss or damage or recklessly and with knowledge that such death of or personal injury or loss or damage would probably result, the carrier's servant or agent shall not invoke limitation of liability provided for in Articles 116 and 117 or in the *Provisions regarding the Limitation of Liability in the Carriage of Passengers between the Ports of the People's Republic of China of 1994* (paragraph 2, Article 118, MC).

774. As analysed in Chapter 5 of Part II *supra*, in principle, where a servant or agent proves that his act was within the scope of his employment or agency, the claimant cannot raise a claim against him for the loss or damage caused by such an act or omission, but can only claim against his employer or principal under Chinese law.

III. Actual Carrier and His Servant or Agent

775. The provisions contained in Chapter V of MC concerning the actual carrier under a contract of carriage of passenger by sea are quite similar to those contained in Chapter IV of MC governing the actual carrier under a contract of carriage of goods by sea.

An actual carrier is defined in Article 108 of MC as 'the person to whom the performance of carriage of passenger, or part of the carriage, has been entrusted by the carrier, and includes any other person to whom such performance has been entrusted under a sub-contract'.

Noticeably, the corresponding term contained in 1974 PAL is 'performing carrier'. The reason of using the term of actual carrier under a contract of carriage of passenger by sea in Chapter V of MC is to be identical with the case of carriage of goods by sea. However, there is no substantial difference in meaning between the actual carrier contained in Chapter V of MC and the performing carrier contained in 1974 PAL.

776. The carrier is at liberty to entrust the performance of a contract of carriage of passenger or part thereof to an actual carrier, unless the contract provides to the contrary. Where so entrusted, the carrier remains responsible for the entire carriage performed by the actual carrier and for the acts or omissions of the actual carrier and of his servants and agents acting within the scope of their employment or agency (Article 111, MC).

The actual carrier shall be responsible for the death of or personal injury to a passenger or the loss of or damage to his luggage caused by an occurrence which takes place during the actual carrier's performance of the carriage. All the provisions governing the responsibility of the carrier also apply to the responsibility of the actual carrier for the carriage performed by him (Article 109, MC). However, a special agreement concluded between the carrier and a passenger, if any, under which the carrier assumes obligations not imposed by MC or waives rights conferred by MC shall be binding upon the actual carrier only where the actual carrier has expressly agreed in writing to the contents thereof. On the other hand, the carrier nevertheless remains bound by the obligations or waivers resulting from such special agreement, whether or not the actual carrier has so agreed (Article 122, MC).

Where and to the extent that both the carrier and the actual carrier are liable, i.e., where the actual carrier is liable due to the fault of him, his servants or agents by virtue of Articles 109 and 117 of MC, then their liability is joint and several (Article 123, MC). However, any right of recourse as between the carrier and the actual carrier shall not be prejudiced (Article 125, MC).

777. By virtue of Article 109 of MC, the provisions governing the carrier's servants or agents shall apply to the servants or agents of the actual carrier. Therefore, the servants or agents of the actual carrier have the same legal status as the servants or agents of the carrier, as stated *supra*.

778. With respect to the death of or personal injury of a passenger or the loss of or damage to his luggage, the aggregate of the amounts recoverable from the carrier, actual carrier and their servants and agents shall not exceed the limits of liability provided for in Article 117 of MC (Article 124, MC), unless anyone of them loses his right to limit liability by virtue of Article 118 of MC.

Part III. Other Transport

Chapter 1. Transport by Road

§1. Applicable Laws

779. The HL, other laws and regulations applicable to road transport in China are referred to in §2 of Chapter 2 of Part I *supra*. Noticeably, HL does not govern the matters in the nature of civil law and there is no special law governing such matters regarding carriage of passengers and goods by road. Instead, the law governing such matters in this regard is mainly CC.

§2. Carriage of Passengers by Road

I. Passenger Ticket

A. *Functions of Passenger Ticket*

780. A passenger ticket is an evidence of a contract of carriage of passenger by road. A contract of carriage is concluded when the carrier or other person on his behalf delivers the ticket to a passenger, unless otherwise agreed upon between the carrier and the passenger or there is practice to the contrary (Article 814, CC). Based upon passenger ticket, a passenger travels by road.

By virtue of Article 815 of CC, a passenger shall travel by road by holding a valid passenger ticket. A passenger who travels without a ticket or with an invalid one shall pay the fare for a ticket and an additional fare in accordance with regulations. If the said passenger refuses to pay, the carrier may refuse to carry him or order him to get off the vehicle.

The passenger shall produce a valid passenger ticket for check on entering or leaving a road station, or on boarding a vehicle or thereon on demand. Nowadays, a passenger may produce his identity card instead of a passenger ticket or have his identity card scanned on the check-in gate of a road station.

B. *Contents of Passenger Ticket*

781. A passenger ticket shall be in the form formulated by the road transport authorities and contain the name of station or other place of boarding and destination, class of seat, fare, vehicle number, date and time of boarding. Normally, the name of passenger is also indicated in the ticket.

C. Validity of Passenger Ticket

782. A passenger ticket is valid only for the date and vehicle number indicated therein. Where a passenger stops traveling during the journey, the ticket shall become invalid. However, where the passenger stops traveling due to his health condition, the fare for the remaining journey can be refunded upon production of proof of his health condition.

D. Change of Vehicle or Getting Refund for Passenger Ticket

783. Where a passenger is unable to travel in accordance with the vehicle number, date or time of boarding, he may demands the change of vehicle number, date or time of boarding at a time not later than two hours before the time of departure.

In the case of cancellation of the vehicle or delay in departure, the carrier is obliged to make rearrangement for the passenger to travel on another vehicle to the same destination as demanded. If the carrier changes the vehicle on his own will and, as a result, the service standard becomes lower, the carrier shall refund the balance to the passenger; where the service standard becomes higher, the passenger shall not pay for the balance or additional fare (Article 821, CC).

784. Where a passenger is unable to continue his journey due to the reasons of the carrier, the ticket fare shall be refunded for the remaining journey without payment of commission, or the carrier shall carry the passenger back to the place of departure gratuitously and refund the fare for the whole journey to the passenger, if the passenger so demands.

II. Basic Obligations of Passenger and Carrier

A. Basic Obligations of Passenger

785. Besides the payment of the fare and boarding the vehicle as indicated in the passenger ticket, the passenger shall be bound by the provisions regarding safety, public order and health during journey.

So far as the fares are concerned, an adult passenger may carry a child of less than 6 years old or 1.2 meters' height free of charge. A child of 6 to 14 years old or 1.2 to 1.5 meters' height may have half-price discount.

B. Basic Obligations of Carrier

786. A carrier engaged in public transport of passengers cannot refuse the reasonable or normal demand for carriage of a passenger (Article 810, CC).

The carrier shall provide a vehicle in good technical condition and in conformity with the class indicated in the passenger ticket.

The carrier shall carry the passengers in accordance with the date, time and vehicle number and carry their baggage to the destination safely within the agreed, stipulated or reasonable time on the agreed or normal route. Where the carrier fails to carry on the agreed or normal route resulting increased fare or transport expenses, the passenger may refuse to pay the increased fare or transport expenses. (Articles 811 and 812, CC).

The carrier shall strictly fulfil the obligation of safety transport and timely inform passengers of the safety precautions (Article 819, CC).

The carrier shall carry a passengers in accordance with the time of departure, vehicle number and seat number indicated on the valid passenger ticket. In the case of delay in carriage or other circumstance under which normal carriage cannot be performed, the carrier shall inform the passenger and make necessary resettlement arrangements, and, where a passenger demands, arrange the passenger to switch to another vehicle number or refund the fare. The carrier shall be liable for the loss suffered by the passenger, unless the loss is not attributable to the carrier (Article 820, CC).

The carrier shall endeavour to assist a passenger in emergent illness, distress or giving childbirth (Article 822, CC).

III. Tariff

787. The calculation and collection of fares and miscellaneous fees for the carriage of passengers, their baggage and parcels as well as goods are governed by the *Law on Pricing* adopted 29 December 1997 by NPC. By virtue of this Law, there are three kinds of prices *viz*. the prices determined by the local governmental authority, the government-guided prices and the market prices. Now, the prices determined by the local governmental authorities are not applicable to the road transport, except the bus services in the cities. The road passenger transport and the road transport of goods under the State mandatory planning are subject to the government-guided prices by which the road transport companies may formulate tariff or negotiate tariff with the passengers or consignors following the basic tariff fixed and within the margins allowed or not exceeding the upper limit fixed by the local governmental authority. In other aspects of road transport of goods, the market prices are applicable and therefore the road transport companies are free to formulate tariff or negotiate tariff with the consignors. The tariffs formulated following the government-guided prices shall be publicized by the road transport companies by virtue of the *Law on Pricing*.

IV. Carriage of Carry-on Articles

788. The carry-on articles of a passenger are excluded from the scope of baggage and are carried under a contract of carriage of passenger by road. They are in the custody of passengers during the journey.

The weight of carry-on articles of a passenger is normally limited as publicized by a road passenger transport company. Within this limit, the carry-on articles are carried by the carrier gratuitously. The carry-on articles in excess of the limit shall be carried as baggage *viz.* checked baggage.

The measurement of a carry-on article shall not exceed the limit as publicized by a road passenger transport company.

789. In order to ensure safety, the passengers shall not carry or put in his carry-on articles, baggage inflammable, explosive, corrosive, radioactive and other dangerous goods which may endanger the life and property on board the vehicle or contrabands. Where a passenger carries or put in his carry-on articles, baggage any of these goods, the carrier is entitled to discharge, destroy or deliver it to the authority concerned, or to refuse to carry if the passenger insists to do so (Article 818, CC).

§3. Carriage of Baggage or Parcel by Road

I. Baggage or Parcel Check

A. *Functions of Baggage or Parcel Check*

790. The carrier or road transport station shall issue a baggage or parcel check after taking over the baggage or parcel from a passenger or a consignor other than a passenger.

A baggage or parcel check is an evidence of the contract of carriage of baggage or parcel by road.

B. *Contents of Baggage or Parcel Check*

791. A baggage or parcel check normally contains: (a) name of station of departure and destination; (b) name, address of the consignor and consignee in the case of a parcel; (c) freight; (d) date of commencement of carriage and deadline of arrival at destination; (e) number of packages and weight.

II. Taking Over of Baggage or Parcel by Carrier

792. A passenger or consignor shall deliver the baggage to the carrier for transport upon production of a valid passenger ticket.

Baggage or parcels shall be properly packed, secured and distinctly marked and suitable for transport. The articles such as confidential documents, valuables, fragile articles, articles that may cause pollution, ammunition, precise instruments, negotiable securities shall be in the custody of passengers during carriage.

III. Delivery of Baggage or Parcel by Carrier

793. The carrier shall carry the baggage to the destination at the same time of arrival of the passengers, unless otherwise agreed upon between the carrier and the passenger.

On arrival of a parcel at destination, the carrier shall notify the consignee thereof in time or make public notice thereof.

The passenger or consignee shall take delivery of baggage or parcel in time on the production of baggage or parcel check and shall pay storage expenses in the case of delay in taking delivery thereof after expiry of the free custody period.

IV. Tariff

794. As mentioned in §2 *supra*, the expenses and miscellaneous fees for the carriage of baggage, parcels by road are subject to the government-guided prices. The tariff shall be publicized by the road transport companies by virtue of the *Law on Pricing*.

§4. Carriage of Goods by Road

I. Concepts and Definitions

795. The following concepts and definitions are concerned in the carriage of goods by road:

- Carrier means a road transport operator who has concluded a contract of carriage of goods by road with the consignor.
- Consignor means a person who has concluded a contract of carriage of goods by road with the carrier.
- Consignee means a person designated by the consignor in the contract of carriage of goods by road to take delivery thereof.
- Terminal operator means an operator of road transport station, warehousing, storage, packing, loading and discharging, handling of goods within a designated area.
- Deadline of carriage of goods means a specific time agreed upon between the carrier and the consignor when the carriage shall commence or the goods shall arrive at destination.
- Period of responsibility of carrier covers the period of time during which the goods is in the charge of the carrier, starting from the time when he takes over

the goods until the time when he delivers the goods to the consignee, provided, however, the carrier and the consignor may reach an agreement concerning the carrier's responsibility with regard to the goods prior to loading onto and after discharging from an vehicle.

II. Road Waybill

A. *Functions of Road Waybill*

796. A road waybill is an evidence of the contract of carriage of goods by road and of the taking over of the goods by the carrier, and a document based upon which the carrier delivers the goods to the named consignee. It also serves as an original document for the record of vehicle operation and industrial statistics.

B. *Contents of Road Waybill*

797. A road waybill normally contains the following particulars:

- name, address and contacting numbers of the consignor, consignee and carrier;
- description, nature, weight, quantity and measurement of goods;
- place of loading and discharge, distance of carriage;
- means of packing of goods;
- date of commencement of carriage and deadline of arrival of goods;
- value of cargo, value-declared carriage or insurance of carriage of goods;
- means of settlement of transport expenses;
- liability for breach of contract;
- way of settlement of disputes.

III. Contract of Carriage of Goods by Road

798. A contract of carriage of goods by road may be in the form of an oral or written contract. Written form includes telefax, EDI, e-mail and other electronic message.

A contract of carriage of goods by road may be in the form of a time contract, single journey contract. A time contract is a contract for the carriage of a certain amount of goods during a specified period of time as agreed upon between the carrier and the consignor. A single journey contract is a contract for a particular carriage of goods from one place to the other.

799. Sub-book One 'General Provisions' of Book Three 'Contracts' of CC shall apply to the matters of conclusion, change, termination, performance and liability for breach of a contract of carriage of goods by road, whatever the form thereof is. Furthermore, section 1 'General Provisions' & section 3 'Contracts of Carriage of

Goods' of Chapter XIX of Book Three 'Contracts' of CC governs the rights and obligations of the carrier, consignor and consignee.

IV. Consignment and Taking Over of Cargo

A. *Obligations of Consignor*

800. The consignor shall make the goods ready and suitable for loading, carriage and discharge in accordance with the time and requirements as agreed upon between him and the carrier, and ensure taking delivery of cargo by the consignee after arrival, failing which the consignor shall compensate for the losses suffered by the carrier.

The consignor shall accurately indicate to the carrier the name of consignee, the description, nature, number of packages, weight, measurement, means of packing and other particulars of the goods, the place of delivery of goods and other information necessary for the carriage. In the case of the wrongful declaration or omission of material information, the consignor shall be liable for the loss suffered by the carrier (Article 825, CC).

Where a permit or approval, inspection or other governmental formality is required for the carriage of goods, the consignor shall submit to the carrier the documents indicating that the required formalities have gone through and such documents shall accompany the goods during carriage (Article 826, CC).

The consignor shall pack the goods in the manner as agreed upon between him and the carrier or, in the absence of such an agreement, in the ordinary manner or, in the absence of ordinary manner, in such a manner as to ensure the safety of carriage, loading, discharge and handling of goods (Article 826, CC). Where special packing is required by regulations, the requirements shall be met. Where there are compulsorily applicable packing standards, the same shall be complied with. Otherwise, the carrier may refuse to carry the goods.

The consignor shall not provide for carriage any inflammable, explosive, noxious, corrosive, radioactive and other dangerous goods, unless agreed upon between him and the carrier. The consignor shall also not provide for carriage any contrabands or goods the transport of which is prohibited by the government.

The consignor shall correctly use the transport marks, packing and storage marks as required by the State in accordance with the nature of goods and the requirement of transport.

801. The consignor may have additional obligations for the carriage of special goods.

In the case of refrigerated goods, the consignor shall notify the carrier of the required temperature to be kept during carriage.

In the case of fresh or live goods, the consignor shall submit to the carrier the instructions concerning the maximum length of time of carriage, care for the goods during carriage.

In the case of awkward and heavy goods, the consignor shall notify the carrier of the nature, weight and dimensions of the goods.

Consignment of containerized goods shall adhere to the requirements concerning such carriage made by the government.

Consignment of dangerous goods shall adhere to the requirements of the *Provisions on the Administration of Road Dangerous Goods Transport*. As required by Article 828, CC, the consignor shall pack, mark and label the dangerous goods in accordance with State regulations, submit to the carrier the written documents indicating the description, nature of the goods and precautions to be taken; otherwise, the carrier may refuse to carry or take preventive measures at the expenses of the consignor.

In the case of live animals or plants which need feeding or care during carriage, sophisticated precise instruments, rare valuables, cultural relics, ammunitions, negotiable securities, currencies or the like, the consignor shall designate a person or persons to escort on an vehicle who shall take charge of care for, custody and delivery of the goods during carriage. In other cases, escorting in carriage is subject to the agreement between the carrier and consignor.

B. *Obligations of Carrier*

802. The carrier shall check and verify the cargo in accordance with the statement in the road waybill or otherwise declared by the consignor.

After taking over of the goods, the carrier or other person on his behalf shall issue a road waybill.

V. Carriage and Delivery of Cargo

A. *Obligations of Carrier*

803. The carrier shall reasonably arrange for a vehicle or vehicles according to the goods which he agreed to carry. The weight of goods to be carried shall not exceed the maximum load of a vehicle and the goods loaded shall not exceed the maximum length, height and width of the load as required.

The carrier shall carry the cargo to the destination on the agreed route or, in the absence of agreed route, on customary route, failing which, the consignor or consignee may refuse to pay any additional transport expenses (Articles 812 and 813, CC).

804. The carrier shall carry the cargo to the destination before the deadline as agreed upon between the parties or, in the absence of such agreement, within reasonable time (Article 811, CC).

B. *Obligations of Consignee*

805. After the arrival of the goods at destination, the consignee shall take delivery of goods in time on the production of a road waybill or other effective delivery document. If he refuses to take delivery of cargo or fails to take delivery in time, he shall pay storage expenses or compensate for the losses suffered by the carrier. Where damage to or shortage of goods is found at the time of delivery, the carrier and the consignee shall jointly prepare a record of goods transport accident and sign on it for confirmation of such damage or shortage.

Where the consignee refuses to take delivery of cargo without any justifiable reasons, or the consignee is unknown, the carrier may deposit the cargo with the department stipulated in regulations (Article 837, CC). After such deposit, the obligations of the carrier under the contract shall be deemed as fulfilled.

VI. Tariff for Domestic Carriage of Cargo by Road

806. As mentioned in §2 *supra*, the road transport of goods under the State mandatory planning is subject to the government-guided prices. In other aspects of road transport of goods, the market prices are applicable. The tariffs formulated following the government-guided prices shall be publicized by the road transport companies by virtue of the *Law on Pricing*.

807. Normally, the freight shall be calculated on the basis of the freight weight of goods and the distance of carriage, but in the case of light goods the freight shall be calculated on the basis of the measurement thereof.

§5. Liability of Carrier

I. Liabilities and Exemptions of Liabilities of Carrier

A. For Death of or Personal Injury to Passengers

808. The strict liability adopted by paragraph 1 of Article 823 of CC regarding the carrier's liability for death of or personal injury to passengers under a contract of carriage of passenger shall apply to the carriage of passenger by road. Thus, the carrier shall be liable for the death of or personal injury to a passenger occurred during the carriage, unless the death or injury was caused by the health condition of the passenger or intentionally caused by him or caused by his gross negligence.

The provisions of paragraph 1 of Article 823 of CC shall apply to a passenger who travels gratuitously or by holding a preferential ticket or without ticket as permitted by the carrier (paragraph 2, Article 823, CC).

809. The scope of compensation for the death of or personal injury of passenger shall be determined in accordance with the Interpretations on Certain Issues regarding Application of Law in the Trial of Cases of Compensation for Loss of Life or Personal Injuries promulgated by SPC on 4 December 2003 and amended on 15 February 2022.

B. For Loss of or Damage to Carry-on Articles

810. By virtue of Article 824 of CC, the carrier shall be liable for loss of or damage to the carry-on articles of a passenger occurred during carriage, if the loss or damage is caused by the fault or intentional act on the part of the carrier.

C. For Loss of or Damage to Goods, Checked Baggage or Parcels

811. Strict liability is also adopted in section 3 'Contracts of Carriage of Goods' of Chapter XIX of Book Three 'Contracts' of CC regarding the carrier's liability for loss of or damage to the goods.

As provided for in Article 832 of CC, the carrier shall be liable for loss of or damage to the goods occurred during carriage, unless the carrier proves that the loss or damage was caused by force majeure, the natural characteristics or ordinary wear and tear of the goods, or by the fault of the consigner or consignee.

By virtue of paragraph 2 of Article 824 of CC, the above provisions of Article 832 of CC regarding the carrier's liability for loss of or damage to the goods shall apply to the baggage or parcels.

812. By virtue of Article 833 of CC, the amount of compensation shall be calculated as agreed upon between the parties or, in the absence of agreement, on the basis of the market price at the time and place where the goods were delivered or should have been delivered.

In the case of value-declared carriage of goods, baggage or parcels, the amount of compensation for the total loss thereof shall be the declared value thereof; in the case of partial loss, it shall be calculated in proportion to the extent of loss or the expenses for repair or restoration.

The value-declared carriage means the carriage of goods, baggage or parcels in which the consignor or passenger has on the voluntary basis declared the value thereof before consignment and paid additional freight or transport fees for the purpose of compensation for the loss or damage within the liability of the carrier in accordance with the declared value.

By virtue of Article 584 of CC, the loss of profit shall be recoverable, provided that it shall not exceed the extent that the carrier had foreseen or could have foreseen as a result of his breach of contract of carriage when the contract of carriage was concluded.

D. For Delay in Carriage of Passengers, Carry-on Articles, Baggage or Parcels or Cargo

813. Where the carrier fails to carry the goods to the destination before the deadline as agreed upon between the parties or, in the absence of such an agreement, within reasonable time, he shall be liable for the losses suffered by the consignee, unless caused by force majeure, the natural characteristics or ordinary wear and tear of the goods, or by the fault of the passenger, consignor or consignee.

814. The carrier's liability for losses suffered by the passenger or consignee resulting from delay in the carriage of passengers, baggage or parcels shall be determined in accordance with Articles 583 and 584 of CC. As a result, the carrier shall compensate for the loss suffered by the passenger or consignee resulting from the delay, unless his liability can be exempted as stated *supra*, provided that it shall not exceed the extent that the carrier had foreseen or could have foreseen as a result of his breach of contract of carriage when the contract of carriage was concluded.

E. *Obligation of Passenger or Consignor to Mitigate Loss*

815. By virtue of Article 591 of CC, where the carrier is liable, the passenger the consignor or consignee shall take appropriate measure to avoid the exaggeration of loss, failing which the exaggerated loss cannot be claimed for. Any expenses incurred in taking such measures shall be borne by the carrier.

II. Limitation of Liability of Carrier

816. Up to now, no Chinese law or regulation contains provisions regarding the limitation of liability of the carrier for the death of or personal injury to passengers, or for the loss of or damage to the goods, carry-on articles, baggage or parcels. Therefore, the carrier cannot limit his liability therefor.

III. Procedures

A. *Time-Bar*

817. The time-bars with respect to carriage by road shall be determined in accordance with Chapter IX 'Time-bars' of Book One 'General Provisions' of CC. Thus, the time-bar for claims for the death of or personal injury to passengers or for the loss of or damage to or delay in delivery of goods, baggage or parcels or other loss arising from breach of contract by road shall be three year counting from the date of death or injury, loss or damage took place (Article 188, CC).

B. *Jurisdiction*

818. In China, unlike the case of maritime transport, there is no special court of law with jurisdiction over the disputes arising from road transport. Thus, the disputes arising from road transport are subject to the jurisdiction of the ordinary courts of law as provided for in CPC.

§6. ROAD TRANSPORT INSURANCE

I. Introduction

819. The road transport insurance including the insurance of road passenger transport and the insurance of road goods transport is subject to IL. The relevant provisions of IL are introduced in Chapter 11 of Part II *supra*.

820. The road transport insurance is operated by PICC Property and Casualty Company Limited and other insurance companies in the insurance market in China mainly on the basis of the clauses formulated by PICC Property and Casualty Company Limited.

821. PICC Property and Casualty Company Limited formulated the Road Goods Transport Clauses in 2009 (hereinafter referred to as 'PICC P&C Domestic Road Goods Clauses 2009') applicable to domestic road goods transport insurance, and Land Cargo Transport Clauses (Vehicle and Train) in 2009 (hereinafter referred to as 'PICC P&C Land Goods Clauses 2009') applicable to the international road goods transport insurance and the international rail goods transport insurance.

II. Insurance of Domestic Road Goods Transport

A. *Subject Matters Insured*

822. Under the PICC P&C Domestic Road Good Clauses 2009, any goods carried by domestic road can be the subject matter of insurance, except fresh vegetables, fruits, live stocks, birds, fish and other live animals. In addition, unless specially agreed upon between the insurer and the applicant and stated in the insurance policy, valuables such as gold, silver, jewellery, diamonds, jade, antiques, ancient books, postage stamps, works of art and rare metals are not covered by the insurance.

B. *Scope of Cover*

823. Under the PICC P&C Domestic Road Goods Clauses 2009, the insurer shall be liable for the loss of or damage to the insured goods or expenses resulting from:

– fire, explosion, lightning, hail, storm, rainstorm, flood, tsunami, subsidence of land, collapse of cliff, abrupt landslide, mud-rock flow;
– collision or capsize of vehicle, collapse of bridge, tunnel or wharf;
– accident occurred during loading or discharge of goods or change of transport vehicles;
– breakage, crook, concavity, split of goods due to vibration, impact or extrusion;
– scatter and disappearance of goods due to breakage of packing;

- leakage of liquid goods due to damage to container including its seal thereof arising from vibration, impact or extrusion, or putrescence or deterioration of liquid goods due to leakage;
- rain on the condition that the safety transport provisions are conformed to;
- scatter and disappearance of goods caused by disorder or direct and reasonable expenses arising from sue and labour or protective measures taken on the occurrence of the above calamities and accidents.

C. *Exclusions*

824. Under the PICC P&C Domestic Road Goods Clauses 2009, the insurer shall not be liable for the loss of or damage to the insured goods arising from any of the following causes:

- war, hostility, military action, seizure, strike, riot or robbery;
- earthquake;
- theft or non-delivery of goods in packages;
- defective quality or shortage in quantity of goods existing before the commencement of insurance liability;
- ordinary wear and tear, inherent vice or specific nature of goods;
- loss of market or delay in transport;
- responsibility of consignor;
- intentional or criminal act of the applicant or the insured;
- illegal goods as recognized by relevant authorities.

D. *Commencement and Termination of Insurance Liability*

825. The PICC P&C Domestic Road Goods Clauses 2009 contains a 'warehouse to warehouse' clause to the effect that the insurance liability shall commence from the time when the insured goods are carried away from the last warehouse or other storage place of the consignor at the place of commencement of carriage after the issuance of the insurance policy or other insurance certificate, and terminate at the time when the insured goods arrive at the first warehouse or storage place of the consignee at destination stated in the insurance certificate, provided that the time limit of termination shall not exceed fifteen days from the time when the insured goods were discharged from the vehicle in the case of failure of the consignee to take delivery of goods in time.

E. *Obligations of Applicant or Insured*

826. Under the PICC P&C Domestic Road Goods Clauses 2009, the applicant or the insured shall fulfil the following obligations:

- The applicant shall fulfil the obligation of disclosure according to the facts, answer to the inquiries of the insurer accurately concerning the subject matter insured or the insured, failing which due to the applicant's intention or gross negligence sufficiently affecting the insurer in deciding whether to agree to cover or increase the insurance premium, the insurer is entitled to terminate the insurance contract; where non-disclosure is due to the applicant's intention, the insurer shall not be liable for the insurance incident occurred before termination of insurance contract and shall not refund the premium; where non-disclosure is due to the applicant's gross negligence and has material influence in the occurrence of the insurance incident, the insurer shall not be liable for the incident occurred before termination of insurance contract, but shall refund the premium.
- The applicant shall pay the insurance premium in one lump upon the issuance of insurance policy or other insurance certificate by the insurer or his agent, failing which the insurer shall not be liable for the insurance incident occurred before payment of premium.
- The insured shall strictly obey to the various provisions of the State and transport authorities concerning safety transport, maintain the safety of the subject matter insured, make sure that the packing of goods be in conformity with the standard provided for by the State and competent authorities, and implement written suggestions concerning eliminating the unsafe factors and hidden danger to the subject matter insured put forward by the insurer to the applicant or the insured, failing which the insurer shall not be liable for the insurance incident or the exaggerated loss or damage arising therefrom.
- Where the extent of danger to the subject matter insured increases remarkably during the period of validity of the insurance contract, the insured shall notify the insurer in time as agreed upon in the contract and the insurer is entitled to either increase the premium or terminate the contract; where the insured fails to notify, the insurer shall not be liable for the insurance incident arising from any remarkable increase of the extent of danger to the subject matter insured.
- Upon notice of the occurrence of loss of or damage to the insured cargo within the insurance coverage, the applicant or the insured shall take reasonable sue and labour or protective measures and notify the insurer's local branch thereof not later than ten days; where notification fails due to the intention or gross negligence resulting in difficulty in determining the nature, causes or extent of loss or damage, etc., the insurer shall not be liable for the part which is unable to be determined, except where the insurer has timely known or could have timely known the occurrence of the insurance incident through other means.

F. Settlement of Claim

827. In his claim for insurance indemnity against the insurer, the insured shall provide various documents in support of the claim including, *inter alia*, (a) the insurance policy or other insurance certificate, waybill, delivery order, invoice or other evidence of the price of goods; (b) the accident record, receipt and delivery record made by the carrier, and the assessment report; (c) the record of goods entering the warehouse made by consignee, survey report, breakdown of loss and vouchers of reasonable expenses incurred directly for the protection of goods; (d) other documents concerning determination of the nature, causes, extent of loss or damage, etc., which the insured is able to provide.

The insurer shall, after receipt of the above documents, immediately determine whether the loss or damage is within the insurance liability and notify the insured of the result. If an agreement on settlement amount is reached between the insurer and the insured, the insurer shall make compensation within ten days.

Where the loss of or damage to the insured goods is within the insurance liability, the insurer shall indemnify for the loss or damage in accordance with the actual loss, if the insured amount is determined by virtue of the insured value of goods, but such indemnity shall be limited to the insured amount. Where the insured amount is less than the insured value, the amount of indemnity for the loss, damage or expenses of sue and labour or protection shall be calculated in the proportion that the insured amount bears to the insured value. The indemnity for loss of or damage to the insured goods and that for the reasonable expenses incurred directly for the sue and labour and protection of goods shall be calculated respectively and each shall not exceed the insured amount.

Where the carrier or other third party shall be liable wholly or partly for the loss of or damage to goods insured within the insurance liability by virtue of law or relevant agreement, the insured is required to claim against the third party first. However, strictly speaking, such a provision is illegal, as the insured may choose to make claim against either the insurer or the third party.

If the insured waives his claim against the third party, the insurer's liability shall be discharged.

Where the insurer pays insurance indemnity as required by the insured, the insured is obliged to issue a letter of subrogation to the insurer, furnish the insurer with relevant documents and assist the insurer in pursuing recovery from a third person. If, due to the intention or gross negligence of the insured, the insurer is unable to exercise his right of subrogation, the insurer may deduct from the indemnity the corresponding amount.

III. Insurance of International Road Goods Transport

A. Scope of Cover

828. The PICC P&C Land Goods Clauses 2009 contain the land risks cover and the all land risks cover.

Under the land risks cover, the insurer shall be liable for the following loss of or damage to the insured goods and/or expenses:

- total or partial loss of goods arising from natural calamities of storm, lightning, flood or earthquake suffered by the insured goods, or collision or capsize suffered

by transport vehicle, or grounding, running on a reef, sinking, collision of transhipment means during transhipment, or arising from an accident of collapse of tunnel or cliff, fire or explosion;
- reasonable expenses paid for the measures taken by the insured for the purpose of rescuing, preventing or mitigating loss of or damage to the goods in danger within the insurance coverage, provided that these expenses shall not exceed the insured amount of the insured goods.

Under the all land risks cover, the insure shall, besides his insurance liability under the land risks cover, also be liable for the total or partial loss of the insured goods resulting from the external causes during the carriage.

B. Exclusions

829. Under the PICC P&C Land Goods Clauses 2009, the insurer shall not be liable for:

- loss or damage due to intentional act or negligence of the insured;
- loss or damage within the responsibility of the consignor of the goods;
- loss of or damage arising from the defective quality or shortage in quantity of the insured goods existing before the commencement of insurance liability;
- loss or damage or expenses arising from ordinary wear and tear, inherent vice or specific nature of the insured goods as well as from loss of market or delay in transport;
- loss or damage or expenses within the scope of cover or exclusions under the war risks cover or the strike risks cover of the land goods transport insurance.

C. Commencement and Termination of Insurance Liability

830. The PICC P&C Land Goods Clauses 2009 also contains a 'warehouse to warehouse' clause to the effect that the insurance liability shall take effect from the time when the insured goods is carried away from the warehouse or other storage place stated in insurance policy to the time when the insured cargo arrives at the last warehouse or storage place of the consignee at destination stated in the insurance policy or other place which is used for the distribution of goods by the insured, including the period on land or of lightering on water during normal transport; where the goods have not been carried to the above warehouse or other storage place, to the time of expiry of sixty days from the time when the goods is carried to the land station where the goods is finally discharged.

D. Obligations of Insured

831. Under the PICC P&C Land Goods Clauses 2009, the insured shall fulfil the following obligations:

- After the insured goods have been carried to the destination stated in the insurance policy, the insured shall take delivery thereof in time; where loss of or damage to the goods is found, the insured shall apply for survey to the insurer's agent authorized for survey or handling claims stated in the insurance policy; where there is shortage of packages of or apparent damage to the insured goods, the insured shall try to obtain evidence of such damage or shortage from the carrier, his authorized party or relevant authority; where damage to or shortage of cargo is within the responsibility of the carrier, his authorized party or relevant authority, the insured shall file a formal claim in writing against them and obtain from them extension of time-bar when necessary; otherwise, the insurer shall not be liable for the relevant loss or damage.
- Where there is a danger to the insured goods within the insurance liability, the insured shall immediately take reasonable rescue measures to avoid or mitigate loss of or damage to the goods; otherwise, the insurer shall not be liable for the exaggerated loss or damage.
- The insured shall, in making claim against the insurer, provide documents including the original insurance policy, transport document, invoice, packing list, weight memo, evidence of damage to or shortage of goods, survey report and breakdown of damages, correspondences for the purpose of making recourse claim against a third party if the liability of a third party is involved, as well as the other evidence or materials which the insured is able to provide relating to determination of the nature, causes, extent of damage, etc.

Chapter 2. Transport by Rail

§1. Applicable Laws

I. Introduction

832. RL, other laws and regulations as well as international treaty applicable to railway transport in China are referred to in §3 of Chapter 2 of Part II *supra*.

II. Concepts and Definitions

833. In the applicable laws mentioned *supra*, the following concepts and definitions are adopted:

- Railways include the national railways, local railways, special railways and special rail lines of which the national railways refer to the railways administered by the National Railway Administration under MOT and operated by China State Railway Group Co., Ltd. known as 'China Railway', the local railways refer to the railways operated by the local governments, the special railways refer to the railways operated by enterprises or other entities exclusively for their internal transport, and the special rail lines refer to the branch railways operated by enterprises or other entities which are connected with the national or other railways.
- Railway transport contract means an agreement which stipulates the rights and obligations of the carrier and passenger or consignor.
- Carrier means a railway transport enterprise which has concluded a contract of carriage with a passenger or consignor, and a railway station, train and the personnel during performance of their duties shall be deemed as representing the carrier.
- Passenger means a person who holds a valid passenger ticket and may include a companying child traveling gratuitously, and a person escorting the goods under a contract of carriage of goods by rail is deemed as a passenger.
- Consignor means a person who has concluded a contract of carriage of goods, baggage or parcel by rail with the carrier.
- Consignee means a person who takes delivery of goods, baggage or parcel based upon a valid proof.
- Baggage means personal belongings and other traveling necessities of a passenger and refers to the checked baggage only.
- Parcel means a small package of goods suitable to be carried in a baggage wagon and carried under a parcel check, and the consignor of a parcel is a person other than a passenger.
- Carry-on article means an article in the custody of a passenger during journey.

§2. Carriage of Passengers by Rail

I. Passenger Ticket

A. *Functions of Passenger Ticket*

834. By virtue Article 7 of the PRPT, a passenger ticket is the basic evidence of a contract of carriage of passenger by rail.

A passenger to travel on board a train shall hold a valid passenger ticket (Article 14, RL). A passenger boarding a train without a ticket or with an invalid one shall pay the fare for a ticket and be charged an additional fare in accordance with regulations. If a passenger refuses to pay, the carrier may order him to get off the train.

A passenger shall produce a valid passenger ticket for check on entering or leaving railway stations and on train on demand (Article 14, RL; Article 27, PRPT). Nowadays, a passenger may produce his identity card instead of a passenger ticket or have his or her identity card scanned on the check-in gate and exit of a railway station.

B. *Contents of Passenger Ticket*

835. As provided for in Article 4 of PRPT, a passenger ticket shall normally contain: (a) name of station of departure and that of destination; (b) train number; (b) wagon number; (c) class of seat or berth; (d) fare; (e) date and time of departure. In practice, a passenger ticket also contains the name and identity card number of the passenger.

C. *Validity Period of Passenger Ticket*

836. By virtue of Article 20 of PRPT, a passenger ticket is valid only for the train number on the date and time indicated therein. However, a train company may stipulate the valid period of a passenger ticket.

D. *Change of or Getting Refund for Passenger Ticket*

837. A passenger may, before the time of departure and within the period of validity of a passenger ticket stipulated by a train company, demand the change of train number, date or time or class, but may be required to pay a commission.

Where a passenger is unable to travel as indicated in the ticket due to his or her own reasons, or is refused to carry by the carrier under PRPT, the passenger may demand to change of or get refund for a passenger ticket, but may be required to pay a commission (Article 30, PRPT).

838. Where, due to the reasons of the carrier, natural calamity or other circumstance preventing normal carriage, the passenger is unable to travel as indicated in the ticket, the carrier is obliged to refund for the passenger ticket or make rearrangement for the passenger to travel on another train to the same destination as demanded by the passenger. If, as a result, the class becomes lower, the carrier shall refund the balance to the passenger; where the class becomes higher, the passenger shall not pay for the balance (Article 31, PRPT).

II. Service for Passengers on Train or in Stations

839. The carrier shall take effective measures to provide good services to the passengers, maintaining cleanliness and hygiene in railway stations and in train carriages, and to supply food and beverages on a train (Article 13, RL).

III. Basic Obligations of Passenger and Carrier

A. *Basic Obligations of Passenger*

840. Besides the payment of the ticket fare and other stipulated transport expenses as mentioned *infra*, a passenger is obliged to board the train as indicated in the passenger ticket, to obey to the law and regulations regarding railway transport, to take good care of the rail equipment or facilities, to maintain the public order and transport safety (Article 6 and 20, PRPT).

B. *Basic Obligations of Carrier*

841. The carrier engaged in public transport of passengers cannot refuse the reasonable or normal demand for the carriage of passengers (Article 810, CC).

The carrier shall notify a passenger in time of the information affecting the carriage in normal way and of the safety instructions (Article 819, CC).

The carrier shall carry a passenger in accordance with the date, time and train number (Article 820, CC). The carrier is obliged to secure safe and timely carriage of passenger, to provide a passenger with good traveling circumstances and service facilities.

The carrier shall endeavour to assist a passenger in emergent illness, distress or giving childbirth (Article 822, CC).

IV. Tariff

842. By virtue of Article 25 of RL, the passenger ticket fares for the carriage of passengers are subject to the prices determined by the governmental authorities or the government-guided prices, while the items and the charging standards of miscellaneous expenses in the carriage of passengers shall be determined by the railway transport companies.

In the case of the government-guided prices, the railway transport companies may formulate tariff or to negotiate tariff with the passengers following the basic tariff fixed and within the margins allowed or not exceeding the upper limit fixed by the governmental department in charge of prices in conjunction with the governmental department in charge of railway transport.

The passenger ticket fares and miscellaneous fees and their standards fixed shall be made public; otherwise, the implementation thereof shall be prohibited (Article 26, RL).

V. Carriage of Carry-on Articles

843. The carry-on articles of a passenger which are in the custody of the passenger during the journey are excluded from the scope of baggage and are carried under a contract of carriage of passenger.

The weight of carry-on articles of a passenger is limited by railway transport companies. Within this limit, the carry-on articles are transported by the carrier gratuitously. The measurement of a carry-on article shall not exceed the limit specified by railway transport companies.

844. A passenger shall not carry as carry-on articles or in carry-on articles the articles the carriage of which are prohibited or restricted, dangerous goods as stipulated in law or regulations, ammunitions and chemical products of which the carrier cannot identify their natures, animals and articles which may impact the public hygiene, articles which may damage or pollute the train carriages.

§3. Carriage of Baggage or Parcel by Rail

I. Baggage or Parcel Check

A. *Functions of Baggage or Parcel Check*

845. By virtue Article 32 of PRPT, a baggage or parcel check is an evidence of a contract of carriage of baggage or parcel by railway.

B. *Contents of Baggage or Parcel Check*

846. By virtue of Article 32 of PRPT, a baggage or parcel check shall contain: (a) number of ticket; (b) name of station of departure and that of destination; (c) number and weight of baggage or parcel; (d) time of carriage; (e) name, address, contacting phone number and other main information of the passenger. Where a railway transport company and a passenger have otherwise agreed, the agreement shall be adhered to.

II. Consignment and Taking Over of Baggage or Parcel

847. By virtue of virtue of PRPT, a passenger shall deliver the baggage to the carrier or railway station of departure for carriage upon the production of a valid passenger ticket and identification proof. The station indicated in baggage check and that indicated in the passenger ticket shall be identical (Article 34).

The packing of baggage or parcel shall be complete and secured, and is suitable for transport. The materials and means of packing shall conform to the standards stipulated by the State (Article 37).

III. Carriage and Delivery of Baggage or Parcel

848. The carrier shall carry the baggage or parcel to the destination before the deadline as agreed upon between the parties or, without such an agreement, before the deadline set by MOT (Article 16, RL).

849. In the case of late arrival of the baggage or parcel at destination, the carrier shall pay liquidated damages. Where the baggage has not been delivered to the passenger for thirty days overdue, or the parcel has not been delivered to the consignee for thirty days overdue, the passenger or the consignee may treat the baggage or parcel as lost and claim against the carrier accordingly (Article 16, RL).

850. As provided for in Article 40 of PRPT, on the arrival of baggage at destination, the carrier shall notify the consignee thereof in time. A railway transport company shall provide at least free storage of baggage for three days or for ten days in the case of late arrival of baggage. The days of free storage shall be appropriately increased in the case of damage to baggage, force majeure or under other circumstances. Where a railway transport company and a passenger have otherwise agreed as to the days of free storage, the agreement shall be adhered to.

IV. Tariff

851. By virtue of Article 25 of RL, the tariff of baggage is subject to the prices determined by the governmental authorities or the government-guided prices, whereas the tariff of parcels shall be determined by railway transport companies.

§4. Carriage of Goods by Rail

I. Rail Waybill

A. *Functions of Rail Waybill*

852. The functions of a rail waybill are not provided for in Chinese law. However, a rail waybill is understood as an evidence of a contract of carriage of goods by rail, of the taking over of the goods by the carrier and a document based upon which the carrier delivers the goods to the consignee at destination. A rail waybill is non-negotiable.

B. Contents of Rail Waybill

853. By virtue of the *Agreement concerning International Carriage of Goods by Rail* (CMIC), a rail waybill applicable in Chinese international railway transport shall contain the following particulars:

- description of train and wagon;
- name of station of commencement and arrival;
- name and address of consignor and consignee;
- statement as to station and formality of transit;
- consignor's apparatus or container for transport;
- description of goods and declared value;
- kind of transport and person responsible for loading;
- date of loading, carriage and arrival of goods;
- consignor's special declaration;
- expenses payable by consignee.

854. A rail waybill for the domestic carriage contains similar particulars, although no statute provides in this regard.

C. Making of Rail Waybill

855. By virtue of Articles 6 and 7 of CMIC, the consignor shall at the time of consignment fill in and sign a rail waybill together with copies thereof and submit them to the railway station of commencement which shall fix its seal on the waybill. When so fixed, a contract of international contract of goods by railway shall be deemed as concluded.

In the domestic transport by rail, however, a contract of goods by railway is concluded when the consignor's offer of carriage is accepted by a railway company or a railway station of commencement on its behalf, unless they have agreed otherwise (Article 483, CC). Thus, the filling in waybill by the consignor or fixing seal by the railway company or station of commencement may be irrelevant to the conclusion of contract, but serves as an evidence of conclusion of the contract.

II. Consignment and Taking Over of Goods

A. Obligations of Consignor

856. As provided for in Article 19 of RL, the consignor shall make an honest declaration in the consignment bill of the description, nature, number of packages, weight, measurement, means of packing and other particulars of the goods delivered to the carrier or the station of commencement for carriage. Where the declaration is found inconsistent with reality after inspection by the carrier, the consignor shall bear the inspection expenses. The carrier may charge the consignor who underpays freight and other expenses as a result of dishonest declaration for additional freight and other expenses according to the stipulations of the former Ministry of Railways (MOR) or now MOT.

Where permit or approval, quarantine or other governmental formalities are required for the carriage of goods in accordance with relevant regulations, the consignor shall submit to the carrier the documents indicating that the required formalities have gone through. Such documents shall accompany the goods during carriage (Article 826, CC).

As provided for in Article 20 of RL, where the goods requires packing, the consignor shall pack the goods according to the State or industrial packing standards or, in the absence of State or industrial packing standards, properly pack the goods so that they will not be damaged during carriage because of inadequate packing; otherwise, the carrier may refuse to carry (Article 20, RL).

While consigning inflammable, explosive, toxic, corrosive, radioactive or other dangerous goods, the consignor shall, in accordance with the State regulations on the transport of dangerous goods, properly pack, mark and label the goods, submit to the carrier written document indicating the description, nature of the goods and precautions to be taken; otherwise, the carrier may refuse to carry or take preventive measures at the expenses of the consignor (Article 828, CC).

In the case of live animals or plants or other goods which requires escorting, the consignor shall designate a person or persons to escort the goods during carriage as agreed upon between the consignor and the carrier.

The consignor shall deliver the goods to the station of commencement on the date designated by the carrier and be responsible for loading, unless otherwise agreed upon between the consignor and the carrier (Article 21, PRCT).

B. Obligations of Carrier

857. Unless the goods are loaded in a container and sealed by the consignor, the carrier or the station of commencement on his behalf shall check and verify the description, number of packages or pieces, transport packing and marks of the goods, and be responsible for loading.

III. Carriage and Delivery of Goods

A. Obligations of Carrier

858. The carrier shall provide suitable train or wagon in accordance with the contract of carriage. Substitute of train or wagon is subject to the agreement of the consignor, safety carriage of goods and convenience of loading and discharge in the case of lack of suitable train or wagon.

During carriage, the carrier shall take effective measures to protect the perishable goods or live animals according to the stipulations set by the former MOR or now MOT and the provisions of contracts (Article 20, RL).

The carrier shall carry the goods to the destination on the agreed route or, in the absence of agreed route, on customary route (Article 812, CC).

The carrier shall carry the goods to the destination before the deadline as agreed upon between the parties or, without such an agreement, before the deadline set by the former MOR or now MOT (Article 16, RL).

Where the carrier is responsible for the discharge of goods, the station of arrival shall send to the consignee a notice of taking delivery.

The station of arrival shall deliver the goods the consignee named in the rail way-bill upon production of proof of taking delivery or proof of identity if the proof of taking delivery has not received or lost.

B. *Obligations of Consignee*

859. By virtue of Article 830 of CC, after the arrival of the goods at destination, the consignee shall take delivery of the goods in time. If he refuses to take delivery or fails to take delivery in time, he shall pay storage expenses or compensate for the losses suffered by the carrier.

Where the consignee refuses to take delivery without any justifiable reasons, or the consignee is unknown, the carrier may deposit the goods with the department stipulated in regulations (Article 837, CC). After such deposit, the obligations of the carrier under the contract of carriage shall be deemed as fulfilled.

By virtue of Article 22 of RL, where the goods are not taken delivery of upon expiry of thirty days from the date on which the notice of taking delivery notice has been sent, or the consignee notifies the carrier of refusal of taking delivery in writing, the carrier shall notify the consignor. Where the consignor fails to reply within thirty days after receiving the notice, the carrier may sell the goods. After deduction of the storage expense from the proceeds of sale, any surplus amount shall be refunded to the consignor. If there is no way to make the refund and such surplus amount has not been claimed by the end of one hundred and eighty days after the sale, it shall go to the State Treasury. If the goods is not suitable for long-time storage, the period of disposal may be reduced as stipulated by MOT.

IV. Tariff for Domestic Carriage of Goods by Rail

860. The fixing of fares and miscellaneous fees for the carriage of goods is mentioned in §2 of this chapter *supra*.

§5. Liability of Carrier

I. Liabilities and Exemptions of Liabilities of Carrier

A. *For Death of or Personal Injury to Passengers or Other Persons*

861. A strict liability is adopted in RL regarding the carrier's liability for death of or personal injury to passengers in railway transport.

862. As provided for in paragraph 1 of Article 58 of RL, the carrier, or railway transport enterprise in the words of RL, shall be liable for the death of or personal injury to persons including passengers caused by a traffic accident or by other accidents resulting from railway operations, unless the death or injury is caused by force majeure or by the victim himself or herself.

Article 823 of CC further provide that the carrier shall not be liable for death of or personal injury to passengers caused by the health condition, intentional act or gross negligence of the passengers.

863. Article 58 of RL also applies to the liability of railway transport enterprise for death of or personal injury to persons other than passengers.

Paragraph 2 of Article 58 of RL further provides that death of or personal injury to a person caused by his or her passing through a level crossing or pedestrian passageway in violation of traffic regulations is deemed as caused by the victim himself or herself and consequently the railway transport enterprise shall bear no liability therefor.

B. *For Loss of or Damage to Carry-on Articles*

864. RL does not contain any provision governing the carriage of carry-on article of a passenger and the liability of the carrier for loss thereof or damage thereto. Thus, his liability shall be determined in accordance with CC.

By virtue of Article 824 of CC, the carrier shall be liable for the loss of or damage to carry-on article of a passenger occurred during carriage, if the loss or damage is caused by fault on the part of the carrier.

C. *For Loss of or Damage to Goods, Baggage or Parcel*

865. A strict liability is also adopted in RL regarding the carrier's liability for loss of or damage to the goods, baggage or parcel in railway transport.

Article 17 of RL provide that the carrier shall be liable for the loss of or damage to the goods, baggage or parcels including missing, shortage, deterioration, pollution thereof occurred during the period from the time of receipt thereof by the carrier for carriage until the time of their delivery by the carrier. Article 18 of RL stipulates the exemptions of liability, i.e.,: (a) force majeure; (b) natural characteristics or ordinary wear and tear of the goods, baggage or parcel; or (c) fault of the consignor, consignee or passenger.

866. By virtue of Article 17 of RL, the amount of compensation shall be calculated on the basis of the actual loss in the case of value-declared carriage of goods, baggage or parcel, but shall not exceed the value declared by the consignor or passenger, or on the basis of the actual loss in the case of value-undeclared carriage thereof, but shall not exceed the amount of limit of liability formulated by the former MOR or now MOT.

Value-declared carriage means the carriage of goods, baggage or parcel in which the consignor or passenger has declared the value thereof on a voluntary basis before consignment and paid additional freight or transport fees for the purpose of compensation for loss or damage within the liability of the carrier in accordance with the declared value.

In the case of value-declared carriage, the amount of compensation shall not exceed the declared value. Where the actual loss exceeds the declared value, the excess amount of loss shall not be compensated for. In the case of partial loss, the amount of compensation shall be calculated in the proportion that the amount of loss bears to the actual value.

Where the value is not declared, the amount of compensation for loss or damage shall be calculated on the basis of the actual value in the case of loss, or the difference in actual value before and after the damage or the expenses for repair or restoration in the case of damage.

By virtue of Article 584 of CC, loss of profit shall be recoverable in the case of loss of or damage to goods, provided that it shall not exceed the extent which the carrier had foreseen or could have foreseen as a result of his breach of contract of carriage when the contract was concluded.

867. In the international carriage of goods under CMIC, the carrier shall not be liable for loss of or damage to live animal during carriage or loss of or damage to goods caused by:

- force majeure;
- spontaneous combustion, damage, rust, deterioration or similar result, extraordinary natural characteristics of goods;
- fault or requirement of consignor or consignee and thus not attributable to carrier;
- loading onto or discharge from wagon by consignor or consignee;
- carriage by open-cover wagon as allowed by railway regulations or agreed upon between the parties;
- failure of the person escorting goods as designated by consignor or consignee to take necessary measures in protecting the integrity of goods;
- defect of container or packing on its surface not discoverable by carrier;
- wastage in transit within stipulated limit.

The liability of the carrier shall be limited to an amount equivalent to the decrease in the value of goods due to damage thereto. In the case of total or partial loss of goods, the amount of indemnity shall be based upon the declared value in rail waybill or, if the value of goods is not declared, upon the price contained in the seller's invoice.

D. For Delay in the Carriage of Goods, Baggage or Parcels

868. By virtue of paragraph 1 of Article 16 of RL, where goods, baggage or parcel is transported to the destination after the deadline as agreed upon between the parties in the contract or after the deadline set out by the former MOR or now MOT, the carrier shall pay liquidated damages for breach of contract, unless delay in delivery is caused by a cause stipulated in Article 18 of RL as indicated *supra*. In the case of carriage of goods, neither the former MOR nor now MOT has set out the way of calculation of deadline of delivery. Thus, where no deadline is agreed upon between the parties, the criterion of reasonable time adopted by Article 811 of CC shall apply.

869. In the case of delay in delivery of goods, baggage or parcel, the carrier shall be liable for any loss thereof or damage thereto caused by such delay, unless his liability can be exempted.

870. If the carrier fails to deliver the goods, baggage or parcel to the consignee or passenger within thirty days after the deadline, the consignor, consignee or passenger may deem it as have been lost and has the right to demand compensation from the carrier for the loss thereof (paragraph 1, Article 16, RL).

871. In the international carriage of goods by rail, by virtue of the CMIC, the penalty for breach of contract in the case of delay in delivery shall be based upon the freight for the goods delayed. Where the time of delay does not exceed 10% of the total time allowed, the sum of penalty shall be equivalent to 6% of the freight. Where the time of delay exceeds 40% of the total time allowed, the sum of penalty shall be equivalent to 30% of the freight. Where the delayed goods suffers damage, the carrier shall make compensation for the damage and pay the penalty for breach of contract, provided that the total amount payable shall not exceed the amount payable by the carrier in the case of loss of the goods.

II. Procedures

A. Time-Bar

872. The time-bars for claims against the carrier for death or personal injury, loss of or damage or delay in delivery are subject to the ordinary time-bars provided for in. Article 188 of CC to the effect that. the time-bars shall be three years from the date on which the person entitled to claim knows or should have known his right was infringed and the person who is liable.

873. The time-bars for claims are subject to suspension as provided for in Article 194 of CC and to discontinuation as provided for in Article 195 of CC.

874. In the international carriage of goods by rail, by virtue of CMIC, the time-bar for claim founded on a contract of carriage against the carrier or for the carrier's claim against the consignor or consignee for transport expenses, loss or damage shall be nine months, while the time-bar for claim for delay in delivery shall be two months.

B. Jurisdiction and Arbitration

875. As introduced in Chapter 3 of Part I *supra*, the cases of disputes arising from or in connection with railway transport are within the jurisdictions of the railway transport courts in the places at provincial level where there are railway transport courts or within the jurisdictions of the intermediate courts of law in places at provincial level where there are no railway courts. The high courts of law are the Courts of Appeal.

876. There is no special law or provisions adopted by SPC governing litigation or arbitration of disputes arising from railway transport. Thus, litigation or arbitration of disputes arising from or in connection with railway transport is governed by CPC and AL as well as the CPC Interpretations and the AL Interpretations. In addition, SPC promulgated the *Provisions on Certain Issues in the Attachment on Goods in Railway Transport* on 22 April 1997 as amended 23 December 2020 indicating the procedural right of a railway transport enterprise to apply to a court of law for the attachment on the goods in railway transport and the related matters of procedure.

877. Disputes arising from or in connection with railway transport may be referred to arbitration in accordance with a valid arbitration agreement between the parties (Article 32, RL).

§6. Railway Transport Insurance

I. Introduction

878. Railway transport insurance includes the railway passenger transport insurance and the railway goods transport insurance.

No specific law governs railway transport insurance in China. Thus, railway transport insurance is subject to IL.

879. Railway transport insurance is operated by PICC Property and Casualty Company Limited and other insurance companies in the insurance market in China mainly on the basis of the clauses formulated by PICC Property and Casualty Company Limited.

PICC Property and Casualty Company Limited formulated the Railway Goods Transport Clauses in 2009 (hereinafter referred to as 'PICC P&C Domestic Railway Goods Clauses 2009') applicable to the domestic railway goods transport insurance.

As mentioned in §6 of Chapter 1 of Part III *supra*, the PICC P&C Land Goods Clauses 2009 are applicable to the international railway goods transport insurance.

II. Railway Passenger Transport Insurance

880. A passenger can have the risks of his or her incidental death or personal injury during railway transport insured with an insurance company on voluntary basis.

The payment of insurance indemnity shall not affect the liability of the carrier for the death of or personal injury to a passenger.

III. Domestic Railway Cargo Transport Insurance

A. *Subject Matters Insured*

881. Under the PICC P&C Domestic Railway Goods Clauses 2009, any goods carried by domestic railway can be the subject matter of insurance, except fresh vegetables, fruits, live stocks, birds, fishes and other live animals. In addition, unless specially agreed upon between the insurer and the applicant and stated in the policy, valuables such as gold, silver, jewellery, diamonds, jade, antiques, ancient books, postage stamps, works of art and rare metals cannot be covered by the insurance.

B. *Scope of Cover*

882. The PICC P&C Domestic Railway Goods Clauses 2009 contain the basic risks cover and the comprehensive risks cover.

Under the basic risks cover, the insurer shall be liable for the loss of or damage to the insured goods or expenses resulting from:

- fire, explosion, lightning, hail, storm, rainstorm, flood, tsunami, subsidence of land, collapse of cliff, abrupt landslide, mud-rock flow;
- collision or going off the rails of train, collapse of bridge, tunnel or wharf;
- loss or damage arising from accident occurred during loading, discharge or transhipment of transport vehicles;
- direct and reasonable expenses arising from sue and labour or protective measures taken on the occurrence of the above calamities and accidents.

Under the comprehensive risks cover, the insurer shall also be liable for the loss of or damage to the insured goods resulting from:

- breakage, crook, concavity, split of goods due to vibration, impact or extrusion;
- scatter and disappearance of goods due to breakage of packing;
- leakage of liquid goods due to damage to container including its seal arising from vibration, impact or extrusion, or putrescence or deterioration of goods preserved in liquid due to the leakage of liquid in which the goods is preserved;
- theft of goods;
- non-delivery of goods due to external causes;
- wetness by rain on the condition that safety transport provisions are conformed to.

C. Exclusions

883. Under the PICC P&C Railway Goods Clauses 2009, the insurer shall not be liable for:

- loss of or damage to the goods arising from war, military action, seizure, strike, robbery or riot;
- loss of or damage to the goods arising from earthquake;
- loss of or damage to the goods arising from nuclear reaction, nuclear radiation or radioactive pollution;
- loss of or damage to the goods arising from ordinary wear and tear, pollution, putrescence or damage arising from inherent vice or specific nature of the insured goods or improper packing of goods;
- loss of or damage to the goods arising from defective quality or shortage in quantity of the insured goods existing before the commencement of insurance liability;
- loss of market or arising from delay in transport;
- loss or damage due to the responsibility of the consignor of goods;
- loss or damage due to the intentional or criminal act of the applicant or the insured;
- loss or damage arising from administrative act or enforcement of law.

D. Commencement and Termination of Insurance Liability

884. The PICC P&C Domestic Railway Goods Clauses 2009 contains a 'warehouse to warehouse' clause to the effect that the insurance liability shall commence from the time when the insured goods is carried away from the last warehouse or other storage place of the consignor at the place of commencement of carriage after the issuance of the policy or other insurance certificate and terminate at the time when the insured goods arrives at the first warehouse or storage place of the consignee at destination stated in the insurance certificate, provided that the time limit of termination shall not exceed fifteen days from the receipt of notice of arrival by the consignee in the case of failure of the consignee to take delivery of goods in time.

E. Obligations of Applicant or Insured

885. Under the PICC P&C Domestic Railway Goods Clauses 2009, the applicant or the insured shall fulfil the following obligations:

- The applicant shall fulfil the obligation of disclosure according to the facts, answer to the inquiries of the insurer accurately concerning the subject matter insured or the insured, failing which due to the applicant's intentional act or gross negligence sufficiently affecting the insurer in deciding whether to agree to cover or increase the insurance premium, the insurer is entitled to terminate the insurance contract; where non-disclosure is due to the applicant's intention, the insurer shall not be liable for insurance incident occurred before termination of insurance contract and shall not refund the insurance premium paid; where non-disclosure is due to the applicant's gross negligence and has material influence in the occurrence of the insurance incident, the insurer shall not be liable for incident occurred before termination of insurance contract, but shall refund the insurance premium paid.
- The applicant shall pay the insurance premium in one lump upon issuance of insurance policy or other insurance certificate by the insurer or his agent, failing which the insurer shall not be liable for insurance incident occurred before payment of the insurance premium.
- The insured shall strictly obey to the various provisions of the State and transport authorities concerning safety transport, maintain the safety of the subject matter insured, make sure that the packing of goods be in conformity with the standard provided for by the State and competent authorities, and implement written suggestions concerning eliminating the unsafe factors and hidden danger to the subject matter insured put forward by the insurer to the applicant or the insured, failing which the insurer shall not be liable for the insurance incident or the exaggerated loss or damage arising therefrom.
- Where the extent of danger to the subject matter insured increases remarkably during the period of validity of the insurance contract, the insured shall notify the insurer in time as agreed upon in the contract and the insurer is entitled to either increase the insurance premium or terminate the contract; where the insured fails to notify, the insurer shall not be liable for the insurance incident arising from any remarkable increase of the extent of danger to the subject matter insured.
- Upon notice of the occurrence of loss of or damage to the insured goods within the insurance coverage, the applicant or the insured shall take reasonable sue and labour or protective measures and notify the insurer's local branch thereof not later than ten days; where notification fails due to the intentional act or gross negligence of the applicant or the insured resulting in difficulty in determining the nature, causes or extent of loss or damage, etc., the insurer shall not be liable for

the part which cannot be determined, provided that the insurer has known or should have known the occurrence of the insurance incident through other means.

F. Settlement of Claim

886. In the claim for insurance indemnity against the insurer, the insured shall provide various documents in support of the claim including, *inter alia*, (a) insurance policy or other insurance certificate, waybill, delivery order, invoice or other evidence of goods price; (b) accident record, receipt and delivery record made by carrier, and assessment report; (c) record of goods entering warehouse made by consignee, survey report, breakdown of loss and vouchers of reasonable expenses incurred directly for the protection of goods; (d) other documents concerning determination of the nature, causes, extent of loss or damage, etc., which the insured is able to provide.

After receipt of the above documents, the insurer shall immediately determine whether the loss or damage is within the insurance liability and notify the insured of the result. If an agreement on settlement amount is reached between the insurer and the insured, the insurer shall make compensation within ten days.

Where the loss of or damage to the insured goods is within the insurance liability, the insurer shall indemnify for the loss or damage in accordance with the actual loss, if the insured amount equals to or higher than the insured value of goods, but such indemnity shall be limited to the insured amount. Where the insured amount is less than the insured value, the amount of indemnity for the loss, damage or expenses of sue and labour or protection shall be calculated in the proportion that the insured amount bears to the insured value. The indemnity for loss of or damage to the insured goods and that for the reasonable expenses incurred directly for the sue and labour and protection of goods shall be calculated respectively and each shall not exceed the insured amount.

Where the carrier or other third party shall be liable wholly or partly for the loss of or damage to goods insured within the insurance liability by virtue of law or relevant agreement, the insured is required to claim against the third party first. However, strictly speaking, such a provision is invalid, as the insured may choose to make claim against either the insurer or the third party.

If the insured waives his claim against a third party, the insurer's liability shall be discharged.

Where the insurer pays insurance indemnity as required by the insured, the insured is obliged to issue a letter of subrogation to the insurer, furnish the insurer with relevant documents and assist the insurer in pursuing recovery from the third person. If, due to the intentional act or gross negligence of the insured, the insurer is unable to exercise his right of subrogation, the insurer may deduct from the indemnity the corresponding amount.

Chapter 3. Coastal Transport and Inland Navigation

§1. INTRODUCTION

I. Carriage by Waterway

887. In China, the domestic maritime transport of goods and the domestic carriage of goods in inland waterways are collectively called as 'carriage of goods by waterway', and the coastal maritime transport of passengers and the carriage of passengers by inland waterway are collectively called as 'carriage of passengers by waterway'. The carriage of goods by waterway and the carriage of passengers by waterway are collectively called as 'carriage by waterway' or 'waterway transport'.

II. Applicable Laws

A. *Laws and Regulations Applicable to Carriage of Goods by Waterway*

888. For more than half a century, two different regimes have been applied to the international maritime carriage of goods and the carriage of goods by waterway. On the other hand, a single regime is applied to the domestic maritime transport of goods and the carriage of goods in inland waterways, i.e., carriage of goods by waterway.

By virtue of paragraph 2 of Article 2 of MC, Chapter IV 'Contract of Carriage of Goods by Sea' including section 7 'Special Provisions regarding Voyage Charter Party' is applicable to the international maritime carriage of goods only, but are not applicable to the domestic maritime transport of goods between two ports or other places within the jurisdiction of China. Noticeably, the maritime transport of goods between the mainland and Hong Kong, Macau or Taiwan is in the nature of domestic transport, but is treated by reference to international transport and thus Chapter IV 'Contract of Carriage of Goods by Sea' of MC is applicable. This chapter also does not apply to the carriage of goods in inland waterways.

As indicated in §4 of Chapter 2 of Part I *supra*, the main law applicable to carriage of goods by waterway is CC. In addition, the *2000 Cargo Regulations* were abolished in 2016, but the contracts of carriage of goods by waterway or the waybills issued thereunder often provide that the contracts are subject thereto. Consequently, the *2000 Cargo Regulations* are in fact still playing their important role in regulating the carriage of goods by waterway including the carriage of goods in inland waterways.

B. *Laws and Regulations Applicable to Carriage of Passengers by Waterway*

889. Chapter V 'Contract of Carriage of Passengers by Sea' of MC applies to both the international maritime transport of passengers and the domestic maritime transport of passengers. The only difference is that the limits of liability of the carrier for the death of or personal injury to the passengers or for loss of or damage to the passengers' luggage stipulated in paragraph 1 of Article 117 of MC does not apply to the carriage of passengers in the domestic maritime transport. Instead, the limits applicable to the carriage of passengers in domestic maritime transport are contained in the *Provisions regarding the Limitation of Liability in the Carriage of Passengers between the Ports of the People's Republic of China* promulgated by the former MOC in 1993. 1974 PAL and its SDR Protocol of 1976 to which China has acceded apply to the domestic maritime transport of passengers with foreign elements except for the provisions of carrier's limitation of liability, but a reservation has been made on its application in this regard.[72]

Besides, CC and the *Passenger Regulations* are applicable to carriage of passengers by waterway as indicated in §4 of Chapter 2 of Part I *supra*.

Discussions in §3 of this chapter are based upon CC and the *Passenger Regulations* and are limited to the carriage of passengers in inland waterways unless otherwise indicated. The matters concerning domestic maritime carriage of passengers are introduced and discussed in Chapter 15 of Part II *supra*.

§2. Carriage of Goods by Waterway

I. Concepts

890. The following are the concepts concerning the carriage of goods by waterway, of which most ones are either the same as or very similar to those in the international maritime carriage of goods:

- Contract of carriage of goods by waterway means is a contract under which the carrier, against the payment of freight, undertakes to carry by waterway the goods shipped by the shipper from one port, station or spot to another port, station or spot within the jurisdiction of China.
- Liner cargo service means regular carriage of goods by waterway on a particular route in accordance with agreed time schedule and calling order.
- Carriage under voyage charter means the carriage of goods in which the shipowners charter out the whole or part of the ship's space to the charterers for the carriage by waterway of the agreed goods from one port, station or spot to another port, station or spot.
- Carrier means the person who has concluded a contract of carriage of goods by waterway with a shipper.
- Actual carrier means the person to whom the performance of carriage of goods or port thereof has been entrusted by the carrier including any other person to whom such performance has been entrusted under a sub-contract.
- Shipper means the person who has concluded a contract of carriage of goods by waterway with a carrier.
- Consignee means the person nominated by the shipper in the contract of carriage of goods by waterway or otherwise to take delivery of goods.

72. *See* §2, Ch. 15 of Part II.

- Goods includes live animals and containers, pallets or similar articles of transport supplied by the shipper for consolidation of the goods.
- Unit Ro/Ro carriage means the carriage of motor vehicles or other movable machines as transport units, whether loaded with goods or not, which roll on to and off the carrying ship by the shippers or their servants.
- Carriage of goods in container means the carriage of goods in a container.

Noticeably, it often occurs in carriage of goods by waterway that the loading or discharging place is not within a port, but is a regular loading or discharging station or spot off a port area, whether at sea or in river or other navigable water.

Unlike the definition of shipper contained in Article 42 of MC, the person who delivers the goods to the carrier by himself or in his name, i.e., mainly the FOB seller in practice, is not treated as a shipper.

II. Conclusion of Contract of Carriage of Goods by Waterway

891. The conclusion of a contract of carriage of goods by waterway is subject to the general provisions governing the conclusion of contract contained in Chapter 2 'Conclusion of Contracts' of Book Three 'Contracts' of CC. Therefore, a contract of carriage of goods by waterway shall be concluded upon agreement reached by the carrier and the shipper. A voyage charter shall be concluded upon agreement reached by the shipowners and the charterers. By virtue of Article 490 of CC, however, whereas a contract of carriage of goods by waterway is in written form, the contract shall be concluded at the time of signature, seal or finger print by the parties thereto, unless one party has performed his main obligation and the other party has accepted such performance in which case the contract shall be concluded at the time of such acceptance.

A contract may be in oral, written or other form. A written form shall include, *inter alia*, telegram, telex, telefax and other means of physically indicating the loaded contents, and EDI, e-mail message and other electronic message of physically indicating the loaded contents and accessible at any time (Article 469, CC). Where the parties conclude a contract by means of letter, electronic message, etc., requiring signing of confirmation letter, a contract shall be concluded at the time of signing the confirmation letter (Article 491, CC).

A contract of carriage of goods by waterway may be a contract of carriage in liner cargo service or a voyage charter party.

The content of a contract of carriage in liner cargo service shall include, *inter alia*, (a) name of the carrier, shipper and consignee; (b) description, number of packages, weight and measurement of the goods; (c) transport expenses and means of settlement; (d) name of vessel and voyage number; (e) port of loading, transhipment and discharge; (f) place and time of receipt and delivery of goods; (g) date or deadline of arrival of goods at destination; (h) means of packing; (i) identification mark of goods; (j) liability for breach of contract; (k) means of dispute settlement.

A voyage charter party shall include, *inter alia*, (a) name of the shipowners and the charterers; (b) description, number of packages, weight and measurement of the goods; (c) transport expenses and means of settlement; (d) name, deadweight, carrying capacity and other particulars of vessel; (e) port of loading and discharge; (f) place and time of receipt and delivery of goods; (g) deadline of shipment; (h) deadline of arrival of goods at destination; (i) laytime for loading and discharging and means of calculation; (j) rate of dispatch money and demurrage; (k) means of packing; (l) identification mark of goods; (m) liability for breach of contract; (n) means of dispute settlement.

III. Obligations and Rights of Shipper

A. *Obligations of Shipper*

892. The shipper shall perform all necessary cargo transport procedures.

Similar to Article 66 of MC, Article 826 of CC provides that where the carriage of goods is subject to approval, inspection or other procedures, the shipper shall furnish to the carrier all relevant documents concerning the procedures the shipper has gone through.

893. The shipper shall make accurate declaration of goods.

Similar to Article 66 of MC, Article 825 of CC requires the shipper to indicate accurately to the carrier the name of consignee, and the description, nature, weight, quantity, place of delivery of goods and other particulars necessary for the carriage of goods. The shipper shall indemnify the carrier against any loss resulting from the inaccuracies of declaration or omission of material information.

894. The shipper shall properly pack and mark the goods.

As required by Article 827 of CC, where packing is required for the carriage of goods, the shipper shall undertake that the packing be in conformity with the agreement between the carrier and the shipper. In the absence of such an agreement, the packing shall meet the requirement the State standards to ensure for the safety of carriage of goods. Otherwise, the carrier may refuse to carry the goods. The shipper shall provide sufficient spare packing materials as required which shall be carried onboard without any additional freight.

Unless in the case of direct carriage where all the goods in one hold or onboard are of the same shipper or consignee, the shipper shall make on the external packing or surface of the goods the indication mark and identification mark including the symbol of consignment, description of goods, port of loading, transhipment and destination, consignee and total number of packages. The indication mark, identification mark and the transport and custody mark shall be legible and secure.

B. *Rights of Shipper*

895. By virtue of Article 829 of CC, the shipper is entitled, before the carrier delivers the goods to the consignee, to demand the carrier to stop carriage, return the goods, change the port of destination or deliver the goods to other consignee, but shall be liable to the carrier for losses resulting therefrom.

IV. Obligations and Rights of Carrier

A. Obligations of Carrier

896. The carrier shall exercise due diligence to make before and at the beginning of the voyage, properly man, equip and supply the ship and to make the holds, refrigerating and cool chambers and all other parts of the vessel in which goods are carried, fit and safe for their reception, carriage and preservation, and maintain the ship's seaworthiness during the voyage.

897. The carrier is obliged to accept the goods for carriage as agreed upon in the contract of carriage.

898. The carrier shall properly and carefully load, handle, stow, carry, keep, care for and discharge the goods carried.

899. The carrier shall carry the goods to the port or other place of discharge on the agreed or customary or geographically direct route (Article 812, CC). However, deviation from the agreed or customary or geographically direct route for the purpose of saving or attempting to save life or property at sea or other reasonable deviation shall not be deemed as any breach of this statutory obligation.

900. The carrier is obliged to carry safely the goods to the agreed place within the time expressly agreed upon, or, in the absence of such agreed time, within reasonable time (Article 811, CC).

Thus, delay in delivery of goods covers two situations. First, the carrier fails to deliver the goods within the time expressly agreed upon. Second, the carrier fails to deliver the goods at the agreed place within a reasonable time, even if no time of delivery was expressly agreed upon. Noticeably, the second situation does not constitute delay in delivery of goods in international carriage of goods by virtue of Article 50 of MC.[73]

The carrier shall be liable for the loss of or damage to the goods caused by delay in delivery and other economic losses suffered by the shipper or consignee caused thereby, unless his liability can be exempted.

901. The carrier shall timely notify the consignee who is known to the carrier of the arrival of the goods at destination (Article 830, CC).

Such notification can be in the form of a letter, telex, telegram, telefax or electronic message. Where the consignee does not timely take delivery of the goods, he shall pay for the custody and other expenses.

73. *See* §6, Ch. 6 of Part II.

B. Rights of Carrier

902. The shipper or consignee is obliged to pay the transport expenses as agreed upon (Article 813, CC). Therefore, the carrier is entitled to freight and other transport expenses as agreed upon. However, by virtue of Article 835 of CC, where the goods are lost during carriage due to force majeure or other cause, the shipper can demand return the freight he has already paid to the carrier; if the freight has not been paid, the carrier cannot claim freight. If part of the goods is lost, the carrier shall collect or refund the freight in proportion to the goods actually delivered.

The amount of freight or calculation thereof and the time, place and method of payment are all subject to agreement between the carrier and the shipper. They can reach an agreement that the freight shall be paid by the consignee before taking delivery of goods at destination. However, if the consignee fails to pay the freight and other transport expenses, the obligation of the shipper to pay these expenses shall not be relieved.

The carrier shall, unless otherwise agreed upon between him and the shipper, have a possessory lien on the corresponding goods where the freight, custody expense and other charges to be paid to the carrier have not been paid in full (Article 836, CC). In the construction of Article 836 of CC, the corresponding goods subject to lien mean that the goods from the carriage of which the freight, custody expenses, demurrage, contribution in general average and other charges have arisen, even if the goods do not belong to the shipper or consignee who is obliged to pay, provided that the value of the goods subject to lien shall be equivalent to the amount of the unpaid freight and other expenses. As an exception, where the carrier and the shipper or consignee are both enterprises, the carrier may exercise a lien on the goods belonging to the shipper or consignee for securing the freight or other charges which the shipper or consignee is obliged to pay and arose from the previous continuous transactions between them by virtue of Article 448 of CC.

V. Liabilities for Breach of Contract

A. Rules of Liability for Breach of Contract

903. CC has adopted the basis of strict liability for breach of contract by both the carrier and the shipper.

By virtue of Article 577 of CC, where a party to the contract fails to fulfil his contractual obligation or his fulfilment is not in conformity with the agreement between the parties, he shall bear the liability in the form of going on with fulfilment, taking remedial measures or compensation for losses, etc. Where, after the party in breach of contract has gone on with fulfilment or taken remedial measures, the innocent party still has suffered loss, the party in breach shall be liable for the loss (Article 583, CC).

In principle, unless otherwise provided for in law, the only exemption of liability for breach of contract is force majeure in the meaning of physical circumstances that cannot be foreseen, avoided and overcome. Article 590 of CC further provides that where the non-performance of contract is caused by force majeure, the liability for non-performance shall be exempted wholly or in part in accordance with the extent of influence thereof on the non-performance, except where force majeure occurred after delay in performance of contract in which case the liability for non-performance shall not be exempted. Where one party is unable to perform the contract due to force majeure, he shall notify the other party thereof in time in order to decrease the loss that the other party may incurs as a result of force majeure and shall provide evidence thereof within reasonable time (Article 590, CC).

Where breach of contract by a party to the contract is caused by a third party, the party in breach of contract shall still bear the liability, whereas any dispute between him and the third party shall be otherwise settled (Article 593, CC).

Where both parties committed breach of contract, each party shall bear corresponding liability for the breach of contract (Article 592, CC).

In the case of anticipatory breach of contract, i.e., where a party to the contract indicates either expressly or by his behaviour that he will not fulfil his contractual obligation, the other party may demand him to bear the liability for breach of contract before the expiry of the time limit of performance of the contract (Article 578, CC).

B. Exemptions of Liability of Carrier and Burden of Proof

904. Besides the principled provisions governing liability for breach of contract in Articles 577 and 590 of CC as introduced *supra*, specific exemptions of liability of the carrier are contained in Article 832 of CC by virtue of which the carrier shall not be liable for the loss of or damage to the goods or delay in delivery thereof occurring during the performance of the contract, if he can prove that the loss, damage or delay has been caused by force majeure, natural character or reasonable wastage of goods, and fault or intentional act of the shipper or consignee.

As a matter of construction, natural character of goods may include the inherent vice of goods; fault or intentional act of the shipper may include any non-conformity of packing or marks to the requirement, inaccuracy of the weight of goods as declared by the shipper, and shipment of dangerous, liquefied or corrosive goods secretly in general goods, etc.

905. Unlike the case of international carriage of goods by sea, the carrier cannot avail of any limitation of liability for the losses resulting directly from the loss of or damage to or delay in delivery of the goods, but shall compensate for all the losses unless his liability can be exempted.

C. Measure of Liability

906. The measure of liability of the party in breach of contract shall be equivalent to the amount of losses suffered by the other party including the loss of profit, provided that the losses shall not exceed the extent the party in breach of contract foresaw or should have foreseen at the time of conclusion of the contract (Article 584, CC).

In the case of breach of contract by one party, the innocent party has the obligation to mitigate loss. If the innocent party fails to take proper measures to mitigate loss, he is not entitled to claim against the party in breach of contract for the loss that could have been mitigated by taking proper measures by him (Article 591, CC). On the other hand, where the innocent party has taken such measures, the reasonable expenses thus incurred shall be borne by the party in breach of contract.

By virtue of Article 585 of CC, the parties to the contract may reach an agreement as to the calculation of compensation for the losses caused by breach of the contract. Where an amount of penalty on breach of contract has been agreed upon between the parties, the party in breach of contract shall pay the agreed amount of penalty to the innocent party, regardless of the amount of loss the innocent party has suffered. However, if the amount of loss suffered by the innocent party exceeds the agreed amount of penalty, the party in breach of contract shall compensate for the balance of the loss. If the agreed amount of penalty is lower or excessively higher than the losses thus caused, a court of law or arbitration organ may increase or appropriately reduce upon a request of a party to the contract.

By virtue of Article 587 of CC, if a deposit has been agreed upon between the parties and paid by one party to the other, the party in breach of contract resulting in non-realization of the purpose of contract is not entitled to demand return of the deposit paid to the other; if the other party is in breach of the contract resulting in non-realization of the purpose of contract, the innocent party is entitled to demand double return of the deposit paid to the party in breach. The amount of deposit is subject to the agreement between the parties but shall not exceed 20% of the principal amount and any mount exceeding this percentage shall be invalid. If the amount of loss suffered by the innocent party exceeds the amount of deposit, the party in breach of contract shall compensate for the balance of the loss.

VI. Carriage of Special Goods

A. Dangerous Goods

907. Similar to Article 68 of MC, Article 828 of CC provides that, at the time of shipment of flammable, explosive, poisonous, corrosive, radioactive and other dangerous goods, the shipper shall, in compliance with the regulations governing the carriage of such goods,[74] have them properly packed, distinctly marked and labelled and notify the carrier in writing of their proper description, nature and precautions to be taken. If the shipper fails to do so, the carrier can refuse to carry the dangerous goods or take corresponding measures to avoid the occurrence of loss at the expense of the shipper.

In the case the shipper fails to notify the carrier as required or notified him inaccurately, therefore, the carrier may have such goods landed, destroyed or rendered

74. The *Regulations Governing the Transport of Dangerous Goods by Waterway* enacted by the former MOC on 4 Nov. 1996.

innocuous when and where circumstances so require, without payment of compensation, and the shipper is liable to the carrier for the loss resulting from the shipment of such goods. Notwithstanding the carrier's knowledge of the nature of the dangerous goods and his consent to carry, he may still have such goods landed, destroyed or rendered innocuous without compensation, when they become an actual danger to the ship, her crew and other persons onboard or to other goods, without prejudice to the contribution in general average.

B. Deck Cargo

908. The carrier is entitled to carry the goods on deck only where an agreement of deck carriage has been concluded with the shipper or such carriage complies with the custom of the trade or with law or administrative regulations.

In the case of authorized carriage of goods on deck, the carrier shall not be liable for the loss of or damage to the goods caused by the special risks involved in such carriage. In the case of unauthorized carriage of goods on deck, the carrier shall be liable for the loss or damage caused thereby.

C. Putrescible Goods, Live Animals and Plants

909. In the case of carriage of putrescible goods, live animals or plants, the shipper and the carrier shall reach an agreement as to the requirements of carriage.

Where the putrescible goods are carried in a refrigerating ship or hold, the temperature of refrigeration shall be agreed upon at the time of conclusion of the contract.

Unless otherwise agreed, where feeding or care is needed during the carriage of live animals or plants, the shipper shall declare the goods as such and appoint an escort onboard during carriage. The feed shall be supplied by the shipper. The carrier shall supply fresh water needed for the carriage of live animals or plants at the expenses of the shipper, unless otherwise agreed upon.

The carrier shall not be liable for the loss of or damage to the live animals or plants arising or resulting from the special risks inherent in the carriage thereof, provided that the carrier shall be bound to prove that he has fulfilled the special requirements of the shipper with regard to the carriage thereof and that the loss or damage has occurred due to the special risks inherent therein.

VII. Non-contractual Claims

A. Consignee's Title to Sue Against Carrier

910. The consignee other than the shipper is a third party to the contract of carriage and therefore is not bound by the contract by virtue of the rule of privity of contract. However, the consignee is entitled to make claim against the carrier for losses arising from loss of or damage to or delay in delivery of goods and the carrier can avail of the exemptions of liability and other defences available to him when the claim is made by the shipper.

In claiming for such losses, the consignee has the burden of proving the extent and amount thereof. By virtue of Article 381 of CC, the consignee shall inspect the goods within the agreed time limit or within reasonable time limit in the absence of an agreed one; where the consignee raises no objection to the quantity, loss of or damage to the goods, it shall be deemed as prima facie evidence of delivery of the goods by the carrier as stated in a waybill or other transport document.

B. Actual Carrier

911. The *2000 Cargo Regulations* before abolishment contained provisions concerning the actual carrier which were very similar to those of Chapter IV of MC. After the abolishment of these Regulations, CC and other laws applicable to domestic carriage of goods by waterway lack the definition and rules of actual carrier. However, the following points are recognized in judicial practice:

First, where the carrier other than the owners of the carrying ship entrusts the performance or part thereof to the shipowners or other actual carrier, the carrier remains responsible for the entire carriage. However, as an exception, where a contract of carriage provides explicitly that a specified part of the carriage covered by the said contract is to be performed by a named person other than the carrier, the contract may also provide that the carrier is not liable for loss, damage or delay in delivery caused by an occurrence which took place while the goods were in the charge of the actual carrier during such part of the carriage.

Second, the actual carrier shall bear tortuous liability for loss of or damage to or delay in delivery of goods if caused by the fault or intentional act or omission on his part.

Third, where and to the extent that both the carrier and the actual carrier are liable, their liability shall be joint and several.

C. Servants or Agent of Carrier or Actual Carrier

912. Unlike Articles 58 and 61 of MC which stipulate that, where an action with regard to loss of or damage to the goods is brought against a servant or agent of the carrier or actual carrier whose act is within the scope of his employment or agency, the actual carrier or his servant or agent is entitled to avail of the immunities and limitation of liability and other defences available to the carrier, CC does not contain any specific provision in this respect. The lack of such provisions conforms to the rules contained in Articles 162, 1191 and 1192 of CC to the effect that no claim can be made against a servant or agent for loss or damage due to the fault thereof within the scope of his employment or agency, unless his act or omission proves illegal.

VIII. Waybill

A. *Functions of Waybill*

913. Waybill, or waybills of carriage of goods by waterway in their full name, are the main transport documents used for more than half a century in the carriage of goods by waterway in China.

A waybill used in the carriage of goods by waterway shall not be confused with an SWB used in international carriage of goods by sea, although they share a lot of similarities.

A waybill serves as an evidence of the contract of carriage of goods by waterway and the taking over of the goods by the carrier. Unlike a bill of lading, however, a waybill is not a document based upon which the carrier undertakes to deliver the goods against surrendering the same. Instead, in the case of a waybill, the carrier shall deliver the goods to the consignee stated therein after verification of the identity of the consignee, unless the shipper nominates another consignee as a result of the exercise of right of control on the goods by virtue of Article 829 of CC.

B. *Particulars of Waybill*

914. A waybill normally contains the following particulars:

- name of carrier, shipper and consignee;
- description, number of packages, weight and measurement of goods;
- transport expenses and means of settlement;
- name of ship and voyage number;
- port of loading, transhipment and discharge;
- place and time of receipt and delivery of goods;
- date of shipment;
- deadline of arrival of the goods at destination;
- means of packing of goods;
- identification mark of goods.

C. *Issuance of Waybill*

915. After the taking over of the goods, the carrier shall issue a waybill as demanded by the shipper or the consignor. Where a waybill is issued by an agent of the carrier or by the master of the carrying ship, it shall be deemed as issued by the carrier.

In practice, the number of waybills is normally six. The carrier, his agent, shipper, port operator at destination and consignee shall separately keep one and the other one shall be signed by the consignee as receipt of the goods and returned to the carrier after the consignee has taken delivery of the goods. However, the carrier may increase or reduce the number of waybills as the circumstances require.

IX. Taking Over and Delivery of Goods

A. *Taking Over of Goods by Carrier*

916. Unless otherwise agreed upon between the carrier and the shipper, the goods in bulk shall be taken over in terms of the weight thereof and the goods in packages or pieces in terms of the number thereof. This means that the carrier shall be responsible for the number of packages or pieces of the goods in packages or pieces, but not for the weight thereof, unless it proves that any proven shortage of goods in weight is caused by the carrier.

The carrier and the shipper can reach an agreement as to the means of determining the weight of goods in bulk. In the absence of such an agreement, the weight of goods in bulk shall be measured by draft survey of a ship. Where the weight cannot be measured by draft survey or other reasonable means, the weight stated in the waybill shall not constitute evidence of the weight of goods taken over by the carrier.

In the case of liquid goods, the shipper and the carrier normally reach an agreement to seal the valves of the tankers and pipelines with materials supplied by the shipper. Before discharge at destination, the carrier shall deliver the goods in accordance with the seals. Therefore, where the seals remain intact, the carrier shall not be responsible for any shortage of the goods.

B. *Delivery of Goods by Carrier*

917. The carrier shall deliver the goods to the consignee stated in the waybill or other consignee nominated by the shipper by virtue of Article 829 of CC. At the time of delivery of the goods, the carrier shall verify the identity of the consignee.

The consignee is obliged to timely take delivery of goods after receipt of the notice of arrival thereof and shall not detain the ship for the purpose of testing the quality of goods. The consignee is also obliged to inspect the goods upon delivery thereof and issue a receipt of the goods he has taken delivery of.

Where the shipper demands the goods to be delivered to two or more consignees, the shipper or the consignees shall be responsible for the allotment thereof and any wastage in weight.

Where loss of or damage to the goods is reasonably anticipated, the consignee may before taking delivery of the goods at the port of destination, and the carrier may before delivering the goods at the port of destination, demand a survey agency to inspect the condition of goods, provided that the party demanding such inspection shall bear the costs thereof, but shall be entitled to recover the same from the other party liable for the damage to the goods, if any. The consignee and the carrier shall mutually provide reasonable facilities for such inspection.

C. Transport Record

918. Transport record is a document customarily used in the domestic carriage of goods by waterway to indicate the apparent loss of or damage to the goods or other circumstances of the carriage. Such a document is normally signed by the carrier and shipper/consignee as well as by port operator and serves as a strong evidence of the extent and cause of loss of or damage to the goods.

X. Special Provisions Regarding Voyage Charter Party

A. Introduction

919. Voyage charter parties are a kind of contracts of domestic carriage of goods by waterway. In practice, except in the domestic liner shipping, the contracts of domestic carriage of goods by waterway are mainly in the form of voyage charter parties.

The provisions of section 1 'General Provisions' and section 3 'Contracts of Carriage of Goods' of Chapter XIX 'Contracts of Carriage' of Book Three 'Contracts' of CC concerning the carrier's rights, obligations and liabilities are applicable to the shipowners under a voyage charter party, and those concerning the shipper's rights, obligations and liabilities are applicable to the charterers under a voyage charter party.

However, the shipowners and the charterers are free to negotiate the provisions concerning laytime, demurrage, dispatch money and other matters of voyage charter party which are not provided for in CC.

B. Duties of Shipowners

920. The shipowners under a voyage charter party are basically in the same position as a carrier under a contract of domestic carriage of goods by waterway and undertakes the following obligations:

- to exercise clue diligence before and at the beginning of the voyage to make the vessel seaworthy, properly man, equip and supply the ship and to make the holds, refrigerating and cool chambers and all other parts of the ship in which goods are carried, fit and safe for their reception, carriage and preservation, and to maintain the ship's seaworthiness during the voyage;
- to carry the goods to the port or other place of discharge on the agreed or customary or geographically direct route except for reasonable deviation;
- to properly and carefully load, handle, stow, carry, keep, care for and discharge the goods carried;
- to carry and deliver goods within the agreed or reasonable time, failing which the carrier shall be liable for the losses resulting from delay in delivery;
- to timely notify the consignee of the arrival of goods at the port or other place of destination.

921. The shipowners shall provide the agreed ship or ship's space and make her ready to load the agreed cargo at the port or other place of loading within the lay-days fixed in the charter party, failing which the charterers may cancel the contract subject to his notice of cancellation of contract after receiving the shipowners' notification of the delay of ship and the expected date of her arrival of the port or other place of loading. The shipowners shall be liable for any loss or damage the charterers have suffered resulting therefrom, unless his liability can be exempted.

Without consent of the charterers, the shipowners shall not substitute the agreed ship, failing which the charterer may reject the ship or cancel the contract.

C. Duties of Charterers

922. The charterers under a voyage charter have the following obligations:

- to pay to the shipowners the agreed freight, dead freight, contribution in general average and other necessary charges paid by the shipowners for and on behalf of the charterers;
- to provide the agreed goods for carriage, unless the agreed goods are replaced with the consent of the shipowners. If the charterers fail to provide the agreed goods and, as a result, the shipowners suffered loss, the charterers shall be liable for compensation, if such loss resulted from a cause for which the charterers shall be responsible. Where the charterers are entitled to replace the good under the charter party, the shipowners shall be entitled to reject the goods replaced and cancel the charter party, should the replacement of goods is detrimental to the interests of the shipowners;
- to load and discharge the goods within the laytime for loading and/or discharge. Where the Charterers fail to load and/or discharge the goods within the laytime, they shall pay to the shipowners the agreed demurrage. On the other hand, where the loading and/or discharge operation has completed ahead of schedule, the charterers are entitled to the agreed dispatch money.

D. Rights and Obligations of Consignee under Voyage Charter

923. The rights and obligations of the consignee under a voyage charter party depend on whether the consignee is the charterers or not.

Where the consignee is the charterers, the consignee shall assume the obligations and enjoy the rights of the charterers as indicated *supra*. At the same time, the consignee shall assume the obligations and enjoy the rights determined in accordance with sections 1 and 3 of Chapter XIX of Book Three of CC. Where the consignee is not the charterers, the obligations and rights between the carrier and the consignee shall be determined in accordance with the waybill issued under the voyage charter and the related provisions contained in sections 1 and 3 of Chapter XIX of Book Three of CC.

XI. Special Provisions Regarding Carriage in Containers

924. Where a container is supplied by the carrier, the shipper shall inspect the container and verify the container number and, when the consignee returns the container to the carrier, the carrier shall also inspect and verify.

Where, as agreed upon between the carrier and the shipper, the shipper is responsible for stuffing and devanning the goods, i.e., in the case of FCL, the goods shall be taken over by the carrier at the port of loading and taken delivery of by the consignee at the port of destination in accordance with the condition of the container, its seal and its number. The waybill shall state accurately the container seal number. Where the container seal number does not conform to that stated in the waybill or is in damaged condition, the parties involved in the receipt or delivery of goods shall make a transport record indicating the inaccuracy or the damaged condition.

Where, as agreed upon between the carrier and the shipper, the carrier is responsible for stuffing and devanning the goods, i.e., in the case of LCL, the goods shall be taken over by the carrier at the port of loading and taken delivery of by the consignee at the port of destination in the same way as non-containerized goods.

Where a container is supplied by the carrier, the consignee shall return the empty container to the carrier after taking delivery of the containerized goods. Otherwise, the consignee shall pay for the detention of the container as agreed.

In the stuffing of goods in a container, no matter who is responsible for it, the goods shall be reasonably stowed and secured. The weight of goods stowed in container shall not exceed the maximum capacity thereof.

XII. Special Provisions Regarding Unit Ro/Ro Carriage

925. In the mode of unit Ro/Ro carriage of goods, the period of performance of contract shall be from the time when the transport unit enters the port of loading to the time when it leaves the port of destination, unless otherwise agreed upon between the carrier and the shipper.

At the time the transport unit enters the port of loading, the carrier shall check the apparent order and condition thereof, issue a waybill and remark the waybill if it is not in apparent good order and condition. At the time the transport unit leaves the port of destination, the consignee shall sign on the waybill and return it to the carrier or his agent after signature. The waybill shall state the number of vehicle, the weight and dimension of the transport unit.

The accidents occurred in practice prove that lashing and fastening of the vehicles and the goods loaded on them on board the carrying ship for the prevention of movement thereof is very important for the safety of the transport units and the ship. Therefore, the shipper is required to lash and fasten the goods loaded on the vehicle or other movable machine. Where a transport unit needs special lashing and fastening onboard, the shipper shall state the case to the carrier at the time of shipment and pay for the corresponding expenses. The carrier shall have the ordinary lashing and fastening materials on board the ship, and lash and fasten the transport units in the ordinary or required manner for the prevention of movement thereof, unless it is agreed that the shipper is responsible for lashing and fastening.

When a transport unit moves on to or off the ship, the drivers shall be bound by the safety regulations and obey to the command on the part of the ship. When a transport unit is located onboard, the engine of vehicle shall be turned off and the vehicle shall be in the braked condition.

No dangerous goods shall be loaded on the transport units, unless otherwise agreed upon between the carrier and the shipper in which case all the requirements for the carriage of dangerous goods onboard shall be complied with.

§3. Carriage of Passengers by Waterway

I. Passenger Ticket

926. A passenger ticket serves as an evidence of the conclusion of a contract of carriage of passenger by waterway between the carrier and the passenger. Unless otherwise agreed upon or there is transaction usage to the contrary, the contract of carriage shall be deemed as have been concluded when the carrier or his agent delivers the passenger ticket to the passenger (Article 814, CC).

II. Obligations of Passenger

927. By virtue of section 2 'Contract of Carriage of Passengers' of Chapter XIX of Book Three of CC and the *Passenger Regulations*, a passenger under a contract of carriage of passenger in inland navigation has the following obligations:

- A passenger shall travel with a valid passage ticket. A passenger traveling without a valid ticket or taking a berth of higher class than booked or going beyond the distance shall pay for the fare or the excess fare as required and, if the passenger refuses to pay, the carrier may refuse to carry, unless permitted by the carrier (Article 815, CC). However, a child passenger below the height of 1.2 m can travel with an adult passenger without passage ticket. If two or more children travel with an adult passenger, the other or others shall each hold a preferential passage ticket of 50% of the normal fare (Article 25, *Passenger Regulations*).
- Where, due to his or her own reason, a passenger is unable to embark the ship at the time indicated in the passage ticket, he or she shall get refund for the passage ticket or change voyage within the agreed time. Otherwise, the carrier may refuse to refund and shall not undertake to carry him or her (Article 816, CC).
- A passenger shall carry cabin luggage not exceeding the stipulated quantity. Otherwise, the excess luggage shall be carried as checked luggage and the passenger shall pay for it (Article 817, CC).
- A passenger shall not carry as cabin luggage or pack in the checked luggage any article of an inflammable, explosive, poisonous, corrosive or radioactive nature or other contraband that would cause danger to the safety of life and property onboard. Should the passenger commit breach of this obligation, the carrier may have the contraband landed, rendered innocuous or sent over to an appropriate

authority without compensation. Should the passenger insist to carry the contraband, the carrier may refuse to carry (Article 818, CC).

III. Obligations of Carrier

928. By virtue of section 2 'Contract of Carriage of Passengers' of Chapter XIX of Book Three of CC, the carrier under a contract of carriage of passengers in inland navigation has the following obligations:

- The carrier shall timely notify the passenger of the important information affecting normal transport and of the safety instructions (Article 819, CC).
- The carrier shall carry the passenger in accordance with the time and voyage as indicated in the passage ticket. Where delay in carriage occurs, the carrier shall arrange for the change of voyage or refund the passage ticket as the passenger demands (Article 820, CC).
- The carrier shall not change the ship at his will as a result of which the service standard is reduced. Otherwise, the carrier shall arrange for the change of voyage or refund the passage ticket as the passenger demands. Where, due to the change of ship, the service standard is increased, the carrier is not entitled to any additional fare (Article 821, CC).
- The carrier shall render assistance to passengers during the carriage in case of urgent disease, giving birth or distress (Article 822, CC).

IV. Liabilities of Carrier

A. For Personal Injury or Death of Passenger

929. CC has adopted the basis of strict liability of the carrier for death of or personal injury to the passengers during the carriage by waterway.

By virtue of Article 823 of CC, the carrier shall be liable for death of or personal injury to a passenger occurred during the carriage by waterway, unless the death or injury is caused by the healthy condition of the passenger or the carrier proves the death or injury is caused intentionally by the passenger or by his or her gross negligence. In any other case, the liability of carrier cannot be exempted, whether the carrier has committed fault or not. This liability also applies to death of or injury to a passenger whose travel does not need a passage ticked or travels by holding a preferential passage ticket or without a passage ticket as permitted by the carrier.

B. For Loss of or Damage to Passenger's Cabin Luggage

930. CC has adopted the basis of fault liability of the carrier for loss of or damage to the passenger's cabin luggage during the carriage by waterway.

By virtue of paragraph 1 of Article 824 of CC, the carrier shall be liable for loss of or damage to the passenger's cabin luggage occurred during the carriage by waterway only if the loss or damage is caused by the intentional act or omission or by the fault on the part of the carrier.

C. For Loss of or Damage to Passenger's Checked Luggage

931. By virtue of paragraph 2 of Article 824 of CC, where the passenger's checked luggage suffers loss or damage during the carriage by waterway, the luggage shall be deemed as goods under a contract of domestic carriage of goods by waterway. Thus, by virtue of Article 832 of CC, the carrier shall not be liable for the loss or damage if he proves that the loss or damage is caused by force majeure, nature of the luggage or reasonable wastage, or fault or intentional act of the shipper or consignee, as introduced in §2 of this chapter *supra*.

§4. Other Matters Concerning Inland Navigation

I. Introduction

932. As mentioned in §1 in Chapter 2 of Part II *supra*, there is no specific law or regulations now in China governing the matters of civil law relating to inland navigation and inland vessels such as collision, salvage, general average, limitation of liability, hull and cargo insurance, vessel's proprietary rights including ownership, possessory lien, mortgage and maritime lien. Therefore, these legal matters are subject to the limited general rules contained in the basic laws, i.e., CC and IL.

As a result, collisions between inland vessels are regulated by the provisions governing tort liability contained in Book Seven 'Tortuous Liability' of CC; hull and cargo insurances are regulated by IL and CC; ownership of, possessory lien and mortgage on inland vessel are regulated by Book Two 'Real Rights' of CC. There is no salvage, general average, limitation of liability and maritime lien in inland navigation.

Obviously, CC and IL cannot meet the need of law with respect to the above matters of law relating to inland navigation and inland vessels. Thus, it is advisable that specific statutory provisions be adopted to regulate these matters. This legislative issue is now under consideration. One possible way is to extend the scope of application of MC to cover inland navigation adjacent to the sea and inland vessels with necessary special provisions.

933. Particularly, as introduced in §1 of Chapter 11 of Part II *supra*, both Chapter XII 'Contract of Marine Insurance' of MC and IL are applicable to the insurances of hull and cargo in domestic coastal transport and the provisions of Chapter XII of MC have priority over those contained in IL in case of and to the extent of repugnancy. Chapter XII of MC, however, does not apply to the insurances of hull and cargo in inland navigation. Therefore, the insurances of hull and cargo in inland navigation are subject to the provisions of IL.

The contracts of insurance of hull or cargo in both domestic coastal transport and inland navigation are subject to the provisions of CC to the extent they are not repugnant to those of MC and/or IL.

Thus, the introduction to and discussions of MC and IL in Chapter 11 of Part II *supra* are also applicable to the insurance of hull or cargo in the domestic coastal transport. On the other hand, only the introduction to and discussions of IL in Chapter 11 of Part II *supra* are applicable to the insurance of hull or cargo in inland navigation. However, those of CC in that Chapter are applicable to the insurance of hull or cargo in both domestic coastal transport and inland navigation.

As indicated in §1 of Chapter 11 of Part II *supra*, PICC P&C has formulated the Coastal & Inland Vessel Insurance Clauses of 2009 (hereinafter referred to as 'PICC P&C Coastal & Inland Vessel Clauses of 2009'), the Inland Vessel Insurance Clauses of 2009 (hereinafter referred to as 'PICC P&C Inland Vessel Clauses of 2009') and the Waterway Cargo Transport Insurance Clauses of 2009 (hereinafter referred to as 'PICC P&C Waterway Cargo Clauses of 2009'). The PICC P&C Coastal & Inland Vessel Clauses of 2009 and the PICC P&C Inland Vessel Clauses of 2009 are almost the same. Noticeably, the PICC P&C Coastal & Inland Vessel Clauses of 2009 and the PICC P&C Inland Vessel Clauses of 2009 are not subject to the same statutory provisions, because the insurance of coastal vessels is subject to Chapter XII of MC and IL, while the insurance of inland vessels is subject to IL only.

II. Coastal and Inland Hull Insurance

A. *Subject Matter Insured*

934. By virtue of the PICC P&C Coastal & Inland Vessel Clauses of 2009, the subject matter insured means a vessel duly registered in China and engaging in coastal trade or combined coastal trade and inland navigation including the hull, machinery, equipment, navigational instruments, and bunker and stores on board the vessel insured.

By virtue of the PICC P&C Inland Vessel Clause of 2009, the subject matter insured means a vessel duly registered in China and engaging in inland navigation including the hull, machinery, equipment and navigational instruments, but not including bunker and stores on board the vessel insured.

B. *Scope of Cover*

935. Under the PICC P&C Coastal & Inland Vessel Clauses of 2009 and the PICC P&C Inland Vessel Clauses of 2009, the coverage includes the total loss cover and the all-risks cover.

936. Under the total loss cover, the insurer shall be liable for the total loss of the insured vessel caused by:

- wind not exceeding Beaufort scale 8, flood, earthquake, tsunami, lightning, ice under the PICC P&C Coastal & Inland Vessel Clauses of 2009, or wind not exceeding Beaufort scale 6, earthquake, lightning, collapse of cliff, landslide, mud-rock flow under the PICC P&C Inland Vessel Clauses of 2009;
- fire or explosions;
- grounding, running on rocks, collision or contacting with any other fixed or floating object (allision);
- capsizing or sinking resulting from one of the above three disasters or accidents;
- missing of the vessel.

937. Under the all risks cover, the insurance covers the total or partial loss of the insured vessel arising from any of the perils insured against under the total loss cover and also the liabilities and expenses in respect of collision or allision, general average, salvage and sue and labour under the PICC P&C Coastal & Inland Vessel Clauses of 2009. However, the PICC P&C Inland Vessel Clauses of 2009 does not cover general average to be contributed by the vessel because there is general average regime in inland navigation.

938. The insurance of collision or allision liability covers the legal liability of the insured for the direct losses and expenses as a consequence of the insured vessel coming into collision or contact with any other vessel, quay, port installations or navigation aids.

Unlike the RDC in PICC P&C Hull Clauses of 2009 which covers 4/4 of the collision or allision liability, this insurance only covers 3/4 of the collision or allision liability. The maximum amount of indemnity for one or all such accidents occurring during the period of insurance not exceeding one year shall be limited to the insured amount.

This insurance does not cover the loss of or damage to the cargo carried on the insured vessel.

939. This insurance also covers the necessary and reasonable expenses of sue and labour, salvage remuneration or award the insured has paid for the measures of sue and labour and salvage in order to avert or minimize loss when an insurance accident of the insured vessel occurs. Under the PICC P&C Coastal & Inland Vessel Clauses of 2009, the insurance of general average covers the insured vessel's proportion of general average contribution the adjustment of which shall be made in accordance with the contract or the applicable law or usages, or, in absence of such contractual provision, law or usage, with the *Beijing Adjustment Rules of 2022*.

Under the PICC P&C Coastal & Inland Vessel Clauses of 2009, the aggregate amount of indemnity for loss of or damage to the insured vessel, general average and salvage, or the amount of indemnity for sue and labour expenses, shall be limited to the insured amount.

C. Exclusions

940. Under the PICC P&C Coastal & Inland Vessel Clauses of 2009 and the PICC P&C Inland Vessel Clauses of 2009, the following losses, liabilities and expenses shall be excluded from the insurance indemnity:

- unseaworthiness of the insured vessel or her incapability of towing including her improper manning or technical conditions, trading limit or use not suitable for navigation (towing) or improper stowage, unless the insured proves that he did not know or has no reason to know the existence of such a situation under a time policy;
- crime committed by the insured, shipowners, ship operator and their representative or master by use of the insured vessel, or their intentional act except general average act or sue and labour act under the PICC P&C Coastal & Inland Vessel Clauses of 2009 or except sue and labour act or salvage act under the PICC P&C Inland Vessel Clauses of 2009;
- ordinary wear and tear, rust, corrosion of the insured vessel;
- liability for loss of damage to other vessel or property caused by waves from the insured vessel during navigation, grounding (vessel's sitting on the water bottom due to ebb tide or cargo loading) or long-term frequent touching of the vessel's bottom on the river bed due to waterway's silt or change of water level in normal navigational waters;
- war, military action, seizure, riot, strike, robbery, governmental requisition or confiscation;
- nuclear substance or material, or nuclear radiation, nuclear testing;
- governmental administrative act or judicial act;
- ordinary maintenance or painting of the insured vessel, damage to her machinery due to breakdown thereof and expenses;
- particular average of rudder, propeller, mast, anchor, anchor chain or affiliated boat under the PICC P&C Inland Vessel Clauses of 2009;
- liability or loss of, damage to or expenses of the vessel towed caused by a towage act, unless the vessel towed is the insured vessel; towing liability under the PICC P&C Inland Vessel Clauses of 2009;
- pollution, prevention or cleanup of pollution;
- wreck removal, or cleanup of port, wharf, waterway or navigable waters;
- loss of life or personal injury;
- aquaculture, fishing apparatus, submarine installations, cables, bridge or bridge under construction and its related installations;
- cargo carried onboard the insured vessel;
- indirect loss, damage or expenses of the insured or a third party including loss of crew's wages, freight, hire and other expenses and interests arising from stoppage of navigation or operation caused by an insurance accident, loss arising from delay in or loss of use of any property, loss of economic activity in water, loss of coastline industry, agriculture or tourism, etc.;
- the insured vessel's engagement in towage or salvage service, direct loading or discharge at sea between the insured vessel and other vessel other than lighter age vessel used in port or coastal waters, or in a voyage of the insured vessel for the

purpose of scrapping or sale for scrapping, unless the insurer was notified of in writing and additional premium has been paid, under the PICC P&C Coastal & Inland Vessel Clauses of 2009;
- other loss, damage or liability not specifically listed within the scope of insurance liability.

D. Obligations of Insured or Applicant

941. Under the PICC P&C Costal & Inland Vessel Clauses of 2009 and the PICC P&C Inland Vessel Clauses of 2009, the insured or the applicant has the following obligations:

- The applicant shall fill in the application form and answer to the insurer's inquiries truthfully. During the period of insurance, the applicant or the insured shall disclose truthfully the events of change of his company or insured vessel affecting the insurer's interest, and shall notify the insurer in advance in writing of the sale, bareboat charter out, change of trading limit, and change of the owners, manager or operator, name, technical condition and use of the insured vessel. The contract of insurance shall remain valid only after the approval and endorsement by the insurer. Otherwise, the insurance contract shall be discharged automatically upon the occurrence of the above events, unless the vessel is carrying cargo or underway in which case the insurance shall remain till the vessel arrives at the next port or last discharge port or port of destination.
- The applicant or the insured shall pay the insurance premium in one lump upon conclusion of the insurance contract, unless otherwise agreed in writing in a time insurance contract. The insurer shall not be liable if an insurance accident occurred before the payment of insurance premium.
- The insured and his representative shall strictly conform to the regulations regarding safety navigation promulgated by MSA and duly arrange for the management, survey and repair of the insured vessel to secure her seaworthiness. Otherwise, the insurance contract shall be terminated automatically.
- Having learnt the occurrence of insurance accident of the insured vessel, the insured shall notify the insurer within forty-eight hours and take reasonable measures to avoid or minimize loss. Where special instructions for the adoption of reasonable measures to avoid or minimize the loss are received from the insurer, the insured shall act according to such instructions. Otherwise, the insurer may make reasonable deduction of the loss exaggerated thereby in compensation.
- Upon the occurrence of insurance accident of the insured vessel, the insured shall act meticulously as shipowners as if he was not an insured and decide repair to damage to the insured vessel and pay for the repair cost after negotiations with the insurer. Otherwise, the insurer may make deduction of the cost increased thereby in compensation.
- Having learnt breach of the insurance contract in respect of cargo, voyage, trading limit, towage, salvage or date of sailing, the insured shall immediately notify

the insurer. This insurance shall remain valid after the insurer has agreed in writing and received additional premium. Otherwise, this insurance shall be terminated automatically as of the date of such violation.

III. Additional Insurances of Coastal and Inland Vessels

942. PICC P&C has formulated the following six sets of insurance clauses of additional risks that are additional to the Coastal & Inland Vessel Clauses of 2009:

- Particular Average of Propeller, Rudder, Anchor, Anchor Chain or Affiliated Boat Clauses.
- Three-fourth Collision & Allision Liability, General Average, Sue & Labour, Salvage Clauses.
- One-fourth Collision & Allision Liability Clauses.
- Tug's Towage Liability Clauses.
- Owner's Liability for Passengers Clauses.
- Owner's Liability for Crew Clauses.

The PICC P&C Coastal & Inland Vessel Clauses of 2009 shall apply to the insurance of additional risks. However, in case of conflict, the additional clauses shall have priority.

IV. Insurance of Cargo Transport by Waterway

A. *Subject Matter Insured*

943. By virtue of the PICC P&C Waterway Cargo Clauses of 2009, the subject matter insured means the cargo carried by waterway in coastal waters, rivers and lakes, excluding fresh vegetables, fruits, live stocks, birds, fishes and other live animals. In addition, unless specially agreed upon between the insurer and the applicant or the insured and stated in the policy, valuables such as gold, silver, jewellery, diamonds, jade, antiques, ancient books, postage stamps, works of art and rare metals are not covered by this insurance.

B. *Commencement and Termination of Insurance Liability*

944. The PICC P&C Waterway Cargo Clauses of 2009 contains a 'warehouse to warehouse' clause to the effect that the insurance liability shall, after the issuance of the insurance policy or other insurance certificate, commence from the time when the insured cargo is carried away from the last warehouse or storage place of the consignor at the place of the commencement of transport and terminate at the time when the insured cargo arrives at the first warehouse or storage place of the consignee at destination stated in the insurance certificate, provided that the time limit of termination shall not exceed fifteen days from the time the insured cargo is discharged from the means of transport.

C. Scope of Cover

945. Under the P&C PICC Waterway Cargo Clauses of 2009, the coverage includes the basic cover and the comprehensive cover.

946. Under the basic cover, the insurer shall be liable for the loss of or damage to the insured cargo or expenses caused by:

- fire, explosion, lightning, hail, storm, flood, tsunami, collapse of cliff, sudden landslide, mud-rock flow;
- collision, grounding or running on rocks of vessel, collapse of bridge or pier;
- sinking or missing of vessel resulting from the above causes;
- loss caused by accident in loading, discharging or transhipment;
- general average sacrifice, contribution in general average or salvage expenses to be borne in accordance with State's provisions or practice;
- scatter and disappearance of cargo due to disorder and reasonable costs paid directly for the sue and labour or preservation of the cargo in the case of the above disasters.

947. Under the comprehensive cover, besides the liability under the basic cover, the insurer shall also be liable for loss or damage arising from:

- breakage, crook, concavity, split of cargo due to impact or extrusion;
- scatter and disappearance of cargo due to breakage of packing;
- damage to containers of liquid cargo, including its seal due to impact or extrusion, or putrescence or deterioration of cargo due to the leakage of liquid in which the cargo is preserved;
- theft;
- wet damage by rain under the condition of conformity with the provisions of safety transport.

D. Exclusions

948. Under the PICC P&C Waterway Cargo Clauses of 2009, the insurer shall not be liable for the loss of or damage to the insured cargo or expenses caused by:

- war, military action, seizure, strike, robbery or riot;
- loss or damage arising from defective quality or shortage in quantity of the insured cargo existing before the commencement of insurance liability;

- ordinary wear and tear, pollution, putrescence or damage arising from vice or specific nature of the insured cargo;
- loss of market or loss or damage arising from delay in transport;
- loss or damage due to the responsibility of the consignor of cargo;
- intentional act or criminal act of the applicant or the insured;
- loss or damage arising from administrative act or enforcement of law.

E. *Obligations of Insured*

949. Under the PICC P&C Waterway Cargo Clauses of 2009, the applicant or the insured shall fulfil the following obligations:

- The applicant or the insured shall fulfil the obligation of disclosure truthfully, answer to the inquiries of the insurer truthfully concerning the subject matter insured or the insured. Where the applicant or the insured fails to perform the above obligation of truthful disclosure due to his intentional act or gross negligence which is sufficient to affect the insurer in deciding whether to agree to cover or to increase insurance premium, the insurer has the right to terminate the contract. The insurance contract shall be terminated upon the arrival of the insurer's notice of termination at the applicant or the insured. Where the applicant or the insured fails to perform the obligation of truthful disclosure due to his intentional act, the insurer shall not be liable for any loss or damage arising from the insurance accident before the contract is terminated without refunding the premium. Where the applicant or the insured fails to perform the obligation of truthful disclosure due to his gross negligence which has significant influence on the occurrence of the insurance accident, the insurer shall not compensate or pay insurance indemnity for any loss or damage arising from the insurance accident before the contract is terminated, but shall refund the premium.
- The applicant or the insured shall pay the insurance premium in one lump upon the issuance of insurance policy or other insurance certificate by the insurer or his agent. Where the applicant or the insured fails to pay insurance premium as agreed, the insurer shall not be liable for insurance accident occurred before the payment of insurance premium.
- The applicant or the insured shall choose with due diligence the carrier and urge him to strictly obey to the various provisions of the State and transport authorities concerning safety transport, agree and assist the insurer in the inspection and survey of the cargo and in the taking of measures of preventing loss of the insured cargo, and shall make sure that the packing of cargo be in conformity with the standard provided for by the State and competent authorities. Where an insurance accident occurs due to failure of the insured in complying with the above agreement, the insurer shall not be liable. Where loss or damage is exaggerated due to such failure, the insurer shall not be liable for such exaggerated loss or damage.
- Where the extent of danger to the subject matter insured increases during the period of insurance, the insured shall notify the insurer in time as agreed upon in the contract. The insurer is entitled to increase the premium or terminate the contract. Where the insured fails to perform the above obligation, the insurer shall

not be liable for the insurance accident arising from the significant increase of the extent of danger to the subject matter insured.

- Upon notice of the occurrence of loss of or damage to the insured cargo within the insurance coverage, the insured shall notify the insurer or local branch or agent of the insurer in time and take reasonable measures to mitigate the loss or damage. In the case of failure of such notice due to the insured's intentional act or gross negligence causing difficulties in determining the nature, causes of the insurance accident or extent of loss or damage, etc., the insurer shall not be liable for the part of loss or damage which cannot be determined, unless the insurer has known or should have known in time of the occurrence of the insurance accident through other way.

Chapter 4. Air Transport

§1. Applicable Laws

I. Introduction

950. As compared with other modes of transport, China has a sound system of law in air transport. The laws, regulations and international treaties applicable to air transport are listed in §5 of Chapter 2 of Part I *supra*.

951. In the international carriage of passengers or cargo by air, the laws and regulations applicable in the order of priority are the 1999 Montreal Convention between China and other states parties to this Convention or the Warsaw Convention as amended at the Hague, 1955 between China and the non-States parties to the 1999 Montreal Convention, CAL, CC and other related basic laws, IACR. In respect of cases not provided for by the laws or regulations or by the international treaties concluded or acceded to by China, the international customs and usages in the international carriage of passengers or cargoes by air may apply (paragraph 2, Article 184, CAL).

In the domestic carriage of passengers or cargo by air, the laws and regulations applicable in the order of priority are CAL, CC and other related basic laws, DACR. Where the laws and regulations do not contain provisions, the customs and usages in the domestic carriage of passengers or cargo by air may apply (Article 10, CC). The *Provisions on Limit of Liability of Carrier in Domestic Air Transport* promulgated by the CAAC on 28 February 2006 shall apply so far as the limits of liability of carrier in domestic air transport of passengers or cargo are concerned.

952. As provided for in Chapter XIV of CAL, in foreign-related matters, the applicable law shall be determined as follows in case of conflict of law:

- to the matters of acquisition, transfer and extinction of the ownership of civil aircraft, the law of nationality of the civil aircraft shall be applicable (Article 185);
- to the matters of mortgage on civil aircraft or civil aviation liens, the law of the location of the court of law which entertains the case, i.e., *lex fori*, shall be applicable (Article 186);
- to the matters of contract of civil air transport, the parties may choose the applicable law, unless otherwise provided for by law, and, in case the parties have made no such choice, the law of the State having the closest connection shall apply (Article 188);
- to the matters of tort liability for damages caused by civil aircraft to third parties on the surface, the law of the place where the tortuous act occurs, or *lex fori* in the case the tortuous act occurs over high seas, shall be applicable (Article 189).

In the case where a foreign law as determined *supra* or international practice shall apply, the application shall in no way violate the public interests of China (Article 190).

II. Concepts and Definitions

953. In the applicable laws mentioned *supra*, the following concepts and definitions are adopted:

- 'Civil aircraft' means an aircraft other than those used in flight missions of military, customs and police services (Article 5, CAL).
- 'Civil airport' means a defined area including any subsidiary buildings, installations and equipment used for the take-off, landing, taxiing, parking and other activities of civil aircraft (Article 53, CAL).
- 'Domestic carriage by air' means any carriage in which, according to the contract of transport by air between the parties, the place of departure, the place of destination, and the agreed stopping place, if any, are all situated within the territory of China (paragraph 1, Article 107, CAL).
- 'International carriage by air' means any carriage in which, according to the contract of carriage by air between the parties, the place of departure, the place of destination or the agreed stopping place, whether or not there is a break in the transport or a transhipment, is not situated within the territory of China (paragraph 2, Article 107, CAL).[75]
- 'Baggage' includes both checked baggage and carry-on articles (carry-on baggage) of a passenger (Article 125, CAL).
- 'Period of carriage by air' means the whole period during which the checked baggage or cargo is in charge of the carrier, whether in an airport or on board a civil aircraft, or, in the case of a landing outside the airport, in any place whatsoever, and does not extend to any carriage by land, sea or river performed outside an airport, provided that if such carriage is used for loading, delivery or transhipment for the performance of a contract of carriage by air, any damage took place during such carriage is presumed, subject to proof to the contrary, to have been the damage taken place during the period of carriage by air (Article 125, CAL; Article 18(2) & (3), Warsaw Convention as amended at the Hague, 1955).
- 'Carrier' or 'Contracting carrier' means any person who has concluded a contract of carriage by air in his own name with a passenger or a consignor or with the agent of a passenger or of a consignor (Article 137, CAL) and the provisions of carrier or actual carrier contained in Chapter IX of CAL apply to the carriage of passengers, baggage or cargo performed by a civil aircraft of a public air transport enterprise, including the gratuitous transport performed thereby, and to the part of transport by air in the case of multimodal transport, but shall not apply to the carriage of mail performed by a civil aircraft (Article 106, CAL).
- 'Actual carrier' means any person to whom the performance of the whole or part of the carriage has been authorized by the contracting carrier and who is not a successive carrier, and in the absence of proof to the contrary, such authorization is deemed to be in existence (Article 137, CAL).

75. This definition is in accord with that contained in para. 2 of Art. 1 of the Warsaw Convention as amended at the Hague, 1955 and para. 1 of Art. 1 of the 1999 Montreal Convention. The Carriage by air between the mainland and Hong Kong or Macau is domestic carriage, but is treated as international carriage.

- 'Public air transport enterprise' means a corporate enterprise engaged in the transport of passengers, baggage, mail or cargo with civil aircraft for the purpose of making profits (Article 91, CAL).
- 'Unit of account' refers to SDR as defined by IMF and its equivalent in the Chinese currency of CNY shall be the amount calculated in terms of the conversion rate from SDR to CNY as prescribed by the State foreign exchange authority at the date of a judgment of a court of law, the date of an arbitration award or the date as agreed upon between the parties concerned (Article 213, CAL).

§2. Carriage of Passengers by Air

I. Passenger Ticket

A. Functions of Passenger Ticket

954. By virtue of Article 111 of CAL and Article 3(2) of the Warsaw Convention as amended at the Hague, 1955, a passenger ticket constitutes prima facie evidence of the conclusion and conditions of a contract of carriage of passengers by air. However, failure of a passenger to produce a passenger ticket or the irregularity or loss of a passenger ticket does not affect the existence or validity of the contract of carriage (Article 111, CAL; Article 3(2), Warsaw Convention as amended at the Hague, 1955).

A passenger ticket may affect the right of the carrier to limit his liability. By virtue of Article 111 of CAL, in the domestic carriage of passengers by air, if a passenger embarks on a civil aircraft without a passenger ticket having been delivered as consented to by the carrier, the carrier shall not be entitled to avail himself of the provisions of Article 128 of CAL concerning limit of liability as mentioned *infra*. In the international carriage of passenger by air, if a passenger embarks on a civil aircraft without a passenger ticket having been delivered as consented to by the carrier, or if the ticket does not include the notice as required by sub-paragraph (3) of Article 110 of CAL indicating the application of an international air transport convention to such carriage, the carrier shall not be entitled to avail himself of the provisions of Article 129 of CAL concerning limit of liability as mentioned *infra*. Similar provision is contained in Article 3(2) of the Warsaw Convention as amended at the Hague, 1955.

By virtue of Article 109 of CAL, in the carriage of passenger, whether international or domestic, the carrier shall deliver a passenger ticket to a passenger by himself or his authorized agent. On the other hand, a passenger to travel on board a civil aircraft shall hold a valid passenger ticket, unless with the consent of the carrier, and shall produce a valid passenger ticket for check.

A passenger ticket is not transferable and can be used only by the named passenger.

B. Contents of Passenger Ticket

955. Article 110 of CAL provides that the contents of a passenger ticket shall be determined by the competent civil aviation authority under the State Council, i.e., CAAC, provided that, in conformity with paragraph 1 of Article 3 of the *Warsaw Convention*, as amended at the Hague, 1955, a passenger ticket shall at least contain the following particulars:

- places of departure and destination;
- if the places of departure and destination are within the territory of China and one or more agreed stopping places are outside the territory, a case rarely occurs, an indication of at least one such stopping place;
- if the ultimate destination, the place of departure or the agreed stopping place of a passenger's journey is not situated within the territory of China, i.e., in the case of international carriage of passenger by air, a notice indicating the international air transport convention applicable to such carriage, if such convention requires the inclusion of the notice in the passenger ticket.

956. The Warsaw Convention as amended at the Hague, 1955 requires in Article 3(1)(e) that a passenger ticket shall contain 'a notice to the effect that, if the passenger's journey involves an ultimate destination or stop in a country other than the country of departure, Warsaw Convention may be applicable and the Convention governs and in most cases limits the liability of the carriers for death or personal injury and in respect of loss of or damage to baggage'. Consequently, all passenger tickets issued by various Chinese airlines in international carriage by air contain such a notice with the same wording as above. As one of the conditions of contract, such a ticket also contains that the carriage hereunder is subject to the rules and limitations relating to liability established by the Warsaw Convention, unless such carriage is not an 'international carriage' as defined by that Convention. The Warsaw Convention is expressly identified as '*the Convention for the Unification of Certain Rules relating to International Carriage by Air* signed at Warsaw, 12 October 1929, or that Convention as amended at the Hague, 28 September 1955, whichever may be applicable'.

The 1999 Montreal Convention does not compulsorily require a passenger ticket to contain such a notice. Article 3(4) of this Convention provides: 'The passenger shall be given written notice to the effect that where this Convention is applicable it governs and may limit the liability of carriers in respect of death or injury and for destruction or loss of, or damage to, baggage, and for delay.' Article 3(5) of this Convention further provides: 'Non-compliance with the provisions of the foregoing paragraphs shall not affect the existence or the validity of the contract of carriage, which shall, nonetheless, be subject to the rules of this Convention including those relating to limitation of liability.'

957. In practice, a passenger ticket in the international carriage issued by a Chinese airline includes the name of carrier, issuer and place of issuance, name of the passenger, flight number, class, date and time of departure, amount and calculation of fare, form of payment, ticket number, conditions of contract and advice to an international passengers on limitation of liability of carrier for loss or personal injury.

Similarly, a passenger ticket in domestic carriage issued by a Chinese airline contains at least: (a) name of carrier; (b) issuer, time and place of issuance; (c) name of passenger; (d) place of departure, stopping and destination; (e) flight number, class, date and time of departure; (e) fare and form of payment; (f) ticket number; (g) carriage information.

C. *Validity Period of Passenger Ticket*

958. A passenger is required to complete the journey or all the journeys stated in the passenger ticket within the validity period (Article 9, DAPR).

If, due to any reason for which the carrier is responsible, a passenger is unable to complete his or her journey within the validity period, the validity of passenger ticket shall be extended consequently.

D. *Change of or Getting Refund for Passenger Ticket*

959. Where a passenger demands the change of flight, date or time of departure, or class, the carrier or his sales agent shall arrange so far as practicable.

In the case of cancellation of flight, earlier departure than scheduled, delay in departure or change of voyage or inability to provide the booked seat, the carrier is obliged to arrange with priority for successive flight or flight of other carrier for the passenger. If, due to the reason of the carrier, the class becomes lower, the carrier shall refund the balance to the passenger; where the class becomes higher, the passenger shall not pay for the balance (Article 821, CC).

Change of carrier on the passenger's own will be subject to the agreement of the carrier or issuer of the passenger ticket. On the other hand, change of carrier in the case of cancellation of flight, earlier departure than scheduled, delay in departure or change of voyage or inability to provide the booked seat not on the passenger's own will be subject to the agreement of the passenger.

960. Where, due to the reasons of the carrier or the passenger, the passenger does not complete his or her journey in part or whole within the validity period of the passenger ticket, he or she can get refund for the ticket within the validity thereof.

Where a passenger demands refund for the passenger ticket on his or her own will, he or she is obliged as a principle to pay a commission at a certain percentage dependent upon the time before the time of departure as scheduled.

If a passenger demands refund for the passenger ticket in the case of cancellation of flight, earlier departure than scheduled, delay in departure or change of voyage or inability to provide the booked seat, i.e., not based upon his or her own will, the ticket fare shall be refunded in full for the whole or remaining journey without payment of commission.

Where a passenger demands refund for the passenger ticket due to his or her illness, upon production of proof thereof issued by a hospital, the ticket fare shall be refunded in full for the whole or remaining journey without payment of commission.

II. Boarding Aircraft

961. A passenger shall check in at the check-in counter at the airport or other designated place upon a valid certificate of identity, go through security inspection and board the aircraft upon production of the boarding card.

962. In the case of delay in boarding, a passenger may demand change of flight or get refund for the passenger ticket at the airport or the place of buying the ticket.

If a passenger demands change of flight, the carrier shall arrange for a successive flight without payment of commission if seat is available in the successive flight. If the passenger demands refund for the passenger ticket, he or she shall pay a commission therefor.

963. In domestic carriage by air, if a passenger boards a wrong aircraft, the carrier shall arrange for the passenger to take the earliest flight to the destination without additional payment, but the passenger may be required to pay commission, or refund the ticket fare. If caused by a reason of the carrier, the passenger may also demand refund for the ticket for the whole or remaining journey, as the case may be, without payment of commission.

964. Under any of the following circumstances, the carrier may refuse to carry a passenger and his or her baggage and shall not be liable for any damages suffered by the passenger due to the carrier's refusal of carriage:

- compliance with law or regulations applicable at the place of departure, destination or stopping places;
- the passenger's behaviour, age, mental or health condition unsuitable for the journey or possible to cause non-comfort or danger to the life or property of the passenger or other persons;
- the passenger's refusal to accept safety inspection;
- failure of the passenger to pay for the ticket fare or other related expenses;
- failure of the passenger to produce a valid traveling certificate.

III. Service for Passengers During Flight or on the Ground

965. During the flight, the carrier shall cater for the passengers dependent upon the duration of the flight. If a passenger becomes ill during carriage, the carrier shall take active measures of assistance (Article 822, CC).

966. If, due to technical maintenance, adjustment of flight, commerce, crew or other reasons for which the carrier is responsible, the flight is delayed or cancelled at the place of departure, the carrier shall cater or provide accommodation for the passengers at his expenses. If such delay or cancellation is caused by weather, sudden incident, air control, safety inspection or passengers' own reason for which the carrier shall not be responsible, the accommodation shall be at the expenses of the passengers themselves. However, if delay or cancellation occurs at any stopping place due to whatever reasons, the carrier shall cater or provide accommodation for the passengers at his expenses. Where delay or cancellation occurs, the carrier shall timely notify the passengers of such information. Should delay or cancellation occurs, the carrier shall arrange for a successive flight or refund of tickets upon demands of a passenger.

§3. Carriage of Passenger's Baggage by Air

I. Baggage Check

A. *Functions of Baggage Check*

967. In respect of the carriage of checked baggage, a baggage check may be combined with or incorporated into a passenger ticket (paragraph 1, Article 112, CAL). In practice, a baggage check is combined with a passenger ticket.

Checked baggage is worded as registered baggage and baggage check is worded as baggage ticket in the Warsaw Convention as amended at the Hague, 1955. In the 1999 Montreal Convention, the words 'checked baggage' and 'baggage identification tag' are used.

Similar to a passenger ticket, a baggage check or baggage ticket has the function of prima facie evidence of the checking of the baggage and of the conditions of the contract of carriage thereof (paragraph 2, Article 112, CAL; Article 4(2), Warsaw Convention as amended at the Hague, 1955). However, failure of a passenger to produce a baggage check, or the irregularity or loss of a baggage check does not affect the existence or validity of the contract of carriage thereof (paragraph 3, Article 112, CAL; Article 4(2), Warsaw Convention as amended at the Hague, 1955).

Likewise, a baggage check may affect the right of the carrier to limit his liability. By virtue of paragraph 4 of Article 112 of CAL, if the carrier carries checked baggage without a baggage check having been delivered in the domestic carriage by air, he shall not be entitled to avail himself of the provisions of Article 128 of CAL concerning the limit of liability as mentioned *infra*. By virtue of paragraph 5 of Article 112 of CAL, if the carrier carries checked baggage without a baggage check having been delivered in the international carriage by air, or if a baggage check does not include the notice required by sub-paragraph (3) of Article 110 of CAL indicating the application of an international air transport convention to such carriage, the carrier shall not be entitled to avail himself of the provisions of Article 129 of CAL concerning the limit of liability as mentioned *infra*. Similar provision is contained in Article 4(2) of the Warsaw Convention as amended at the Hague, 1955.

968. By virtue of Article 4(1) of the Warsaw Convention as amended at the Hague, 1955 which is applicable to the international carriage of baggage by air, a baggage check shall be delivered by the carrier or his agent for the carriage of checked baggage.

Since a baggage check is combined with a passenger ticket in practice and the passenger ticket is not transferable, the baggage check is also not transferable.

B. Contents of Baggage Check

969. As required by paragraph 1 of Article 112 of CAL, a baggage check shall, in addition to the particulars as required by Article 110 of CAL as mentioned *supra*, contain the number of packages and weight of the baggage and, if a declaration of interest in delivery at destination is required, the sum of declared interest.

By contrast, Article 4(3) of the Warsaw Convention as amended at the Hague, 1955 requires same particulars as those for a passenger ticket to be contained in a baggage check. This requirement does not apply where a baggage check is combined with or incorporated in a passenger ticked. That is, in such a case, no other particular is required for a baggage check.

II. Consignment and Taking Over of Baggage

970. The carrier shall make public the weight of baggage which each passenger is entitled to carry gratuitously and the conditions of carriage. Specific free baggage allowance is contained in the passenger information in a passenger ticket and baggage check.

A passenger shall deliver the baggage to be checked to the check-in counter at the airport of departure or other check-in point for weighing or counting the number of packages, while the check-in point on behalf of the carrier shall label the baggage with a baggage tag, insert the weight and number of packages on the baggage tag and deliver baggage tag to the passenger for his or her claim of the baggage at destination or place of stoppage in transit. Checked baggage shall be in the custody by the carrier during transport. Dangerous goods, contrabands and goods unsuitable for carriage due to their packing, shape, weight, measurement or quality are prohibited to be carried as baggage. Carriage of arms, ammunitions, knifes and live animals are restricted. No fragile or corrosive article, currency, pearl, valuable metal, gold and silver product, negotiable security and other valuable goods, commercial documents, passport and other proof documents or samples shall be carried in checked baggage. The carrier is entitled to inspect at the check-in point or ask an authority concerned to inspect the passenger's baggage under legal process for the safety of carriage.

A passenger shall properly pack, lock and secure his or her checked baggage suitable for safety loading, carriage and discharge under normal process.

The carrier shall provide service for value-declared checked baggage in excess of the limit of carrier's liability against a surcharge according to stipulations.

III. Carriage and Delivery of Baggage

971. The carrier shall carry the checked baggage on the same flight as the passenger takes. Where this is actually impossible, the carrier shall state the reason thereof to the passenger and arrange for the carriage by the next flight under safety conditions.

972. A passenger shall claim the checked baggage at the destination or place of stoppage in transit upon production of the baggage tag. The carrier via the terminal operator at the airport of destination or place of stoppage in transit shall deliver the checked baggage against the baggage tag. Where a passenger cannot produce the baggage tag, he or she shall produce proof to the satisfaction of the carrier.

Where a passenger does not raise any objection in writing, it shall be deemed as prima facie evidence that the baggage has been delivered in sound condition. In domestic carriage, where baggage sustains delay, loss or damage, the carrier or his agent shall fill in an incident record together with the passenger.

§4. Carriage of Cargo by Air

I. Air Waybill

A. Functions of Air Waybill

973. An air waybill has the function of prima facie evidence of the conclusion of the contract of carriage of cargo by air, of the receipt of the cargo by the carrier and of the conditions of carriage (paragraph 1, Article 118, CAL; Article 11(1), Warsaw Convention as amended at the Hague, 1955; Article 11(1), 1999 Montreal Convention).

The statements in an air waybill relating to the weight, dimensions and packing of the cargo as well as those relating to the number of packages shall be prima facie evidence of the facts stated; those relating to the quantity, volume and conditions of the cargo shall not constitute evidence against the carrier except so far as they both have been checked by him in the presence of the consignor and are stated in the air waybill, or relate to the apparent condition of the cargo (paragraph 2, Article 118, CAL; Article 11(2), Warsaw Convention as amended at the Hague, 1955; Article 11(2), 1999 Montreal Convention).

The carrier has the right to require the consignor to make out an air waybill and a consignor has the right to require the carrier to accept the air waybill. However, failure of the consignor to produce an air waybill, or the irregularity or loss of air waybill, shall not affect the existence or validity of the contract of transport (Article 113, CAL; Article 5, Warsaw Convention as amended at the Hague, 1955).

Same as in the case of carriage of passenger and baggage, an air waybill may affect the right of the carrier to limit his liability. By virtue of paragraph 1 of Article 116 of CAL, if the cargo is carried without an air waybill having been made out as consented to by the carrier in the domestic carriage by air, the carrier shall not be entitled to avail himself of the provisions of Article 128 of CAL concerning the limit of liability as mentioned *infra*. By virtue of paragraph 2 of Article 116 of CAL, in the international carriage by air, if cargo is carried without an air waybill having been made out as consented to by the carrier, or if the air waybill does not include the notice required by sub-paragraph (3) of Article 115 of CAL indicating the application of an international air transport convention to such carriage, the carrier shall not be entitled to avail himself of the provisions of Article 129 of CAL concerning the limit of liability. Similar provision is contained in Article 9 of the Warsaw Convention as amended at the Hague, 1955.

B. Contents of Air Waybill

974. Like the case of a passenger ticket, by virtue of Article 115 of CAL, the contents of an air waybill shall be determined by CAAC, provided that an air waybill shall at least contain: (a) place of departure and destination; (b) if places of departure and destination are within the territory of China, but one or more agreed stopping places are not within the territory of China, an indication of at least one such stopping place; and (c) if places of departure, place of destination or agreed stopping place is not within the territory of China, and the air waybill shall indicate that the carriage shall be subject to an international convention on carriage by air as required by the applicable convention, an indication to this effect.

975. Likewise, the Warsaw Convention as amended at the Hague, 1955 requires in Article 8(c) that an air waybill shall contain a same notice as required in Article 3(1)(e) in the case of a passenger ticket as stated in §2 *supra*. The 1999 Montreal Convention provides in Article 5 that an air waybill or the cargo receipt shall include: (a) an indication of places of departure and destination; (b) if places of departure and destination are within the territory of a single State Party, but one or more agreed stopping places being within the territory of another State, an indication of at least one such stopping place; and (c) indication of weight of the consignment.

976. As required by Article 115 of CAL, CAAC has laid down in Article 9 of IACR that an air waybill shall, besides the contents as required by Article 115 of CAL, contain, *inter alia*,: (a) place and date of its execution; (b) name and address of consignor; (c) name and address of first carrier; (d) nature of cargo; (e) number of packages, method of packing, particular marks or numbers upon them; (f) weight, quantity and volume or dimensions of cargo; (g) apparent condition of cargo and of packing; (h) freight, date and place of payment and the person who is to pay it if it has been agreed upon; (i) if cargo is sent for payment on delivery, the price of cargo, and amount of expenses incurred if the case so require; (j) number of parts of air waybill; (k) documents handed to the carrier to accompany the air waybill; (l) if agreed upon, time fixed for the completion of carriage and a brief note of the route to be followed.

Obviously, the particulars so required are basically those contained in Article 8 of the 1929 Warsaw Convention.

977. Similarly, as required by Article 115 of CAL, CAAC has laid down in Article 4(2) of DACR that the basic contents of an air waybill shall be: (a) name, address, telephone number and postal code of consignor and consignee; (b) description of cargo; (c) number and means of packages, marks of cargo; (d) actual value of cargo; (e) declared value of cargo; (f) ordinary carriage or urgent carriage; (g) statement of nature, storage, carriage or others of cargo.

C. Making of Air Waybill

978. An air waybill shall be made out by the consignor in three original parts and be handed over to the carrier with the cargo (paragraph 1, Article 114, CAL; Article 6(1), Warsaw Convention as amended at the Hague, 1955).

The first part shall be marked 'for the carrier' and shall be signed and sealed by the consignor; the second part shall be marked 'for the consignee' and shall be signed and sealed by both the consignor and the carrier; the third part shall be signed and sealed by the carrier and handed by him to the consignor after the cargo has been accepted (paragraph 2, Article 114, CAL; Article 6(2), Warsaw Convention as amended at the Hague, 1955).

The carrier shall sign air waybill prior to the loading of the cargo on board the aircraft and the signature of the carrier may be stamped, while that of the consignor may be printed or stamped (Article 6(2), (3) & (4), Warsaw Convention as amended at the Hague, 1955).

If, at the request of the consignor, the carrier makes out the air waybill, he shall be deemed, subject to proof to the contrary, to have done so on behalf of the consignor (paragraph 3, Article 114, CAL; Article 6(5), Warsaw Convention as amended at the Hague, 1955).

The 1999 Montreal Convention in Article 7 contains similar provisions. The only difference is that the signature of the carrier and that of the consignor may be printed or stamped.

II. Obligations of Consignor

A. Responsibility for Correctness of Cargo Particulars

979. The consignor shall be responsible for the correctness of the particulars and statements relating to the cargo that he inserts in the air waybill. Otherwise, the consignor shall indemnify the carrier against all damages suffered by him or by any other person to whom the carrier is liable, by reason of the irregularity, incorrectness or incompleteness of the particulars and statements inserted in the air waybill (Article 117 of CAL; Article 10, Warsaw Convention as amended at the Hague, 1955).

Article 10 of the 1999 Montreal Convention contains similar and more detailed provisions.

B. Provision of Required Information and Documents

980. The consignor shall furnish such information and documents as are necessary to meet the formalities provided by laws and administrative regulations before the cargo is delivered to the consignee by the carrier. Otherwise, the consignor shall be liable to the carrier for any damage occasioned by the absence, insufficiency or irregularity of any such information or documents, unless the damage is due to the fault of the carrier, his servants or agents. The carrier is under no obligation to check such information or documents unless otherwise provided by laws and administrative regulations (Article 123, CAL).

Article 16 of the Warsaw Convention as amended at the Hague, 1955 and Article 16 of the 1999 Montreal Convention contain the similar provisions.

III. Rights of Consignor and Consignee

981. By virtue of Article 119 of CAL the consignor has the right of disposition of cargo in transit, in line with those of Article 829 of CC. Article 12 of the Warsaw Convention as amended at the Hague, 1955 and Article 12 of the 1999 Montreal Convention contain the similar provisions.

Thus, subject to his liability to carry out all his obligations under the contract of transport of cargo by air, the consignor shall have the right to dispose of the cargo by withdrawing them at the airport of departure or destination, or by stopping them in the course of the carriage on any landing, or by requiring the cargo to be delivered at the place of destination or in the course of the carriage to a person other than the consignee named in the air waybill, or by requiring them to be returned to the airport of departure, provided that the consignor shall not exercise this right in such a way as to prejudice the carrier or other consignors and he shall pay any expenses occasioned by the exercise of this right.

If it is impossible to carry out such orders of the consignor for the disposition of the cargo, the carrier shall inform him forthwith.

If the carrier obeys the orders of the consignor without requiring the production of the part of the air waybill delivered to the consignor, he will be liable, without prejudice to his right of recovery from the consignor, for any damage which may be caused thereby to any person who is lawfully in possession of that part of the air waybill.

The right of disposition of cargo in transit conferred on the consignor has certain time limit and shall cease at the moment when the consignee's right of disposition of cargo begins in accordance with the provisions of Article 120 of CAL or Article 13 of the Warsaw Convention as amended at the Hague, 1955 or Article 13 of the 1999 Montreal Convention as mentioned *infra*, unless the consignee declines to accept the cargo or cannot be communicated with in which case the consignor shall resume his right of disposition.

982. In accordance with Article 120 of CAL or Article 13 of the Warsaw Convention as amended at the Hague, 1955 or Article 13 of the 1999 Montreal Convention, except where the consignor has exercised his right of disposition, the consignee shall be entitled, on arrival of the cargo at the place of destination, to require the carrier to deliver the cargo to him on payment of the charges due and on complying with the conditions of transport set out in the air waybill. However, this right shall be defeated if the consignor has exercised his right of disposition of cargo as mentioned *supra*. Noticeably, the consignee's right is called the consignee's right of requisition of air waybill and cargo in CAL and the Warsaw Convention as amended at the Hague, 1955. However, the 1999 Montreal Convention unified the consignor's right and the consignee's right to be the right of disposition of cargo.

Unless otherwise agreed upon, it shall be the duty of the carrier to give a notice to the consignee as soon as the cargo arrives.

If the carrier admits loss of cargo, or if the cargo has not arrived on the expiry of the agreed or stipulated period of time after the date on which it ought to have arrived, the consignee shall be entitled to force against the carrier the rights which flow from the contract of carriage of cargo by air.

983. The consignor's right of disposition of cargo and the consignee's right thereof can be enforced respectively, each in his own name, whether he is acting in his own interest or in the interest of another, provided that he carries out the obligations imposed by the contract of carriage of cargo by air (Article 121, CAL; Article 14, Warsaw Convention as amended at the Hague, 1955; Article 14, 1999 Montreal Convention).

The consignor's right of disposition of cargo and the consignee's right thereof and the exercise thereof shall not affect the relations between the consignor and the consignee or the mutual relations of third parties whose rights are derived either from the consignor or from the consignee. In addition, the statutory provisions concerning the consignor's and the consignees' right and the exercise thereof can be changed by agreement between the carrier and the consignor, provided that any terms of the contract which are different from these statutory provisions shall be expressly stated in the air waybill (Article 122, CAL; Article 15, Warsaw Convention as amended at the Hague, 1955; Article 15, 1999 Montreal Convention).

§5. Liability of Carrier

I. Compulsory Application of Statutory Liability

984. The statutory provisions concerning the liability of the carrier for death of or personal injury to a passenger occurred in the carriage by air, or for loss of or damage to baggage or cargo occurred during the period of carriage by air, or for damages in delay in the carriage of passenger, baggage or cargo in the carriage by air shall be applied compulsorily.

Article 130 of CAL provides that any provision in the contract of passenger, baggage or cargo or in the transport documents which tends to relieve the carrier of the liability provided for in CAL, or to fix a lower limit of liability of the carrier than that laid down in CAL, shall be null and void, but the nullity of any such provision shall not involve the nullity of the whole contract of carriage by air. This means that the liability of the carrier provided for in CAL is minimum and any decrease in liability shall be null and void. However, Any increase in liability besides those set out in CAL shall not be prejudiced.

Similar provision is contained in Article 23 of the Warsaw Convention as amended at the Hague, 1955 or Article 27 of the 1999 Montreal Convention.

II. Liabilities and Exemptions of Liabilities of Carrier

A. *For Death or Personal Injury or Delay in Carriage of Passenger*

985. The carrier shall be liable for death of or personal injury to a passenger, if the accident took place on board the civil aircraft or in the course of any of the operations of embarking on or disembarking from the civil aircraft (Article 124, CAL; Article 17, Warsaw Convention as amended at the Hague, 1955; paragraph 1, Article 17, 1999 Montreal Convention).

However, the carrier is not liable if the death or injury resulted solely from the state of health of the passenger (Article 124, CAL).

In addition, if the carrier proves that the death of or personal injury to a passenger was caused by or contributed to by the fault of the passenger, the carrier may be wholly or partly exonerated from his liability in accordance with the extent of the fault that caused or contributed to such damage, whether the claimant is the passenger himself or herself or not (paragraph 1, Article 127, CAL).

Under the 1999 Montreal Convention, the general exoneration from liability provided for in Article 20 shall apply to damage arising from destruction or loss of or damage to the cargo, or death of or personal injury to a passenger, or destruction or loss of or damage to any carry-on articles or checked baggage of a passenger, or delay in the carriage by air of passengers, baggage or cargo. That is, if the carrier proves that the damage was caused or contributed to by the negligence or other wrongful act or omission of the person claiming compensation or the person from whom he or she derives his or her rights, the carrier shall be wholly or partly exonerated from its liability to the claimant to the extent that such negligence or wrongful act or omission caused or contributed to the damage.

B. *For Loss of or Damage to Baggage*

986. By virtue of Article 125 of CAL, the carrier shall be liable for loss of or damage to any carry-on articles or checked baggage of a passenger, if the occurrence took place on board the civil aircraft or in the course of any of the operations of embarking on or disembarking from the civil aircraft of the passenger or during the period of carriage by air.

However, the carrier shall not be liable, if such loss or damage resulted solely from the inherent defect, quality or vice of the baggage. In addition, in the carriage of baggage including checked baggage and carry-on articles of a passenger, if the carrier proves that the loss of or damage to any baggage was caused by or contributed to by the fault of the passenger, the carrier may be wholly or partly exonerated from his liability in accordance with the extent of the fault that caused or contributed to such damage (paragraph 1, Article 127, CAL).

Similarly, by virtue of paragraph 2 of Article 17 of the 1999 Montreal Convention, the carrier is liable for damage sustained in case of destruction or loss of, or of damage to, checked baggage upon condition only that the event which caused the destruction, loss or damage took place on board the aircraft or during any period within which the checked baggage was in the charge of the carrier. However, the carrier is not liable if and to the extent that the damage resulted from the inherent defect, quality or vice of the baggage. In the case of unchecked baggage including personal items, the carrier is liable if the damage resulted from its fault or that of its servants or agents. In addition, the general exonerations from liability provided for in Article 20 of the 1999 Montreal Convention shall also apply as stated *supra*.

C. For Loss of or Damage to Cargo

987. By virtue of paragraph 4 of Article 125 of CAL, the carrier shall be liable for loss of or damage to any cargo, if the occurrence took place during the period of carriage by air, unless he proves that the loss of or damage resulted solely from one or more of the following causes: (a) inherent defect, quality or vice of cargo; (b) defective packing of cargo performed by a person other than the carrier or his servants or agents; (c) an act of war or an armed conflict; (d) an act of public authority carried out in connection with the entry, exit or transit of the cargo.

Similar provisions are contained in Article 18 of the 1999 Montreal Convention. In addition, the general exonerations from liability provided for in Article 20 of the 1999 Montreal Convention shall also apply as stated *supra*.

Noticeably, paragraph 4 of Article 18 of the 1999 Montreal Convention contains a detailed definition of period of carriage by air. This period does not extend to any carriage by land, by sea or by inland waterway performed outside an airport. If, however, such carriage takes place in the performance of a contract for carriage by air for the purpose of loading, delivery or transhipment, any damage is presumed to have been the result of an event which took place during the carriage by air. If a carrier, without the consent of the consignor, substitutes carriage by another mode of transport for the whole or part of a carriage intended by the agreement between the parties to be carriage by air, such carriage by another mode of transport is deemed to be within the period of carriage by air.

In addition, paragraph 2, Article 127 of CAL provides that if the carrier proves that loss of or damage to the cargo was caused by or contributed to the fault of the person claiming compensation or the person from whom he derived his right, the carrier shall be wholly or partly exonerated from his liability in accordance with the extent of the fault that caused or contributed to such damage.

D. For Delay in the Carriage of Passenger, Baggage or Cargo

988. By virtue of Article 126 of CAL, the carrier shall be liable for damages occasioned by delay in the carriage by air of passengers, baggage or cargo, unless he proves that he and his servants or agents have taken all necessary measures to avoid the damage or it was impossible for him or them to take such measures.

Similar provisions are contained in Articles 19 and 20 of the Warsaw Convention as amended at the Hague, 1955 and Article 19 of the 1999 Montreal Convention. In addition, the general exonerations from liability provided for in Article 20 of the 1999 Montreal Convention shall also apply as stated *supra*.

However, neither CAL, nor the Warsaw Convention as amended at the Hague, 1955, nor the 1999 Montreal Convention contains the definition of delay in carriage. Article 811 of CC provides that the carrier shall carry the passenger or cargo safely to the destination within the time agreed upon or reasonable time shall apply. By virtue of this provision, delay in carriage occurs if the carrier fails to carry the passengers, baggage or cargo to the agreed destination within the time agreed upon or, in the absence of the agreed time, within reasonable time. The time of arrival at the destination announced by the carrier shall be deemed as the agreed time, unless otherwise agreed upon.

III. Limitation of Liability of Carrier

A. *In International Carriage by Air*

989. The limits of liability of the carrier applicable to the international carriage of passengers, baggage or cargo contained in Article 129 of CAL in terms of SDR are the same as those provided for in Article 22 of the Warsaw Convention as amended at the Hague, 1955.

The statutory limit of liability is applicable to a case where the proven damages exceed the amount of limit. Otherwise, the carrier shall be liable for the actual loss or damage.

990. The liability of the carrier for death of or personal injury to each passenger is limited to the sum of 16,600 SDR. However, a passenger may agree with the carrier a higher limit of liability.

The 1999 Montreal Convention significantly increased the limit of liability to 100,000 SDR for each passenger. The carrier can avail of such limitation if the carrier proves that: (a) such damage was not due to the negligence or other wrongful act or omission of the carrier or its servants or agents; or (b) such damage was solely due to the negligence or other wrongful act or omission of a third party.

991. Paragraph 1 of Article 22 of the 1999 Montreal Convention provides that in the case of damage caused by delay in the carriage of persons, the liability of the carrier for each passenger is limited to 4,150 SDR. However, neither CAL nor the Warsaw Convention as amended at the Hague, 1955 provides limit of liability the carrier for damage caused by delay in the carriage of persons.

992. The liability of the carrier for loss of or damage to or damages arising from delay in carriage of checked baggage or cargo is limited to a sum of 17 SDR each kilogram, unless the passenger or consignor has made, at the time when the checked baggage or cargo was handed over to the carrier, a special declaration of interest in delivery at destination and has paid a supplementary sum of expense if the case so requires, in which case the carrier shall be liable to pay a sum not exceeding the declared sum, unless he proves that the sum declared by the passenger or consignor is greater than the actual interest of the checked baggage or cargo in delivery at destination.

Noticeably, the 1999 Montreal Convention does not differentiate checked baggage from unchecked baggage so far as the carrier's liability and limitation of liability are concerned. Paragraph 2 of Article 22 provides that in the carriage of baggage, the liability of the carrier in the case of destruction, loss, damage or delay is limited to 1,000 SDR for each passenger unless the passenger has made, at the time when the checked baggage was handed over to the carrier, a special declaration of interest in delivery at destination and has paid a supplementary sum if the case so requires, in which case the carrier will be liable to pay a sum not exceeding the declared sum, unless it proves that the sum is greater than the passenger's actual interest in delivery at destination.

In the case of loss of or damage or delay of a part of checked baggage or cargo, or of any object contained therein, the weight to be taken into consideration in determining the amount to which the carrier's liability is limited shall only be the weight of the part of checked baggage or cargo concerned. Nevertheless, when the loss of or damage or delay of a part of the checked baggage or cargo, or of an object contained therein, affects the value of other checked baggage covered by the same baggage check, or, of other cargo covered by the same air waybill, the total weight of such checked baggage or cargo shall also be taken into consideration in determining the limit of liability of the carrier. Under the 1999 Montreal Convention, the above provision is also applicable to unchecked baggage, i.e., carry-on baggage of a passenger.

993. Under CAL or the Warsaw Convention as amended at the Hague, 1955, the liability of the carrier for carry-on baggage of a passenger is limited to 332 SDR per passenger, regardless of the weight thereof.

994. With respect to carriage of passenger by air to or from or with an agreed stopping place in the United States of America, it is contained in the *Advice to International Passengers on Limitation of Liability* in the passenger ticket and baggage check issued by a Chinese airline, *inter alia*, that the liability of the carrier and certain other carriers, parties to special contracts of carriage in applicable tariffs, for death of or personal injury to passengers is limited in most cases to proven damages not exceed USD 75,000 per passenger, and that this liability up to such limit shall not depend on negligence on the part of the carrier. This limit is inclusive of legal fees and costs except that in case of a claim brought in a State where provision is made for separate award of legal fees and costs, the limit shall be the sum of USD 58,000 exclusive of legal fees and costs.

Likely, the *Notice of Baggage Liability Limitations* in the passenger ticket and baggage check issued by a Chinese airline contains, *inter alia*, that liability for loss, delay or damage to baggage is limited unless a higher value is declared in advance and additional charges are paid; for most international travel (including domestic portions of international journey), the liability limit is approximately USD 9.07 per pound (USD 20.00 per kilogram) for checked baggage and USD 400 per passenger for unchecked baggage; for travel wholly between US points, the Federal rules require any limit on an airline's baggage liability to be at least USD 1,250 per passenger; excess valuation may be declared on certain types of articles.

B. Domestic Carriage by Air

995. Article 128 of CAL requires CAAC to formulate the limits of carrier's liability in domestic carriage by air to be put in force after approval by the State Council. This Article also sets out that, if the passenger or the consignor has made at the time when the checked baggage or cargo was handed over to the carrier a special declaration of interest in delivery at destination and has paid a supplementary expense of carriage if the case so requires, the carrier shall be liable to pay a sum not exceeding the declared sum, unless he proves that the sum declared by the passenger or consignor is greater than the actual interest of the checked baggage or cargo at the time of delivery at destination.

996. The limitation of liability of the carrier for death of or personal injury to passengers in the domestic carriage by air prevailing now is contained in the *Provisions on Limit of Liability of Carrier in Domestic Air Transport* promulgated by CAAC on 28 February 2006. By virtue of these Provisions, the limit of liability of the carrier for the death of or personal injury to each passenger is CNY 400,000, now approximately USD 54,800. In practice, however, the actual amount of compensation may be much higher as a result of settlement negotiations.

997. By virtue of the *Provisions on Limit of Liability of Carrier in Domestic Air Transport*, the liability of the carrier for loss of or damage to checked baggage is limited to CNY 100 per kilogram of the actual weight of the checked baggage lost or damaged. If the weight of the checked baggage cannot be determined, the weight shall be calculated upon the gratuitous weight of checked baggage as introduced *supra*. The limit of liability for loss of or damage to the carry-on baggage is limited to CNY 3,000 per each passenger.

998. By virtue of the *Provisions on Limit of Liability of Carrier in Domestic Air Transport*, the liability of the carrier for loss of or damage to cargo in the domestic carriage by air is limited to CNY 100 per kilogram of the cargo lost or damaged, unless the value of the cargo has been declared by the passenger in which case the carrier shall be liable to pay a sum not exceeding the declared sum, unless it proves that the declared sum is greater than the actual value in which case the carrier shall be liable in the sum of the actual value.

Where the cargo is carried to destination beyond the agreed time, the carrier shall be liable as agreed upon in the contract of carriage of cargo.

IV. Loss of Right to Limit Liability

999. By virtue of Article 132 of CAL which contains the same provision as that of Article 25 of the Warsaw Convention as amended at the Hague, 1955 or paragraph 5 of Article 22 of the 1999 Montreal Convention, the carrier shall not be entitled to avail himself of the provisions of Articles 128 and 129 thereof concerning the limits of liability, if it is proved that the damage in the carriage by air resulted from an act or omission of the carrier, his servants or agents, done with intent to cause damage or recklessly and with knowledge that damage would probably result, provided that, in the case of such act or omission of a servant or agent of the carrier, it is also proved that he was acting within the scope of his employment.

V. Non-contractual Claims

A. *Tort Liability of Carrier*

1000. Article 131 of CAL provides that any action for damages occurred in the carriage by air, however founded, can only be brought subject to the conditions and limits of liability set out in this Law, without prejudice to the question who the persons entitled to bring suit are and what their respective rights are. Similar provision is contained in Article 24 of the Warsaw Convention as amended at the Hague, 1955 and Article 29 of the 1999 Montreal Convention.

This means that, so far as death of or personal injury to passengers, or loss of or damage to baggage or cargo, or delay in the carriage by air is concerned, the liability and limits of liability of the carrier shall be determined by CAL or other applicable laws, even if the claim for damage is founded in tort.

B. *Legal Status of Servants or Agent of Carrier*

1001. Same as Article 25A of the Warsaw Convention as amended at the Hague, 1955 or Article 30 of the 1999 Montreal Convention, Article 133 of CAL provides that, if an action is brought against a servant or agent of the carrier arising out of damages during the carriage by air, such servant or agent, if it is proved that he acted within the scope of his employment or agency, shall be entitled to avail himself of the limits of liability as provided for in Articles 128 and 129 of CAL. The aggregate of the amounts recoverable from the carrier, his servants and agents shall not exceed the statutory limits of liability of the carrier. However, if it is proved that the damages in the carriage by air resulted from an act or omission of the servant or agent of the carrier done with intent to cause damage or recklessly and with knowledge that damage would probably result, the servant or agent is not entitled to avail of the limitation of liability provided for in Articles 128 and 129 of CAL.

1002. The statutory provision of Article 133 of CAL is not concerned with the question when and how a servant or agent of the carrier can be sued against for damages occurred during the carriage by air, but shall apply to a case where the servant or agent of the carrier is sued against by virtue of applicable basic law.

However, as discussed in §9 of Chapter 6 of Part II *supra*, under the principled provisions of CC, as a rule, the servant or agent of the carrier shall not be liable for the damages caused by his act or omission, if it proves that his act or omission is within the scope of employment or agency. Instead, an action can be brought only against the carrier who is responsible for act or omission of his servant or agent done within the scope of employment or agency. That is, the carrier shall bear vicarious liability.

VI. Successive Carriage

1003. Successive carriage by air means the carriage of passengers, baggage or cargo performed successively by two or more air carriers.

Provisions concerning successive carriage by air contained in Articles 108 and 136 are almost the same as those of Articles 1(3) and 30 of the Warsaw Convention as amended at the Hague, 1955 or Article 36 of the 1999 Montreal Convention.

By virtue of Article 108 of CAL, carriage by air to be performed by several successive air carriers is deemed to be one undivided transport, if it is regarded by the parties to the contract of transport by air as a single operation, whether it has been agreed to be under a single contract or a series of contracts.

Article 136 of CAL sets out detailed provisions governing the liabilities of the successive air carriers.

In the case of carriage to be performed by various successive carriers, each carrier who accepts passengers, baggage or cargo shall be subject to the provisions of CAL, and shall be deemed to be one of the contracting parties to the contract of carriage in so far as that part of the carriage is performed by him in accordance with the contract.

In the case of carriage of this nature, a passenger or his or her successor can take an action only against the carrier who performed the part of transport during which the accident or delay occurred, save in the case where, by express agreement, the first carrier shall assume liability for the whole journey.

As regards checked baggage or cargo, a passenger or consignor shall have the right of action against the first carrier, and the passenger or consignee shall have the right of action against the last carrier, and further, each may take action against the carrier who performed the part of transport during which the destruction, loss, damage, or delay took place. These carriers shall be jointly and severally liable to the passenger or to the consignor or consignee.

VII. Carriage by Air Performed by Actual Carrier

1004. The provisions of section 4 'Special Provisions Governing Carriage by Air Performed by Actual Carrier' of Chapter IX of CAL governing respectively the responsibility of actual carrier in the carriage of goods or passengers by air are very similar to those contained in Chapter IV and Chapter V of MC governing the responsibility of actual carrier in the carriage of goods or passengers by sea, and are similar to the provisions of Articles 39 to 41 of Chapter V of the 1999 Montreal Convention.

1005. As a rule, both the contracting carrier and the actual carrier shall, except as otherwise provided for in this section, be subject to the provisions of Chapter IX of CAL; the contracting carrier shall be responsible for the whole carriage contemplated in the contract of carriage by air, while the actual carrier shall be responsible for the carriage which he performs (Article 138, CAL).

As regards the acts or omissions of an actual carrier and of his servants or agents acting within the scope of their employment or agency, they shall, in relation to the carriage performed by the actual carrier, be deemed to be also those of the contracting carrier. On the other hand, the acts or omissions of the contracting carrier and of his servants or agents acting within the scope of their employment or agency shall, if they relate to the carriage performed by the actual carrier, be deemed to be also those of the actual carrier, provided that no such act or omission shall subject the actual carrier to the liability exceeding the statutory limits (Article 139, CAL).

A special agreement concluded between the carrier and the consignor or passenger, if any, under which the contracting carrier concerned assumes obligations not imposed by this chapter or waives the rights conferred by this chapter or any special declaration of interest in delivery at destination contemplated in Articles 128 and 129 of CAL shall not affect the actual carrier unless agreed to by him (Article 139, CAL).

Any claim to be made or order to be given under the provisions of this chapter shall have equal effect whether addressed to the contracting carrier or to the actual carrier, provided that the orders given by the consignor as referred to in Article 119 of CAL concerning stoppage in carriage or change of destination or consignee shall only be effective if addressed to the contracting carrier (Article 140, CAL).

In relation to the carriage performed by the actual carrier, any servant or agent of the actual carrier or of the contracting carrier shall, if he proves that he acted within the scope of his employment, be entitled to avail himself of the provisions of Articles 128 and 129 of CAL concerning the limitation of liability of the carrier unless he acted in a manner which prevents the limitation of liability from being invoked under the provisions of Article 132 of CAL (Article 141, CAL).

1006. In relation to the carriage performed by the actual carrier, the aggregate amounts recoverable from the actual carrier and the contracting carrier, and from their servants or agents acting within the scope of their employment or agency, shall not exceed the highest amount which could be awarded against either the contracting carrier or the actual carrier under CAL, and none of the persons mentioned shall be liable for a sum in excess of the limit of liability applicable to him, unless he acted in a manner which prevents the limitation of liability from being invoked under the provisions of Article 132 of CAL (Article 142, CAL).

In relation to the carriage performed by the actual carrier, an action may be brought against him or the contracting carrier separately, or against both together;

the carrier against whom an action has been brought shall have the right to require the other carrier to join in the proceedings (Article 143, CAL).

1007. Except as provided for in Article 143 of CAL, nothing of all the above provisions shall affect the rights and obligations between the actual carrier and the contracting carrier which shall be determined in accordance with the contract concluded between them and law applicable thereto (Article 144, CAL).

VIII. Procedures

A. *Complaint of Damage to Baggage or Cargo*

1008. By virtue of Article 134 of CAL, receipt by a passenger of checked baggage or receipt of cargo by the consignee without complaint shall be prima facie evidence that the checked baggage or cargo has been delivered in good condition and in accordance with the documents of transport.

In the case of damage to checked baggage or cargo, the passenger or consignee shall complain to the carrier forthwith after the discovery of the damage, and at the latest, within seven days from the date of receipt in the case of checked baggage or fourteen days from the date of receipt in the case of cargo. In the case of delay, the complaint shall be made at the latest within twenty-one days from the date on which the checked baggage or cargo have been placed at the disposition of the passenger or consignee.

Every complaint shall be made in writing upon the documents of transport or by separate notice dispatched within the stipulated periods of time.

Failing complaint within the stipulated period of time, the passenger or consignee shall be deprived of the right to claim compensation from the carrier, save in the case of fraud on the part of the carrier.

B. *Time-Bar*

1009. By Article 135 of CAL, the time for bringing up an action concerning carriage of passengers, baggage or cargo by air is limited to two years reckoned from the date of the arrival of civil aircraft at the destination, or from the date on which the civil aircraft ought to have arrived, or from the date on which the carriage stopped.

The time limit shall be applicable, regardless of whether the claimant is the carrier, passenger, consignor or consignee, or whether the claim is founded in contract or in tort.

1010. The time limit provided for in Article 135 of CAL is subject to suspension or discontinuance as provided for in Articles 194 and 195 of CC.

Thus, within the last six months of the time limit, if, on account of force majeure or other cause preventing the claim from being made, the time limit shall be suspended, and counting thereof shall be resumed when the cause of suspension no longer exists (Article 194, CC).

The time limit shall be discontinued as a result of bringing an action, or starting arbitration in accordance with an arbitration agreement, or the claimant's demand of the other party to fulfil the obligation, or admission to fulfil his obligation by the party against whom the claim is brought up (Article 195, CC).

C. Jurisdiction and Arbitration

1011. Disputes arising from the carriage of passengers, baggage or cargo by air are subject to the jurisdiction of ordinary courts of law in China by virtue of CPC.

Therefore, a lawsuit brought concerning a dispute arising from a contract of carriage by air shall be within the jurisdiction of the court of law of the place of departure or the place of destination or the place where the defendant has his domicile (Article 28, CPC). A lawsuit brought concerning claims for damages caused by an air accident shall be under the jurisdiction of the court of law of the place where the accident occurred or where the aircraft first landed thereafter, or where the defendant has his domicile (Article 30, CPC).

The parties to a contract of carriage by air may agree to choose in their written agreement one of the courts of law with jurisdiction as determined in accordance with Articles 27 and 30 of CPC to exercise jurisdiction over the case (Articles 25 and 244, CPC).

1012. The parties to a contract of carriage by air may reach an arbitration agreement either before or after the dispute arises and refer the dispute arising therefrom to arbitration accordingly by virtue of AL and CPC.

§6. Air Cargo Transport Insurance

I. Introduction

1013. Air cargo transport insurance including both domestic air cargo transport insurance and international air cargo transport insurance is operated by PICC Property and Casualty Company Limited and other insurance companies in the insurance market in China mainly on the basis of the clauses formulated by PICC Property and Casualty Company Limited.

PICC Property and Casualty Company Limited formulated the Domestic Air Cargo Transport Clauses in 2009 (hereinafter referred to as 'PICC P&C Domestic Air Cargo Clauses 2009') applicable to the domestic air cargo transport insurance, and the Air Cargo Transport Clauses in 2009 (hereinafter referred to as 'PICC P&C International Air Cargo Clauses 2009') applicable to the international air cargo transport insurance. In addition, PICC Property and Casualty Company Limited formulated the Air Cargo Transport War Risks Clauses in 2009 as additional clauses to the PICC P&C International Air Cargo Clauses 2009.

1014. CAL does not contain any provision governing air cargo transport insurance. Therefore, air cargo transport insurance is subject to the provisions of IL. The introduction to and discussions of IL in Chapter 11 of Part II *supra* are also applicable to air cargo transport insurance.

A contract of air cargo transport insurance is also subject to the provisions of Book Three 'Contracts' of CC to the extent they are not repugnant to those of IL.

II. International Air Cargo Transport Insurance

A. Scope of Cover

1015. Under the PICC P&C International Air Cargo Clauses 2009, the coverage includes the air cargo risks cover and the air cargo all risks cover.

Under the air cargo risks cover, the insurer shall be liable for:

- total or partial loss of cargo arising from lightning, fire, explosion, or abandonment of civil aircraft due to heavy weather or other accident of danger, or collision, capsize, falling down or accidental missing of aircraft during transport;
- reasonable expenses arising from measures taken by the insured for the purpose of avoiding or mitigating loss of or damage to cargo in the case of danger covered, provided that these expenses shall not exceed the insured amount of the cargo concerned.

Under the air cargo all risks cover, the insurer shall, besides the liability under the air cargo risks cover, also be liable for the total or partial loss of the cargo insured arising from external causes.

B. Exclusions

1016. Under the PICC P&C International Air Cargo Clauses 2009, the insurer shall not be liable for the following loss of or damage to the insured cargo or expenses:

- loss or damage arising from intentional act or fault of the insured;
- loss or damage due to the responsibility of the consignor of cargo;
- loss or damage arising from defective quality or shortage in quantity of the insured cargo existing before the commencement of insurance liability;
- loss, damage or expenses arising from ordinary wear and tear, vice or specific nature of the insured cargo, drop of market or delay in transport thereof;
- loss, damage or expenses within the scope of cover or exclusions under the air cargo transport war risks clauses or strike risks clauses.

C. *Commencement and Termination of Insurance Liability*

1017. The PICC P&C International Air Cargo Clauses 2009 contains a 'warehouse to warehouse' clause by which the insurance liability shall commence from the time when the insured cargo is carried away from the warehouse or storage place at the place of the commencement of transport stated in the insurance policy, and terminate at the time when the insured cargo arrives at the last warehouse or storage place of the consignee at destination stated in the insurance policy or at other storage place where the cargo will be distributed by the insured or be further carried away not in normal process. However, if the insured cargo is not carried to the above warehouse or storage place, the insurance liability shall terminate thirty days after the insured cargo has been discharged from aircraft at the last place of discharge. Where the insured cargo will be transhipped to a place other than the destination stated in the insurance policy within the thirty days, the insurance liability shall terminate at the time of transhipment.

1018. Where, due to delay in carriage, deviation, enforced discharge, reloading or transhipment of cargo beyond the control of the insured, or change of flight or termination of contract of carriage arising from the exercise of right conferred on him by the contract of carriage, the insured cargo is carried to a place other than the destination stated in the insurance policy, the cargo shall be held covered on the condition that the insured notifies the insurer of the information the insured has known and that the insured has paid additional insurance premium as necessary. Under such a circumstance, the insurance liability shall terminate as follows:

- where the insured cargo is sold at a place other than the destination stated in the insurance policy, the insurance liability shall terminate at the time of delivery of the insured cargo, but in no case shall exceed thirty days after the cargo is discharged from the aircraft at the place of discharge;
- where the insured cargo is still carried to the destination stated in the insurance policy or other destination within the above period of thirty days, the insurance liability shall terminate as stated in the 'warehouse to warehouse' clause contained in the PICC P&C International Air Cargo Clauses 2009 as mentioned *supra*.

D. *Obligations of Insured*

1019. Under the PICC P&C International Air Cargo Clauses 2009, the insured shall fulfil the following obligations:

- after the insured cargo has been carried to the destination stated in the insurance policy, the insured shall take delivery thereof in time; where loss of or damage to the cargo is found, the insured shall apply for survey to the insurer's agent responsible for survey or handling claims stated in the insurance policy; where there is shortage of packages of or apparent damage to the insured cargo, the insured shall try to obtain evidence of damage to or shortage of cargo from the carrier, his authorized party or relevant authority; where damage to or shortage of cargo is within the responsibility of the carrier, his authorized party or other relevant party, the insured shall file a claim in writing against them and obtain from them an extension of time-bar when necessary; if the insured fails to fulfil the obligations, the insurer shall not be liable for the loss or damage concerned;

– where there is danger to the insured cargo within the insurance liability, the insured shall immediately take reasonable measures to avoid or mitigate loss of or damage to cargo, failing which the insurer shall not be liable for the loss or damage exaggerated thereby;
– the insured shall, in making claim against the insurer, provide documents including the original insurance policy, waybill, invoice, packing list, weight memo, evidence of damage to or shortage of cargo, survey report and breakdown of damages, and correspondences in making claim against a third party if the liability of a third party is involved, as well as documents and materials concerning determining the nature, causes of the insurance accident, extent of damage, etc., as the insured is able to provide, failing which the insurer is not liable for the part of damage which the insurer is unable to determine as a result of such failure.

The PICC P&C International Air Cargo Clauses 2009 do not provide the obligation of the applicant or the insured of truthful disclosure, answering to the inquiries of the insurer truthfully concerning the subject matter insured or the insured. Thus, such obligation and the legal effect of failure in fulfilling the obligation are subject to Article 16 of IL.

III. Domestic Air Cargo Transport Insurance

A. *Subject Matters Insured*

1020. Under the PICC P&C Domestic Air Cargo Clauses 2009, any cargo carried by domestic air can be the subject matter of insurance, except fresh vegetables, fruits, live stocks, birds, fish and other live animals. In addition, unless specially agreed upon between the insurer and the insured and stated in the policy or other insurance certificate, valuables such as gold, silver, jewellery, diamond, jade, antique, ancient book, ancient painting, postage stamp, work of art and rare mental are not covered by the insurance.

B. *Scope of Cover*

1021. Under the PICC P&C Domestic Air Cargo Clauses 2009, the insurer shall be liable for the following losses of or damage to the insured cargo or expenses:

– loss or damage arising from fire, explosion, lightning, hail, storm, flood, tsunami, subsidence of land, collapse of cliff;

- loss or damage arising from collision, capsize, falling down of aircraft or missing of aircraft for a period of more than three months, discharge of cargo in case of danger and jettison of cargo in heavy weather or other accident of danger;
- loss or damage arising from breakage, crook, concavity, split of cargo due to vibration, impact or extrusion;
- loss or damage arising from scatter and disappearance of cargo due to breakage of packing;
- loss or damage arising from damage to container of liquid cargo including its seal, semi-liquid cargo or other cargo to be preserved in liquid due to vibration, impact or extrusion, or arising from putrescence or deterioration of cargo due to the leakage of liquid in which the cargo is preserved;
- loss or damage arising from theft or non-delivery of cargo;
- loss or damage arising from force majeure or wetness by rain during loading or discharge or ground transport in airport;
- direct and reasonable expenses arising from sue and labour or protection of cargo in the case of accident of calamity within insurance coverage.

C. *Exclusions*

1022. Under the PICC P&C Domestic Air Cargo Clauses 2009, the insurer shall not be liable for loss of or damage to the insured cargo arising from any of the following causes:

- war, military action, seizure, strike, robbery or riot;
- nuclear reaction, nuclear radiation and radioactive pollution;
- ordinary wear and tear, pollution, putrescence or damage arising from inherent vice or specific nature of the insured cargo;
- defective quality or shortage in quantity of the insured cargo existing before the commencement of insurance liability;
- loss of market or delay in transport;
- the responsibility of the consignor of cargo;
- intentional or criminal act of the insured or the applicant;
- administrative act or enforcement of law.

D. *Commencement and Termination of Insurance Liability*

1023. The PICC P&C Domestic Air Cargo Clauses 2009 also contains a 'warehouse to warehouse' clause to the effect that the insurance liability shall commence from the time of receipt of cargo by the carrier and the issuance of the policy or other insurance certificate and terminate at the time when the insured cargo arrives at the first warehouse or storage place of the consignee at destination stated in the insurance certificate, provided that the time limit of termination shall not exceed fifteen days from the receipt of notice of arrival by the consignee in case the consignee fails to take delivery of cargo in time.

1024. The PICC P&C Domestic Air Cargo Clauses 2009 contain a 'held covered' clause as in the PICC P&C International Air Cargo Clauses 2009 as mentioned *supra*.

E. Obligations of Insured

1025. Under the PICC P&C Domestic Air Cargo Clauses 2009, the applicant or the insured shall fulfil the following obligations:

- the applicant shall fulfil the obligation of truthful disclosure, answer to the inquiries of the insurer truthfully concerning the subject matter insured or the insured; if the applicant fails to fulfil the above obligation of truthful disclosure due to his intentional act or gross negligence which is sufficient to affect the insurer in deciding whether he agrees to insure or not or increasing the premium, the insurer has the right to terminate the contract; the contract of insurance shall be terminated upon arrival of the insurer's notice of termination of contract at the applicant or the insured; if the applicant intentionally did not fulfil the obligation of truthful disclosure, the insurer shall not be liable for any loss arising from the perils insured against before the contract is terminated without refunding the insurance premium; if the applicant did not fulfil the obligation of truthful disclosure due to his gross negligence which has significant impact on the occurrence of the insurance accident, the insurer shall not be liable for any loss arising from the perils insured against before the contract is terminated, but shall refund the insurance premium;
- the applicant shall pay the insurance premium in one lump upon the issuance of insurance policy or other insurance certificate by the insurer or his agent; if the applicant fails to pay the insurance premium as agreed, the insurer shall not be liable for any insurance accident occurred before payment of insurance premium;
- the insured shall strictly obey to the various provisions of the State and transport authorities concerning safety transport, accept and assist the insurer in the inspection and survey of the insured cargo and taking of measures of preventing loss of or damage to the insured cargo, and shall make sure that the packing of cargo be in conformity with the standards provided for by the State and competent authorities; if failure of the insured in complying with the above agreement, the insurer shall not be liable; if such failure results in exaggeration of loss or damage, the insurer shall not be liable for the exaggerated loss or damage;
- if the danger to the subject matter insured increases significantly during the period of validity of contract, the insured shall notify the insurer timely, and the insurer is entitled to demand increase of insurance premium or terminate the contract; if the insured fails to fulfil the obligation of such notification, the insurer shall not be liable for the insurance accident caused by the significant increase of danger to the subject matter insured;
- upon notice of the occurrence of loss of or damage to the insured cargo within the insurance coverage, the applicant or the insured shall take sue and labour and protective measures, and immediately notify the local branch of the insurer not later than ten days; failure of timely notification due to intentional act or gross

negligence which results in difficulty in determining the nature and causes of accident and extent of damage, etc., the insurer shall not be liable for the part which is unable to be determined, except where the insurer has known or should have known timely the occurrence of the insurance accident.

§7. Liability for Damage to Third Parties on the Surface

I. Introduction

1026. As introduced in §1 of this chapter *supra*, China has not ratified or acceded to the 1952 Rome Convention and its Protocol of 1978.

However, Chapter XII 'Liability for Damage to Third Parties on the Surface' of CAL contains provisions governing such liability in detail.

The provisions of this chapter apply to the matters of liability for death of or personal injury to or damage to property of any person on the surface including water surface caused by any civil aircraft during flight or by any person or thing falling therefrom (Article 157, CAL), but shall not apply to: (a) damage caused to a civil aircraft during flight or to persons or cargo on board such aircraft; (b) damage which is regulated either by a contract between the person who suffers such damage and the operator or person entitled to use the civil aircraft at the time the damage occurred, or by the law relating to workman's compensation applicable to a contract of employment between such persons; and (c) nuclear damage (Article 172, CAL).

'During flight' of a civil aircraft means the period beginning from the moment when power is applied by a civil aircraft for the purpose of actual take-off until the moment when the landing run ends. In the case of a civil aircraft lighter than air, the expression 'during flight' relates to the period from the moment when it becomes detached from the surface until it becomes again attached thereto (paragraph 2, Article 157, CAL).

II. Responsible Person

1027. By virtue of Article 158 of CAL, the liability for compensation contemplated by Article 157 shall attach to the operator of a civil aircraft.

'Operator' means the person who is making use of the civil aircraft at the time the damage is caused. However, if the control of navigation of a civil aircraft is retained by the person from whom the right to make use of the civil aircraft is derived, whether directly or indirectly, that person shall still be deemed as the operator. The operator shall be considered to be making use of a civil aircraft when his servants or agents are using the civil aircraft in the course of their employment or agency, whether or not within the scope of their authority.

The registered owner of a civil aircraft shall be presumed to be the operator and shall be liable as such, unless he proves in the proceedings for the determination of his liability that some other person was the operator and, in so far as legal procedures permit, takes appropriate measures to make that other person a party in the proceedings (paragraph 4, Article 158, CAL). Such a provision is helpful for the identification of the operator of a civil aircraft.

1028. If a person makes use of a civil aircraft without the consent of the person entitled to its navigational control and causes damage to third parties on the surface, the person entitled to the navigation control shall be jointly and severally liable with the unlawful user, unless he proves that he has exercised due care to prevent such use (Article 159, CAL).

III. Liability and Exemptions

1029. A strict liability is imposed upon the operator of a civil aircraft and other persons who are liable as mentioned *supra*.

By virtue of Articles 157, 160 and 161 of CAL, the operator of a civil aircraft or other persons who are liable shall be liable for the death or personal injury or the damage to property caused by a civil aircraft during flight or by any person or thing falling therefrom, unless his liability can be exempted or reduced in any of the following cases:

- the damage is not a direct consequence of the incident giving rise thereto;
- the damage results from the mere fact of passage of a civil aircraft through the airspace in conformity with air traffic regulations concerned of the State;
- the damage is the direct consequence of armed conflict or civil disturbance;
- the operator of a civil aircraft or other person who would otherwise be liable has been deprived of the right to use the civil aircraft by a public authority of the Sate according to law;
- the operator of a civil aircraft or other person who would otherwise be liable proves that the damage is caused solely or partly by the fault of the person who suffers the damage or of the latter's servants or agents, provided that there shall be no such exoneration or reduction if, in the case of the fault of a servant or agent, the person who suffers the damage proves that his servant or agent was acting outside the scope of his authority.

1030. Where two or more civil aircrafts have collided or interfered with each other during flight resulting in damage for which the right to compensation is contemplated in Article 157 of CAL, or where two or more civil aircrafts have jointly caused such damage, each of the civil aircrafts concerned shall be considered to have caused the damage and the operator of each civil aircraft shall be liable (Article 162, CAL), i.e., the operators shall bear joint and several liability. In such or similar case, the right of recourse of an operator liable for the damage in accordance with the provisions of CAL against any other operator shall not be prejudiced (Article 165, CAL).

Neither the operator, owner, any person liable under Article 159 of CAL, nor their respective servants or agents shall be liable for damage on the surface caused by a civil aircraft during flight or any person or thing falling therefrom otherwise than as expressly provided for in CAL, unless any such person caused the damage deliberately (Article 164, CAL).

IV. Liability Insurance or Guarantee

A. *Compulsory Liability Insurance or Guarantee*

1031. In order to protect the interests of third parties on the surface, the operator of a civil aircraft shall be covered by insurance against liability for third parties on the surface or obtain corresponding guarantee by virtue of Article 166 of CAL.

The insurance or guarantee furnished in accordance with Article 166 of CAL shall be specifically and preferentially assigned to the payment of claims by third parties on the surface (Article 169, CAL).

In addition, in order to secure that third parties benefit from the liability insurance, Article 170 of CAL provides that any sum due to the operator from the insurer shall be exempted from seizure and execution by creditors of the operator until the claims of third parties have been satisfied.

B. *Direct Action Against Liability Insurer or Guarantor*

1032. By virtue of Article 168 of CAL, a third party on the surface who has suffered damage for which the operator of a civil aircraft shall be liable may bring a direct action against the liability insurer or guarantor of the operator where the insurance or guarantee is continued in force under the provisions of CAL as mentioned *infra* and the operator becomes bankrupt or where the third parties suffering damage have the right of direct action against the liability insurer or guarantor under the law governing the contract of insurance or guarantee.

C. *Defences Available to Liability Insurer or Guarantor*

1033. Where a direct action is brought by the third parties against the liability insurer or guarantor of the operator, the insurer or the guarantor may avail of the following defences by virtue of Article 167 of CAL:

- defences available to the operator;
- defence of forgery;
- that the damage occurred after the insurance or guarantee ceased to be effective, provided that if the insurance or guarantee expires during flight, it should be continued in force until the next landing specified in the flight plan, but no longer than twenty-four hours;

– that the damage occurred outside the geographical limits provided by the insurance or guarantee, unless flight outside of such limits was caused by force majeure, assistance justified by the circumstances or an error in piloting, operation or navigation.

Except these defences, the insurer or guarantor may not avail himself of any ground of nullity of the insurance or guarantee or any right of retroactive cancellation in setting up defence with respect to direct actions brought by the person suffering damage (paragraph 2, Article 168, CAL).

V. Time-Bar

1034. The actions concerning indemnity for the damage to third parties on the surface, whether brought against the operator of a civil aircraft or his liability insurer or guarantor, shall be subject to a period of limitation of two years from the date of the incident which caused the damage, but in no case shall such a period go beyond a period of three years from the date of the incident which caused the damage (Article 171, CAL).

§8. Rights in Civil Aircraft

I. Introduction

1035. As introduced in §1 of this chapter *supra*, China has not ratified or acceded to the *Convention on the Recognition of Rights in Aircraft* signed at Geneva on 19 June 1948.

However, Chapter III 'Rights in Civil Aircraft' of CAL contains provisions governing the rights in civil aircraft including ownership of, mortgage and lien on, and right of lessee of a civil aircraft. In addition, as regards registration of rights in a civil aircraft, the State Council enacted the *Regulations on the Registration of Rights of Civil Aircrafts* (hereinafter referred to as 'Civil Aircraft Registration Regulations') on 21 October 1997 which came into force as of the same date, and CAAC enacted the *Implementation Provisions of the Registration of Rights of Civil Aircraft* (hereinafter referred to as 'Civil Aircraft Registration Provisions') on 1 September 1999 which came into force as of 1 November 1999.

As defined in Article 10 of CAL, the rights in a civil aircraft include the rights in the airframe, engines, propellers, radio apparatus of a civil aircraft and all other articles intended for use therein, whether they are installed thereon or separated temporarily therefrom.

1036. CAL has adopted the system of registration of rights in civil aircrafts.

By virtue of Article 11 of CAL, the persons having the following rights in a civil aircraft shall register the rights respectively with CAAC:

- ownership of a civil aircraft;
- right for the acquisition and possession of a civil aircraft through an act of purchase;
- right to possess a civil aircraft in accordance with a lease contract covering a lease term of six months or over;
- mortgage on a civil aircraft.

For the purpose of registration of the rights in civil aircrafts, CAAC maintains a register of the rights in civil aircrafts. The matters registered concerning the rights in civil aircraft shall be recorded in the same register of rights and these registered matters may be made available to the public for inquiry, reproduction or extraction (Article 12, CAL).

1037. Unless a civil aircraft is the subject of a forced sale by auction in accordance with law, the nationality registration of a civil aircraft or the registration of rights thereof shall not be transferred abroad before the registered rights in the aircraft are compensated for or before the consent of the persons entitled to the aforesaid rights is given (Article 13, CAL).

1038. To the extent of non-repugnance to the corresponding provisions of CAL, the ownership of or mortgage on a civil aircraft is subject to provisions of Book Two 'Real Rights' of CC regarding ownership of property or mortgage on property; the right of lessee of civil aircraft is subject to Chapter XIV 'Contract of Lease' or Chapter XV 'Contract of Financing Lease' of Book Three 'Contracts' of CC.

II. Ownership of and Mortgage on Civil Aircraft

A. *Ownership of Civil Aircraft*

1039. As required by Article 14 of CAL, the acquisition, transference and extinction of ownership of a civil aircraft shall be registered with CAAC. Otherwise, they shall not act against a third party.

The transfer of ownership of a civil aircraft shall be made by virtue of a contract in writing.

Where a State-owned civil aircraft is authorized by the State to be operated, administered or utilized by a legal person, the provisions of CAL concerning the owner of a civil aircraft shall be applicable to such a legal person (Article 15, CAL). That is, such a legal person is deemed as the owner of the civil aircraft concerned.

1040. In applying for the registration of ownership, the applicant shall submit the originals or certified copies of the Certificate of Nationality Registration of Civil Aircraft, the document evidencing the acquisition of ownership of a civil aircraft and other documents required by CAAC (Article 5, Civil Aircraft Registration Regulations).

As provided for in Article 10 of the Civil Aircraft Registration Regulations, a Certificate of Ownership Registration of Civil Aircraft shall be issued by CAAC after registration. The following items shall be recorded in the register:

- nationality, nationality mark and registration mark;
- name, address, representative of the owner or co-owner;
- date and mode of acquisition of ownership;
- name of manufacturer, date and place of manufacture;
- value and technical data;
- date of ownership registration.

Loss or missing of a civil aircraft or alteration of ownership thereof shall be registered with CAAC. In the case of loss or missing, a corresponding certificate shall be issued to replace the original one; in the case of alteration, the items of alteration shall be recorded in the original certificate (Article 17, Civil Aircraft Registration Regulations; Articles 17 and 19, Civil Aircraft Registration Provisions).

B. Mortgage on Civil Aircraft

1041. As required by Article 14 of CAL, the establishment of mortgage on a civil aircraft shall be registered with CAAC jointly by the mortgagee and the mortgagor. Unless registered, no mortgage may act against a third party.

Once a mortgage is established on a civil aircraft, the ownership of the mortgaged civil aircraft shall not be transferred without consent of the mortgagee (Article 17, CAL).

1042. In the application for the registration of mortgage, the mortgagee and the mortgagor shall submit the originals or certified copies of the Certificate of Nationality Registration of Civil Aircraft, the Certificate of Ownership Registration of Civil Aircraft or other document evidencing the ownership thereof, the contract of mortgage on the civil aircraft and other documents required by CAAC (Article 7, Civil Aircraft Registration Regulations).

By virtue of Article 12 of the Civil Aircraft Registration Regulations, a Certificate of Registration of Mortgage on Civil Aircraft shall be issued by CAAC after registration. The following items shall be recorded in the register:

- nationality, nationality mark and registration mark of the mortgaged civil aircraft;
- name, address and representative of the mortgagee and the mortgagor;
- amount of credit secured, the interest rate and the period for repayment of the debt;
- date of registration of mortgage.

Extinction of the credit secured or alteration of mortgage on a civil aircraft shall be registered with CAAC. In the case of extinction, a corresponding certificate shall be issued to replace the original one; in the case of alteration, the items of alteration shall be recorded in the original certificate (Article 17, Civil Aircraft Registration Regulations; Articles 17 and 19, Civil Aircraft Registration Provisions).

III. Lien on Civil Aircraft

A. *Definition*

1043. A lien on a civil aircraft is defined as the right of the claimant to take priority in compensation against the owner or lessee of the civil aircraft which gave rise to the said claims (Article 18, CAL). Claims secured by lien are those for the remuneration for rescuing a civil aircraft or necessary expenses incurred for the custody of a civil aircraft (Article 19, CAL).

B. *Registration of Lien on Civil Aircraft*

1044. Unlike a maritime lien under MC, the claimant whose claim is secured by lien on a civil aircraft shall register his claim with CAAC within three months commencing from the date of the end of rescue or custody (Article 20, CAL). Unless registered, the claim shall not be secured by lien on civil aircraft.

1045. By virtue of Article 13 of the Civil Aircraft Registration Regulations, a Certificate of Registration of Lien on Civil Aircraft shall be issued by CAAC after registration. The following items shall be recorded in the register:

- nationality, nationality mark and registration mark of the civil aircraft;
- name, address, representative of the lien creditor;
- name, address and representative of the owner, operator or lessee;
- amount of claim secured, reason giving rise to the lien and date on which the lien gave rise;
- date of registration of lien.

Extinction or alteration of lien on a civil aircraft shall be registered with CAAC. In the case of extinction, a corresponding certificate shall be issued to replace the original one; in the case of alteration, the items of alteration shall be recorded in the original certificate (Article 17, Civil Aircraft Registration Regulations; Articles 17 and 19, Civil Aircraft Registration Provisions).

C. *Enforcement of Lien and Priorities in Compensation*

1046. A lien on a civil aircraft shall be enforced by a court of law by attaching the civil aircraft that gave rise to the lien (Article 24, CAL).

With respect to the claims secured by lien on a civil aircraft, a claim which arose later shall be satisfied first from the proceeds of the sale by auction of the civil aircraft (paragraph 2, Article 18, CAL).

A lien on a civil aircraft shall have priority over a mortgage thereon (Article 22, CAL).

The expenses incurred in the enforcement of judgment of a court of law and in the course of sale by auction for the common interests of claimants shall be deducted and paid first from the proceeds of the sale by auction (Article 21, CAL).

D. Termination of Lien on Civil Aircraft

1047. By virtue of Article 25 of CAL, a lien on a civil aircraft shall be extinguished at the expiry of three months commencing from the date of the end of rescue or custody, except that the claimant has registered his claim according to the provisions of Article 20 of CAL and that the claimant and the debtor have reached an agreement on the amount of the said claim or legal action concerning the claim has started.

A lien on a civil aircraft shall not be extinguished because of the transfer of ownership of the civil aircraft concerned, except that the civil aircraft was the subject of a forced sale by auction in accordance with law, nor shall a lien be extinguished where a claim secured by lien is transferred in which case the lien attached thereto shall be transferred accordingly (Articles 23 and 25, CAL).

IV. Lease of Civil Aircraft

A. Contract of Lease of Civil Aircraft

1048. As required by Article 26 of CAL, a contract of lease of a civil aircraft including financing lease and other lease shall be concluded in writing.

B. Financing Lease of Civil Aircraft

1049. Financing lease of a civil aircraft is defined in Article 27 of CAL as a kind of lease in which the lessor acquires a civil aircraft pursuant to the selection of the lessee with respect to the supplier and civil aircraft and leases it to the lessee who shall pay hire periodically.

During the period of financing lease, the lessor shall be legally entitled to the ownership of the civil aircraft and the lessee shall be legally entitled to the rights of possession, utilization and earnings thereof (Article 28, CAL). The lessor is obliged to ensure the lessee to possess and use the civil aircraft without interference, while the lessee shall take proper care of the civil aircraft and keep it in the condition as it was delivered subject to fair wear and tear and to any modification of the civil aircraft as agreed to by the lessor (Article 29, CAL). During this period, the lessee may transfer the right of the possession of the civil aircraft and other rights under the contract of lease only with the consent of the lessor and without jeopardizing the interests of third parties (Article 32, CAL).

When the contract of financing lease comes to an end, the lessee shall return the civil aircraft to the lessor in the same condition as it was delivered subject to fair wear and tear, unless the lessee exercises a right to purchase the civil aircraft or to hold the civil aircraft on lease for a further period in accordance with the contract (Article 30, CAL).

C. *Registration of Lease of Civil Aircraft*

1050. Where a lease of a civil aircraft, whether in the form of financing lease or not, covers a period of six months or longer, the lessee shall register his right of possession of the civil aircraft with CAAC. Otherwise, no such lease may act against a third party (Article 33, CAL).

1051. As provided for in Article 11 of the Civil Aircraft Registration Regulations, a Certificate of Registration of Right of Possession of Civil Aircraft shall be issued by CAAC after registration. The following items shall be recorded in the register:

- nationality, nationality mark and registration mark;
- name, address and representative of the possessor (lessee), owner or lessor;
- date of acquisition of the right of possession and the agreed conditions of possession;
- date of registration of possession.

Termination or alteration of the contract of lease of a civil aircraft shall be registered with CAAC. In the case of termination, a corresponding certificate shall be issued to replace the original one; in the case of alteration, the items of alteration shall be recorded in the original certificate (Article 17, Civil Aircraft Registration Regulations; Articles 17 and 19, Civil Aircraft Registration Provisions).

Chapter 5. Multimodal Transport

§1. Introduction

I. Applicable laws

1052. The laws and administrative regulations applicable to multimodal transport of goods or passengers in China are referred to in §6 in Chapter 2 of Part I *supra*.

II. Concepts and Definitions

1053. The following concepts and definitions are adopted in the laws and regulations in China applicable to multimodal transport or recognized in academic circle or practice:

– Multimodal transport contract means a contract under which the 'MTO' undertakes to carry the goods as against the payment of freight for the entire transport from one place where the goods are received in his charge to the destination and to deliver them to the consignee by two or more different modes of transport and, to be regulated by MC, one of the modes of transport shall be international carriage by sea (Article 102, MC).
– MTO means a person who has entered into a multimodal transport contract with the shipper either by himself or by another person acting on his behalf (paragraph 2, Article 102, MC).
– International multimodal transport of goods means an international carriage of goods by at least two different modes of transport on the basis of a contract for such carriage from a place in one country at which the goods are taken in charge by the MTO to a designated place of delivery situated in a different country.
– Document for international multimodal transport of goods (hereinafter referred to as 'multimodal transport document') means a document which serves as an evidence of a multimodal transport contract and the taking in charge of the goods by MTO, and an undertaking by MTO to deliver the goods in accordance with the terms of the contract.
– Sectorial transport carrier means a person who enters into a sectorial transport contract with MTO and undertakes to perform part of the multimodal transport.
– Shipper means a person by whom or in whose name and on whose behalf a multimodal transport contract has been concluded with MTO and who delivers the goods to MTO or sectorial transport carrier for transport.
– Consignee means the person entitled to take delivery of the goods from MTO.
– Delay in delivery means that the goods have not been delivered within the time expressly agreed upon or, in the absence of such expressly agreed time, within reasonable time (Article 811, CC).
– International container means a container which complies with the technical standards issued by ISO.

§2. GENERAL STATUTORY PROVISIONS

I. Multimodal Transport Document

1054. As required by Article 840 of CC, MTO shall issue a multimodal transport document when receiving the goods for transport from the shipper. The document may be issued by a person authorized by MTO. Furthermore, MTO may issue a negotiable or non-negotiable document at the request of the shipper.

By mutual consent between MTO and the shipper, the document may take the form of electronic message in place of paper document.

A multimodal transport document is in many cases in the form of multimodal transport bill of lading, especially where the first section of transport is maritime transport.

If a document is issued in a set of more than one original, it shall indicate the number of originals issued. Copies of the document shall be marked as non-negotiable.

1055. A multimodal transport document normally contains the following particulars:

- description and general nature, number of packages, weight, measurement, apparent order and condition of goods and type of packing;
- container numbers, type and quantity of containers and seal numbers;
- an express statement as to the character of dangerous or refrigerated goods or other special goods and precautions to be taken;
- name and principal place of business of MTO;
- name of shipper;
- name or other description of consignee;
- place and date of taking in charge of goods by MTO;
- place of delivery of goods and date of delivery as agreed between the parties;
- mode of taking in charge and delivery of goods;
- payment of freight;
- place or places of transhipment;
- other particulars which the parties may agree to insert in the document, if and to the extent that such particulars are not inconsistent with the applicable laws and regulations;
- signature of MTO or of a person acting under his authorization;
- place and date of issue.

1056. Where, upon his taking in charge of the goods, MTO has known or has reasonable grounds to suspect that the particulars about the goods stated by the shipper or contained in the multimodal transport document do not accurately represent the goods actually received, or he has had no reasonable means of checking such particulars, he shall insert in the document reservations specifying those inaccuracies, grounds for suspicion or the absence of reasonable means of checking. If MTO fails to insert reservation of the apparent order and condition of the goods or containers on the document, he is deemed to have received the goods and containers in an apparent good order and condition.

Except for the particulars in respect of which and to the extent to which reservations have been thus made, the multimodal transport document issued by MTO shall be prima facie evidence of the taking in charge by him of the goods as described therein.

II. Responsibility of MTO

1057. Article 103 of MC provides that the responsibility of MTO with respect to the goods under a multimodal transport contract covers the period from the time when he takes the goods in his charge to the time when he deliver them.

During this period, MTO shall be responsible for performance of a multimodal transport contract or procurement of the performance thereof and for the entire transport, enjoy the rights of a carrier and assume his obligations (Article 838, CC). However, MTO may enter into separate contracts with the sectorial carriers of different modes defining their responsibilities with regard to the different sections of transport under a multimodal transport contract, provided that such separate contracts shall not affect the responsibility of MTO with respect to the entire transport (Article 104, MC; Article 839, CC).

1058. MTO shall be responsible for notifying the consignee of the arrival of goods at the destination in accordance with the address of consignee or notify party stated in a multimodal transport document.

The consignee shall take delivery of goods in accordance with the mode of delivery of goods as stipulated in the document and acknowledge receipt thereof on the document. MTO shall be discharged from his obligations against surrender of an original document, if two or more original documents have been issued.

Delivery of goods means the handing over of goods to the consignee in accordance with the law or practice of the particular trade applicable at the place of delivery, or the handing over of goods to an authority or a third party to whom the goods shall be handed over pursuant to the law or practice of the particular trade applicable at the place of delivery.

III. Liability of MTO

1059. As a rule, the liability of MTO for loss of or damage to goods and the limitation liability is dependent upon the section in which the loss or damage has occurred and the law applicable to that section.

In detail, where Chinese law is applicable, if loss of or damage to goods occurred in an ascertained section of multimodal transport, the provisions of the relevant laws and regulations governing that specific section in the State where the loss or damage occurred shall be applicable to the matters concerning the liability of MTO and the limitation of liability (Article 105, MC; Article 842, CC).

Thus, where the loss or damage occurred in China, or where the loss or damage occurred on the high seas in maritime transport or in the airspace over the high seas in transport by air with the place of loading or discharge in China, and Chinese law is applicable, if the loss or damage occurred in the section of international maritime transport, Chapter IV of MC as introduced in Chapter 6 of Part II *supra* shall be applied; if the loss or damage has occurred in the section of coastal maritime transport or inland navigation, the laws and other regulations as introduced in Chapter 3 of Part III *supra* shall be applied; if the loss or damage occurred in the section of transport by road, the laws and other regulations as introduced in Chapter 1 of Part III *supra* shall be applied; if the loss or damage has occurred in the section of transport by rail, RL, other laws and regulations as introduced in Chapter 2 of Part III *supra* shall be applied; if the loss or damage occurred in the section of transport by air, CAL, the laws and regulations as introduced in Chapter 4 of Part III *supra* shall be applied. Such a regime is called 'network liability system'.

Noticeably, where if the loss or damage has occurred in a section of multimodal transport within a foreign country, the law of that country governing that section shall be applied, even if the contract of multimodal transport as a whole is subject to Chinese law.

If the section of transport in which the loss of or damage to goods occurred cannot be ascertained, i.e., with respect to the concealed loss of or damage to goods, the liability and limitation of liability of MTO shall be dependent upon whether one mode of transport involved is international maritime transport or not.

Where Chinese law is applicable, if one mode of transport involved is international maritime transport, the loss of or damage to goods shall be deemed as occurred in international maritime transport and thus MTO shall bear liability in accordance with the stipulations regarding the carrier's liability and the limitation of liability set out in Chapter IV of MC (Article 106, MC). If no international maritime transport is involved, the liability of MTO shall be determined in accordance with Chapter XIX of Book Three of CC as a result of which MTO shall bear strict liability and shall not avail of any limitation of liability for the loss of or damage to goods (Article 842, CC), and the exemptions of liability are limited to force majeure, natural characteristics or ordinary wear and tear of goods, and fault of the consigner or consignee (Article 832, CC).

The so-called network liability system as supplemented by the statutory provisions with respect to the concealed loss of or damage to goods is called 'amended network liability system' which is adopted in Chinese law regarding the liability and limitation of liability of MTO.

IV. Responsibility and Liability of Shipper

1060. The shipper shall guarantee to MTO at the time when the goods were taken in charge by MTO the accuracy of the particulars relating to the description and general nature, packing, number of packages or pieces, weight, measurement and marks of goods.

1061. In the case of carriage of dangerous goods, the shipper shall, at the time of shipping such goods, act in accordance with the relevant regulations concerning the transport of such dangerous goods and shall have them properly packed, distinctly marked or labelled to indicate their dangerous nature. Furthermore, the shipper shall inform MTO in writing the standard nomenclature and nature of the dangerous goods and the safety precautions to be taken.

If the shipper fails to inform MTO or if the information provided is incorrect, MTO may have the goods unloaded, destroyed or disposed of by appropriate means, as the circumstances may require, without compensation, provided that MTO did not know the nature of the dangerous goods, nor consented to carry. The shipper shall be liable to MTO for all losses resulting from the shipment of such goods.

Notwithstanding the MTO's knowledge of the nature of the dangerous goods and his consent to carry, he may still have such goods landed, destroyed or rendered innocuous without compensation, when they become an actual danger to the means of transport, persons or other goods.

1062. If loss is caused to MTO due to the fault of shipper at the time of consigning the goods for transport, the shipper shall be liable for such loss, even if the shipper has transferred the multimodal transport document to a third party (Article 841, CC).

Selected Bibliography

Chen, X., *Insurance Law*, Beijing, 2000.
Cooke, J., *e.a.*, *Voyage Charters*, London, 2001.
Cui, J., *Contract Law*, Beijing, 2021.
De Wit, R., *Multimodal Transport*, London, 1995.
Garner, B., *Black's Law Dictionary*, Minnesota, 1999.
Hill, C., *Maritime Law*, London, 1998.
Hu, Z., *e.a.*, *Rotterdam Rules: Consequences and Countermeasures*, Beijing, 2014.
Hu, Z., *e.a.*, *Admiralty Law*, Beijing, 2016.
Hu, Z., *e.a.*, *Revising Chinese Maritime Code: Fundamental Theories and Main Regimes*, Beijing, 2021.
Huybrechts, M., *e.a.*, *Monograph of Belgian Transport Law*, Alphen, 1994.
Jin, Z., *Maritime Litigation*, Dalian, 2001.
Liang, H. & Chen, H., *Law on Real Rights*, Beijing, 2020.
Ministry of Transport, *China Transport Development Report of 2023*, Beijing, 2023.
Moguffie, K.C., *Collision as Sea*, London, 1961.
Schoenbaum, T., *Admiralty and Maritime Law*, Minnesota, 2004.
Si, Y. & Hu, Z., *e.a.*, *Maritime Law*, Beijing, 2023.
Si, Y. & Hu, Z., *Q & A of Chinese Maritime Code*, Beijing, 1993.
Sun, S., *Textbook on Carriage of Goods by Sea*, Beijing, 2022.
Supreme People's Court, *Gazette*, Beijing, 1993–2023.
Tetley, W., *Marine Cargo Claims*, Montreal, 1988.
Wei, Z., *e.a.*, *Civil Law*, Beijing, 2000.
Wilford, M., *e.a.*, *Time Charters*, London, 1995.
Williams, H., *Chartering Documents*, London, 1999.
Wilson, J., *Carriage of Goods by Sea*, London, 2008.
Zhang, Y., *International Conventions on Maritime Transport*, Beijing, 2018.
Zhang, X., *Interpretations of the Civil Code of the People's Republic of China*, Beijing, 2017.
Zhang, W., *Civil Procedural Law*, Beijing, 2023.
Zheng, R., *Marine Insurance: Law and Practice*, Shanghai, 2021.

Selected Bibliography

Index

The numbers here refer to paragraph numbers.

www.ingramcontent.com/pod-product-compliance
Lightning Source LLC
Chambersburg PA
CBHW071410230926
51846CB00001B/47
* 9 7 8 9 4 0 3 5 0 3 0 9 7 *